Religion   (1958)

THE
GREAT
RELIGIOUS
LEADERS

BY CHARLES FRANCIS POTTER

A REVISION AND UPDATING OF
"THE STORY OF RELIGION"
IN THE LIGHT OF
RECENT DISCOVERY AND RESEARCH
INCLUDING THE QUMRAN SCROLLS

SIMON AND SCHUSTER
New York 1958

FIRST PRINTING

LIBRARY OF CONGRESS CATALOG CARD NUMBER: 58–13791
MANUFACTURED IN THE UNITED STATES OF AMERICA
BY GEORGE MCKIBBIN & SON, NEW YORK

Earth's crammed with heaven,
And every common bush afire with God;
But only he who sees, takes off his shoes—
The rest sit round it and pluck blackberries.
                    —ELIZABETH BARRETT BROWNING

Contents

vii

Introduction

T HIS IS *the story of religion as it has been developed by the leaders of religions. In choosing from many possible characters the best representatives for this series, those founders of religions, sects or movements have been selected who made significant contributions to the progress of religion itself.*

The source material is often discouraging to one seeking the determinative events in the lives of these pioneers. The eulogies of defending disciples are almost as untrustworthy as the slanted statements and even deliberate falsehoods and calumnies of the orthodox enemies, who always and naturally feel duty-bound to attack any apostle of new and therefore heretical religious ideas. Some scholars consider the task of delineation impossible in the case of the earlier men because of the paucity of material and its frequently legendary nature.

Recognizing clearly the validity of their argument in certain instances, one is nevertheless impelled to the task because of the real need of a popular biographically "humanized" presentation of the main outlines of what is technically termed in the colleges and theological seminaries "Comparative Religion."

Moreover, the available material for a proper appraisal of the earlier religious leaders has been greatly increased of late not only by amazing archaeological discoveries but even more by advances in the anthropological study of primitive, racial, and folk psychology, which now forbids us to dismiss myth and legend as unreliable sources of information.

Rudolf Bultmann's much-discussed theological theory named "entmythologisierung" is improperly understood as mere demythologizing. He and his school would not so much remove myths from religion as interpret religion by the myths, recognizing the ancient folk legends, common to all religions, as the universal language of man's deeper unconscious. Psychology is presently superseding or at least reinterpreting dogmatic theology, in the more advanced Christian circles.

Much more space is given herein to Christianity than to any other religion simply because since its advent most progress in religion in general has been made within that faith. This may be due to the assimilative policy initiated so early by Paul and cleverly developed later by Augustine, of winning the race for religious supremacy in the Roman empire by adopting, adapting, and incorporating into Christianity the best ideas and practices of rival religions, including even their myths. Anyone really familiar with the actual history of Christianity always visualizes an "Inc." after its name.

Consequently, any history of religion chronologically approached falls into two general sections, pre-Christian and Christian. There are two apparent exceptions, Islam (long miscalled Mohammedanism in spite of Moslem protests) and Sikhism, but these religions were obviously anachronistic. The former is mainly a revival and purification of primitive Semitic religion adapted to seventh-century-A.D. Arabia, and the latter is essentially an interesting humanistic attempt, launched before its due time, by the guru Nanak to harmonize the faiths of Hindus and Moslems on the basis of their common humanity.

Now, since Christianity is really not one religion, as commonly supposed, but many, and exhibits within its multiform divisions all the varieties of religious experience which can be found outside it, an analysis of present-day Christianity reveals its extensive borrowings from previous and contemporary ethnic faiths and also discovers numerous persistent atavistic survivals of all primitive forms of religion. Animism lives again in sacred pools of healing waters and holy grottoes in the Holy Land itself. Polytheism has not been abandoned: it has only gone underground, for the old gods have simply been reincarnated and baptized as Christian saints, to whom prayers are made requesting the same services as before.

Fetishism, taboo, and magic still flourish under the cross of Christ. Indeed, the cross itself, in miniature, is worn as a charm to avert evil, and the Lord's Prayer (its Essenic phraseology slightly sublimated), inscribed on tiny medals, gems, or rings, has become a magic amulet, increasingly popular among modern psycho-primitive Christians, although the wearing of amulets was condemned by the church as long ago as A.D. 721.

Such vestigial relics and throwbacks, common enough today among several branches of Christianity, betray the origin and evolution of the religion of man as clearly as his wisdom teeth and vermiform appendix reveal the evolution of his body, and their removal is sometimes similarly necessary to his mental and spiritual health.

The term superstition *has been used, occasionally and reluctantly, in this book, but only in places where no other word would convey the meaning to the general reader. The dictionaries define* superstition *as irrational belief, or fearful belief not based on reasonable grounds, but no belief seems unreasonable to the one who holds it: at any rate, no one admits believing a superstition. It is always the other person who is superstitious, for it has become a derogatory term applied to a religion or a religious act by one who holds what he considers a higher religion. And of course there are those to whom all religion seems superstition. It is obvious that the meaning of the term is not fixed but varies with the frame of reference of the person using it. Wearing a bit of brown cloth on a string about one's neck under the clothing is a part of the religion of millions of devout Christians; to other Christians it is a clear case of the survival of primitive superstitious protective magic. Yet these latter may "knock on wood" in a protective superstitious gesture still surviving from a Druidism older than the Christianity which supposedly conquered it.*

"Comparative Religion" also is a loose term of variable meaning. Just as Comparative Anatomy was the study of the similarities of structure in man and the "lower" animals, Comparative Religion

was at first the noting of the likenesses but more particularly of the differences between Christianity and the other ethnic faiths, often referred to as "pagan" or "heathen." But nowadays, although the comparative method may be used, the comparisons are not apt to be so openly odious, nor is the professor's thumb so often pressed down on the Christian side of the scales. And the study course is likely to be called The Philosophy of Religion, The History of Religion, The Psychology of Religion. These new names indicate rapidly growing new disciplines, heralding the arrival at last of the much-needed scientific approach to religion.

In the old days, Christian theologians began with God and built their whole theological structure on certain basic assumptions about the deity—what he must be, to be God. They assumed that, of course, God must have created the earth and man. He was perfect, necessarily, unchangeable, existed everywhere at once, knew everything even before it happened, and was all-powerful. The Latin names for these attributes—immutability, omnipresence, omniscience, omnipotence—still echo in the halls of orthodox theological seminaries and Bible institutes.

Christian theology, having thus determined, established, decreed and ordained the nature of God, proceeded to examine the nature of much-more-visible man and found him, by contrast with the perfect Almighty God, quite a worm of the dust, evil by nature and unable to help himself. Gradually, however, and after "great argument about it and about" by "doctor and saint," there was developed for the salvation of poor lost man an elaborate theological scheme centering in the person and work of Jesus the Christ. But from a scientific viewpoint this whole structure of theology is insecure because based on unproved assumptions.

The new sciences of religion, however, proceed from the known to the unknown. They begin with man and his recorded religious experiences and study the various phenomena in order to appraise and assess the values of religion for human life, both for the individual and for society. A new definition of religion itself is already emerging. Whereas Cicero was satisfied to call it "the pious worship of God," and Dr. Allan Menzies as recently as 1902 won acclaim for terming it "the worship of higher powers from a sense of need," there is a tendency today to question the necessity of including the supernatural in a comprehensive definition of religion.

The idea of religion without God is shocking to Christians, Jews, and Moslems, of course, who affirm that their religions were revealed by God; but Buddha and Confucius long ago founded non-theistic religions, and some modern Unitarian Humanists consider the orthodox idea of God a positive hindrance to the progress of real religion. Many liberals of Christian and non-Christian faiths today like Dr. A. Eustace Haydon's humanistic conception of religion as "the shared quest of the good life." That definition naturally seems pale and anemic to the traditional Christian who stresses the absolute need of being "washed in the blood of the Lamb."

Nevertheless, it has lately become obvious that an adequately inclusive definition must recognize both varieties of religion, theistic and nontheistic. The author's present definition of religion and religions is as follows:

Religion is the endeavor of divided and incomplete human personality to attain unity and completion, usually but not necessarily by seeking the help of an ideally complete divine person or persons.

Religions are systems of belief and practice which arise among the disciples of some man who has attained a satisfying measure of success in his endeavors to unify and complete his personality.

Since, then, every religion begins as some individual's personal religious experience interpreted to and reproduced in others, the story of religion can best be told in the lives of the world's religious leaders, setting forth how the faiths they founded were reflections of their own souls' conflicts and harmonies.

It is a very significant fact that the word religion does not once occur in the Old Testament. There was no need of the word, for everything was religious. Religion and life were one.

In all primitive societies it was so. Law was simply the will of the gods. Morals were determined by religious taboos. Art was first occupied with carving semblances of the gods and decorating their shrines. Primitive man's love of rude rhythm was expressed vocally in repetitious hymns and responses, and bodily in monotonous rocking, jerking, rolling, and prancing at festivals in honor of the deities. Hence came music and the dance. Drama's earliest appearance was in religious ritual at the shrine. And the remnants of early literature that have come down to us have uniformly been sacred scriptures.

Religion was thus the mother of the arts and sciences, but the children grew up and left home. We have a special word for religion now because it is only one of the many interests of man. The history of civilization has been characterized by the progressive delimitation of the sphere of religion.

What is left to religion now? There are some believers who find a sufficient field for their religion in the still unexplained phenomena, the residuum of mystery, but the area of the unknown is being so rapidly reduced (even the celestial realms, traditionally in all religions the special domain of the gods), that those are wiser who are going back to the idea that religion is necessarily concerned with all of life.

A new synthesis is being made, as has often been done before, and of an eternally recurring need. When certain elements of life are divorced from religion and given separate spheres of their own, there is produced in the average person a feeling of confusion and impotence because life lacks unity. Life's various interests clash, and life itself, in vigorously protesting existentialism, thrusts up its demand for a fresh faith.

In the fullness of time some great soul, torn with the apocalyptic conflict within his own personality, by great travail gives birth to a unifying concept of life, a new interpretation of all existence, a new religion. The guardians of orthodoxy may condemn the advanced ideas as dangerous and heretical, but because the vaguely felt desires and hopes of many weary people are reflected and explained, focalized and unified by the prophet in his new philosophy and faith, the long-frustrated folk turn eagerly toward the new light.

In some such manner were all these religions born.

I

AKHENATEN

[1388–1358 B.C.]

"THE FIRST INDIVIDUAL

IN HISTORY"

IT IS HARD to account for this Akhenaten. He seems to stand outside all history, like the Nazarene. They have rightly called him "the first individual in history."[1] He was also the first pacifist, the first realist, the first monotheist, the first democrat, the first heretic, the first humanitarian, the first internationalist, and the first person known to attempt to found a religion.

Born out of due time, several thousand years too soon, he seems to us today, as we try to appraise him. Biologists speak of "saltations," jumps ahead in physical evolution. Perhaps Akhenaten's precivilized mind indicated a sort of spiritual saltation, a leap forward in intellectual evolution. In the history of religion his chapter is a parenthesis, for he took his leap ahead alone. He did not carry his race with him. When he died his disciples forsook him and fled. His religion was a bright spot in the darkness of the superstitious polytheism of the Egypt of the second millennium B.C. It shone but briefly, like a comet, and rapidly passed from the ken of mankind. For three thousand years and more Akhenaten was lost to view.

1 Breasted, *Religion and Thought in Ancient Egypt,* p. 339.

1

The Return of Akhenaten

Then suddenly, in our own time, archaeology restored him to a surprised world and the modern mind has found him to be "the most interesting figure of antiquity."[2] Less than a century ago Akhenaten was referred to as Amenhotep IV, one of the obscure and unimportant kings of the latter part of the eighteenth Egyptian dynasty, but several archaeological discoveries of major importance have since made it possible to read the original letters of his correspondence, to walk on the actual stones of the beautiful floor of his palace, to examine the tombs of his near relatives, to look at his likeness, painted and sculptured by contemporaneous artists, and even to view his mummified body.

Amarna

Nearly two hundred river miles south of Cairo a native woman in the year 1887 was digging for fertilizer among the crumbled walls of old ruins on the bank of the Nile. Ancient mud bricks decompose into a phosphate in much demand among modern Egyptian farmers. But the walls, which thirty centuries ago had resounded to the laughter and the wailings of a long-forgotten royal family, had rich secrets to reveal before they utterly crumbled away. The peasant woman's tool struck into a little hidden chamber where lay hundreds of bricks, not building bricks but clay tablets thickly pitted with small wedge-shaped impressions. She sold them to a neighbor for ten piastres, about a half dollar. The neighbor showed them to dealers, who sent samples to France only to be told the tablets were forgeries. Thereafter they became widely scattered, and many were lost or broken from careless handling. Some were ground to powder because they were carried about in sacks from dealer to dealer by ignorant persons.

When experts finally began to suspect that the tablets were valuable, and deciphered them, they waked up to the fact that the peasant woman had found "the place of the records of the palace of the king" and that the tablets were really the diplomatic correspondence between two kings of Egypt and the rulers of near-by nations.

2 Baikie, *The Amarna Age*, p. 234.

Only three hundred and fifty of the priceless tablets were finally saved, including some found in 1891, but there were enough to throw a flood of light on the fourteenth century B.C. The two Egyptian kings were Akhenaten and his father, Amenhotep III. The bulk of the letters were from subject chieftains in Syria and give us an invaluable picture of conditions in Palestine just before and at the beginning of the Hebrew invasion. Others were from Babylonian, Hittite, Mitannian and Cyprian rulers. Nearly all the tablets are written in Babylonian, which was then evidently the language of diplomacy. They are called the Tell el-Amarna letters from the district where they were found, and the entire historical period from the sixteenth to the thirteenth centuries B.C., not merely in Egypt but in all the Mediterranean and Mesopotamian areas as well, is now known as the Amarna Age.

In 1903 the tomb of Thutmose IV, the paternal grandfather of Akhenaten, was discovered at Thebes, and two years later that of Yuaa and Tuau, his maternal grandfather and grandmother. Two years after that, in 1907, the tomb of Queen Tiy, Akhenaten's mother, was discovered, and although her mummy had been removed, the tomb contained a mummy which was later identified as that of Akhenaten himself. These tombs had all been entered by robbers in ancient times and had been despoiled of many of their treasures, but in 1922 another discovery was made which electrified the world.

The tomb of Tutankhamen, the son-in-law of Akhenaten, was opened and found filled with priceless relics dating from the later years of the eighteenth dynasty. All these discoveries brought the strange Akhenaten very much nearer to us. Tutankhamen himself is of no particular consequence in the history of religion. He simply restored the old orthodox religion which his father-in-law had attempted to replace by Atenism. But the opening of the Tutankhamen tomb, by making possible the verification of hitherto suspected but uncertain facts and by the supplementing of meager material with an abundance of related data, has helped in the reconstruction of the picture of the times of Akhenaten. Several novelists have taken advantage of the fascinating new story-material thus made available. It is noticeable that they have chosen Akhenaten and not Tutankhamen as the major character in their historical novels.

How Akhenaten Looked

From the various archaeological discoveries, which have included paintings, busts and statues, we have a much better conception of Akhenaten's personal appearance than of many religious leaders who lived much later.

"Reveal me as I am," this most consistent of realists told the artists for whom he sat, and they did—misshapen head, long neck, sagging belly, abnormal thighs, and all. The result is that in the long line of pharaohs, he stands out from his somewhat stereotyped predecessors and successors with startling individuality, unashamedly grotesque.

Strangely enough, the queen too and the little princesses are pictured with some of the less objectionable anatomic peculiarities. Perhaps this was due to the artist's desire to minimize the king's affliction by making others share it; perhaps the artist decided that since the king was misshapen, it must be accepted as the style of the day; but it is entirely possible that Queen Nefertiti and her daughters were really thus afflicted, for there are good reasons for supposing that she was her kingly husband's own sister! The whole interbred royal line of the eighteenth dynasty may have suffered from congenital abnormalities, carefully ignored by royal artists save by honest Akhenaten's express command.

Was his brain abnormal too? Did that distorted skull indicate a royal imbecile? Certainly he must have seemed insane to his contemporaries. Within a few years after his death, they were calling him "that criminal." They even took his own mother's body away from the same tomb lest it be contaminated by the presence of the dishonored corpse of her peculiar heretic son.

Dr. William F. Albright (in his fascinating study of monotheism and the historical process, *From the Stone Age to Christianity,* 2nd ed. revised, 1957, p. 220) goes so far as to infer that Akhenaten's physical abnormalities reveal him as definitely pathological, and that this fact, together with his accession age of but eleven years, makes it "absurd" to call him the promulgator of the new teaching, Atenism, or "the first individual in history," as Breasted did. So Albright suggests that Akhenaten was "the tool of others," his mother, perhaps, or his wife Nefertiti, or "some unidentified favorite."

But the line between insanity and genius is hard to draw. Most geniuses are misunderstood by their contemporaries, and all religious heretics risk being judged demented. The thoughts of this homely man were high and noble and blazed a trail in religion like the path of ugly Socrates in philosophy. Had Akhenaten but had a Plato or a Paul, perhaps the history of religion would have been different and Egypt instead of Palestine the Holy Land of modern monotheism.

The Boyhood of Akhenaten

It was a rich heritage into which Akhenaten entered at birth. Egypt was leading the nations in military power at the beginning of the fourteenth century B.C. and had led them for two hundred years. The pyramids were over fifteen hundred years old, and the Egyptians of Akhenaten's day looked back upon the Pyramid period from the same distance as we look back upon the Romans. The eighteenth dynasty had begun two centuries before, when Aahmes I (Ahmose or Amasis) had driven out the foreign "Hyksos" or shepherd kings and had subjugated Palestine and Phoenicia. Other kings had continued the conquests, notably, Thothmes III (Thutmosis, Tahutimes), the empire builder, well known for his obelisks. The list of plunder in one battle alone, the battle of Megiddo on the edge of the Plain of Esdraelon, later famous in Bible history, gives us a hint of the incredible wealth pouring into the Egyptian coffers.

By the time of Amenhotep III, the power and wealth of Egypt were very great, and the royal family lived in luxury. The king was called Amenhotep the Magnificent, and his court at Thebes was of such richness and splendor that Solomon's in all its glory was insignificant in comparison.

"The Kings of Palestine and Syria were tributaries to the young Pharaoh: the princes of the seacoast cities sent their yearly impost to Thebes; Cyprus, Crete, and even the Greek islands were Egyptianized; Sinai and the Red Sea coast as far south as Somaliland were included in the Pharaoh's dominions; and the Negro tribes of the Sudan were his slaves. Egypt was indeed the greatest state in the world, and Thebes was a metropolis at which the ambassadors, the merchants, and the artisans from these various countries met together. Here they could look upon buildings undreamed of in their own lands and could participate in luxuries unknown even in Babylon. The wealth of Egypt was enormous. Golden vases in vast quantities adorned the table of the king and his nobles, and hundreds of golden vessels of different kinds were used in the temples. The splendor and gaiety of the court at Thebes remind one of the tales from the Arabian Nights. One reads of banquets, of splendid festivals on the water, of jubilee celebrations, and of hunting parties."[3]

Amenhotep III, while yet a boy of twelve or thirteen, had come to the throne and had married a girl still younger named Tiy, of whose ancestry we know nothing but of whose character and ability there can be no doubt. When they had been married ten years, he built a palace across the river from Thebes. It was beautifully adorned with paintings on ceiling, walls and pavement, all representing scenes from nature. Portions of painted ceiling and pavement recently excavated reveal startlingly realistic pictures of wild ducks, pigeons, fish, and wild cattle. The next year the rich young ruler made his wife a present of an enormous swimming pool, really an artificial lake. An inscription telling of it has been translated:

Year 11, third month of the first season, day 1, under the Majesty of . . . Amenhotep III., given life; and the Great King's Wife Tiy, who liveth. His Majesty commanded to make a lake for the Great King's Wife, Tiy, in her city of Tjarukha. Its length is 3,700 cubits; its width, 700 cubits. His Majesty celebrated the feast of the opening of the lake in the third month of the first season, day 16, when His Majesty sailed thereon in the royal barge, Tehen-Aten, "The Sun-Disk gleams."[4]

The water festival celebrating the completion of this mile-long lake must have been a gorgeous affair and an occasion of great satisfaction to the young ruler of an empire whose resources were so great and so well organized that a lake of this size could be completed in a fortnight. The great heaps of excavated soil were made into garden-covered hills, much like the famous Hanging Gardens of Babylon which Nebuchadrezzar erected over eight centuries later for his Median queen when she longed for the hills of her homeland.

Now Amenhotep the Magnificent and Tiy his Great Wife were already the parents of four princesses when a son was born to them,

---

[3] Weigall, *Akhenaten, Pharaoh of Egypt*, pp. 29–30.
[4] Baikie, p. 91.

probably in the year 1388 B.C. He was named after and later succeeded his father as Amenhotep IV but is better known now as
Akhenaten. Great care was taken of the child, for it soon became
apparent that Amenhotep III would not last long. Twice did Tushratta the King of Mitanni (North Syria) send an image of Ishtar to
be used to cure the ailing king of Egypt.

The boy was reared in a most luxurious and effeminate environment. His four older sisters probably did their best to spoil him.
There must have been many more women than men in the palace,
for by this time Amenhotep the Magnificent had taken other wives.
These included Gilukhipa and Tadukhipa, princesses from Mitanni. An inscription states that Gilukhipa brought with her 317
"harem-ladies." Tadukhipa probably brought as many, and the
Great Wife Tiy would hardly allow her train of personal attendants
to be outnumbered by the retinues of the lesser wives. That she
knew how to maintain her supreme position is indicated by the
facts that she is mentioned as chief wife even in the inscription
recording the marriage of Amenhotep III and Gilukhipa, and that
her husband gave her the artificial lake shortly after that marriage.

At the age of thirteen in the year 1375 B.C. the boy succeeded to
the throne of Egypt at his father's death. Three wise kings of the
East, Burraburiash, king of Babylon, Shubbiluliuma, king of the
Hittites, and Tushratta, king of Mitanni, sent letters to the young
king of Egypt, letters of condolence and congratulation. Incidentally, instead of sending gifts of gold they very pointedly asked for
them. Tushratta's letter was touching in more ways than one. When
he had heard of the death of Amenhotep III he had wept, he had
fasted, he had "sat unmoving through the midst of that night."
And the letter ends characteristically with a reminder that "in my
brother's land gold is as common as dust." But Tushratta gives the
young king good advice:

As to all the words of Nimmuria (Neb-maat-ra, Amenhotep III), thy
father, which he wrote to me, Tiy, the Great Wife of Nimmuria, the
Beloved, thy mother, she knows all about them. Enquire of Tiy, thy
mother, about all the words of thy father which he spake to me. All the
words together, which I discussed with your father, Tiy, thy mother,
knows them all; and no one else knows them.[5]

5 Baikie, p. 241.

The Strange Marriages of Akhenaten

The Great Tiy was evidently queen regent for some time and directed the course of her son with wisdom. True, she sanctioned, and probably arranged, something which seems to us quite strange. She allowed this boy, just entering his teens, to marry two women, who, to say the least, would not today be considered eligible.

First, the boy married Tadukhipa, one of his father's widows. Then he married Nefertiti, his own full sister. These marriages of Akhenaten have greatly troubled some historians. They have tried to interpret the data in some other way—for instance, that Amenhotep III never married Tadukhipa himself but imported her for his son, and that Nefertiti was at most only a half-sister. They have been reluctant to admit what the monuments clearly indicate. But a knowledge of comparative religion clears at once both difficulties.

The first marriage was quite moral according to the customs of ancient peoples, which not only permitted a king to take over his father's young widows as part of his harem but even, it seems, required him to do it as proof of his ability to succeed his father! This custom was current among the Hebrews, for instance, where the man who got possession of the royal widows or concubines immediately after the king's death had a claim to the throne. Thus Abner, "captain of Saul's host," shortly after Saul's death took Rizpah, Saul's concubine, for his own and thus "made himself strong" as a likely successor to the throne.

The David stories in the Old Testament yield two more instances of the custom. He had so many wives and concubines that there was quite a scramble for the kingship even before his death. Absalom tried to make sure of the succession by cohabiting with ten of his father's concubines "upon the top of the house . . . in the sight of all Israel." This was by the advice of Ahithophel, "and the counsel of Ahithophel which he counselled in those days, was as if a man had enquired at the oracle of God." But inasmuch as Absalom died before his father did, the succession was unsettled. Solomon was chosen by David to succeed him, but immediately after the king's death, another son of David, named Adonijah, who desired to marry the beautiful concubine selected to keep David warm, was put to death by Solomon because he feared it was a ruse on Adonijah's part to seize the throne.

Nor was this an exclusively Hebrew custom. Frazer mentions many other instances,[6] including the legendary Oedipus who killed his father Laius, king of Thebes, and married the widow; Aegisthus at Mycenae; Hamlet's uncle in Denmark; Gyges in Lydia; and Edbald and Ethelbald in England. A particularly notable example is that of Canute the Dane, who to the surprise of later historians, when he had conquered England, married almost "sight unseen" the much older Emma, widow of the former king of England, Ethelred, thus assuring his right to the throne.

But how should the marrying of his father's widow be necessary to secure to a prince the throne of his father, which was coming to him anyway by the right of hereditary succession? The answer to that question reveals a very ancient custom, so old that we know of it mostly through such survivals as this. Once, the royal line of succession to the throne ran through the women instead of through the men—that is, there was a matriarchate instead of a patriarchate. The sex habits of early days were more promiscuous than now. Many a child did not know its father, but they all knew their mothers. If there were to be any royal line at all it had to be through the women. That man was king who was the current consort of the queen. Of a queen of the ancient Picts it was said:

Indeed she was a queen and, but that her sex gainsaid it, might be deemed a king; nay (and this is yet truer), whomsoever she thought worthy of her bed was at once a king, and she yielded her kingdom with herself. Thus her sceptre and her hand went together.[7]

Enough of this old matriarchate idea was surviving in Egypt in the times of Akhenaten so that he strengthened his hold on the throne by marrying Tadukhipa. The same reason lay back of his marriage to Nefertiti, his own sister, which also has parallels in many nations.[8] Probably the marriage of prince with princess is a temporary custom of the long period of transition from matriarchate to patriarchate. The son inherits and rules, but his claim to the throne is stronger if he is not only the son of the king but also the husband of the king's daughter. That this explanation is correct is confirmed by the fact that a boundary stone has been discovered

[6] Sir James G. Frazer, *The Golden Bough*, Vol. 2, Ch. 18.
[7] *Golden Bough*, Vol. 2, p. 281.
[8] *Golden Bough*, Vol. 4, p. 193 note, Vol. 5, p. 316, and especially Vol. 6, pp. 213–216.

which contains Nefertiti's titulary, or list of royal titles, which claims that she was queen in her own right.

The wisdom of Queen Regent Tiy[9] now becomes apparent. When she arranged that her young son, who had just become king, should marry first one of his father's widows and then his father's daughter, she added to his own right of succession two other claims and made his succession right triply sure. She knew that her son was not physically strong and also that there were clouds on the horizon. He would need all the power she could gain for him. His father, Amenhotep III, had been neglecting the outlying provinces, and enemies were consequently gathering. The time had come for a king of Egypt to make a demonstration of military power. The Amarna letters contain many pleas to Akhenaten from subject princes who were being hard-pressed by rising nations beyond them.

But Akhenaten was not interested in military conquests, not because he was an effeminate weakling but because he was interested in other matters entirely. He was raising a family, creating a new art and founding a new religion. His love for Nefertiti and his growing family of daughters is one of the beautiful things of all time. The paintings and low reliefs which have come down to us depict his almost shameless love-making in public. Tadukhipa is entirely in the background. He adored the beautiful sister-wife, Nefertiti, in whom his own physical abnormalities reappeared, but so softened and altered as to have a unique charm. Those who have seen the brown sandstone head and the more famous and often copied painted limestone bust now in Berlin, depicting that engaging and intriguing young beauty of old Egypt, do not wonder at his infatuation.

It was not in good taste for him to be seen riding in a chariot with his wife and daughters, but Akhenaten was a breaker of many old traditions. His patronage of the new art shows that. The priceless specimens of the work of the new school of realistic artists, who admitted that the king himself taught them, reveal to us that a new spirit was abroad in Egypt. Both Akhenaten's attitude toward his family and his theory of art were a part of the third interest which kept him at home from expeditions of pillage and war.

That third interest was the new Aten religion.

9 The New York Metropolitan Museum of Art has a fascinating little black statuette, thirty-three centuries old, of the enigmatic Queen Mother Tiy.

The Rise of Atenism

Some years before Akhenaten was born, a golden pleasure boat had led the procession at that festival which had dedicated the artificial lake. We do not know who named the boat, probably Queen Tiy herself, but its name was very significant. A heresy was launched with the boat, for it was named, not for the great ruling god of Thebes, Amen, but for a new god, Aten (or Aton). Its name was "Tehen-Aten" or "Aten-gleams," which almost might be translated "Sunshine," or "Sunlight."

Egypt had a very complicated theology, the ramifications of which would require a volume to explain. There were many gods, each with a local center of worship, but Ra, the sun-god, was everywhere recognized. Amenism, with its center at the royal capital, Thebes, was the official religion, and the priests of Amen were the orthodox conservers of tradition. The conquests of Thothmes III created an empire-consciousness and with it came a growing tendency to give more honor to the sun-god Ra, because not only in all parts of Egypt but also in all the Mediterranean and Mesopotamian countries, the sun was worshiped. The priests of Amen recognized this tendency by incorporating Ra into Amen, who was now frequently referred to as Amen-Ra.

But this compromise was not enough for the progressives in the court circles, and the word *Aten* began to grow in favor. Aten was really the name of the sun disk, but it came to mean more than that. Early in the reign of the young king Amenhotep IV there was included in his titulary the strange phrase "High-Priest of Harakhti-Rejoicing-in-the-Horizon, in His Name, 'Heat-which-is-in-Aten.'" This titulary was carved on a tablet at a new quarry whence the king was securing stone for a new temple, a temple to "Heat-which-is-in-Aten" to be erected in Thebes itself!

The essence of the theology of Atenism is in that clumsy phrase "Heat-which-is-in-Aten." Akhenaten seems to have been anxious to keep Atenism nonmaterialistic. There was to be no graven image of Aten, for Aten had no physical body. Here was emphasis laid on the life or power or heat or energy which so obviously came from the sun. It was not the sun that was to be worshiped but the central power of it, which seemed so greatly to influence all life on the earth. Akhenaten may even have had a vague conception of what Bergson in our day has called the *élan vital* or vital impulse.

With true artistic taste Akhenaten devised a symbol to illustrate what he meant. There began to appear before long, on the walls of temple and tombs, pictures of various scenes in the life of the king, pictures which have lasted even until today. Above each scene is portrayed the disk of the sun with distinct rays descending to certain parts of the bodies of the human beings in the picture and to other prominent objects. Each ray terminates in a miniature hand and some of the hands hold the *ankh,* the ancient Egyptian symbol of life, which looks like an oval resting upright on the letter *T*. The *ankh* was borrowed by many religions and is found in Christian art as the *crux ansata* or handled cross. It was obviously of phallic significance originally.

Plainly the teaching of the entire symbol of disk, rays, hands and *ankh* was that all life and all blessings come from the energy of the sun. There could be no better trade-mark for the modern devices for curing by light rays than one of these three-thousand-year-old pictures.

Very rapidly the new religion gained power, as any religion does at first which has a ruling monarch as patron. The nobles fell into line, but the priests of Amen prepared to defend the old religion. Not content with having a temple to Aten in the city of Amen, Akhenaten ruled that Thebes itself should be thereafter called "The City of the Brightness of Aten." Then he proceeded to even more drastic measures which indicate that his mother's regency was over and he had taken the reins of full power. Queen Tiy had been too wise to go to the excesses in which the young religious fanatic now indulged.

The Religious Revolution

At once he made his position very clear by changing his own name from Amenhotep IV to Akhenaten (otherwise variously written Akhnaton, Ikhnaton and Khuenaten), meaning "He in whom Aten is satisfied." It was both an announcement and a challenge. Amen was to be obscured by Aten. The change of name occurred about the sixth year of the young king's reign, when he was nineteen years of age. The die once cast, Akhenaten commenced immediately a vigorous campaign to supplant the old faith with the new. He forbade the worship of Amen, officially closed the Amen temples, and became so obsessed by his reforming spirit that he ordered the obliteration of the name of Amen wherever it occurred in the many inscriptions. A most consistent and thorough iconoclast he was, indeed, who caused even his own father's name to be chiseled away from the buildings Amenhotep III had erected.

Still further, so ardent a monotheist was this youthful revolutionist in religion that he tried to eradicate all the gods of Egypt. Even the word *gods* was removed from the monuments. But it is far easier to rub out a word, even if the word be written in stone characters, than to remove from the minds of living men their regard for the religion which that word symbolizes. Opposition developed.

The Thebans did not take kindly to the sudden change of religion and, led by the priests of Amen, made their disapproval known. Promptly Akhenaten punished them in the most severe fashion by removing the royal court from Thebes. Perhaps he recognized the futility of trying to set up a new religion where the old was so strongly intrenched by prestige and long possession. Erase the name of Amen, close the temples, stop the ritual, still Thebes was the city of Amen.

With characteristic originality, Akhenaten determined to symbolize the universality of Atenism by creating three new religious capitals, one far down the Nile from Thebes, another in Syria and the third in Ethiopia. Of the Syrian one we know nothing today. The Ethiopian city was called "Gem-Aten" and the Egyptian, Akhetaten, "The Horizon of Aten."

The City of the Horizon

By the eighth year of his reign, such progress had been made in the building of Akhetaten that Akhenaten moved from Thebes with his wife Nefertiti and his three infant daughters Meritaten, Maketaten and Ankhsenpaaten, together with his courtiers and attendants. In the new environment, free from the weight of tradition and hostile atmosphere in Thebes, the new religion grew more beautiful. Tell el-Amarna has its charm today, but when it was Akhetaten, the City of the Horizon, it must have been the delight of poets and artists.

The excavations at Tell el-Amarna have revealed enough of the remains of the buildings so that, with the aid of the pictures on the

walls of the near-by tombs of the nobles of the court, we are able to
reconstruct imaginatively the remarkable Utopia which Akhenaten
created more than three thousand years ago. One of Akhenaten's
nobles describes Akhetaten as, "The mighty City of the Horizon
of Aton, great in loveliness, mistress of pleasant ceremonies, rich in
possessions, the offering of the sun being in her midst. At the sight
of her beauty there is rejoicing. She is lovely and beautiful: when
one sees her it is like a glimpse of heaven."[10]

Never has there been, before or since, such a community founded
as a religious experiment. Kings had built cities before and religious
leaders have built small communities since, but here was a religious
king building on a royal scale an entire city of homes, palaces,
temples and recreation halls, the whole place dedicated to Aten
and conceived as an expression of the spirit of Atenism. Such a
synthesis of life and religion is unique in the world's history. Life
was rich and beautiful, joyous and free, not in spite of but because
of religion. For the religion was one from which the master mind
of Akhenaten had banished superstition and fear and into which
he had introduced sunshine and happiness.

What Akhenaten Taught

By a fortunate circumstance we know what Akhenaten actually
taught. The writings of other founders of religion have suffered
from the hands of many copyists and editors. Until the 1945 discovery of the Qumran manuscripts, commonly called the Dead Sea
Scrolls, the oldest manuscript of the Hebrew Bible dated from the
ninth or tenth century A.D. The oldest nearly complete manuscript
of the New Testament belongs to the fourth century A.D. Both had
suffered many changes before then. It is much the same with the
sacred scriptures of other religions. But we may today look upon
the original text of the teachings of Akhenaten as it was written
during his lifetime under his supervision upon the walls of the
tombs of his contemporaries. And the theology of Atenism com-
pares most favorably with that of any religion whatsoever. The
startling thing to us is its extreme modernism. It is as broad and
universal as life itself.

The fortunate preservation of the very originals of the scriptures
containing the teachings of Akhenaten was due to the fact that the

10 For more detailed description, see Weigall, pp. 175-185.

custom of the nobility to cover the walls of their tombs with traditional inscriptions of the stereotyped phrases of Amenism was forbidden in Akhetaten. The question arose as to what should be done
with the blank spaces. Someone had the inspiration to use the spaces
for writing down the hymns which Akhenaten was composing for
the services held in honor of Aten. These hymns expressed the spirit
of the new religion and outlined its simple theology.

Most of these are short, but the tomb of the noble Ay, "master of
all the horses of His Majesty," has inscribed upon its walls a longer
hymn which takes high rank among the religious treasures of the
world. It is well worth quoting complete in Professor Breasted's
beautiful translation.[11]

Thy dawning is beautiful in the horizon of heaven,
O living Aton, Beginning of life!
When thou risest in the eastern horizon of heaven,
Thou fillest every land with Thy beauty;
For Thou art beautiful, great, glittering, high over the earth;
Thy rays, they encompass the lands, even all Thou hast made.
Thou art Ra, and Thou hast carried them all away captive;
Thou bindest them by Thy love.
Though Thou art afar, Thy rays are on the earth;
Though Thou art on high, Thy footprints are the day.

When Thou settest in the western horizon of heaven,
The world is in darkness like the dead.
Men sleep in their chambers,
Their heads are wrapped up,
Their nostrils stopped, and none seeth the other.
Stolen are all their things that are under their heads,
While they know it not.
Every lion cometh forth from his den,
All serpents, they sting.
Darkness reigns,
The world is in silence:
He that made them has gone to rest in His horizon.

Bright is the earth, when Thou risest in the horizon,
When Thou shinest as Aton by day.
The darkness is banished
When Thou sendest forth Thy rays;

[11] *A History of Egypt,* pp. 371–376.

The two lands [of Egypt] are in daily festivity,
Awake and standing upon their feet,
For Thou hast raised them up.
Their limbs bathed, they take their clothing,
Their arms uplifted in adoration to Thy dawning.
Then in all the world they do their work.

All cattle rest upon the herbage,
All trees and plants flourish;
The birds flutter in their marshes,
Their wings uplifted in adoration to Thee.
All the sheep dance upon their feet,
All winged things fly,
They live when Thou hast shone upon them.

The barques sail upstream and downstream alike.
Every highway is open because Thou hast dawned.
The fish in the river leap up before Thee,
And Thy rays are in the midst of the great sea.

Thou art He who creates the man-child in woman,
Who makest seed in man,
Who giveth life to the son in the body of his mother,
Who soothest him that he may not weep,
A nurse [even] in the womb.
Who giveth breath to animate every one that He maketh.
When he cometh forth from the body . . .
On the day of his birth,
Thou openest his mouth in speech,
Thou suppliest his necessities.

When the chicken crieth in the egg-shell,
Thou givest him breath therein, to preserve him alive;
When Thou hast perfected him
That he may pierce the egg,
He cometh forth from the egg,
To chirp with all his might;
He runneth about upon his two feet,
When he hath come forth therefrom.

How manifold are all Thy works!
They are hidden from before us,

O Thou sole God, whose powers no other possesseth.
Thou didst create the earth according to Thy desire,
While Thou wast alone:
Men, all cattle large and small,
All that are upon the earth,
That go about upon their feet;
All that are on high,
That fly with their wings.
The countries of Syria and Nubia,
The land of Egypt;
Thou settest every man in his place,
Thou suppliest their necessities.
Every one has his possessions,
And his days are reckoned.
Their tongues are divers in speech,
Their forms likewise and their skins,
For Thou, divider, hast divided the peoples.
Thou makest the Nile in the nether world,
Thou bringest it at Thy desire, to preserve the people alive.
O Lord of them all, when feebleness is in them,
O Lord of every house, who risest for them,
O sun of day, the fear of every distant land,
Thou makest [also] their life.
Thou hast set a Nile in heaven,
That it may fall for them,
Making floods upon the mountains, like the great sea,
And watering their fields among their towns.

How excellent are Thy designs, O Lord of eternity!
The Nile in heaven is for the strangers,
And for the cattle of every land that go upon their feet;
But the Nile, it cometh from the nether world for Egypt.
Thus Thy rays nourish every garden;
When Thou risest they live, and grow by Thee.

Thou makest the seasons, in order to create all Thy works;
Winter bringeth them coolness,
And the heat [the summer bringeth].
Thou hast made the distant heaven in order to rise therein,
In order to behold all that Thou didst make,
While Thou wast alone,

Rising in Thy form as Living Aton,
Dawning, shining afar off, and returning.

Thou makest the beauty of form through Thyself alone,
Cities, towns, and settlements,
On highway or on river,
All eyes see Thee before them,
For Thou art Aton [or Lord] of the day over the earth.

Thou art in my heart;
There is no other that knoweth Thee,
Save Thy son Akhnaton.
Thou hast made him wise in Thy designs
And in Thy might.
The world is in Thy hand,
Even as Thou hast made them.
When Thou hast risen they live;
When Thou settest they die.
For Thou art duration, beyond mere limbs;
By Thee man liveth,
And their eyes look upon Thy beauty
Until Thou settest.
All labor is laid aside
When Thou settest in the west.
When Thou risest they are made to grow....
Since Thou didst establish the earth,
Thou hast raised them up for Thy son,
Who came forth from Thy limbs,
The King, living in truth ...
Akhnaton, whose life is long;
[And for] the great royal wife, his beloved,
Mistress of the Two Lands ... Nefertiti,
Living and flourishing for ever and ever.

The reader who is familiar with the Psalms of David will have noted the many parallelisms between this hymn and the 104th Psalm, similarities in language and especially in thought. The composition of the Hebrew Psalm is assigned by scholars to the Greek Period of Hebrew History, 332–168 B.C.[12] hence the Egyptian hymn is at least a thousand years older. Even if David wrote the Psalm, as

[12] Briggs, Psalms, Vol. II, in *International Critical Commentary.*

tradition has it, the Egyptian composition is over three centuries older. If anyone was guilty of plagiarism, it was not Akhenaten.

The Passing of Akhenaten

The idyllic life of the City of the Horizon was very brief. Like every religious community dedicated to ideas far in advance of those of its day it did not last a generation. It barely outlasted its founder, who lived only a decade at Akhetaten, from his twenty-first to his thirtieth and last year. From the known facts we infer that the first part of the decade was a period of happy, enthusiastic building. The city had been laid out only two years before it was occupied and consequently there were many parts to be developed and completed after the colonists arrived. But the shadows which Queen Tiy had foreseen had become deeper and darker. Before long the clouds obscured even the sun of Atenism, and there must have been gloomy days in Akhetaten toward the end. When we read the Amarna letters we easily understand how it happened and how inevitable it was.

There rises in the letters from Akhenaten's correspondents, the kings of Assyria, Babylon, Mitanni, and Hattu, a wail of complaint that his presents to them were not on the scale of those which his father had sent. Evidently Akhenaten had to cut expenses some-where when he created a great and gorgeous city. Other complaints came from vassal princes on the Syrian frontier that the people of the countries beyond were pressing them hard. They begged for Egyptian armies to defend their cities, but the help they asked for did not come. Their letters were full of lies, but it was true they were being hard-pressed.

They were asking a pacifist to fight for them. When Akhenaten developed his doctrine of the universal love of God, he was logical enough to live up to its corollary, the universal brotherhood of man. In his hymn to Aten,

> The countries of Syria and Nubia,
> The land of Egypt;
> Thou settest every man in his place,
> Thou suppliest their necessities,

he was announcing the spiritual brotherhood of nations, and he refused to make war against any of those upon whom the sun shone.

He prided himself upon his honesty and truthfulness, calling himself "Ankh em Maat," "Living in Truth," and he would not say one thing in his words and the opposite in his deeds.

When, then, one visualizes Akhenaten as a sincere truth-lover and a consistent pacifist living in a world where his enemies were accomplished liars and experienced warriors, at a time when any policy but trickery and force was looked on as a sign of weakness, it is easy to see why Akhenaten's reign was brief. His untimely death was as inevitable as that of Jesus and for much the same reasons.

The action of Christian rulers at the time of the first World War suffers in comparison with the action of Akhenaten three thousand years before. Woodrow Wilson's conduct was a possible exception and affords an interesting parallel.[13]

When the Egyptians knew that their king's policy was ruining the empire, internal troubles developed. The hostile priests of Amen found their cause strengthened by the increasing disaffection. Whether the growing difficulty of keeping his faith and his empire both intact proved so great a burden that it affected the king's health, or whether ill health prevented him from coping with the situation adequately—which was cause and which effect, we cannot surely tell today, but the combination was enough to kill any man of as sensitive and nervous a disposition as that of the young king. It may be that the fact that the names of Akhenaten's later daughters (he had seven, and no son) end in "ra" instead of "aten" indicates an attempt at compromise by returning to the worship of the older form of the Egyptian sun-god, but it is unlikely, for all other signs indicate that the king held out to the bitter end.

Just before his death he made two attempts to stem the tide. He celebrated his jubilee. It was customary for Egyptian kings to do that thirty years after their accession. Akhenaten stretched a point and dated the beginning of the thirty years at his birth. He knew well that if he waited till thirty years from his coronation, there would be no jubilee and he knew that jubilees of any sort strengthened the loyalty of wavering subjects. He also appointed a co-regent. He had no son but he had sons-in-law of the nobility. His eldest daughter, Meritaten, had been married to Smenkhkara and his third daughter, Ankhsenpaaten, to Tutankhaten. Either of these sons-in-law was eligible, because both were married to daughters of the king. Akhenaten chose Smenkhkara as co-regent and

[13] See Simeon Strunsky, *King Akhnaton.*

lived less than a year thereafter. Just what disease took him off at last we do not know, but the abundant evidence of his physical peculiarities and the known weakness of his ancestors lead us to infer that the inbred royal line was naturally decadent and had little resistance to offer to any disease.

The Great King was buried in his already prepared tomb in the hills back of his beloved city, with ceremony and with great sadness, for everyone must have known that they were witnessing the obsequies of the last great king of the eighteenth dynasty. Smenkhkara ruled but a few months and accomplished nothing. The task was too great. All that we know of him is that a label on a wine container was discovered in the ruins of Akhetaten, bearing the date of the second year of his reign. The husband of the third daughter succeeded to the throne. Of him we know much, for he was that Tutankhaten who abjured Atenism, capitulated to Amenism, changed his name to Tutankhamen, and whose unspoiled tomb was opened to startle our world in 1922.

The triumphant priests of Amen found revenge sweet. Tutankhamen and his queen, now "Ankhsenpaamen," evidently placed themselves wholly at the disposal of the restoration party, for they reigned six, perhaps nine, years, but the queen must have felt twinges of conscience many times. The court was restored to Thebes, Akhetaten was abandoned to desolation and decay, Akhenaten's mummy was brought to the tomb of his mother Queen Tiy, and he was officially referred to as "that criminal"!

Why Atenism Fell

Atenism, which started out so gloriously, fell so ignominiously, for several reasons. First, its initiation had been too abrupt. The polytheism of Egypt had hardly evolved from animism, as the animal-headed images of its gods amply showed. To expect a whole race to change to monotheism in a decade was expecting too much. To expect it to change to a monotheism so pure that the god was a disembodied philosophical idea was beyond reason. Again, Atenism was almost a court fad, the diversion of bored nobility. Only in Akhenaten himself was it a passionate obsession. The people of Egypt probably did not know what it was all about. They might have appreciated their king's democratic religion had his publicity methods been better and had they not had the servility complex which causes the slave to despise the master who demeans himself by recognizing the slave as an equal.

Finally, the unfortunate political situation made impossible the long period of peace necessary for the development of the new religion. In itself Atenism might have appealed to Syria and even to other nations, for Aten was much like Adonis. But Akhenaten's foreign policy, while it was a result of his religion, was in reality the death of his religion, for it would have necessitated his own abdication, even if his own death had not intervened.

Akhenaten's Importance in the History of Religion

When the outstanding characters in the history of religion are arranged in chronological order, one would naturally expect to find the earlier religious leaders appearing as representatives of the more primitive religions. The concept of deity should develop from crude animism, through polytheism, to anthropomorphic tribal god and then on to highly ethical and spiritual monotheism.

This is indeed the general outline of the progress of the religion of mankind, but the leaders of men have usually been in advance of their fellows. Necessarily so, or they would not have been leaders. But some leaders have been more in advance of their contemporaries than others. If a prophet is a little way ahead of his people he can lift their religion to his. If he is somewhat farther in advance, they rise a little and then sink back toward, but not to, their former level. But if he is too far ahead of them for them to comprehend him, they may follow a little way or for a short time and then sink back in despair or reaction into a worse orthodoxy than before. That was the way with Akhenaten and his people. Orthodox Amenism was stronger ten years after his death than it was at his birth. Egyptian religion never even remotely approached his level afterward.

But Atenism will come again and better than Atenism. The Eternal Life and Light at the heart of the universe must continually manifest itself until death and darkness vanish. Moses evidently caught the gleam, dimly at least, and passed it on. It flared up again in the prophets of Israel, Iran and Qumran, and in Jesus Christ became the light of the world. It died down again as men obscured the light with revived orthodoxies, but there are signs today of another dawning. All races and religions have caught the gleam and followed it, sometimes near and often afar, but ever hopeful.

Atenism would not do for a complete religion today. The Hymn to Aten is spiritual and beautiful but it lacks ethical content. It has much about God's relation to man, but too little of man's relation to God, and nothing of man's relation to man, save a vaguely implied brotherhood. Still it nourished one great soul. With reverence we look upon the newly opened pages of history and speak softly and with respect of our hitherto unknown friend, Akhenaten. We see him through the mists of thirty-three centuries but know in our hearts that he will be the contemporary of our great-grandchildren.

We agree with Arthur Weigall[14] that "He has given us an example three thousand years ago which might be followed at the present day: an example of what a husband and a father should be, of what an honest man should do, of what a poet should feel, of what a preacher should teach, of what an artist should strive for, of what a scientist should believe, of what a philosopher should think. Like other great teachers, he sacrificed all to his principles, and thus his life plainly shows—alas!—the impracticability of his doctrines; yet there can be no question that his ideals will hold good 'till the swan turns black and the crow turns white, till the hills rise up to travel, and the deeps rush into the rivers.' "

When they found the embalmed body of Akhenaten in 1907 in the Valley of the Tombs of the Kings, in his mother's tomb from the walls of which her son's name had been erased, they discovered a prayer evidently addressed to Aten and composed by the king himself. It was engraved on gold foil placed just beneath Akhenaten's feet, and it read, as Dr. Alan Gardiner[15] translates it,

I breathe the sweet breath which comes forth from Thy mouth. I behold Thy beauty every day. It is my desire that I may hear Thy sweet voice, even the north wind, that my limbs may be rejuvenated with life through love of Thee. Give me Thy hands, holding Thy spirit, that I may receive it and may live by it. Call Thou upon my name unto eternity, and it shall never fail.

[14] Weigall, p. 251.
[15] Weigall, p. 249.

II

MOSES

[THIRTEENTH CENTURY B.C.]

WHO DISCOVERED THE PERSONALITY OF GOD

O F ALL HUMAN BEINGS, the one who has most influenced the others is Moses. Over three thousand years ago he was buried "in a valley in the land of Moab," yet his era is only now ending, if indeed it will ever end.

Not only did all his words become religious precepts and moral law to his own undying people, the Hebrews, but they have echoed and re-echoed down the centuries. Christianity and Islam are direct outgrowths of the Judaism which Moses founded, and are still rooted in his ethical system. Muhammad hailed Moses and Jesus as the greatest prophets of old. Jesus said, "I came not to destroy the Law [of Moses] but to fulfill it." In later years Puritanism in England and America was a revival in Christianity of the legalism of Moses and found its justification therein; and Mormonism, that well-organized present-day Puritanism, is but a recent reverberation of the thundering prohibitions of the book of Exodus.

In government as well as in religion, Moses is still mighty after three millenniums. The laws of the Christian world are traced to his lips, and millions who recognize no religious fealty to him or his God are still influenced in their legal loyalties, tremendously and inescapably, by his ancient pronouncements in the shadow of Sinai. It may be that Mosaic prohibitions will eventually be replaced by the spiritual persuasions of Christianity. It may be that capital punishment, which says, "Whoso sheddeth man's blood, by man shall his blood be shed," will someday be superseded by a less vindictive justice. A careful inquiry must reveal, however, that, as yet, "eye for eye and tooth for tooth" is the guiding spirit of more existing legislation than is inspired by the principles of the Sermon on the Mount.

When we leave the fields of religion and law, and pass to the industrial world, we find Moses still supreme. There, his principles obtain, rather than those of Christ. Many Christians are in business in America, but their business is not run on Christian principles, and they admit it. Indeed, under the present system, it cannot be, for the present system is mainly Mosaic. It is still considered rather clever and a good joke to "spoil the Egyptians" when you have a good chance, especially after the Egyptians have "spoiled" you.

Idealistic individuals, conspicuous by their rarity, have occasionally tried to run their business more or less according to the Golden Rule of doing to others as they would have others do to them, a conscientious attempt to "Christianize" industry. But even if they had succeeded in applying the Golden Rule, that success would not have made industry Christian. The Golden Rule was taught in seven different religions, including the Jewish, long before Christ was born. Very few businessmen, if any, have ever tried out the more distinctively Christian principles of giving to all who beg, taking no thought for the morrow, turning away from none who would borrow, and giving an opponent a second chance to smite. Nonresistance is hardly characteristic yet of the men of industrial and commercial circles, even in Christian countries. It is hard enough in business to live up to the ethics of Moses.

In actual daily living, most Christians profess Christianity but practice Mosaism—that is, if they live up to the Ten Commandments, they think they are doing pretty well and do not worry much about the Beatitudes and the Sermon on the Mount. Christianity is an ideal; Mosaism, a reality.

There is, therefore, no sphere of human life today in Europe or America where the influence of Moses is not overwhelmingly felt, whether for good or bad. The very fact that the teachings of Moses are all-pervasive and generally accepted blinds us to the magnitude of his influence. We make light of him, but we live by his laws. The boy on the streets chants in derisive doggerel,

Holy Moses, the king of the Jews,
Wore his stockings without any shoes.

The professor in his study dissects documents, examines evidence and balances data to prove that Moses never lived. Meanwhile there comes round the corner the protector of both urchin and sage, the officer of the law, whose rhythmic steps on the sidewalk beat out slowly and steadily the eternal words of Moses, "Thou shalt not murder; thou shalt not steal!"

Was Moses Mythical?

If Moses has been so immeasurably important to the human race, why is it that some scholars have questioned his historical existence? It is a strange and interesting fact that the greater a man is, the more probable will be the denial, some centuries after his death, that he ever existed at all!

There is a fairly regular process by which this comes about. By his outstanding character the great man attracts attention and a following during his lifetime. After his death, his admiring disciples gather in group meetings to testify how wonderful a man the master was. Stories related by enthusiasts seldom lose anything in the telling. Disciples dote especially on tales of infant precocity foreshadowing the adult wisdom of their teacher. Simple folk commonly connect the unusual with the supernatural. Consequently, when their limited vocabularies fail to express adequately their deep emotional appreciation, the growing tendency to extravagant praise soon reaches its natural climax in the ascription of partial or even complete deity to their beloved great one.

Then fresh legends arise. The distinct outlines of the outstanding individual become blurred as he is idealized and made totemic and epic. The cutting edge of the prophet's personality is dulled with nacreous tradition until the character of the nucleus is forgotten in the beauty of the pearl. Cycles of stories group themselves around the hero, and old myths are attached to him, myths that were formerly related of other all-wise ones, legends selected from the whole zodiac of human experience, and then the apotheosis is complete. Centuries pass, and some analytic historian, examining the sacred scriptures of the faith built around this great teacher's personality, announces gravely, "The historicity of this character is very doubtful. We have here probably only a group of sun myths nucleating around an alleged person."

In the case of Moses, this evolution from historic person, through periods of appreciation, eulogy, idealization, enhaloing, and mythologizing, to an actual denial of historicity, is easily traceable. The Hebrews never quite accomplished the full deification of Moses, however, perhaps because the tradition remained that he had insisted, "Thou shalt have no other gods than Yahweh." But they did partially apotheosize him. They spoke of him as so transfigured that the skin of his face emitted rays, which a poor translation rendered, "horns." This mistake is perpetuated in Michelangelo's magnificent statue of Moses in the Church of San Pietro-in-Vincoli, Rome. Had the sculptor made the horns longer and curved, Moses might have entered the divine company of Jupiter Ammon, Azazel, Hathor, Kneph, Yama, Pan, and other horned deities.

The author of the apocryphal Assumption of Moses, who lived during the lifetime of Jesus, certainly considered Moses to be more than a mere man. In this anonymous apocryphon, of increased importance and interest since the discovery of the very similar Qumran (Dead Sea) manuscripts, Moses is said to have pre-existed before creation with God (as Christians later claimed Christ had) and was "prepared before the foundation of the world to be the Mediator of God's covenant with His people (Assumption of Moses 1:14 and 3:12). Moses is even called (11:16) "the Lord of the Word . . . God's chief prophet throughout the earth, the most perfect teacher in the world." All the world was to be the sepulcher for his secretly interred body (11:8) after Michael the Archangel won it away from the devil (Assumption of Moses, R. H. Charles, 1897, page 106. See the Bible Epistle of Jude 1:9), while Moses' soul was assumpted to the heavens, where God appointed him to be the great intercessor for the sins of the Jews.

The final step in the process, the denial of the historicity of Moses by the higher critics, we have witnessed in our day. Their reasons for doubting his existence include, among others, (1) the parallels between the Moses stories and older ones like that of Sargon, (2) the absence of any Egyptian account of such a great event as the Pentateuch asserts the Exodus to have been, (3) the attributing to Moses of so many laws that are known to have originated much later, (4) the correlative fact that great codes never suddenly appear full-born but are slowly evolved, (5) the difficulties of fitting the slavery, the Exodus, and the conquest of Canaan into the known chronology of Egypt and Palestine, and (6) the extreme probability that some of the twelve tribes were never in Egypt at all.

Any one of these reasons is sufficient to cause us to ponder seriously the question of the historicity of the traditional Moses, but all of them together are not enough to force us to deny the existence of a great Moses, for all of them can be (and have been) accounted for much more easily than we can explain without Moses the Exodus from Egypt and the development of a fleeing horde of superstitious slaves into the organized One-God-worshipers whose fighting phalanxes startled and subdued Canaan. As the late Professor Charles Foster Kent said, "If all the Pentateuchal books had been lost, it would still be necessary to postulate a personality like that of Moses to explain the character of the Israelites as they figure in later history."[1]

The Man behind the Traditions

Too long have we left Moses in the mists of obscurity whence doubting critics have said he can never emerge. Many legends dim his outlines and contradictions cloud our view of him, but that very fact predicates the presence of a great person behind the mists. The new type of historian is learning to appreciate myth as the vehicle for conveying more significant facts than are cut in cuneiform tablets, and to recognize contradictory records as the evidence of the varying impressions made upon smaller men by the great men of all time.

Historical criticism, of the destructive and dry-as-dust type which in the nineteenth century characterized German theological circles, is giving way to a new form which uses psychology and which refuses to spend all its time in the dissection of documents. The old school of higher critics disposed of Moses, Homer, Zoroaster, Buddha, and Jesus as mythical characters, and has been at work on Muhammad, Omar Khayyam, and even as late a figure as Shakespeare. These critics did a necessary service, in a way, but too often the operation killed the patient. There is now, happily, a strong tendency in the other direction, and it is due to an improved tech-

[1] *History of the Hebrew People*, 1:39–40.

nique of appraisal which follows Von Ranke's axiom, "I do not go back *to,* but back *of,* the documents."

After all, it is a confession of failure of method and technique when a scholar cannot see the forest for the trees, or when he deduces that no vase ever existed because he finds only a few unmatched shards left. If a scientist can reconstruct a skeleton of an extinct dinosaur from a single thigh bone so accurately that it matches a complete skeleton later discovered, and if an astronomer's prediction from the irregularities of several orbits that a new planet will be found in a certain location is later verified when a larger telescope is employed, then, surely, it is not too much to hope that we can find the real Moses.

As a matter of fact, the eclipse of Moses is nearly over. The penumbra of theological scholasticism is rapidly passing away, and one may venture to suggest a somewhat new conception, which differs from the Moses of the Sunday School Quarterly and differs still more from the anemic ghostly figure of the higher criticism. While one works over the vague, contradictory sources and the still more exasperating quarrels and quibbles of commentators and scholars, there slowly rises the mighty figure of a man—a man of his own crude times of lust and fighting, deceit and superstition, but a man withal of such power of purpose and with such indomitable faith in his God that it is not surprising that miracle stories have gathered about him. There is a power in a great human personality that laughs at space and time and even overleaps the confining traditions of eulogistic disciples. Carleton Noyes says, "These garnishments of romance do not disguise the essential personality of Moses as a man of signal capacity for leadership, of exceptional skill in administration, and an authentic religious genius. The reality of Moses has overcome tradition."[2]

Much of the majesty of the character of Moses has been unperceived by those who have not contrasted the religion which he found with the religion which he left. Perhaps nowhere in history has any one man taken such a long stride forward and carried a nation with him. His life seems actually to have been the historical bridge between animistic polytheism and ethical monotheism—that is practically to say, from superstition to religion. Of course, his predecessors' superstitions were primitive religion and his own religion had a large content of credulity, but through the windows

2 *The Genius of Israel,* 49.

of his personal experience our human race saw a bright light where hitherto had been darkness.

To picture Moses accurately, then, we must admit a content of magic and even of animism, which prevents our regarding his religion as wholly acceptable to us. In his deeds and in his decalogues are reflected strange, uncouth, and barbaric practices which do not commend themselves to us. The man who emerges when we turn the light of comparative religion upon him is not altogether lovely and of good report by present-day standards of ethics and morality.

Serpent-worship, fetishes, ordeals to determine guilt, polygamy, offerings of hair, strange vows, ceremonial defilement, belief in evil spirits, magic, the efficacy of blood, the sacrifice of birds and animals, and phallic worship—all these elements of superstition and primitive religion seem to have been sanctioned or tolerated by Moses. The "spoiling" of the Egyptians, the harsh treatment of captives and the idea of women as property do not agree with our ethical ideals. False witness might not be borne against another Hebrew in court, but one was permitted to sell bad meat to strangers. When we realize that such ideas were in the mind of this Moses whose influence has been so potent in the world for three millenniums, we are still more anxious to push aside the veil of tradition and find the secret of his power.

Tradition tells us that "Moses was the meekest man." The only recorded incidents upon which any reputation for meekness could possibly have been built are two, one where he keeps discreetly silent when his sister Miriam protests at his taking a Cushite (Ethiopian) woman as a second wife, probably bigamously, and the other at the burning bush where he exhibits natural reticence when it is suggested that he soon make a public address before a hostile audience with the royal box occupied. When we go behind the tradition of meekness and interpret his character by his deeds, we discover a powerful fellow who kills an Egyptian with one blow of his fist, and whose irascibility is exhibited on more than one occasion. His own people said the reason he was not permitted to enter the promised land was an outbreak of bad temper (Numbers 20:7–12). Surely if "the man Moses was very meek, above all the men which were upon the face of the earth" (Numbers 12:3), the other men upon the face of the earth at that time must have been very rough persons.

The secret of Moses' influence upon posterity lay not in his being the meekest of men. Something tremendous happened to him, a great religious experience, the power of which he was able to convey to his own impressionable race, whence it has come to us. In order to understand that religious experience and its effect, we must follow his life story.

The Life of Moses

Bible accounts divide the life of Moses into three periods of forty years each, the first ending with his flight into Midian, the second with his leaving Midian on his mission to rescue his countrymen, and the third coinciding with the forty years in the wilderness. This tradition may be correct in dividing his life into three periods, but we must remember the Semitic fondness for the round number forty, as representing almost anything over ten and under a hundred. Judging from the lives of other men, twenty is a more likely age for the murder and running away, and thirty for the mission to Egypt. Allowing forty years for the trek to Palestine would bring his death at seventy.

Concerning his youth we know almost nothing. We are told in Exodus 6:20, "And Amram took him Jochebed his father's sister to wife; and she bare him Aaron and Moses." But whoever wrote the earlier and more familiar account of "Moses in the Bulrushes" in the second chapter of Exodus was evidently unaware of his hero's parents' names. After telling of the edict of the king of Egypt that all male children of the Hebrew captives should be killed at birth, the unknown author relates,

And there went a man of the house of Levi, and took to wife a daughter of Levi. And the woman conceived and bare a son: and when she saw him that he was a goodly child, she hid him three months. And when she could no longer hide him, she took for him an ark of bulrushes, and daubed it with slime and with pitch, and put the child therein; and she laid it in the flags by the river's brink. And his sister stood afar off, to wit what would be done to him.

And the daughter of Pharaoh came down to wash herself at the river; and her maidens walked along by the river's side; . . . and, behold, the babe wept. And she had compassion on him and said, This is one of the Hebrews' children. Then said his sister to Pharaoh's daughter, Shall I go and call to thee a nurse of the Hebrew women, that she may nurse the child for thee? And Pharaoh's daughter said to her, Go. And the maid went and called the child's mother. And Pharaoh's daughter said unto her, Take this child away, and nurse it for me, and I will give thee thy wages. And the woman took the child, and nursed it. And the child grew, and she brought him unto Pharaoh's daughter, and he became her son. And she called his name Moses: and she said, Because I drew him out of the water.

The story of the infant hero, hidden from a baby-killing king, is in various versions very frequently found in comparative mythology.[3] It has even been attached to Jesus.[4] Probably the story was connected with Moses by some Hebrew editor who, hunting for tales of the hero's youth and finding none, seized upon the name itself as a clue, knowing the common custom of naming a child from some circumstance of its infancy.

"Moses" is, in the original Hebrew, *Mosheh,* and might easily be derived from the Hebrew verb *mashah,* to draw out (of the water). But the Egyptian word *mes* or *mose* means son or child, and we know how commonly a little boy is called "sonny." Even if the name is from *mashah,* it may mean deliverer or savior. This seems the best explanation, and "Deliverer" he probably was named, or re-named, by the grateful Hebrews because he had appeared and delivered them from their bondage.

Hebrew (and Christian) tradition has accepted this infancy narrative as sober fact. Among the legends of the Jews are many interesting additions and embellishments, of which Christians have too long been ignorant.[5] These accounts are only slightly if any less valuable to the student of religion than the parts of the Moses cycle which happened to be included in the canonical Bible. It is too bad, for instance, that we have not known how clever a father Moses had, and how near Moses came to not being born at all!

The Clever Father of Moses

When the royal edict had first gone forth that all male Hebrew children were to be killed, Amram had put his clever brain to work and devised a brilliant scheme to outwit the cruel Egyptian king. The way to circumvent the killing of Hebrew male children was

3 See Frazer, *Folk-Lore in the Old Testament,* Vol. II, pp. 437–455.
4 Matthew 2: 13–21.
5 See Ginsberg, *Legends of the Jews,* Vol. II, Ch. IV.

simply for the Hebrews to have no children at all! So Amram, who knew only one rather drastic method of birth control, had promptly divorced and left his wife, and his example had been followed by the other Hebrew men.

Now Miriam, who could not have been more than nine years old at the time, had showed remarkable precocity at this crisis. She approached her father and said,

Father, thy decree is worse than Pharaoh's decree. The Egyptians aim to destroy only the male children, but thou includest the girls as well. Pharaoh deprives his victims of life in this world, but thou preventest children from being born, and thus thou deprivest them of future life, too. He resolves destruction, but who knows whether the intention of the wicked can persist? Thou art a righteous man, and the enactments of the righteous are executed by God, hence thy decree will be upheld.

Moved by her arguments, Amram had led the return of the husbands and remarried Jochebed, and the child of the reconciliation was Moses.

Moses' Foster Mother

From all these legends, both Biblical and non-Biblical, we can learn very little accurate information about Moses, save that he probably spent his youth in Egypt. An old tradition, preserved in Stephen's speech in the New Testament in Acts 7, stating that "Moses was learned in all the wisdom of the Egyptians" is not to be found anywhere in the Old Testament, but may have been built upon the passage in Exodus 2:10 to the effect that Pharaoh's daughter adopted Moses as her son, but is more likely taken right from Philo's Life of Moses, 1:5. Hebrew legend says that this princess' name was changed to "Bithiah," which means "daughter of God," because of her kind deed, and that she later married Caleb, who became a famous fighting captain of the Hebrews in the wilderness and in the conquest of Canaan. Artapanus, however, asserts that her name was Merris, wife of Chenephres, King of Upper Egypt, but Josephus says her name was Thermuthis.

Whether Moses was adopted by a princess or not, he may well have studied the wisdom of the Egyptians, for he was of an inquiring turn of mind and priests have ever been willing to educate possible converts. An ignorant man would hardly have been able to do what he later did. If it be objected that his later laws show more similarity to the legislation of the Euphrates than to that of the Nile, it must be remembered that communication between those two districts was well enough developed long before Moses so that one could learn much about the former from the wise men of the latter. Moreover, additions attributed to Moses were made to his laws at a later time, when the Jews were under Babylonian influence.

The Smiting

There is, it is true, very little Egyptian influence traceable in the religion of the Hebrews, but, as we shall soon see, that little is very important. The main reason we are inclined to believe that Moses was brought up in Egypt is the fact that it seems logical and consistent with his character that the sufferings of the Hebrews so impressed him that he went back to lead them forth from bondage. The reason assigned by tradition for his leaving Egypt and going to Midian—namely, the killing of an Egyptian whom he saw striking a Hebrew slave—seems also probable.

It is startling to realize that the real career of so great a religious leader started with a murder, and the tendency of commentators and preachers has been to minimize the incident. But his first reaction to the sufferings of his countrymen revealed by its violence the tremendous effect it had upon his powerful imaginative nature. That impression was deepened rather than effaced by the meditative years of his exile in Midian, whither he fled after his crime.

The Courtship

In Midian Moses found a wife and a religion. The first meeting of Moses and Zipporah was at the usual place where pastoral men and maidens met, and the courtship conformed to pattern. As Jacob won Rachel[6] by helping her water her flock of sheep, so Moses won Zipporah in the same fashion when she appeared at the well with her six shepherdess sisters.

Later Hebrew tradition was not content with the simple narrative as recorded in Exodus 2:15–22, but embellished it with mira-

[6] Genesis 29:2–10. See also Genesis 24:10–67 for Isaac and Rebekah's somewhat parallel courtship.

cle. The hostile shepherds who rudely watered their own flocks with the water which Jethro's daughters had drawn continued their persecution by trying to assault them. Failing in this, they threw the girls down the well. Moses arrived in time to save them. Then he watered all the sheep, magnanimously including those of the un-gentlemanly shepherds. This was easy for him, for when he had drawn one bucketful, the water flowed in such miraculous volume that it was not necessary to draw another, and it continued to flow until Moses left the well.

The theme is a common one in comparative mythology. So flowed the milk from the pitcher of Philemon and Baucis[7] and the oil from the widow's cruse (I Kings 17:8–16). Whoso shares, finds the supply unfailing.

Legend gives us interesting details of Moses' proposal and court-ship. He had been particularly taken with one of the seven daugh-ters of Jethro and asked her to marry him. She replied, "My father has a tree in his garden with which he tests every man that ex-presses a desire to marry one of his daughters, and as soon as the suitor touches the tree, he is devoured by it." Not at all amazed or embarrassed, Moses pulled up the tree and brought it to Jethro, who, afraid of the power of such a magician, suddenly thrust Moses into a pit to die.

But Zipporah was not to be cheated of her prospective husband so easily. She always appears, both in the Bible and out, as a woman of ideas and initiative, as quick to act as the "sparrow" she was named for, and not afraid of gods or men. For seven years (!) she used her access to the family larder to keep Moses supplied not only with necessary food but even with dainties. Then she casually said to her father, "I recollect that once upon a time thou didst cast into yonder pit a man that had fetched thy tree from the garden for thee, and thou didst commit a great trespass thereby. If it seemeth well to thee, uncover the pit and look into it. If the man is dead, throw the corpse away, lest it fill the house with stench. But should he be alive, then thou oughtest to be convinced that he is one of those that are wholly pious, else he had died of hunger."

"Thou host spoken wisely," said Jethro. "Dost thou remember his name?"

Zipporah, thinking hard, said, "I remember he called himself Moses the son of Amram."

7 Ovid, *Metamorphoses*, viii, 610–715.

Thereupon Jethro called into the pit, "Moses! Moses!" When Moses answered cheerily, "Here am I," Jethro pulled him out and gave him the clever girl and a handsome dowry, making only one stipulation: that one child should be raised as a member of his father's race and the next as one of his mother's. The first child was, according to the legend, circumcised as a Hebrew, but the second one, by the agreement with Jethro, could not be. The name given to the first child, Gershom, reveals that Moses' marriage did not bring him happiness. Gershom means "a stranger here," and Moses sighed, as he named the child, "I have been a stranger in a strange land." The name given the second son, Eliezer, sounded like another sigh, "God help [me]."

The Meditations of Moses

The names Moses gave his children indicated not only his unhappiness but one of the causes of it. He may have been disappointed in his wife but there was something more than that at the bottom of his discontent. The "stranger" kept thinking of his own race in slavery in Egypt. That led him to meditate on the ways of God with men. As a shepherd he had plenty of time to think. Every great religious leader has come forth with a message after a long period of meditation in a lonely place.

In the wastes of Midian, the musing shepherd Moses, tending the flocks of his father-in-law Jethro, put together several things from his own experience and produced a new religion. Like Buddha, seven centuries later in India, it was the fact of human suffering which first made him think deeply. He still remembered, indeed he could not forget, the bleeding backs of his enslaved countrymen in Egypt. If he, a mere man, cared so much, why didn't the gods care?

The great gods of Egypt could not be expected, of course, to help the Hebrews, and the Hebrews had only their little household idols, the tribal *teraphim,* and the shadowy nature gods, the *elohim,* either kind of doubtful value in a crisis like this. If they only had one great god to help them now! Then Moses remembered the heretic king of Egypt, Amenhotep the Fourth, who had ruled Egypt only the century before, who had dared to establish the religion of one god, the sun god Aten, and who had changed his own name to Akhenaten. For only a brief period had monotheism been the official religion of Egypt. The great mass of the people had not understood it and had probably never ceased to worship the old gods, but the dreamy idealistic young king Akhenaten had left a historical record, which had doubtless come to the attention of Moses during the latter's Egyptian studies.

Akhenaten had been mistaken surely, Moses mused, for if Aten had really been the one great god, then he could never have been overthrown. But perhaps, after all, there *was* one great god, greater even than Aten. Perhaps this unknown god had caused all things, even the sun, and really cared for suffering human beings, and would deliver the Hebrews from bondage and help them escape to some better land!

The Theophany

Then, like a flame of light, as to many a mystic, it seemed to Moses that God came and spoke to him. Describing it later, he said that, as he walked along leading the flock to the back of the wilderness, near to the Mountain of God (Horeb-Sinai), he saw first a burst of flame with an angel in its midst. Then he noticed that the flame came from a bush which burned but was not consumed, and from the bush God spoke, saying that He had long been the God of the Hebrews, even in the days of the fathers, that He knew about the oppression of His people, had heard their cry, and knew their sorrows.

"Go down, Moses!"

Then came the surprising commission, "Come now, therefore, and I will send *you* unto Pharaoh, that *you* may bring forth my people the children of Israel out of Egypt." Thus comes the divine call to every prophet—a sense of a great wrong to be righted, a task to be done, and then a sudden blinding realization that the task is one's own.

The Significance of the Burning Bush

The Story of the Burning Bush has always been recognized as of great significance to mankind. Countless sermons have been preached upon it: every Sunday-school scholar has studied it again and again; and literature is full of allusions to it. To the student of comparative religion it is of unusual value, not only because it bears all the marks of authenticity but in several other important respects as well.

First of all, it is a fine example of a theophany—that is, a religious experience which is interpreted by the one who has it as including a direct contact with deity through one or more of the senses. In this case, according to Moses' account, although he did not actually *see* God, he did see a flame-encircled angel of the Lord, and he distinctly *heard* the voice of God. In all theophanies the hearing of the prophet seems much more acute than his vision.

Then, the unusually long conversation between Moses and God reveals the fact that the subjective side in such an experience is paramount. Children at play are able to imagine and converse at length with an unseen playmate. In adult years the persistence of this personalizing ability assists greatly in religion. Moses was wrestling with a personal problem after all. His conscience was contrasting his present peaceful pastoral existence with the troubles of his fellow Israelites in Egypt. It is worth noting that all three of the accounts of the burning bush, which a later editor wove into one but which we can disentangle, mention that Moses was moved by the suffering of the Egyptian exiles. Like every theophany, particularly like Paul's on the Damascus Road, Moses unconsciously personified his pleading conscience into the very voice of God.

Finally, the student of comparative religion cannot fail to remark the significance of several of the connected circumstances.

Sacred Localities

It was in a sacred locality that the call came. Just as Mecca was a holy place untold centuries before Muhammad turned men's faces thither, so Horeb-Sinai had already seen many worshiping nomads prostrate on its lower slopes. A new religion does well to build on the old. It was also a lonely spot where the theophany occurred. Most "calls" of prophets have come to them in deserts or wildernesses or some other solitary place, and there is a definite psychological reason for it. The feeling of awe is frequently the beginning of religion.[8] Hebrew legend has it that Moses noted the mountain

[8] For an excellent description of the awesome feelings produced by the desert, see Keyserling's *Travel Diary of a Philosopher*, pp. 20–21.

was a holy spot, for birds did not light on it, and as he neared it, it moved forward to meet him. He took off his shoes because he stood on holy ground.

Sacred Trees and Shrubs

It is also significant that it was in a bush that God made His appearance to Moses. We do not know what particular kind of bush it was, for the Hebrew *seneh* (possibly connected with the name Mt. Sinai itself) is used only here, but most commentators take it to have been a bramble bush. In the Septuagint (Greek) version of the Book of Exodus and in the New Testament references the Greek word *batos* is used, which means thorn bush. It has been suggested that flaming azalea blossoms would explain both the blazing appearance and the fact that the bush was not consumed.

Many peoples have believed that God dwells in trees, groves and shrubs. The Zoroastrians held all plants sacred, as the givers of health and immortality. The Greeks venerated Zeus at the oak of Dodona: the famous oak or terebinth of Abraham at Mamre was worshiped for centuries, not only by Jews but even by Christians, until Constantine in the fourth Christian century stopped the superstitious practice by building a church there! Agamemnon was a priest of tree worship. Buddha found peace under the Bo tree.

Survivals of the belief in a peculiar magic power residing in trees and bushes are to be found in our customs today. "Oak and Ash and Thorn" are still magic words in England. When we "knock on wood" to avert sickness, we are summoning the spirit of the tree to protect us. In country districts men still hunt locations for wells by holding a "witch" hazel twig before them which is expected to point to the desired water. It must be a hazel twig; why, they do not know. But the hazel in Ireland was long known as the tree of knowledge. To come upon a witch-hazel bush alight with its yellow blossoms in early winter when no other blooms are to be seen is to most persons a surprising and almost uncanny experience. It helps one to understand a little how Moses felt when he found God in the burning bush.

Nearly every religion has its sacred trees of life, of knowledge, and healing. We find them not only in Genesis, Enoch, and Revelation, but on "willow-pattern" Chinese plates as well. The Yule log, the lighted tree, and the blazing-berried holly, none of which has

the slightest connection with Christianity but all of which good
Christians use at Christmastime, proclaim them ardent if ignorant
tree-worshiping pagans for that day at least, while the innocent
kissing under the "golden bough" of the mistletoe is an atavistic
survival of a practice which once was not so innocent. The "Holy
Thorn of Glastonbury," the crown of thorns on Jesus' brow, and
the flaming thorn bush of Moses were all akin, not only botanically
but also in their religious significance.[9] Let anyone who doubts the
latent tree-adoration spirit remaining in even sophisticated circles
watch the faces of a group hearing read or sung Joyce Kilmer's

> *I think that I shall never see*
> *A poem lovely as a tree.*

In such deep-seated admirations survives the essence of aesthetic
religion, distilled from the blind passions of animism. In primitive
religion's rank but fertile soil lie embedded the roots of our best
poetry and art.

Sacred Lights

The most important fact about the bush, however, to one studying theophanies, the circumstance which identifies it beyond doubt
as typical, is its incandescence. The point is emphasized by the
phrases "in a flame of fire," "the bush burned with fire," and "Moses
hid his face."

When man is suddenly confronted with a great duty and realizes
his divine call to a mission, a great light breaks upon him. As we
shall see in our survey of the theophanies of the notable leaders of
religion, this physical manifestation seems an almost invariable
accompaniment of a religious awakening. Perhaps someday the
physiological psychologists will explain this phenomenon to us, why
it is that the shock of an overwhelming realization of a divine "call"
produces the sensation of a brilliant light.[10] It may be a flaming fire,
a lightning flash, a hot coal from the altar, a burning bush, a light
from heaven, tongues of flame on the head, the shining sun, day-

[9] For further examples of sacred trees, see Frazer's *Golden Bough*, Vol. I, Ch. I,
and *Encyclopedia of Religion and Ethics*, Vol. XII, article on "Trees and Plants."

[10] See James, *Varieties of Religious Experience*, pp. 251-254, for case examples.
Are these "photisms" mere hallucinations or are they rare phenomena in man parallel
to heliotropism and phototaxis in plants and animals?

break, or a white dove from the opened heavens. Does the vision produce the light or the light the vision?

Not Consumed

One word more about the burning bush: the thing that led Moses to it was the fact that it was not consumed. The idea of perpetual light is another common element in religion, the idea of everlastingness, of the eternal God. The sacred flame which the vestal virgins of Rome so carefully guarded, the perpetual fires of the Persians, the fiery cresset on the tent pole of Alexander the Great, the everlasting light in the synagogue, the continual jets of flaming gas under the Hindu temple in the Himalayas, the devoutly worshiped everlasting blue fires of petroleum at Baku on the Caspian Sea, the perpetual holy fires in the temples of the Kiziba, Congo, and Uganda districts of Africa and in the square temples of the Natchez Indians in Mississippi, the unfailing candle in Roman Catholic churches, and the ever-burning lamp in the Holy Sepulcher at Jerusalem: these are all related to the unconsumed bush of Moses.[11] Well do the Scottish churches take as their emblem the Burning Bush with the motto, *"Nec tamen consumebatur."* It is a symbol of religion itself.

Moses Protests

When Moses heard the call of God to go back to Egypt and bring his people out of bondage, he protested his unworthiness, as more than one prophet has done. "Who am I, that I should go unto Pharaoh, and that I should bring forth the Children of Israel out of Egypt?"

And the account says that God promised to be with him and gave him a sign—namely, that the rescued exiles would worship God on that very mountain. In other words, this thrill of power he now felt in the sacred place would not only go with him but be communicated to his whole people as well. Still he demurred: "When I tell them that the God of their fathers has sent me, they will say, 'What is His name?' And what shall I tell them?" Thus he questioned himself, and the answer came: "You shall say 'Yahweh [Jehovah], the God of your fathers, has sent me.'"

[11] For further examples, see Frazer, *Golden Bough,* Vol. II, Ch. XVII.

Changing Gods

Now Moses knew very well that this great God Yahweh of whom he had just caught a flaming vision and whom he was now resolving to present to the Hebrews in Egypt as their God had not been the "God of their fathers." At least, the fathers had not known it, if He was. But Moses also knew enough about religion and people not to expect human beings to accept eagerly a totally new God. So he very carefully resolved to tie up the new god with the old religion.

There is in the sixth chapter of Exodus a statement which is of intense interest to the student of the evolution of religion. It is placed in the narrative as occurring after Moses had got to Egypt again, but it really belongs in the burning bush episode,

And God spake unto Moses and said unto him, I am Yahweh: and I appeared unto Abraham, unto Isaac, and unto Jacob, by the name of El Shaddai, but by my name Yahweh was I not known unto them.

This passage is evidently an editorial note by some priestly writer centuries later and betrays rare critical acumen. This editor perceived, dimly perhaps, the fact of the evolution of the idea of God. Whom Abraham called El Shaddai, Moses called Yahweh. We can now supplement that comment of an early student of comparative religion and fill in the gaps in the evolution of the character of this god, El Shaddai, by tracing his various incarnations backward from our own time.

Recently, in the form of "Goshamity," El Shaddai has been a favorite rural New England swear word of the milder sort, practically a mere euphemism like "Oh, Lordy" or "Goldarn." In the New Testament, Almighty is used only nine times, eight of them in the Book of Revelation, and simply means "All powerful" (Greek, *Pantokrator*). In the many places in the Old Testament (thirty in the Book of Job) where the name of the ancient deity Shaddai occurs, the King James and Revised Standard versions translate it "Almighty," which is really a late derived and refined interpretation. In the early days it had a rougher connotation, and Shaddai was a nature storm god, like the Carib Hurukan. Shaddai was even the violent devastator, like the Hindu Shiva the Destroyer.

Finally, in the old "Song of Moses" (Deuteronomy 32:17) and Psalm 106:37, the plural form *Shedim* is translated "devils" in

King James and "demons" in the Revised Standard. The apotheosis is complete. The Canaanite dread demon placated by human sacrifice ("Yea, they sacrificed their sons and their daughters unto Shedim" Psalm 106:37) becomes the El Shaddai God Almighty of Abraham, then an attribute of Yahweh, and eventually a euphemistic exclamation.

It has been remarked that Moses made the Hebrew tribes into a nation by giving them a God, and that is more or less true, but that God was not made *de novo*. With the wisdom in dealing with men which so frequently characterized him, and out of his own religious conviction, Moses conveyed to his people the idea of one great personal God by using concepts already at hand. He knew the value of the point of contact in teaching. He would not "pour spring water unawares upon a gracious public full of nerves." His was the task of leading a people from animism to monotheism, from superstition to religion, and he did a piece of work which deserves admiration. Zoroaster and Muhammad were later to do much the same thing, but to Moses belongs the glory of the pioneer.

Early Hebrew Animism

The pre-Mosaic religion of the Hebrews was a mixture of animism and fetishism. Certain places and objects were worshiped as sacred. The natural feeling of awe which came upon nomads when they viewed a mountain, a majestic tree, or the starry host of heaven, grew into a superstitious recognition of the power resident there. This power was not definitely personal in the sense that a manlike person or being was supposed to be living in the mountain, but it was vaguely personal in that there was felt to be the need of keeping on the right side of the power, which was human enough at least to be jealous of its rights. These powers, or gods, were called *elohim* (singular, *eloha* or *el*) and among them were El Elyon, the God Most High, El Shaddai, the Almighty God, El Sabaoth, the God of the Heavenly Hosts, and many others.

In a very interesting passage, especially in the Hebrew, Genesis 14:17–24, we have an actual record of the fact that Abraham worshiped El Elyon with the aid of Melchizedek, ancient King of Salem, the City of Peace (*Uru-salim,* hence, Jerusalem). This mysterious Melchizedek, priest of El Elyon, is mentioned again in Psalm 110, nine times in the New Testament Epistle to the Hebrews and has turned up again in the Genesis Apocryphon (formerly called the Lamech Scroll), and in other Essene books.

It is worth noting that in Genesis 1:1, which is translated, "In the beginning God created the heaven and the earth," the Hebrew word translated *God* is really the plural *elohim,* the gods. In process of time, as Moses' monotheism became successful, all these *els* or *elohim* became absorbed in Yahweh, who said, according to Moses, jealously, "Thou shalt have no other gods but Me," and *elohim* was therefore regarded as singular, God, although the plural ending *im* remains.

The great *elohim* of the ancient Hebrews were not expected to be of much assistance in minor matters of the daily life of tent and camp. Something more tangible was needed for simple minds to grasp. Hence arose the *"teraphim,"*[12] images and fetishes which could be carried about.[13] Contrasted with the *elohim* and the *teraphim,* Moses' conception of one great good personal God who cared for His people certainly indicates a remarkable advance.

The Origin of Yahweh

Some scholars maintain (the so-called Kenite hypothesis) that Yahweh was the local god of the Kenites, and that Moses' father-in-law was a priest of that tribe who initiated the Hebrews into Yahweh worship. In other words, they say that Moses got both his wife and his god from the same man. Yahweh may well have long been a local nature god connected with Horeb-Sinai, but wherever Moses got the name, he certainly made Yahweh pre-eminently the God of the Hebrew people.

12 References in the Bible (Genesis 31:19–35; Judges 17:5 and 18:14; First Samuel 19:13–16; Second Kings 23:24; Ezekiel 21:21; Hosea 3:4; and Zechariah 10:2) lead us to infer that these teraphim may possibly have been wooden man-shaped idols or even mummified human heads. It is more likely, however, that they were large phalluses, for the Hebrew word *toreph* means, according to old Hebrew commentators, pudendum, and, as we shall see later, sexual elements were by no means lacking among Hebrew religious customs. Dr. William F. Albright, in his book *From the Stone Age to Christianity,* 1957, page 311, points out that the authors of some of these Bible passages apparently used the word *teraphim* (literally, "vile things") as a general classification which included, rather unfairly, even the harmless figurines of pregnant and large-busted nude females, used as charms by women "expecting."

13 Lucky coins, pocket pieces, rabbits' feet, elks' teeth, swastikas, and other crosses are modern examples of fetishism, a form of primitive religion which is singularly persistent even among Christians.

It is likely that, instead of the haughty and rather fatuous "I-am-that-I-am" or "I-am-who-I-am" of the King James and Revised Standard Versions (Exodus 3:14), Yahweh originally meant "He-who-causes-to-be." That has been interpreted variously as The Creator, The Fulfiller of Promises, and, more recently, as The God of Procreation, and even The God of Passionate Love.

There were undoubtedly phallic elements in Yahwehism up to the time of the prophets and later, some of which were adopted from Canaanite religion and some of which were original in it, but the central meaning which the name Yahweh had for Moses was evidently something like The Living God of Life. That included naturally a certain sponsorship of the sexual relation, as numerous Old Testament passages indicate.

The Personality Idea

But the great overwhelming conviction which drove Moses down into Egypt again although there was a price on his head, and which sustained him in his trying interviews with Pharaoh and even through the weary wilderness, was the belief that the hitherto unknown God of the Hebrews had revealed Himself as a Living Person, jealously protecting His chosen people in their every concern.

This was the new idea in religion which Moses brought to the Hebrews and which from them passed to Christianity. At the burning bush occurred the birth of the greatest concept of historic religion, *the personality of God*, ethical personal monotheism. Akhenaten of Egypt also had the idea, in a measure, but it perished with him, save as Moses may have caught it in his Egyptian studies. But Akhenaten was more the contemplative theorist, the poet and artist. Moses wrought the idea out into a living practical religion for suffering, toiling mankind.

Religion, as we know it, began with Moses, and the religion of many has stopped there. What was good enough for Moses is good enough for them. You may criticize Moses' anthropomorphic conception of a god with a physical body and with such human limitations as jealousy and vengeance, but you will not carp long if you compare his god with the deities of contemporary nations, or with the gods of early Israel. Besides, even the religions of today are still somewhat anthropomorphic. So are philosophy and science. This is no real condemnation, for, to think at all, most men must think in manlike terms.

The Strange Affair at the Inn

Inspired by his new-found religion and anxious to inform his people that Yahweh would bring them out of bondage, Moses started for Egypt, taking his wife Zipporah and his two infant sons, all three mounted upon an ass. Whatever fears he may still have had of being punished for his crime of murder were evidently allayed when the Lord (with whom Moses was soon conversing quite freely, according to Exodus 3 and 4) "said unto Moses in Midian, Go, return into Egypt: for all the men are dead which sought thy life" (Exodus 4:19). Here again we are reminded of a parallel incident in the life of Jesus, recorded in Matthew 2:20, when an angel told the Holy Family in Egypt to return to "the Land of Israel: for they are dead which sought the young child's life."

On the way a singular event occurred, which, in the light of comparative religion, gives us an insight into the strange beliefs and customs of the times of Moses. Three brief verses, Exodus 4:24-26, contain it, but they have caused considerable wonderment to the average Bible reader.

And it came to pass by the way in the inn, that Jehovah met him and sought to kill him. Then Zipporah took a sharp stone, and cut off the foreskin of her son and cast it at his feet, and said, Surely a bloody husband thou art to me. So he let him go: then she said, A bloody husband thou art, because of the circumcision.

The story becomes clearer if we use Dr. Charles Foster Kent's translation,

And on the way at the lodging place, Jehovah fell upon him, and sought to kill him. Then Zipporah took a flint and cut off the foreskin of her son, and touched [Moses'] person with it, and said, Surely you are a bridegroom of blood to me. So [Jehovah] let him alone. Thus she originated the saying 'A bridegroom of blood' with reference to circumcision."[14]

When Zipporah saw that the hand of the Lord had been laid in

[14] Kent, "Beginnings of Hebrew History" in *The Student's Old Testament*, Vol. I, p. 155.

affliction on her husband, probably in the form of a sudden sickness, she took measures, the best she knew, to cure him. Yahweh was displeased, and she could think of but one reason—Moses had not been circumcised. That is, Yahweh had been insulted because the customary sacrifice had not been offered, so Zipporah appeased the angry deity by circumcising the child in the stead of the father. This act was more noble than appears on the surface, for one of her two sons, Gershom, had already been circumcised, and by operating on Eliezer she was risking her father's wrath by violating the solemn agreement made at her wedding. (See page 36.)

By substitution, then, Zipporah made Moses a "husband of blood" and therefore safe from Yahweh's wrath. It was probably part of an ancient ritual of marriage that the bride should say to the recently circumcised groom, "A husband of blood thou art to me," and the later editor of this narrative thought that the saying originated from this incident and said so in verse 26, which accounts for the repetition of the phrase.

Moses versus Circumcision

What did Moses himself think about circumcision in general and the affair at the inn in particular? In the fifth chapter of Joshua there is an account of a wholesale circumcising of the Hebrews at the end of their wilderness wanderings just as they entered Canaan. The explanation given as to why such a large number had to be operated on at one time was that while all who came out of Egypt had been circumcised, those who were born in the wilderness had not. Now if circumcision was practiced by the Hebrews in Egypt until they left, and if it was resumed immediately after Moses' death when they entered Canaan, and if Moses was commander-in-chief, high priest and supreme dictator during the entire wilderness wanderings, there is only one possible inference to be drawn—namely, that Moses did not believe in circumcision and tried to abolish it.

One cannot say that the lapse in the practice was due to the lack of facilities in the desert, for the custom had flourished for centuries, and still does, among nomads who always live in the desert. We are confirmed in our conclusion by the testimony of the passage describing the affair at the inn, which certainly reveals that Moses had not been circumcised even at the time of his marriage. Evidently, then, Moses was opposed to the rite and continued to refuse it for himself. Probably Zipporah's performance with all its primitive roughness finally disgusted him with the whole idea, and when the opportunity came, he endeavored to extirpate this phallic survival from the customs of his race. Such action was consistent with his other efforts to elevate the religion of the Hebrews.

But the weight of the practice of centuries was too strong for him, and if he kept them from it for a generation, they reverted to it immediately after his death. Many centuries later, the Hebrews actually claimed that circumcision was part of the Mosaic law, but we know that Leviticus 12:1–8, where the assertion is made, was an addition by priests probably as late as the Babylonian captivity, as was the account in Genesis 17 of the alleged Abrahamic origin of circumcision.

Jesus, according to John 7:22, recognized some inconsistency in his racial traditions on this very point, for after saying (Moffatt's translation), "Moses gave you the rite of circumcision," he corrected himself and added, "not that it came from Moses, it came from your ancestors." The brief narrative of Exodus 4:24–26, therefore, is of great significance to those who would study primitive religion and throws more light on Moses' struggle to purify the Hebrew religion than many longer and more familiar passages. In fact, some students of the history of religion[15] think another, probably more ancient, version of the strange affair at the inn preserves a more important clue to the age-old superstitions connected with honeymoons. In this version, a demon trying to kill Moses is driven off only when Zipporah circumcises Moses and touches the demon with the foreskin. We may even have here a substitute sacrifice for the first-night-with-the-bride privilege originally thought to belong to a demon, or god, or spirit, as in the similar story in the apocryphal Book of Tobit.

In that case, the demon Asmodeus loved the maid Sara and killed her seven successive husbands on their wedding nights, but the eighth bridegroom exorcised the devil with fish-liver smoke. Zipporah, a thousand years before, evidently did not know that fumigatory method. In the much later feudal age, the Lord of the Manor sometimes claimed the *jus primae noctis* when a serf married, and it is said that the traditional clergyman's right to the bride's first kiss is the last vestigial survival of the ancient custom.

15 Interpreter's Bible, 1952, Vol. I, p. 882.

"Let My People Go!"

Just what happened during the period after Moses arrived in Egypt before the flight of his countrymen began, may someday be better known if the excavators continue their work. Since the Tutankhamen discovery, Moses seems somehow much nearer to us. But it is still impossible from our present knowledge to date the Exodus (and therefore Moses) any more specifically than about the thirteenth century B.C., and it may have been during the fourteenth.

Formerly it was supposed that Ramses II reigned from 1292 to 1225 B.C. and was the Pharaoh of the Oppression, largely because he colonized Goshen, the district in which the Bible says the Hebrews lived, and also because he caused to be built there the treasure cities Pithom and Ramses on which the Hebrews labored. It was also supposed that the Pharaoh of the Exodus must have been the son of Ramses II—namely, Merneptah, who reigned for about twenty years after his father. This would bring the latest possible date for the Exodus about 1205 B.C. But some scholars now date the reign of Ramses II from 1340 to 1273 B.C., which would make the latest date of the Exodus about the middle of the thirteenth century B.C. To complicate the matter, an inscription was discovered in 1896 A.D. which gives evidence that in the fifth year of Merneptah—that is, about 1268 B.C., there were Israelites already in Palestine.

We know from the Amarna Letters that in 1400 B.C. the Hebrews were not yet in Palestine, so, if the trip took forty years, the Exodus may have taken place between 1440 B.C. and 1308 B.C. There is still sufficient justification, however, for placing the date of the Exodus about the middle of the thirteenth century B.C. because the Israelites who were in Palestine in the fifth year of Merneptah may have been other tribes than those who came up out of Egypt. There is strong reason for believing that several Hebrew tribes which settled Canaan were never in Egypt at all.

A Protestant Archbishop of North Ireland named James Ussher worked out a system of dating Biblical events which was published in 1660 A.D. after his death and which for many years was printed at the top of the pages of the King James Version of the Bible. It has therefore been taken by many for "gospel truth." Ussher dated the Exodus at exactly 1491 B.C., but inasmuch as he dated the creation of the world at 4004 B.C., and as it is now positively known that highly developed civilizations were flourishing long before that time, his chronology can hardly be regarded as trustworthy.

The Tournament of Magic

Magic was a large element in the Egyptian religion, and Moses' adoption of Yahweh as the one great personal God did not, according to the Biblical account, prevent him from contesting with the Egyptian magicians in a long tournament of necromancy, very much as Zoroaster did in the court of King Vishtaspa. In those days, and for long afterward, the only divine credentials recognized were miracles. Jesus protested vehemently at the practice, saying in exasperation, "Except ye see signs and wonders ye will not believe," but the belief that miracles are a proof of divinity still prevails among the ignorant.

In spite of the fact that Moses and Aaron were supplied by Yahweh himself with magic rods (remarkably similar in their powers to the rods and staffs in the mythology of other nations, and the forerunners of the wands of the modern stage magicians), they did not triumph at first. Jannes and Jambres, the leading Egyptian magicians, are not mentioned by name in the Old Testament but are named in Second Timothy 3:8, in the apocryphal Gospel of Nicodemus, chapter 5, and also in Origen, Pliny, and Apuleius.

These champions matched Moses and Aaron, trick for trick. One Hebrew legend says that Jannes and Jambres, reputed to be sons of Balaam, reminded the Hebrew leaders that in bringing magic tricks to Egypt they were "carrying straw to Ephrain," and Pharaoh said they were bringing "brine to Spain or fish to Accho," which were evidently ancient equivalents of "carrying coals to Newcastle." Legend says too that Pharaoh brought in his wife and even schoolchildren who all duplicated the early tricks of Moses and Aaron.

The Bible story says that even when Yahweh determined to punish Pharaoh and his people by sending upon them two plagues, the first, the turning of all the water of the Nile into blood, and the second, the bringing of multitudes of frogs into the houses of the Egyptians, both calamities accomplished by waves of the magic wands of Moses and Aaron, even then the Egyptians duplicated the feats, and Pharaoh refused to let the Hebrews go. The primitive and naïve character of these accounts is apparent, even if one could explain how the Egyptian magicians could turn the Nile into blood when "all the waters" (Exodus 7:20) had already been turned into blood.

We are not today quite as credulous as the chroniclers who, some centuries afterward, set down the story of the ten miraculous plagues sent by Yahweh, one after another, to compel Pharaoh to let the Hebrews go, but we can easily understand that a series of natural calamities may have made it possible for Moses to play upon the superstitious fears of the regent. Or Moses, enthusiastic in his faith in Yahweh, may have himself believed them to have been providentially sent.

An Ancient Slander

There is a persistent calumny that the real reason the Jews left Egypt was because they were so filthy that Pharaoh drove them out. This story, which was widely circulated in early Christian centuries, and is still current, is largely due to Tacitus and is found in his *Histories,* Book V, Chapter III, but it is also credited to Chaeremon and Diodorus Siculus, who all wrote before 117 A.D. Nomads, accustomed to the tent life in the desert where frequent removals of the camp obviated the need of sanitation systems, may have needed instruction in such matters when they first settled in the villages and cities of Goshen. The sheiks of the desert today are not as attractive as romantic film stories may picture them.

But the slander was probably due to race prejudice and doubtless was only a malicious inference based upon the story that there were many pestilences in Egypt just before the Hebrews left. Certainly the laws in the Mosaic code concerning cleanliness and sanitation are notable for their stringency. It is much more credible that the Hebrews left Egypt of their own accord than that they were driven out. Pharaoh would not willingly have lost valuable wageless laborers, nor would he have pursued the tribes with an army if he had driven them out because of filthiness.

The Red Sea

The "miracle" of the Red Sea passage (Exodus 14) may have been a natural phenomenon. Winds have blown waters back since in well-authenticated instances.[16] That the escaping tribes should interpret their rescue as due to the intervening hand of Yahweh and should add miraculous details in later years is also natural.

The Passover

Later Hebrews dated the Passover feast from the Exodus. Probably the very ancient feast of the vernal equinox, celebrated in various forms all over the world from time immemorial, was transformed into the Passover, just as Christians later appropriated it for their springtime festival of the resurrection of Christ, still bearing the name of the Teutonic goddess of spring, Austro or Eostre. In all likelihood, the gladness of the season and their relief over leaving Egyptian bondage were blended together that vernal day when they found themselves on the safe side of the Red Sea, after the discomfiture of their pursuing enemies. And during the long pilgrimage to the Promised Land, on the springtime anniversary of that day, Miriam the sister of Moses would assemble her dancing girls. Timbrels in hand, they would dance and chant joyously,

> *Sing ye to Yahweh, for he hath triumphed gloriously:*
> *The horse and his rider hath he cast into the sea.*

(*Note*—If Moses had been forty years old when he first left Egypt and had lived forty years in Midian, he would have been eighty at the time of the Exodus, and Miriam about ninety when she led the dancers! But then, it was spring.)

On the Road to the Promised Land

Moses' greatest task was to transfer to the motley mob he had led forth from Egypt his own inspiring conviction of the constant presence of a living God. In the methods which Moses employed to produce this conviction among the tribesmen, it is comparatively easy to find the resemblance to his own experience in attaining his faith in Yahweh. When he had led his people across the Red Sea, he headed straight for Horeb-Sinai, the mountain of God, where he had received his call and commission from Yahweh. And, of course, the famous beacon, the pillar of cloud by day and of fire by night, was his own burning bush, magnified for them.

[16] See Hastings, *Bible Dictionary*, Vol. I, p. 802.

Constantly he was telling them that it was Yahweh who had sent the pestilences which gave them their chance to escape, who had parted the waters of the Red Sea for them, and who was leading them into the Promised Land of Plenty, flowing with milk and honey. Repeatedly, like a clever teacher of simple folk, he drilled into their superstitious souls, filled with animistic fears, his conviction that there was a personal God, Yahweh, a god who cared, and who, moreover, had chosen them as His own peculiar people. It was hard to justify that statement at times when food and water were scarce, but patiently he built up their faith and established a racial religious consciousness which is even today a marked attribute of their widely scattered descendants.

Besides this, he had before him the herculean labor of welding unorganized serfs into a fighting machine to conquer the fortified country, Canaan, which was his ultimate goal. Pacifist sentiments could have no place in his pedagogy. Also he had to make provision for food, drink, and clothing in a wild country. Sanitation was a problem when the camp stayed for any length of time in the same place. Dissension broke out in camp frequently and there was rebellion at his authority.

The Wives of Moses

There was in the period of the wilderness wanderings a quarrel between Moses and his sister Miriam about his intimate relations with some woman. The Bible account in Numbers 12:1–16 says that it was over an Ethiopian (Cushite) woman whom Moses had married. (Hebrew, "taken.") Some scholars, including many Jewish commentators, identify this woman as Zipporah, because no account of Zipporah's death had been given. It is difficult, however, to identify with the Ethiopian or Cushite woman the Midianite Zipporah, for Midian is nowhere connected with Ethiopia or Cush. Furthermore, the Bible narrative distinctly implies that the taking of the Ethiopian woman was a recent occurrence. Moses had married Zipporah long before.

The simplest explanation of the incident is that Miriam was incensed at the lack of dignity shown by a man of Moses' position in taking a Negro girl, probably a slave, to share his tent. Perhaps Moses turned to the carefree, amiable disposition of the Negro girl as a welcome relief from his sparrow-pecked existence with Zipporah. Josephus makes the Ethiopian woman Moses' first wife, and of high degree, and tells a romantic story about her:

Before Moses left Egypt the first time, he was a mighty general in command of an Egyptian army which fought the Ethiopians and laid siege to their impregnable royal city, Saba. Tharbis, daughter of the Ethiopian king, was walking on the city wall when she saw Moses leading his troops and fell in love with him at first sight. So strong was her passion for him that she sent to him by a trusted servant a proposal of marriage. Moses agreed, evidently without having seen the girl, but made a condition—namely, that she should arrange to deliver the city into his power. The more than willing princess accepted the condition, and, says Josephus, "No sooner was the agreement made, but it took effect immediately; and when Moses had cut off the Ethiopians, he gave thanks to God, and consummated his marriage, and led the Egyptians back to their own land.[17]

Moses may have had more than two wives, unless his alleged fathers-in-law, Reuel of Exodus 2:15–22, Raguel of Numbers 10:29, and Hobab of Judges 4:11 are all the same person as the Jethro (or Jether) of Exodus 3:1, 4:18, and 18:1–27, as certain scholars would have us believe! Whether he had more than one at a time, we cannot tell, but polygamy was neither a novelty nor a sin in those days. And even in more recent days other prophets have had divine revelations permitting plural marriages.

We know from Exodus 18:2 that Moses sent his wife Zipporah and the children back to her father. Just when or why we do not know. Another noncanonical source says that it was shortly after he entered Egypt and upon the advice of his brother Aaron, who pointed out that there were already enough sad people in Egyptian captivity without bringing any more. Perhaps the rather ponderously minded Moses, "slow of speech and of a slow tongue," had by this time found his alert, sparrowlike wife too vivacious for comfort and was glad of an excuse to send her back to her father in Midian. He may have divorced her, as one legend affirms. Indeed, his sending her back to her father practically amounted to that anyway. It seems to have been "a clear case of incompatibility."

Jethro later (Exodus 18:1–12) brought Zipporah and the two children to Moses in an obvious attempt at reconciliation. When

17 *Antiquities*, Book II, Ch. X, Sec. 2.

they met, Moses kissed his father-in-law, but nothing is said about his kissing, or even noticing, his former wife. Jethro keeps mentioning her and the children, but Moses ignores her completely and takes Jethro off to talk politics. Whatever version we accept of Moses' marital career, it is plain that he had no easy time and evidently discovered, as Muhammad did, and as most prophets do, that while a founder of a religion can serve both God and women, it is difficult for him to serve both simultaneously. Bishop Hall implied as much when he said, "He hath need to be more than a man, that hath a Zipporah in his bosom, and would have true zeal in his heart."

The Ten Commandments

One of Moses' many problems in the wilderness, perhaps the greatest, was the making of wise laws to maintain proper social relations between antagonistic individuals, groups, and tribes. And he did his work well. He was long credited with having written the first five books of the Bible, called the Pentateuch, even though the last one contained his obituary, but even an amateur scholar today knows that the present form of those books and probably also the original written documents date from much later. But Moses was undoubtedly the author of many of the laws embedded in the present books, and to be author of the Ten Commandments is fame enough for any composer. A very natural question when the Ten Commandments are mentioned is, "Which Ten Commandments do you mean?"

For there are many decalogues in Exodus, Leviticus, and Deuteronomy. Professor Charles Foster Kent,[18] following up the work of Professors Bertheau, Ewald, Dillman, Briggs, and Paton, has detected *ten* sets of Ten Commandments in Exodus, chapters 20 to 23, and the parallel passages in Deuteronomy, besides the ones in the Holiness Code of Leviticus, chapters 17 to 26. But there are really only two clearly defined and differing great decalogues, the familiar one of Exodus 20:1–17, which is commonly taught in Sunday schools and which is repeated with slight changes of order and phraseology in Deuteronomy 5:6–21, and the less familiar one of Exodus 34:14–26.

[18] *Student's Old Testament,* Vol. IV, Ch. III, especially pp. 26–28.

The decalogue in Exodus 20 is, in abbreviated form, as follows,

Preface. I am the Lord thy God, which have brought thee out of the
land of Egypt, out of the house of bondage.

    I. Thou shalt have no other gods before me.

    II. Thou shalt not make unto thee any graven image . . .

    III. Thou shalt not take the name of the Lord thy God in vain . . .

    IV. Remember the sabbath day, to keep it holy. . . .

    V. Honour thy father and thy mother . . .

    VI. Thou shalt not commit murder.

    VII. Thou shalt not commit adultery.

    VIII. Thou shalt not commit theft.

    IX. Thou shalt not bear false witness against thy neighbor.

    X. Thou shalt not covet thy neighbor's house, thou shalt not
covet thy neighbor's wife . . . nor anything that is thy neighbor's.

The Order of the Ten Commandments

While Jews and Christians agree upon the substance of the decalogue of Moses, Jews are divided from Christians and Christians
from each other on the subject of the proper numbering of the
Ten Commandments. For instance, if you asked a Jewish child to
recite the first commandment, he would reply by giving the preface
"I am the Lord thy God . . ." but most Protestant children would
say, "Thou shalt have no other gods before me." But a Lutheran
or Roman Catholic would include with that the next clause, "Thou
shalt not make unto thee any graven image."

A play was presented on Broadway entitled *The Seventh Commandment*. The title was evidently designed to imply delicately
that the play had to do with adultery, but while some people caught
the implication, others thought it connoted theft.

We really ought to standardize the Ten Commandments.

The Greek Catholics, most Protestants and most modern scholars
accept the order as given above. The Jews take the preface as the
first commandment. It isn't really a commandment, but it emphasizes a very important event in Jewish history. Then they combine
the first and second as given above into one commandment and call
it the second, evidently considering polytheism and idolatry similar enough sins to be classed together.

The Roman Catholics and the Lutherans also combine the first and second into one, but they call it the first. That makes it necessary for them to split one of the other commandments in order to make ten. They both choose the tenth, the one on coveting, but they divide it differently. While the Lutherans make the ninth commandment prohibit the coveting of the neighbor's house, and the tenth, his wife, the Roman Catholics reverse the order, following the Deuteronomic version.

So, if the Jews take the preface as a commandment, and the Lutherans and Roman Catholics split the tenth into two, there are really Twelve Commandments for children to learn if an "interfaith" religion is to be taught in the public schools!

The Other Decalogue

The less familiar Ten Commandments of Exodus 34 may be abbreviated as follows,

   I. Thou shalt worship no other god . . .   (verse 14)
  II. Thou shalt make thee no molten gods.   (verse 17)
 III. The feast of unleavened bread shalt thou keep . . .   (verse 18)
  IV. All that openeth the womb is mine . . . (that is,
      every first-born male, cattle or human)   (verse 19)
   V. Six days shalt thou work, but on the seventh
      day thou shalt rest . . .   (verse 21)
  VI. Thou shalt observe the feast of weeks, of the first
      fruits of wheat harvest, and the feast of ingathering
      at the year's end. . . .   (verse 22)
 VII. Thou shalt not offer the blood of my sacrifice with
      leaven;   (verse 25a)
VIII. Neither shall the sacrifice of the feast of the
      passover be left unto the morning.   (verse 25b)
  IX. The first of the first fruits of thy land thou shalt
      bring unto the house of the Lord thy God.   (verse 26a)
   X. Thou shalt not seethe a kid in his mother's milk.   (verse 26b)

There is much in this ancient decalogue of interest to students of primitive religion. Parallels with other religions can be found in Frazer's *Golden Bough* and the *Encyclopedia of Religion and Ethics*. Because of the pastoral and nomadic character of this code, many scholars have called it the original (or earliest-known He-

brew) Ten Commandments and have said that the decalogue in
Exodus 20, which we have so long recited as the very words which
Moses took down at God's dictation, must be dated much later,
when the teaching of the great prophets of Israel had produced a
higher morality.

It is true that the sort of ethics taught in Exodus 20:1–17 was
more emphasized in the time of the prophets than in the days of the
Conquest of Canaan and during the reigns of the early kings of
Israel and Judah, but the reformation in the time of the prophets
may have been the flowering of the principles of which Moses sowed
the seed. Again, the code of Exodus 20:1–17 was not impossible of
conception at the time of Moses, for it is not such a tremendous advance upon the Code of Hammurabi, who was king of Babylonia
from 1728 to 1686 B.C., four centuries before Moses. Details and
comments added by later editors may seem to date this decalogue in
a period when Moses was long dead, but the core of it, at least, was
probably of his composition. In spite of the many volumes written
by critics, there is yet no unanswerable argument compelling us to
deny the Mosaic authorship of the familiar Ten Commandments.

The Ten Commandments Today

This is by no means to say that the commandments are perfect,
cannot be improved upon, and are a sufficient moral guide for
today. The noble art of sculpture, which makes "likenesses" of
many things "in heaven above and earth beneath," may have been
an immoral occupation when simple people worshiped "graven
images," but it is hardly to be classed today as the sinful occupation
which the second commandment would make it. Nor is the code
complete. There is in it no "Thou shalt not lie," because deceit was
then no great sin, especially if practiced on foreigners. Indeed, a
perusal of the Pentateuch gives one the impression that deceit was
considered merely a permissible form of cleverness.

Jesus evidently felt the lack in the decalogue of a command
against deceit, and deliberately added, "Do not defraud," when reciting the commandments to the rich young ruler. Jesus and Paul
exercised the right of revising, rearranging, adding to, and even
omitting several of the Ten Commandments. In the four New
Testament lists (Matthew 19:18, 19; Mark 10:19, Luke 18:20; and
Romans 13:9) there are four different arrangements, and none of

them give more than five of the commandments of Exodus 20. Yet any suggestion of altering, adding to, or subtracting from the Ten Commandments today meets a storm of criticism from the defenders of the literal, infallible Bible. And an attempt as recently as 1957 to reconcile the various versions in a composite "nondenominational" compromise for use in the public schools of New York State was a failure.

Why There Were Ten Commandments

All the laws of Moses were taught orally, for although Moses could probably read and write, a literacy test of the Hebrew tribes would doubtless have been a waste of time. Very cleverly he prepared his many laws in groups of tens, that the people might remember them, finger by finger, in oral recitation. It is still a convenient way of teaching children the Ten Commandments.

What Moses Really Did

The remarkable thing about Moses' work, and it cannot be too often emphasized, is the fact that, by his earnestness, patience, perseverance, and ingenuity, he brought a race so far on the road of religious evolution in so short a time, from the shades of animistic polytheism to at least the dawn of ethical monotheism, in one lifetime! Of the difficulties he met in his task, a reader of the quaint account becomes well aware, but Moses was surprisingly resourceful. By ingenious devices, like the pillar of cloud and fire, he constantly reminded them of the presence of Yahweh. With masterly cunning he utilized and transformed existing superstitions into Yahweh ritual.

Moses and Superstitions

Such relics of animism and primitive religion as the rites of the red heifer (Numbers 19), the release of the scapegoat (Leviticus 16), the elevation of the healing serpent (Numbers 21:4–9), and the ordeal of the magic bitter water for suspected adulteresses (Numbers 5:11–31), while they seem to us revolting examples of superstition and have many parallels in the religion of undeveloped races,[19] were

[19] See Frazer, *The Golden Bough,* Index.

nevertheless countenanced by Moses. But he was careful to connect them all with Yahweh worship and removed some of their objectionable features. He probably had to leave the people a few superstitions or they would have turned away from him altogether.

"The ark of the covenant," the sacred chest with twenty other names, was about four feet long by two and a half wide and deep, of wood with gold overlay. Its original contents have never been really known, and wild guesses have ranged from meteorites (like Islam's Kaaba stone), phallic serpents, and teraphim, to the pot of manna, Aaron's rod, and Moses' decalogue tablets mentioned twelve centuries later by the author of Hebrews 9:4. The Moslems still later assured the faithful that the Ark actually contained carved ruby figures of the prophets to come, including Muhammad. Students have noted a remarkable similarity to the sacred, nontouchable boxes carried about by the Cherokee Indians.[20] The Ark played a large part in the history of the Hebrews, and a surprising number of Bible readers have confused it with Noah's ark (wondering that the Hebrews should have carried such a cumbersome craft around with them on dry land). Its use was doubtless a concession to an ancient custom among the nomad Hebrews, but Moses sublimated it by making it of rare wood with golden fittings, and taught his people that it was Yahweh's traveling abiding place and a reminder of their covenant with their God who would protect them as long as they were loyal to Him.

"By Nebo's Lonely Mountain"

On the edge of the land of promise, his task done, victory in sight, and his successors trained and ready, Moses died. The great prophet, mystic, reformer, organizer, leader, judge, and law-giver had come to the end of his road.

There is something very humanly touching in the old narrative and it is no wonder that it has been embellished in legend and poetry. We read that "his eye was not dim nor his natural force abated."[21] He was accorded the unique journalistic distinction of writing his own obituary in advance and correctly! Jewish rabbis assert solemnly and beautifully that God drew out the spirit of Moses with a kiss.

[20] See Frazer, *The Golden Bough*, Vol. X, p. 11.
[21] Deuteronomy 34:5–7.

Some admirers of Moses find the most satisfying description of his last rites in the old familiar "Fifth Reader" poem by Mrs. Cecil Alexander, beginning,

> *By Nebo's lonely mountain*
> *On this side Jordan's wave,*
> *In a vale in the land of Moab,*
> *There lies a lonely grave.*
> *And no man dug that sepulchre,*
> *·And no man saw it e'er;*
> *For the angels of God upturned the sod*
> *And laid the dead man there.*

Others of us like best, however, the old legend preserved for us by Josephus[22] that as Moses was talking on a mountain with Joshua the general and Eleazar the high priest, a cloud obscured him and suddenly he vanished and was never seen again. And we find the legend echoed—cloud, two men and all—in the later assumption stories about Enoch (II Enoch 67:1–2) and Jesus (Acts 1:9–11).

The legend which Josephus has preserved expresses so well the fact that while Moses' body disappeared, he never really died. His influence lived on and his personality is still potent. So very well was his work done that his laws and teachings not only served during the wilderness sojourn and the years of the conquest of Canaan but formed the core of later legislation and religious customs in the periods of the judges, the kings, the prophets, and the priests. Still later they were adopted by the Christians, who spread them around the world. Moses' commandments and his faith in a personal god are even now the moral code and daily religion of millions.

His burning bush still lights our world.

22 *Antiquities*, Bk. IV, Ch. VIII, Sec. 48.

MOSES   [II]

III

ZOROASTER

[660–583 B.C.]

WHO DISCOVERED THE DEVIL

How zoroaster discovered the devil and, incidentally, paradise
and the last judgment and the resurrection of the dead, is one
of the most interesting chapters in the story of religion.

Every great religion is some noble soul's conflict written large.
In the lonely desert the prophet faces the temptations of his lower
self and emerges victorious to tell the world the epic lesson he has
learned. Round the core of his personal experience is built a religion for his whole tribe, satisfying and helpful to them as far as he
is a typical tribesman triumphant over their common temptations.

Moses in the Midianite wilderness found not his God only but
the great God of the Hebrews who later was worshiped by many
nations. Zoroaster's demonic adversary gradually developed into
the Ahriman of his fellow Persians and later became the Satan of
the post-exilic Jews, the Belial of the Qumran Essenes, Jesus'
"Prince of the World," Paul's "Prince of the Powers of the Air,"
and the Devil of Christianity.

In the evolution of religion, the devil has played a useful part for
so long that it requires an effort of imagination to think back to the
time when men had no personal devil. Historically he came into

existence with Zoroaster's realization of the need of rousing in mankind the hatred of unworthy things. The devil was really Zoroaster's object lesson to teach his people ethical discrimination, which they sadly lacked. The doctrine was a very valuable device for focusing primitive thought upon the importance of recognizing and overcoming evil. Upon the devil during his long life have been concentrated righteous indignations which otherwise might have remained dormant.

Much as we deplore the superstitions attaching to the doctrine of the existence of the devil, we must admit that, historically, men seem to have been obliged to learn to hate the devil before they could learn to love God. The danger, of course, is that men may fear the devil so much that they worship him as they worship God.

But Zoroaster never worshiped Ahriman: he hated and fought him. The thing that saved Zoroaster from dualism and kept him essentially monotheistic was his sublime faith that Ahriman and the dark hosts of evil would finally be overcome by the righteous God Ahura Mazda and the angels of light. Every dark night in the valleys of doubt had been dissipated by the rising of the sun of truth over the Persian mountain tops. Zoroaster's firm conviction of the final triumph of good over evil has worked itself into the very fabric of the world's thought, giving hope to humble millions who pray, "Deliver us from the Evil One. Thy kingdom come."

Numerically considered, Zoroastrianism is today the smallest of the world's living religions, with about ninety thousand adherents in India, known as Parsees (Persians), and a few thousand faithful Gabars near Yazd in present-day Persia. Yet it lives, unrecognized, in the churches of its successful rivals and quietly influences their most cherished doctrines. Because Judaism, Christianity, and Islam all owe a great debt to Zoroastrianism, and because Zoroastrianism is built around its prophet's personal religious experience, it is important to know the main events in the life of this virile and unique man.

The Life of Zoroaster

It is no small task to discover the historical Zoroaster. Scholars have doubted his existence and even some who admit his historicity despair of ever finding the man behind the myths. But careful scholarship has patiently studied the Persian scriptures, called the

Avesta, and has found a real person. In the seventeen Gathas or psalms, the oldest part of the Avesta and which scholars think were written by Zoroaster himself, there is revealed a consistent and powerful character. The other parts of the Avesta are of later origin and contain many legends, but there is historical truth in even a legend when it is properly evaluated.

Racially Zoroaster was of that white Indo-European stock which at the dawn of history had recently divided into two great sections. One was spreading west to settle Europe. The other section, the Aryans, divided again into two groups. One group settled in what is now India and the other in the land until recently called Persia, but then, and now again, known as Iran.

Many word roots and racial customs from the original mother country still survive in all these lands. The words *brother, father,* and *mother* are practically the same in Latin, Greek, English, and German as they were in the Old Persian Avestan and in the Old East Indian Sanskrit. We recognize our kinship with Zoroaster when we know that his word for brother was *bratar.* An Englishman can find other familiar word roots now and then in the text of the Zoroastrian scriptures. An orthodox American Christian will discover startlingly familiar concepts in the Avestan description of heaven, hell, and the last judgment.

Somewhere in the western part of Iran Zoroaster was born. There has been much debate as to when. The Zoroastrian tradition, corroborated by Arabian sources, placed the beginning of the prophet's public teaching 272 years before the death of Alexander the Great, which would definitely locate the birth of Zoroaster at 660 B.C. and his death, 583 B.C. The Greek classics, through a mistake, dated him at 6000 B.C. A Theosophist writer claimed for him the antiquity of 20,000 B.C. and said that, even at that, he was really the seventh to bear the name Zoroaster. From a single word in an Assyrian inscription some scholars date him 1000 B.C., but the two greatest authorities on his date, Casartelli and Jackson, after painstaking research, take as correct the traditional date of B.C. 660–583.

It was during Zoroaster's lifetime, then, that the Jews were carried captive to Babylon and shortly after his death that they were returned to Jerusalem by Cyrus the Great, himself a Zoroastrian, called by the Sumerians and Accadians "the savior of oppressed peoples" and by the grateful Jews "the Lord's Anointed."

The significance of this coincidence (of the Jewish captivity in

Babylon, and the rise of Zoroastrianism which brought about the return of the Jews to their homeland) has never been sufficiently recognized by either Jewish or Christian historians or theologians, although it radically changed the religions of both.

Naming the Boy

The name given to the boy born into the Spitama (or White) family in 660 B.C. was not exactly Zoroaster. That is the Greek form of the real Avestan name Zarathustra, familiar to us in Nietzsche's *Thus Spake Zarathustra*. *Ustra* means camel. *Zarath* with *ustra* may mean "tormenting the camel." Since children in primitive tribes were frequently named for their first conspicuous action, we may have here the preservation in his very name of a typical boyish prank of the Persian prophet, the first event in his biography.

Later scriptures, of the Pahlavi period, spell his name, Zartusht. Indeed, his name appears in extant scriptures with no less than twenty-three variant spellings. We shall use, however, the Greek form, Zoroaster, most familiar to Western eyes. His father and mother had the strange names of Pourushaspa and Dughdhova, and tradition traces his genealogy back through a royal line of forty-five generations to Gayomart, the Adam of the Iranian mythology.

Zoroaster is said to have been the middle one of five sons and to have had three wives, who all survived him. Whether he was polygamous or given to divorce we are not informed. Nor are we told the names of the first two wives. By the first he had a son and three daughters, and by the second, a widow, he had two sons. Although the third and favorite wife, Hvovi, had no children, she is destined, so we are solemnly assured, eventually to bear three posthumous sons to Zoroaster, the first two to be millennial prophets, and the last to be the Messiah, Saoshyant. To believe this requires a greater act of faith than believing Zoroaster's birth from a fifteen-year-old virgin who had been visited by a shaft of light. It is interesting to note in this connection that Zoroaster's lineage is traced to Gayomart through his father, Pourushaspa, just as that of Jesus is traced by Luke through seventy-five generations to Adam through Joseph.

The Youth of Zoroaster

Through the legends, it is hard to discover the exact circumstances of Zoroaster's youth. The story that he was placed with a wise teacher by the time he was seven, however, seems quite credible, and the hints of precocity and rebellion are probably well founded, even if the details verge on the miraculous. The antipathies and hatreds of his manhood are so virulent that they must have been deep-rooted in his childhood, and give us by psychoanalytic inference a picture of a young life shocked by the cruelty, falsehood, necromancy, and superstition around it. As Dr. Jackson says, "We seem to have a sort of background of Dr. Faustus and the Europe of the Dark Ages."

Probably, as tradition asserts, he followed the custom of the time and at the age of fifteen assumed the rights of manhood, including a share of his father's property. That he selected as part of his share a sacred girdle which later became a symbol of the religion he founded seems a likely and typical action of the unusually serious youth. From fifteen to thirty we hear little of him. These years are comparable to the "eighteen silent years" of Jesus from the appearance in the temple at twelve to the beginning of his ministry at thirty, youthful years of "long long thoughts" and serious study.

Evidently the lad grew ashamed of his name "camel-tormentor" and tried to live down his reputation of cruelty to animals. Several stories illustrating his youthful compassion tell us that he fed other people's cattle from his father's barn, that he ran away from home to a place where he helped distribute food to the poor in time of famine, and that he brought bread to a dying dog. Upon his arrival with the bread he found the dog and her five puppies all dead. The deep impression this made upon his boyish consciousness is evidently reflected in the stern penalties prescribed in the Zoroastrian code for anyone who harms a female dog with young.

Another story of this period of his life may indicate his tendency to assume a radical attitude toward ancient social customs, for it asserts that he actually had the effrontery to ask that he might see his bride's face before he was married to her!

The Scientist in the Cave

Somewhere in this interval before he was thirty, tradition asserts very credibly that there was a long period of wilderness meditation. We cannot believe, with his later disciples, that he existed in the desert for years on one cheese which miraculously renewed itself, nor that the heavenly fire which illuminated the mountain where

Zoroaster had his cave was anything more unusual than an electric storm or a volcanic eruption. The cave idea is very persistent in the old legends and may easily have had a factual origin. Caves seem to figure sooner or later in the life stories of many great religious leaders.

Picture the earnest young truth-seeker, then, on the mountain by his cave entrance, one of the first men to think long and seriously on the problems of human destiny. We know that here was no ordinary young man, for the fragmentary references to the period of his meditation and call depict his nature as versatile and thoughtful, inquisitive and inventive.

He appears as an amateur scientist, studying and conducting experiments with fire and light, with which he afterward mystified royalty. Later Greek writers, who recognized in him a kindred inquiring spirit prying into the secrets of nature, said that he had in his cave some sort of miniature representation of the solar and planetary system. This star-gazing youth, studying the planets through the clear nights of the Iranian mountains, was the first of the Magi, the astrologers of the east, the forerunners of modern astronomers.

The Call to Preach

He appears also as a student of sociology and social evolution, for one of the most significant features of the earliest Avestan scriptures is the frequent glimpses of Zoroaster in the rôle of agricultural missionary to a semi-nomadic people. He confesses himself that his call came through "the wail of the kine." Like Moses, he protested his unfitness. Who was he to plead the cause of the cattle, who were suffering in the unsettled conditions of tribal warfare? With a sort of primitive humor, he said that the kine themselves would object to "a lord who is a powerless, feeble, pusillanimous man." But like Moses, too, he became a great leader who steadied and welded wandering tribes into a powerful established nation through the influence of a new religion. He seems to have planned definitely during his wilderness sojourn this creative, controlled evolution of his people. It was part of his divine call to service.

Zoroaster's call, however, was not primarily to scientific and economic work. There was a genuine religious experience, a mystic exaltation of spirit, a veritable vision of God.

But first the devil came. At the door of his mountain cave the prophet wrestled with his own despairs in an emotional conflict so fiercely fought that evil seemed present in person. He was oppressed by the fact that superstition and primitive fear darkened the lives of his people; he was also troubled at the Turanian raids which made life a misery for them. Like Buddha a century later in India, he felt deeply the problem of human suffering, but his solution of the enigma was different. In the inspiration of a moment he identified all these troubles and sufferings as the work of a malignant spirit, the Prince of Lies, the Demon of Doubt and Despair. "I will not give in," he agonized. "This great demon of darkness will be conquered by the god of light.

"I will go forth and preach to my people, tell them that their old gods of fear and superstition are but agents of the great Lie Demon, Angra Mainyu, and tell them that the Turanians raiding our poor cattle are also sent by this Evil One. But I will also proclaim that the time is coming when Angra Mainyu will be completely vanquished by Ahuramazda, the Supreme God of Light and Truth." As he made this high resolve his spirit felt purged and there came to him great peace and exaltation of soul.

Pure of heart, he saw God in a wonderful vision which ranks in Zoroastrianism with Christianity's vision of John on Patmos. This theophany is described in elaborate detail by later writers, for they recognized its importance in the life of their leader. They dated their chronology from this great moment, with rather more insight than most calendar makers. By their reckoning the thirty-first year of King Vishtaspa became the first Year of the Religion (1 A.R.). At dawn on the fifteenth day of the month Artavahisto (May 5, 630 B.C.), the Revelation came.

The story goes that at daybreak Zoroaster stood upon the bank of the third channel of the sacred river Daiti. As he lifted some of the holy water he suddenly saw a figure coming to him from the south bearing a shining staff. It was the archangel Vohu Manah, nine times as large as a man. He bade the enrapt Zoroaster lay aside his body and follow him to the audience room of the great Ahuramazda and his holy angels.

In the presence of God and the angels Zoroaster first noticed that he himself cast no shadow. He laid this to the exceeding brightness of the angels. The unusual nature of his surroundings evidently affected his scientific acumen. Otherwise he would have recalled that his material body was still down by the riverside, making its only permissible shadow there. Still forgetting that he was incorporeal, "he went forward and sat down in the seat of the enquirers" and was taught the cardinal principles of the True Religion. Mysterious signs and secrets were shown him which miraculously forecast coming events in the history of Zoroastrianism. Then he returned to earth, assumed his body and, following his instructions from Ahuramazda, preached for two years to the religious leaders of his country.

What was the actual experience which came to Zoroaster by the riverbank that May dawn after his night of wrestling with the devil? It is impossible for any mystic to describe his own trance temperately and accurately. There seem to be, however, two common elements in these calls which come to prophets. They all speak of a great light or flame and they are all commissioned to preach. Paul on the Damascus road or Moses by the burning bush or Zoroaster by the bank of the Daiti—brothers all.

It was the brightness of God's presence which most intrigued Zoroaster. Ahuramazda means Lord of Wisdom, but wisdom and truth and light seem to have been almost interchangeable in the prophet's vocabulary, and light and fire came to play a very important part in Zoroastrianism. Parsees today deny that they worship fire, and it is true that they have been remarkably free from idolatry all through their history, but they certainly do give fire the central place in their ceremonies. Out of this vision came a great contribution by Zoroaster to the evolution of religion—namely, the firm belief that some great day the Lord of Truth and Light would triumph over the Lord of Evil and Darkness. This millennial hope has since brought inspiration to men of many races and creeds.

The Message

When, however, we examine the actual exhortations of Zoroaster's message, the Kerygma with which he went forth to save the world, we find concepts foreign to our ideas of relevance. His sermon had four points: "Worship Ahuramazda. Magnify the archangels. Damn the demons. Marry your nearest relative."

It sounds to us like an irrelevant anticlimax, and the preachment fell on cold ears. Like many another enthusiastic young missionary, Zoroaster thought his message would carry its own conviction. He had not learned how to present his new truth to minds full of old ideas. He forgot that his hearers had not shared his celestial experience and when, instead of trying to persuade them, he demanded their allegiance, they laughed at him. Then he got angry and cursed them. And although Zoroaster was a master of anathema, this method proved to be of little value in making converts.

The failure of his early missionary efforts in his home country of western Iran made him decide on a change of policy and territory. He made a long journey far to the southwest, well down toward India, into the land of Seistan between Afghanistan and Beluchistan. He had plenty of time to think matters over on the way and evidently decided to alter his message a little. For the time being he did not preach the unpopular next-of-kin marriage. He urged the ruler of the country to praise righteousness, curse the demons, and adopt the new religion. To laud the good and curse the bad was easy enough, and the ruler went that far but balked at any creedal subscription.

Zoroaster had added healing to his repertoire and carried with him some holy water of the sacred river Daiti, which this ruler desired to sample. The young missionary refused to give it unless the king would profess the faith but made a parting tantalizing demonstration of the hormonal power of the water by miraculously rejuvenating a prematurely senile four-year-old bull.

Visions

Homeward the disappointed prophet turned and for some years wandered about, preaching without success. In fact, there were ten long pilgrim years between the Revelation and the first convert. During that time six other celestial visions were vouchsafed him, each affording additional information about heavenly matters, and setting the pattern for the later apocalypses of Enoch, John of Patmos, Dante, Bunyan, and Joseph Smith. It is reported that each "conference" was with a different archangel and that each archangel enjoined upon him certain duties in the realm in which that angel was a specialist. One quaint old commentary informs us gravely that the prophet got so well acquainted with these heavenly beings that he recognized them by sight.

Vohu Manah (Good Thought) in the second vision urged him to take good care of all useful animals. Zoroaster's conscience was still troubling him even in heaven. Asha (Righteousness) charged him with the care of fires of all sorts. Kshathra (Power) advised him about metals and mines. Armaiti (Piety) gave him the oversight of boundaries and districts. Haurvatat (Health) told him about the use of water. Ameretat (Immortality) in the last of these celestial interviews informed him about plants.

When we get a hint from the old scriptures that Zoroaster's visions all occurred during the five months of winter we begin to understand the method of his yearly program in the decade of his thirties. The places where the revelations occurred are all in western Iran. It would seem that Zoroaster made summertime preaching excursions to the east and that the winter periods of "going into conference" with the heavenly powers and principalities were times of study and meditation near his home. The thoughtful young prophet was really making a synthesis of life's problems, both practical and theoretical. Abstract virtues and concrete duties were gradually correlated in his mind by the simple device of personifying each virtue into an archangel in charge of certain real duties of life. There is evident a happily appropriate connection between some of the angels' names and their respective realms—this in spite of the difficulties of translation.

Zoroaster thus built up a system of philosophy, theology and ethics for which the world is his debtor. His was the first great philosophy of religion. He had learned the need of a preachable theology, an attractive religion. Though lonely and often discouraged, as the fragmentary records pathetically reveal, he persistently alternated summer contacts with raw human life and winter meditations about its meaning and end, until his storehouse of original thought was so rich and varied that the world's thinkers have mined it ever since. Plato and Pythagoras and Herodotus among the Greeks were indebted to him, to say nothing of Roman, Jewish, Christian and Moslem philosophers and theologians. When we learn how properly to evaluate the world's original thinkers, we shall accord Zoroaster a more prominent place than we have hitherto given him.

The Temptation

As Zoroaster was leaving his last heavenly consultation, having received the complete revelation to be later set down in the Avesta, the Bible of Zoroastrianism, he was warned that he was about to be tempted again by the fiends of evil, and this temptation was a very subtle one. He had been studying and preaching for years. He was forty years old and had not yet gained a single convert. It was only natural that he should feel tired and inclined to return quietly to the religion of his parents. The temptation took place "at the abode of Pourushaspa," when he was back home on a visit. Angra Mainyu, the crafty devil, appealed to the oldest human tie when he said to Zoroaster, "Thou art the son of Pourushaspa; I was worshiped by thy mother."

But the prophet, fresh from his vision, was not to be trapped, even when Angra Mainyu asked on what authority and by whose weapon he expected to triumph. It was asking a weary prophet without followers who he was anyhow, to be challenging the status quo in religion. Whatever doubts were in Zoroaster's mind, and there were doubts, else no temptation, nevertheless the brave man boldly answered, "By my own weapon I will vanquish you and it is the best one."

Then he recited the prayer which was to become the "Lord's Prayer" of Zoroastrianism. It is called the "Honover," which is short for "Ahuna vairo," the first two words of the prayer, just as Christians call the Lord's Prayer, "Our Father," or in Latin, "Pater Noster." The Honover sounds like a verse from the Old Testament with which it is contemporary: "The will of the Lord is the law of righteousness."

Then the devil left him for a season, and soon an angel came, not to minister unto him but to tempt him further. It seems that this was to all appearances a beautiful female angel, but really a fiend in disguise. If it were not for the Bible verse which says that Jesus was tempted in all points like as we are, an unprejudiced student comparing the two temptations would be likely to think that the Persian prophet had a harder testing. But Zoroaster triumphed again. He exorcised he demon and was left alone. What personal history lies behind this picturesque narrative we shall probably never know, but we can speculate that, since this temptation took place in his old home town, some former neighborhood sweetheart still angelically attractive in Zoroaster's eyes may have, by her promissory addresses to the homesick and world-battered prophet, added to his inclination to return to the faith of his fathers.

Recantation of his new-made faith was soon put out of the question, however, by the startling event which immediately followed the temptation. A convert appeared! And, wonder of wonders, it was a relative! His own cousin, Metyomah, adopted the faith. We are told that the conversion took place "in the forest of reedy hollows which is the haunt of swine of the wild-boar species," a spot which even A. V. W. Jackson, the indefatigable biographer of Zoroaster, cannot locate geographically yet certainly picturesque enough to stimulate the imagination.

Did Metyomah take pity on his lonesome, discouraged, tempted cousin, mooning around his old boyhood nature haunts after years of fruitless wandering? If so, Metyomah deserves a special place in Paradise: such sacrifice should be rewarded well. What more embarrassing than playing lone first chick to a proud old hen!

After the first flush of success Zoroaster was soon again despondent and complained, "In ten years only one man has been attracted by me." Notwithstanding his discouragement and poverty he traveled and worked hard for two years more. Wistfully and naïvely he prayed for material and spiritual benefits in the same breath, "Tell me truly, Ahura, whether I shall indeed, O Right, earn that reward, even ten mares with a stallion and a camel, which was promised to me, O Mazda, as well as through Thee the future gift of welfare and immortality." The "camel-tormentor" was now ironically tormented by lack of one, but he kept bravely, if complainingly, on. Then real success came.

King Vishtaspa

The two years following the conversion of Metyomah had been spent trying to win King Vishtaspa to the new faith. Now Vishtaspa was a mighty monarch to the east of Iran whose realm was especially devoted to those aspects of the old religion which were most distasteful to Zoroaster. Superstition and dark magic throve, and the Kais and the Karaps, the chief priests and scribes, were very powerful.

Straight into the enemies' camp Zoroaster marched. It was a desperate move, a gambler's play. One is minded of Jesus with his face steadfastly set toward Jerusalem. Only here was no band of disciples: Zoroaster went alone, wisely deciding that one follower was worse than none. The old account is worth noting here:

After the continuance of the last questioning of the ten years of conference [he took] his departure alone, by the advice and command of

Ahuramazda, to the residence of Vishtaspa and the precinct of that terrible conflict. [His duel of wits with the magicians of Vishtaspa's court was always referred to by his later followers as the "terrible conflict."] And the religion was taught by him, with a powerful tongue—through the speech of wisdom, through manual gestures, through definite words, through explanation of many doubts, and through the presentation of the visible testimony of the archangels, together with many miracles.

A picturesque legend tells how "two oppressive and infidel kings" got in Zoroaster's way as he was going to King Vishtaspa. The prophet prayed and an accommodating cyclone blew the two kings into the air and held them there until birds flocked thither, evidently resenting the invasion of their domain, "and with beaks and talons tore off their flesh until the bones fell to the ground." Or, to demythologize a bit, Zoroaster brooked no opposition in his campaign for converts and moved heaven, earth and air until he got to the king.

At the end of two years the king was suddenly converted with eighty-nine others, many of royal blood. Zoroaster cannily insured and celebrated his success by marrying the daughter of the king's counselor. In the course of time Zoroaster married off his own daughter to the grand vizier and composed a quaint bridal hymn which survives in the oldest part of the Avesta.

Debates and Magic

Interesting stories are told of Zoroaster's first appearance in the court of the king. "In his hand was a cube of fire with which he played without its hurting him." Immediately the wise men and priests engaged him in a "conflict" of debates. Thirty-three questions were put to the intruder. The debate lasted three days, and of course Zoroaster passed the intelligence test one hundred per cent. Then he proceeded to read the king's inmost thoughts and those of the others in a most disconcerting way. The king began to get interested and the plot thickened.

The beaten priests, in true storybook fashion, bribed Zoroaster's new servant and planted incriminating evidence of witchcraft in his room. When the heads and tails of cats and dogs were "discovered" Zoroaster was imprisoned. But the king's equine Black Beauty became very sick at the moment of Zoroaster's incarceration.

The prophet promised to restore the animal's health, upon conditions.

The distressed quadruped's feet had been strangely drawn up into its belly, and Zoroaster demanded four rewards, one for curing each leg. As the king promised each boon the corresponding leg was straightened. For his veterinary services Zoroaster won the fourfold fee: the king accepted the new religion; the king's son, Isfendiar, became a crusader for the faith; the queen was converted; and the plotting priests were killed. It was almost a kingdom for a horse.

Beneath all these fables lie discernible facts. An amateur scientist from a naphtha country should be able to manage the "cube of fire" with comparative ease, and a lover of animals might have some skill as a veterinarian. A clever king who perceived the value of the prophet's preaching of civilization to a nomadic tribe might, for economic and political reasons, espouse a new faith.

The Conquering Faith

At any rate the king kept his word, and the new religion spread quickly by conquest. Zoroastrianism militant grew with incredible rapidity. The details of the campaigns need not concern us here. The legends read like the tales of King Arthur's court or feats of the heroes of the *Iliad*. Like the fire which was its sacred symbol, the faith spread throughout Iran.

The words of Zoroaster became "the law of the Medes and Persians which changeth not." In just a century after Zoroaster's death, a Zoroastrian king with a countless host was thundering at the gates of Athens. From India's coral strand to the Grecian peninsula the faith of the lone prophet was the religion of the East. In the crusading which followed King Vishtaspa's conversion Zoroaster passed the happiest days of his life. He was ever a fighter, and for twenty-five years, until his violent death at the age of seventy-seven, he had plenty of opportunity.

In a great debate of many days, still sung of in the East, he defeated a wise Brahman, Cangranghacah, who traveled from India to vanquish him. This antagonist was so surprised to have Zoroaster read a manuscript which answered in advance all the points he had intended to make that he became a Zoroastrian missionary and converted eighty thousand in Hindustan.

Zoroaster also defeated a Greek in debate, but the Hellenes did not embrace the prophet's religion, although they admired Iranian culture and later praised Persian art. Pythagoras was said to have visited him, but it must have been prenatally, as the best chronologers think Zoroaster died in 583 B.C. and Pythagoras was born in 582 B.C. Plato is said to have planned a Persian trip two centuries later to consult Zoroaster's disciples but was prevented by the outbreak of war between the two countries.

In the great war with the "infidel" Turanians, Zoroaster was much occupied. Whether or not the aging prophet actually used the sword we do not know. Tradition says that he died at the hand of an invading Turanian, but that in the moment of death the old man hurled his rosary and killed his murderer. His soul went marching on. The next century saw the triumph of his faith, as vast armies, inspired by his religion, made the empire of the Medes and Persians the greatest in the world.

Why did Zoroastrianism spread so rapidly, once it got started? Because it had an attractive, preachable theology, with vivid imagery and definite duties, and a hope for the future of the individual and the race. Especially attractive was its doctrine of the devil and his coming overthrow, which explained the evils of the present and promised their alleviation. It was a religion easy to "sell" because it was just what men had been looking for for a long time. Even the followers of Moses succumbed somewhat to its attraction.

The Debt of Judaism to Zoroaster

A careful Bible student with any historical sense is forced to recognize how very plainly the fact stands out that the Hebrews borrowed the devil from the Zoroastrians.

The Jews were taken into captivity in Babylon in 586 B.C., three years before Zoroaster's death. Before the captivity they had no devil in their theology. Fifty years later Cyrus the Zoroastrian conquered the Babylonians and restored the Jews to their homeland. For two centuries they were ruled by Zoroastrian kings until the coming of Alexander the Great. The theology of *post-exilic* Judaism had a devil. Since the Zoroastrian religion of that time strongly emphasized a chief among evil spirits called "The Adversary," and since the *post-exilic* Jews called their devil "Satan," which means "The Adversary," there is only one possible inference.

If anyone wishes to see a literal verification of this, he has but to turn to the Bible itself. In Second Samuel, the twenty-fourth chapter, written before the exile, you will find the singular statement that Jehovah moved David to number the people and then punished the poor people for David's sin (!) by killing seventy thousand of them with a pestilence. In First Chronicles, the twenty-first chapter, the later account of the same event written after their exile, it is Satan who suggests the census. Evidently the Jews had been somewhat troubled by the very obvious inconsistency of having Jehovah function both as the author of evil and its punisher, and therefore gladly welcomed the clever Zoroastrian surrogate who relieved Jehovah of such an embarrassing inconsistency. Thus Zoroaster's influence spread.

The Debt of Christianity to Zoroaster

When we turn to the New Testament we find in the beginning of the first book, Matthew, an old story dear to the hearts of all Christians which relates that the earliest visitors to the cradle of the infant Jesus were Wise Men from the east who said they had seen his star and had come to worship him. The Greek word translated "Wise Men" is *magoi* or *magi,* which enables us to identify these dignified travelers as Zoroastrian priests. The same word is used in the first chapter of the book of Esther to describe the Seven Wise Men of Persia who "sat first in the kingdom" of Ahasuerus (or Xerxes), that Zoroastrian king "who reigned from India even unto Ethiopia, over a hundred and seven and twenty provinces."

No wonder early Christendom rejoiced at the story that priests of this ancient religion had brought to the feet of the Christ-child precious gifts of gold, frankincense and myrrh, perhaps thus expressing their hope that this babe was the Saoshyant, or Savior, that Zoroastrianism had long awaited. But Christianity got more than gold and perfumes from the followers of the Prophet of Persia.

When the Babe of Bethlehem grew to manhood, fulfilled his ministry, and was dying on the cross, one of his last sentences revealed that he expected to go immediately to "Paradise." To the penitent thief on the cross beside his, Jesus said, "Today shalt thou be with me in Paradise" (Luke 23:43). Now, "paradise" was the *Zoroastrian* abode of the blessed after death. The very word was Persian. The Hebrew word was Sheol for the abode after death of both good and bad. The place where Adam and Eve lived was not Paradise, as we sometimes call it, but a "garden." Paradise, a separate place for the good, was not used by the Hebrews till they had taken both the word and the idea from the Zoroastrians. So the Bible accounts of both the birth and death of Jesus reveal his contact with Zoroastrians and their ideas.

Many other doctrines in the Christian religion in all likelihood came from the Persian religion through the Jews—for instance, the resurrection of the dead, the final triumph over the devil, the coming of the Messianic Son of Man, the Last Judgment with its separation of the good and the bad, the belief in evil spirits, and the belief in legions of guardian angels. None of these is found in Judaism before the days of the exile, and they are all found in it afterward, or in its sects, and were all adopted by Christianity.

We suspect now that the particular sect of Judaism through which these concepts were channeled was the Essene Covenanters with headquarters at Qumran.

If a Christian were asked what great religious leader was, according to scripture, born of a virgin, was saved in infancy from a jealous and powerful foe, confounded wise men by his youthful sagacity, began to preach at the age of thirty, was tempted by the devil in the wilderness, cast out demons, cured a blind man, performed many other helpful miracles during his ministry, and taught that there is one supreme God of light, truth and goodness—he would probably say at once, "Jesus Christ: at least, that is what the Bible teaches."

If that same question were asked of a Parsee, he would answer just as quickly, "Zoroaster, for so the Zend Avesta teaches."

Indirectly but powerfully, the religions of Mithraism and Manicheism, popular in the Roman Empire, particularly in the third and fourth Christian centuries, contributed from their considerable content of Zoroastrianism to the Christianity then being formulated.

Moreover, Zoroaster's visits to heaven were echoed in Christian literature. The Book of Enoch (really several apocalyptic books probably written by Essenes) was in the Christian Scriptures for three centuries until it was supplanted by the Book of Revelation. The Enochan literature, obviously read by Jesus and Paul, is plainly Zoroastrian in its imagery and theology. And so is the Book of Revelation itself. And down through the ages Dante's *Divine*

Comedy, its Irish precursor, Adamnan's *Vision of Heaven and Hell,* and its English successor, Milton's *Paradise Lost,* have preserved the same literary and theological tradition.

Great indeed is the debt Christianity owes the Prophet of Iran. If the orthodox Christian ideas of the future life were denuded of all Zoroastrian elements the most picturesque parts would have to go.

It is time Zoroaster got credit for the favorite apocalyptic tenets of the Pentecostal Essenes of the Acts of the Apostles (chapter 2), and their present-day imitators, the Fundamentalist sects known variously as Assemblies of God, Churches of God, and Pentecostalists, all repeating, very opportunely, in the lurid light of atomic-bomb tests, the identical ecstasies, trances, and glossalalia (speaking with "tongues") that characterized early Christianity's apocalyptic age.

Yet, with the customary forgetfulness of all borrowers, few Christians even know of the debt. It is interesting to note that Christendom's belated and only acknowledgment has come, not from theologians but from a man of science, the free-thinker Edison, who named his improved electric lamp for Zoroaster's Lord of Light and Wisdom, Ahura Mazda!

Zoroaster's spirit is well reflected in one of the *gathas* or hymns of the Avesta, composed by the prophet himself and given here in the free rendering of a modern Zoroastrian, Mr. D. J. Irani,

With Truth moving my heart,
With Best Thought inspiring my mind,
With all the might of spiritual force within me,
I kneel in homage to Thee, my Master, with the songs of Thy loving
    praise ever on my lips!
And even at the last when I shall stand at Thy Gateway as a supplicator,
I shall hear distinct the sweet echo of my prayers from Thy Abode of
    Songs.

IV

JEREMIAH

[650–575 B.C.]

THE GREATEST OF THE HEBREW
PROPHETS

THE GREATEST of the prophets has been the least understood.
Jeremiah's life was one long martyrdom to principle, a heroic
tragedy of such noble dimensions that only Akhenaten or Socrates
or Jesus may be spoken of in the same breath.

He was the original "man of sorrows," and the misunderstandings
which made his life so tragic still becloud his name. Very few people remember anything about Jeremiah beyond the fact that he
wept. He has the reputation of being the world's greatest pessimist,
and his very name, in the form *jeremiad*, has passed into our language as a sarcastic synonym for a woeful wail. Give the word *Jeremiah* in a word-reaction psychological test, and nine out of ten, even
Bible students, will respond, "Lamentations."

He was, it is true, a prophesier of the unpleasant consequences
of evil deeds. He did wail and lament the inevitable destruction of
Jerusalem. But his pessimism has been overemphasized, and there
has been a consequent obscuration and neglect of his important
contribution to the evolution of religion.

Jeremiah and Jesus

If Jesus had been born six and a half centuries sooner or Jeremiah that much later, they would have been great friends, for they had much in common. The fifty-third chapter of Isaiah, with its beautiful description of the Suffering Servant of God, the Man of Sorrows acquainted with grief, despised and rejected of men, was probably written concerning Jeremiah as representing the real spirit of Judaism, but it has been adopted by Christendom as a prophetic picture of Jesus of Nazareth. The similarity between the two was noticed even in the time of Jesus. When he questioned his disciples who men thought he was, the reply was that some took him for Jeremiah come again to life.

Jeremiah was the Jesus of the Old Testament and Jesus the Jeremiah of the New. The resemblances were many. They were both, so we are informed, sanctified from the womb to the special service of God. Both were probably celibate,[1] sacrificing home joys that they might be entirely devoted to their hard task. They were both looked upon as heretics and destructive critics and charged with blasphemy and treason for predicting the destruction of the temple. In fact, when Jesus called it a den of thieves he was quoting Jeremiah. They both, in an agony of disappointment, reproached God for forsaking them, Jesus moaning, "My God, my God, why hast thou forsaken me?" and Jeremiah bitterly demanding, "Wilt thou be altogether unto me as a liar, and as waters that fail?" And they were both persecuted, their deaths planned by those they loved and were trying to save.

Indeed, the matter is much deeper, for Jeremiah named the New Testament seven centuries before it was written[2] and Jesus at the most solemn moment of his life, in one of his best-attested statements, accepted and adopted Jeremiah's doctrine of the "new covenant." If Jewish synagogues and religious schools and Christian churches and Sunday schools should study Jeremiah simultaneously for a year, with special reference to the relation of Jeremiah to Moses and Jesus, the breach between these two great religions would be greatly lessened.

[1] Jeremiah 16:2. Christian tradition always has Jesus unmarried. See also Matthew 8:20.

[2] Compare Jeremiah 31:31–34 with Hebrews 8 and Hebrews 12:24. *Testament* and *covenant* are synonymous.

The Book of Jeremiah

One reason why Jeremiah is not appreciated is because the Book of Jeremiah in the Old Testament is, as it now reads, so difficult to understand. Dr. A. S. Peake says,[3]

No clear principle seems to have determined its arrangement, so that anyone who reads the book straight through finds himself in a state of constant bewilderment as he moves backwards and forwards along the prophet's career, or, still worse, has no clue to the situation or period of the prophet's life reflected in the portion he may be reading. But even if the book were arranged in its chronological order[4] and the circum-stances which gave rise to each section were precisely known, the reader might still complain with justice that its style is often diffuse and pedes-trian, it abounds in stereotyped formulae and constant repetition, and draws not a little on earlier writings. It is accordingly not strange that a rather unfavorable verdict has commonly been passed on Jeremiah's literary power.

But amid the confusion there are certain gems of thought and aptly turned phrases that have become golden currency in the world's conversation. Who has not heard the following quotations?

Jer. 31:15—Rachel weeping for her children refused to be comforted for her children, because they were not.

Perhaps more familiar is the wording in Matthew 2:18 which, like many New Testament quotations of Old Testament passages,[5] has been inaccurately quoted, "Rachel weeping for her children, and would not be comforted, because they are not."

Jer. 8:11—... saying, Peace, peace; when there is no peace.

Jer. 8:20—The harvest is past, the summer is ended, and we are not saved.

3 New Century Bible, Jeremiah, Vol. I, p. 48.

4 For such arrangement, see Kent, *Student's Old Testament*, Vol. 3, or Moffatt, *The Old Testament, A New Translation*, Vol II, p. 814. Dr. Moffatt's translation makes Jeremiah a refreshingly new and interesting book.

5 Sometimes even the author is misnamed. Matthew 27:9 attributes to Jeremiah the passage about the thirty pieces of silver which is really found in Zechariah 11:13. Mark 1:2 (Revised Standard Version) quotes as from Isaiah a famous saying in Mal-achi 3:1.

Jer. 8:22—Is there no balm in Gilead?

Jer. 12:5—If thou hast run with the footmen, and they have wearied thee, then how canst thou contend with horses?

Jer. 13:23—Can the Ethiopian change his skin, or the leopard his spots?

Jer. 18:6—As the clay is in the potter's hand, usually quoted, "As clay in the hand of the potter."

Religious literature has few passages which exceed in startling impressiveness Jeremiah's cutting arraignment of apostate Israel,

Jer. 2:12, 13—Be astonished, O ye heavens, at this, and be horribly afraid, be ye very desolate, saith the Lord. For my people have committed two evils; they have forsaken me, the fountain of living waters, and hewed them out cisterns, broken cisterns, that can hold no water.

These quotations and other less familiar sections of Jeremiah's sermons become important material for the student of religion when they are placed against the background of the prophet's life and times.

Jeremiah's Strange Ancestress

It has been said that to produce a great man you must begin several generations back of his grandfather. It may have been Jeremiah's priestly ancestors that gave him his religious bent. We read that he was "the son of Hilkiah of the priests that were in Anathoth." Of his mother, not a word has been told us in the Bible. Anathoth had been one of the official residences of the priests of Yahweh for some centuries and was especially noted as the retiring place of the great priest Abiathar when he was unfrocked by Solomon.

But among Jeremiah's female ancestors, according to an unashamed and persistent tradition, was one of the sort seldom boasted of. In that queer and fascinating body of Hebrew lore, some of which found its way into our Bible but part of which was discreetly omitted, is the frequent recital of the large role played by a famous professional prostitute in the genealogy of several noted Hebrew leaders, including Jeremiah.

Many years before, when the Jews under Joshua were approaching Jericho, two spies, who had been sent ahead to secure information, had spent the night in the house of a harlot. She had concealed them and had enabled them to escape from the suspicious ruler of the city. As a reward, when the victorious Jews sacked the city, "Joshua saved Rahab the harlot alive." Legend has it that Joshua married her, and that she bore him children, in spite of the fact that she was then fifty years old and had been a prostitute since the age of ten.

The Jews hold her to have been the ancestress of eight famous priests and prophets (including Jeremiah, Baruch, and Ezekiel) besides the prophetess Huldah. Indeed she seems to have rivaled Jonathan Edwards in the ability to procreate genius. Christian tradition asserts that this famous woman had a child by another man, named Salmon, and that from this child, Boaz, descended Jesus himself.

The superstition that "love children" are apt to be geniuses is a very old and widespread one. The author of the genealogy of Jesus in Matthew made full use of it, for besides Rahab the harlot, he mentions only three other women, Tamar, Ruth, and Bathsheba, all of unconventional morals. But that Jeremiah's immediate ancestry was proper and pious we have little doubt. His priestly father Hilkiah probably maintained at Anathoth the better tradition of Yahweh worship. Jeremiah's later horror at the licentiousness of the admixture of Baal worship which had crept into the religion of Yahweh at Jerusalem probably reflects the puritanism of his boyhood surroundings.

The Infancy Narratives

Of his birth and childhood, the Bible tells us nothing, but extra-canonical Hebrew legends fill in the gap with miracles, as usual. It is amazing how the human mind, especially the Oriental, can invent and believe the most preposterous yarns about the infancy of its heroes. The precocity of the future prophet manifested itself, naturally, in the very early age at which he began to talk. Before he was born, indeed, he shouted that he would not leave his mother's womb until he was named. His father first suggested "Abraham" and then many other worthy names, only to have them flatly rejected as inappropriate by his son-to-be.

In the emergency Elijah came down from heaven and proposed "Yirmeyahu" (Yahweh raises up) because, he said, in the lifetime of this child "Yahweh" would "raise up" an enemy against Jerusalem. How very similar this is to the story in Matthew of Joseph's heavenly visitor who named the unborn child in Mary's womb Jesus because he would "save" his people from their sins. Elijah's suggestion was adopted.

"This," said the child, "is my name. I shall be called Yirmeyahu, adding in this way the last part of thy name to my own," and forthwith was born, and was found to be already circumcised! Yirmeyahu, or Jeremiah, was a common name, for there are seven others of that name in the Old Testament. The child continued to converse immediately after birth, wailing disconsolately, "Destruction upon destruction I bring upon earth."

The most startling part of the conversation of the newborn babe related to the adulterous conduct of his mother, who naturally was surprised and indignant. But the infant reassured her by saying, "Not thee do I mean, my mother, not to thee doth my prophecy refer; I speak of Zion, and against Jerusalem are my words directed."[6]

These infancy narratives are very obviously mistaken interpretations of part of the first chapter of that book of memoirs which has come down to us in a sadly altered edition as the Book of Jeremiah in the Old Testament. That chapter contains, not the story of the author's birth and boyhood but his call to be a prophet, one of the most interesting theophanies in the history of religion.

God in the Almond Tree

Jeremiah saw God in an almond tree, as Moses did in a thorn bush. The almond is the first tree to bloom. In Palestine its leafless branches waken to new life as early as January and are suddenly covered with white blossoms an inch or more in diameter. This striking characteristic of the tree was the source of its popular name among the Hebrews, "*shaked*," or wake-tree, much as the trillium is popularly and poetically called by Americans the "wake-robin." The young prophet, disheartened by the dissolute religion of his time, was thrilled with new hope one day when he contemplated a branch of an almond tree. It seemed to him a sign and message from God. Just as the blossoming branch promised, even in winter,

6 Ginsberg, *Legends of the Jews,* Vol. IV, p. 294.

the advent of spring, so God would soon waken new life in a seemingly dead faith.

The King James Version of the two verses (Jer. 1:11, 12) does not make the meaning clear. The conversation between Jeremiah and Yahweh is better translated as follows,

Jeremiah, what seest thou?
I see a branch of a wake-tree.
Thou hast seen well, for I am wakeful to perform my word.

The play upon words, *shaked* meaning almond tree, and *shoked* meaning watchful or wakeful, was a form of primitive pun which much appealed to Hebrews. To us it seems crude, but it had its value in fixing religious messages in simple minds. And it is no worse than many puns still popular in the Bible Belt, such as the assertion that Adam must have been created in the late afternoon since God made him a little before Eve.

The Steaming Cauldron

The bright light which commonly appears at theophanies took two forms with Jeremiah: first, the snowy whiteness of the almond blossoms and, shortly afterward, the blazing of an outdoor fire, on which a huge iron pot was boiling vigorously. A breeze from the north was fanning the flames and blowing the steam from the seething contents southward. From this incident Jeremiah deduced a message from God that "Out of the north an evil shall break forth upon all the inhabitants of the land."

Well did Jeremiah know what the evil from the north was. The Scythians were coming!

Zephaniah the prophet, the forerunner of Jeremiah, as John the Baptist was of Jesus, was already preaching and warning of the wrath to come, "The great day of the Lord is near . . . a day of wrath, a day of trouble and distress, a day of trumpet and alarm . . ." Jeremiah felt that God was calling him to follow in the footsteps of Zephaniah. But he hesitated to start out and preach.

To Preach or Not to Preach

He felt that the nation needed to be warned and he felt called to help do the warning, but he held back. Legend has it that he said,

"O Lord, I cannot go as a prophet to Israel, for when lived there a prophet whom Israel did not desire to kill? Moses and Aaron they sought to stone with stones; Elijah the Tishbite they mocked at because his hair was grown long; and they called after Elisha, 'Go up, thou bald head!' "

Jeremiah was sufficiently acquainted with the lore of his people to be hesitant about assuming the role of prophet. He was torn with indecision, and his mental struggle is vividly pictured in that first chapter of his memoirs. Urging him to the work was the knowledge that he came from generations of religious leaders and that he had been dedicated by his parents even before his birth to the service of Yahweh,

Then the word of the Lord came unto me, saying,

Before I formed thee in the belly I knew thee; and before thou camest out of the womb I sanctified thee, and I ordained thee a prophet unto the nations.

Then said I, Ah, Lord God! behold, I cannot speak: for I am a child.

But the Lord said unto me, Say not, I am a child: for thou shalt go to all that I shall send thee, and whatsoever I command thee thou shalt speak.

Be not afraid of their faces: for I am with thee to deliver thee, saith the Lord.

Then the Lord put forth his hand, and touched my mouth. And the Lord said unto me, Behold, I have put my words in thy mouth.

See, I have this day set thee over the nations and over the kingdoms, to root out, and to pull down, and to destroy, and to throw down, to build, and to plant.

At just what age he received his call to prophesy we do not know, but he was probably in his early twenties. Scholars generally date his birth about 650 B.C. His own statement that the call came in the thirteenth year of King Josiah (i.e., 627–626 B.C.) would make him twenty-three or twenty-four years old. Hebrew legend has him the exact age of Josiah, and since Josiah began to reign at the tender age of eight years, Jeremiah would by that reckoning have been twenty-one at the time of his call.

A young man in his early twenties need not have hesitated over-long at assuming the role of prophet. His offering his youth as a reason was apparently an excuse. His real reason for hesitation was probably the realization that his message would be an unpopular one. Well did he know that his was to be the unwelcome task of the destructive critic so much abhorred by all "right-minded" orthodox people. He would have to "root out, pull down and destroy" the established worship of the day with all its shameful but popular ritual. He must tell the people that the Scythians were coming as God's agents to punish them.

It was a call to certain unpopularity and probable death, but he braced himself to meet the challenge of duty. It seemed to him then in his moment of high resolve that God spoke to him, saying, "Thou therefore gird up thy loins, and arise, and speak unto them all that I command thee: be not dismayed at their faces, lest I confound thee before them."

The Barbarians Are Coming

While the Scythians were overrunning the lands to the north and east and sweeping down toward Palestine on their way to Egypt, the young prophet started out, saying to his careless countrymen, who were so heedless of approaching doom, "Behold a people cometh from the north country, and a great nation shall be raised from the sides of the earth. They shall lay hold on bow and spear; they are cruel and have no mercy; their voice roareth like the sea; and they ride upon horses, set in array as men for war against thee, O daughter of Zion."

As the hordes of barbarians came nearer, the people began to listen to Zephaniah and Jeremiah. Uneasiness increased in Jerusalem and all the countryside. Rumors of the merciless mounted men who rode in array and harried the land had been coming from the north for months and the rapidity of their progress was terrifying. When Assyria and Egypt were afraid, what would Jerusalem do? Paralyzed by fear, the Hebrews could only wait. Jeremiah told them of the boiling cauldron he had seen, and prophesied that the northern invaders would come to the very walls of Jerusalem and that Yahweh would use these enemies to punish the Hebrews who had "burned incense to other gods and worshiped the works of their own hands." But the Scythians did not enter Hebrew territory.

"When they had reached Palestine," says Herodotus,[7] "Psammetichus, the Egyptian king, met them with gifts and prayers, and prevailed on them to advance no further." The relief in Jerusalem

7 Book I, Ch. 105.

found vent in great rejoicing, and the inhabitants paused in their orgy of celebration only long enough to laugh and jeer at Zephaniah and Jeremiah.

It was too much for Zephaniah, and he evidently prophesied no more. Jeremiah, too, remained silent for several years. He was forced to readjust some of his ideas. He had been convinced that he had spoken the word of Yahweh, but he must have made some mistake.

Deuteronomy

His warnings had failed to turn his people back to Yahweh, but other men were at work to secure the same end. In the year 621 B.C., the Book of Deuteronomy was "found" in the temple while repairs were being made. Deuteronomy means "second Law," and the book was a new revision of the laws of Moses, evidently composed by righteous priests of the temple as part of the much-needed reformation program.

King Josiah lent his sanction to the new movement and ordered the public reading of the book in the temple. King and people both promised to keep the laws of the new code. The paraphernalia of Baal worship was removed from the temple and burned. The valley of Hinnom, where child sacrifice had been practiced, was "defiled" and the custom forbidden. The various centers of Baal worship throughout the land were desecrated and even the worship of Yahweh was forbidden anywhere save at Jerusalem.

Did Jeremiah Write Deuteronomy?

It would be very natural to suppose that Jeremiah wrote the book of Deuteronomy for, as Renan pointed out, it "was composed in the time of Jeremiah, among the associates of Jeremiah, and according to the ideas of Jeremiah."[8] He began preaching five years before the book was found. Ahikam, who was one of the leaders in publishing the book, was Jeremiah's friend, and Hilkiah, the priest who "found" the book, may possibly have been the Hilkiah who was Jeremiah's father. More than that, there are many phrases and

[8] *History of the People of Israel,* p. 193. Ernst Renan's interpretations of Biblical history, once considered heretical and even blasphemous, are now spoken of more respectfully, especially since the discovery of the remains of the Qumran Library.

clauses identically the same in the books of Deuteronomy and Jeremiah, and Driver states that "even where the words are not actually the same, the thought and the oratorical form—the copious diction, and sustained periods—are frequently similar."

Nevertheless, the hundred parallels between Deuteronomy and Jeremiah have been proved by the painstaking work of scholars to be due, not to the Jeremian authorship of Deuteronomy but to the fact that Jeremiah read the book and mastered it so thoroughly that he quoted it freely and almost unconsciously. Its phrases became part of his vocabulary.

Whether the young man was permitted by his friends to read the book before its publication is unknown, but it is evident that soon after its appearance Jeremiah was actively preaching "in the cities of Judah and in the streets of Jerusalem, saying, 'Hear ye the words of this covenant, and do them.' "

Rejected at Home

But Jeremiah had not been preaching long before he met opposition of a personal sort which much surprised him, for it came from his townspeople. It is so disconcerting to a young prophet to find himself without honor among his own folk.

When Abiathar had been deposed and sent to Anathoth, his place had been given to Zadok. It was the Zadokite[9] priests in Jerusalem who had sponsored the Deuteronomic reformation and who had probably introduced the provision for centralizing Yahweh worship in Jerusalem, a provision that took away from the Anathoth priests even the one privilege they had left, of officiating at the local shrine in their own town. It was adding insult to injury. The intense rivalry between the two priesthoods is what makes it difficult to believe that the priest Hilkiah who discovered the book could have been the Hilkiah who was the father of Jeremiah.

It is easy to understand, then, the plot of the men of Anathoth against Jeremiah. He was deemed a traitor to his family and town,

[9] The "Sadducees" of the New Testament were probably derived partly from the Zadokites, and so were the Pharisees. But the Essenes of Qumran, the Sons of Zadok, more nearly observed the spirit of the Deuteronomic reformers. It is significant that the Book of Deuteronomy was so prized at Qumran that fragments of fourteen manuscripts were found in Cave IV alone, and Dr. F. M. Cross inferred (*Revue Biblique*, Jan. 1956, p. 56) that to judge by the quantity, "*C'était le plus populaire des livres biblique à Qumrân.*"

and his life was plotted against. He had evidently been telling again and again his almond-tree story. That phrase about God being wakeful to perform his word made a fine text for a sermon, for the "word" was, of course, the newly discovered book.

"But," says Jeremiah ruefully, "I was like a lamb or an ox that is brought to the slaughter; and I knew not that they had devised devices against me, saying, 'Let us destroy the "tree" with the fruit thereof, and let us cut him off from the land of the living, that his name may be no more remembered.' " Probably the young prophet was as much disturbed by the scornful treatment of his favorite sermon illustration as he was by the threat against his own life. The whole incident distressed him greatly. He remonstrated with God because the wicked prosper and those who deal very treacherously are happy.

Then he reminds himself that he has hardly started out on his ministry and must not lose heart at his first persecution. Or as he recorded it, God said to him, "If thou hast run with the footmen, and they have wearied thee, then how canst thou contend with horses?"

The reformation of religion under Josiah was outwardly successful. With a strong hand the laws of the book of the Zadokite priests were enforced. The old local sanctuaries, some of which had been sacred places devoted to the worship of various gods ever since men had lived in Palestine, were abandoned, and the Jerusalem temple and priesthood grew in power. But after Jeremiah's first espousal of the reform, he seems to have lost his enthusiasm. He may have become too discouraged after he discovered the plot against him, but it is more likely that he felt no great urgency to preach. The people were prosperous and were faithful in the temple worship, and idolatry was suppressed. There was nothing to get excited about.

Jeremiah was not interested in preaching to prosperous people unless they were openly wicked. He was by nature a prophet who flourished in times of calamity. He probably felt vaguely disturbed at the growing power of the priesthood and the consequent trend toward the substitution of ritual for righteousness; but during the last decade of Josiah's reign, from 618 B.C. to 608 B.C., the reform movement was still young and strong, and the dangers of priestly dominance had not yet become apparent.

Armageddon and After

But when Josiah died in 608 B.C., conditions changed almost overnight. When Josiah "fought at Armageddon" he "battled for the Lord," and lost. Armageddon was a later name for Megiddo, a city overlooking the Plain of Esdraelon, where many famous battles have since been fought.

Esdraelon is on the highroad from the Nile to the Euphrates, and the defeat of Josiah's army by Pharaoh Necho was only a minor event in a great contest for world power between Egypt and Assyria. Jerusalem simply had a new overlord. They paid tribute to Egypt instead of Assyria. But the death of Josiah was no minor event for the Hebrews. It shook their sense of security and raised religious doubts.

Josiah's second son, Jehoahaz, was made king by the people but reigned only three months before he was taken to Egypt by Pharaoh Necho, who put Josiah's eldest son, Eliakim, on the throne at Jerusalem. The account in II Kings 23:34 says that the Pharaoh changed Eliakim's name to Jehoiakim, a statement which gives the Egyptian ruler credit for more interest in Hebrew theology than was likely. He probably did not know the god "El" from the god "Yahweh."

Jehoiakim had not long been king before Jeremiah had plenty to prophesy about. In a violent reaction from the reforms of Josiah, the people returned to the superstitions and immoralities which had characterized their worship before the discovery of Deuteronomy. Jeremiah's suspicions about the value of a reformation enforced by law were justified. When the enforcement ceased, there was no strength of character in the individual to enable him to carry out the covenant he had pledged to keep.

Besides, the common impression was that no serious harm could come to Jerusalem. Was not Yahweh's house, the temple, a guarantee of safety? What matter if they did enjoy themselves? As long as the temple ritual was kept up Yahweh would be satisfied.

There were really two parties in Jerusalem. The reform party was led by the Zadokite priesthood, sponsored by Josiah during his life and supported for a time by the free-lance prophet Jeremiah. The other group was the "heathen" party, ousted by Josiah but restored to power by Jehoiakim. This was made up of those who welcomed the admixture of Canaanite and Babylonian culture with its luxurious and licentious customs and strange religious practices.

The Prophet Attacks Licentiousness

Three of these "heathen" religious practices appear to have excited Jeremiah's wrath in particular, the worship of the Queen of Heaven, the worship of stocks and stones, and the sacrifice of children to Molech in the valley of Hinnom. He was constantly preaching against these practices. Some of his sermons against them come from the pre-reform period, some from the reign of Jehoiakim, and some from later. It is difficult, in the present condition of the book of Jeremiah, to determine which utterances belong to each period. It is also hard to discover whether the worshipers thought they were worshiping Yahweh or the foreign gods in these ceremonies, for a great deal of syncretism and amalgamation had gone on for centuries.

The Queen of Heaven

The Queen of Heaven, however, had nothing to do with Yahweh. She was the planet we know as Venus, personified as the goddess, Ishtar. In Babylon Ishtar was called the Queen of Heaven, and the cult is said to have been introduced into Jerusalem during the reign of Jehoiakim's great-grandfather, Manasseh.

But the goddess had been known only too well by the Hebrews long before the time of Manasseh. They found her one of the chief deities of the Canaanites when they came into the land of promise. The Phoenicians, known in the Bible as Philistines, paid her high honor. She was the patron goddess of Sidon, and the Sidonian ships had her figure on their prows, her extended right hand holding a crown, exactly as some automobiles had her on their radiator-caps several decades ago.

Hiram, King of Tyre, according to Menander, quoted by Josephus,[10] built a temple to Ashtart. One of her priests was the father of the infamous Jezebel who married and corrupted King Ahab of Israel. Solomon himself built a "high place" near or on the Mount of Olives for the worship of Ashtart, or Ashtoreth, as the

[10] *Antiquities*, VIII: V:3.

Hebrews called her. Periodically her worship was revived in Jerusalem, and the last revival there was after the death of Josiah. The Hebrew women were especially attracted to her worship, and they easily persuaded their husbands and children to unite with them in some of the customs connected with her ritual.

Jeremiah protested mightily against such practices in a passage which reveals the simple and rather attractive family preparations for worshiping Ashtoreth, the Queen of Heaven,

Seest thou not what they do in the cities of Judah and in the streets of Jerusalem?

The children gather wood, and the fathers kindle the fire, and the women knead their dough, to make cakes to the queen of heaven, and to pour out drink offerings unto other gods, that they may provoke me to anger.

Do they provoke me to anger? saith the Lord: do they not provoke themselves to the confusion of their own faces?

Therefore thus saith the Lord God; Behold, mine anger and my fury shall be poured out upon this place, upon man, and upon beast, and upon the trees of the field, and upon the fruit of the ground; and it shall burn, and shall not be quenched.

From Jer. 44:16–22, which tells how the Hebrew women insisted on worshiping Ashtoreth even when exiled in Egypt in Jeremiah's old age, we learn that the cakes were shaped in the form of the goddess. The Authorized Version of Jer. 44:19 renders the Hebrew "did we make her cakes to worship her," but Dr. Moffatt's translation is better, "made cakes in the shape of her."

Sacred Cakes

It was an ancient and widespread custom of many religions. "In many parts of the world cakes stamped with symbols or with the actual form of a divinity, or dough or paste images of gods or goddesses, are commonly found and are frequently ritually eaten."[11] In some countries these cakes were made of the first grain to be harvested, and it was quite likely the custom in Palestine, for Ashtoreth was the goddess of fertility and evidently combined the virtues later resident in both Aphrodite and Demeter.

11 *Encyclopedia of Religion and Ethics*, Vol. III, p. 58. See also Frazer, *The Golden Bough*, Index, "cakes."

Jeremiah might denounce all he pleased. The women knew. And they told him plainly, for the account says,

All the women who were standing by shouted loudly to Jeremiah, "We will not listen to this word of yours. . . . No, we mean to keep without fail this oath of ours to offer sacrifices to the Queen of Heaven . . . as we used to do . . . in the towns of Judah and on the streets of Jerusalem. Then we had plenty of food, we prospered and came to no harm. But ever since we gave up sacrificing to the Queen of Heaven and pouring out libations in her honor, we have been in utter need, and at the mercy of the sword and of famine."[12]

What a long succession of sacred cakes through the ages, lineal descendants of the ones baked and ritually eaten for Ashtoreth! Think of the wedding cakes, with "lucky" symbols in them. How carefully and ritually they must be cut and the pieces put under pillows to dream on! In England, the top tier of the wedding cake is the christening cake, carefully put by, a silent Christian appeal to Ashtoreth, goddess of fertility, that she may bless the union and make it fruitful.

"Hot cross buns," to be eaten during Holy Week, must have the image of the cross on them. Even more directly of "heathen" origin are the Simnel cakes bearing the figures of Christ or His Mother Mary.[13] One does not need to be a scholar to see in a Simnel cake stamped with the shape of the Virgin a Christian version of the very confections Jeremiah condemned. Perhaps the "gingerbread dolls" hung even yet on New England Christmas trees have a more ancient lineage than the cooks suspect.

But more notable than Simnel cakes or gingerbread men, a distant descendant by a different line and of a higher spiritual quality, is the bread or wafer of the Christian communion or mass. The ancients ate cakes shaped like their deity that they might partake of the virtues of the god or goddess. It was a comparatively refined way of doing what the savage did when he ate the lion's heart that he might have courage. Eat the god and become like him. It is a long way from Ashtoreth cakes to "this is my body broken for you. Eat ye all of it. This do in remembrance of me." It is a long way, but the trail is plain and the trail is upward. Religion has no higher

---

[12] Jeremiah 44:15–18, Moffatt's translation.

[13] *Encyclopedia of Religion and Ethics*, Vol. III, p. 60.

sublimation in its ritual. Devout worship, a sincere desire to become like one's chosen ideal god, has been in history a great force elevating man from the mud to the stars.

Ashtoreth was Ishtar, Queen of Heaven, the planet Venus, and no one can lift his eyes to the evening skies and behold that star without rejoicing with exceeding great joy. But when insincerity and ignorance crept into Ashtoreth worship, it became a licentious orgy.

And it is alleged that when the ignorant Christian priests of the Middle Ages hurried through the mass that they might get back to less spiritual pursuits, the sacred words *Hoc est corpus meum* (this is my body) became *Hocus pocus,* which, with its abbreviation *hokum,* has come to signify a performance calculated to produce a desired effect on an ignorant audience. And the still often-heard ejaculation, "hocus-pocus," is the semantic protest of the cynic, the doubter, and the unimpressed.

The Fallen Virgin

It was the licentious part that troubled Jeremiah. He was so strict with himself, never marrying lest he be hindered in his chosen work as wandering prophet, that he was doubly severe on others. Evidence in plenty there was around him. "On every high hill and under every green tree" he found wanton worshipers. It seemed to him that the whole nation had gone after the strange gods. Jeremiah personified the nation as a fallen virgin, as Hosea had done before him. He pictured the betrothal of the virgin Israel to Yahweh, her lover in the wilderness, and then, in unsparing language, condemned the fickle virgin's desertion of Yahweh for the gods of Canaan, with whom she wantoned openly.

Sacred Stocks and Stones

In Jeremiah 2:27 there is a puzzling phrase, the explanation of which throws light on the religious customs of the time and reveals the nature of the revived animism which the prophet was fighting. He bitterly condemned those who were "saying to a stock 'thou art my father'; and to a stone, 'thou hast brought me forth.' "

The "high places," where the Hebrews had learned from the

Canaanites to worship, had the ancient sacred symbols which the
Phoenicians had brought from Crete, one of wood and one of stone.
The wooden object had evidently been a tree originally but was
now a branchless pole, called an *asherah*. The stone object was a
pillar or obelisk and was a *massebah*. It appears that the asherah
was thought of as representing a male divinity and the massebah,
a female, and that both were deities of fertility and reproduction.

At great festivals held on the high places the Hebrews indulged
in licentious orgies, having been taught by the Canaanites that such
practices ensured the fertility of the soil and the herds, by a sort
of sympathetic magic. As Jeremiah put it, with double meaning,
the nation had "committed adultery with stones and with stocks."

The children born because of these promiscuous religious celebrations were considered children of the deities of the high places.
The god was their father and the goddess their mother. No disgrace
was attached to such children; they were, rather, honored. According to Jeremiah 2:26, kings, princes, priests, and prophets proudly
boasted of such origin. To us, it seems almost incredible that such
immoral customs were ever associated with religious worship. We
might feel inclined to doubt Jeremiah's word, but recent excavations have corroborated the prophet beyond doubt.

At Gezer, a Canaanite city on the border between the Hebrews
and the Philistines, was an ancient high place, the remains of which
have been carefully studied by experts.[14] Dr. Frazer says,[15]

Here the English excavations have laid bare the remains of a sanctuary with the sacred stone pillars or obelisks [masseboth] still standing in
a row, while between two of them is set a large socketed stone, beautifully squared, which perhaps contained the sacred stock or pole [ashe-
rah]. In the soil which had accumulated over the floor of the temple
were found vast numbers of male emblems rudely carved out of soft
limestone; and tablets of terra-cotta, representing in low relief the
mother goddess, were discovered throughout the strata. These objects
were no doubt votive offerings presented by the worshipers to the male
and female deities who were represented by the sacred stock and the
sacred stones; and their occurrences in large quantities raises a strong
presumption that the divinities of the sanctuary were a god and goddess
regarded as above all sources of fertility.

14 See R. A. S. Macalister, *Bible Side-lights from the Mound of Gezer.*
15 Frazer, *The Golden Bough*, Vol. V, p. 108.

Child Sacrifice

But Jeremiah's wrath was most excited by a third practice of his contemporaries, the sacrifice of children by "passing through the fire" to Molech. There is no escape from the horrible conclusion that "passing through the fire" meant burning the children as a sacrifice, for Jeremiah explicitly says so in several parts of his memoirs.

Whether the child was placed on the red-hot arms of the image, or placed on the arms, from which it rolled into a fiery pit,[16] or was burned on an altar before the idol, is not clear. Possibly the child was mercifully killed before its body was burned. The story of Abraham's thwarted attempt to sacrifice his son Isaac gives us a faint hope in that direction. The circumstance that Jeremiah quotes Yahweh as saying that He had not commanded such an abominable sacrifice leads one to infer that some Hebrews, at least, believed that they were worshiping Yahweh when they gave their children to the flames. Was child sacrifice of the first-born part of Yahweh worship?[17]

Baal meant simply "lord," and *Molech* may be derived from *melek,* king, and either term may have been applied to Yahweh.[18] Probably, however, Jezebel, the Tyrian wife of Ahab, was responsible for bringing her baal or god, named Molech, Melech, or Melkarth, into the pantheon of Israel. By the time of Jeremiah, two centuries and a half later, the common people were doubtless so confused by the intermixture of foreign elements with their religion that they did not know which baal they were worshiping, and thought that Jeremiah was making a needless and pedantic theological distinction.

The Earthen Jar

But Jeremiah had no sympathy with Molech worship, whatever its origin. Early in the reign of Jehoiakim, when the prophet found that the Molech cult was being resumed in a valley just outside

---

16 See Diodorus Siculus, XX, 14.
17 Frazer, *The Golden Bough,* pp. 168–179.
18 See Hosea, 2:16 and Hastings' *Dictionary of the Bible,* I:210 and III:416.

Jerusalem, he determined to strike a smashing blow against it. Taking with him from the temple several leading lay and professional religionists, either for protection or as witnesses, he started for the accursed valley. He had to pass through the "Gate of Potsherds," so-called because the potters just inside the gate found it convenient to cast the debris of their shops outside it.

From one of the shops Jeremiah took an earthen jar and led the growing procession through the gate and out to the valley. Standing on the slope, within hearing of the worshipers and those who came with him, he delivered a speech of condemnation which must have startled every hearer,

Thus saith the Lord of hosts, the God of Israel; Behold I will bring evil upon this place, the which whosoever heareth, his ears shall tingle. Because they have forsaken me, and have estranged this place, and have burned incense in it unto other gods, whom neither they nor their fathers have known, nor the kings of Judah, and have filled this place with the blood of innocents:

They have built also the high places of Baal, to burn their sons with fire for burnt offerings unto Baal, which I commanded not, nor spake it, neither came it into my mind: Therefore, behold, the days come, saith the Lord, that this place shall no more be called Tophet, nor the valley of the son of Hinnom, but the valley of slaughter.

And I will make void the counsel of Judah and Jerusalem in this place; and I will cause them to fall by the sword before their enemies, and by the hands of them that seek their lives; and their carcasses will I give to be meat for the fowls of the heaven, and for the beasts of the earth. And I will make this city desolate, and an hissing; every one that passeth thereby shall be astonished and hiss because of all the plagues thereof.

And I will cause them to eat the flesh of their sons and the flesh of their daughters, and they shall eat every one the flesh of his friend in the siege and straitness, wherewith their enemies, and they that seek their lives, shall straiten them.

When he had his audience's shocked attention by his vivid description of the cannibalism of the coming siege, he crashed the earthen jar to the ground to announce his climax and said, "Thus saith the Lord of Hosts: Even so will I break this people and this city, as one breaketh a potter's vessel, that cannot be made whole again: and they shall bury them in Tophet, till there be no place to bury."

Then Jeremiah returned to the city and stood in the court of the temple and prophesied the destruction of Jerusalem and the towns round about because the people had "hardened their necks that they might not hear" the words which Jeremiah spake for Yahweh.

In the Stocks

Such open impudence could not be permitted to go unnoticed. Pashur, the officer who was supposed to keep order in the temple, struck Jeremiah and then put him in the stocks, an instrument of torture and humiliation, commonly used for too obstreperous prophets. For the rest of that day, all the night, and part of the next day, Jeremiah was thus exposed to the gibes of the passers-by. Whether or not he continued to preach from the stocks we are not told. It would have been difficult, because he was in the embarrassing position of a preacher who had sought publicity and had suddenly received too much.

At any rate we do know that the prophet was very angry when he was released. First he turned on Pashur, and nicknamed him *Magormis-sabib,* or Terror, and prophesied that the official would be a terror to himself and all his friends. Then he complained bitterly to Yahweh because of the mockery and derision he had undergone. In a most revealing passage Jeremiah tells how he had tried to stop preaching Yahweh's word but could not,

Then I said, "I will not make mention of him, nor speak any more in his name." But his word was in mine heart as a burning fire shut up in my bones, and I was weary with forbearing, and I could not stay.

This whole twentieth chapter uncovers the torment of the prophet's soul. No one can read it without being touched by the alternation of indignation and despondency with confidence and joy. Jeremiah reached the nadir of despair when he cursed the day of his birth, cursed the man who had announced to his father that a son had been born to him, and wished that his mother's womb might have been his tomb. These words were taken by the author of the Book of Job as a text for his famous third chapter. Later men, noting the similarity of the thought and language, inferred that Jeremiah wrote the Book of Job.

On Trial for His Life

In spite of his experiences in the stocks, the prophet was soon preaching again with even greater boldness, for he prophesied the destruction of the temple itself unless the people turned from their evil ways and obeyed the law of Yahweh. Here was heresy indeed, and not merely heresy but treason, for the temple was then to the Hebrews what now the king is to a Briton or the flag to an American.

Jeremiah found all Jerusalem arrayed against him immediately —priests, prophets, people, and even the princes of Judah. A demand for his death arose. He was solemnly called to account, but he repeated his prophecy before the whole assembly. His only defense was that he had spoken nothing save what God had told him to speak. He was really demanding what was many centuries later called "benefit of clergy."

"Of a truth," he said, "the Lord hath sent me unto you to speak all these words in your ears." He spoke as one having authority, the highest authority, and his confidence won him his life. The princes and the people said to the priests and the prophets—that is, the laymen said to the enraged clergy, "This man is not worthy to die: for he hath spoken to us in the name of the Lord our God."

Then arose some of the older men in the assembly and cited a precedent. Micah the Morasthite, in the days of Hezekiah, had likewise prophesied the destruction of Jerusalem and the temple and had not been killed. And Jeremiah's friend Ahikam stood up for him. So they let Jeremiah go. Free speech was vindicated.

Jeremiah versus Jehoiakim

Vindication emboldened the prophet further. He attacked the king himself with scathing words. Here again Jeremiah was courting destruction, for Jehoiakim had just shown signal vindictiveness in dealing with another prophet who had roused the royal anger.

This prophet, Uriah, had fled from Jehoiakim's wrath to Egypt, but the long hand of the angry king had reached him even there and haled him back to Jerusalem. Then the king had had him killed by the sword and his body cast into a grave "of the common people"—that is, into the Potters' Field of the time. It was a great dishonor not to be buried with one's "fathers" in the family burying place. Jeremiah, fully cognizant of the fate of Uriah, approached the king and, after condemning recent royal injustice, prophesied that Jehoiakim's body would be worse treated than Uriah's. It would be dragged outside the city and given the burial of an ass— that is, it would not be buried at all.

Jeremiah was full of righteous indignation not only at Jehoiakim's execution of Uriah, who appears to have been a disciple of Jeremiah, but also at the king's unjust treatment of the workmen who had been building him a palace, "panelled with cedar and painted with vermilion." Jehoiakim had evidently been so hard pressed to pay the tribute demanded by his overlord, Pharaoh Necho, that he had resorted to trickery to get his palace built for nothing, for when it was finished, he simply refused to pay the workmen.

Perhaps the knowledge that Jeremiah had the right on his side prevented the king from punishing the prophet. A trial of Jeremiah by public assembly might give unpleasant publicity to the king's own trickery.

Carchemish

The king soon had plenty to occupy his attention besides house-building and quarreling with prophets. In 605 B.C. Pharaoh Necho was defeated at the great battle of Carchemish in North Syria by Prince Nabu-kudurri-usur of Babylon, who was prevented from following up his victory by the death of Nabu-apal-usur, his royal father. History is indebted to Jeremiah for the only known record of that decisive battle which determined the fate of western Asia for many years.

The scripture transliteration of Nabu-kudurri-usur is Nebuchadrezzar (sometimes Nebuchadnezzar). The name is very familiar to Bible readers as it occurs nearly ninety times in the Old Testament. During his long reign of over forty years this Babylonian (sometimes called Chaldean) king became an almost fabulous personage to the Hebrews and they have many legends about him, one of which makes him the son of Solomon and the Queen of Sheba!

But Jeremiah, with his usual political sagacity, foresaw the importance of Nebuchadrezzar and his probable relation to Hebrew affairs. He began warning his countrymen and the surrounding nations as well, predicting the inevitable spread of Babylonian power. Probably his prophecies have been touched up by later editors to make them accord more accurately with the actual events, but there is little doubt that Jeremiah early recognized Nebuchadrezzar as a powerful leader of a rising world state, before whom Syria, all Palestine, and even Egypt must eventually bow in homage.

Jeremiah saw in the Chaldean king the agent of Yahweh to punish the Hebrews. One is reminded of the way Christians of the Middle Ages looked on Attila the Hun as the Scourge of God.

The Leopard's Spots

The prophet pointed out to his countrymen how he had been warning them for ten years but to no avail. They had hardened their hearts, and one might as well expect them to change now as to expect an Ethiopian to change his skin or a leopard his spots.

Therefore thus saith the Lord of hosts; Because ye have not heard my words, Behold, I will send and take all the families of the north, saith the Lord, and Nebuchadrezzar the king of Babylon, my servant, and will bring them against this land, and against the inhabitants thereof, and against all these nations round about, and will utterly destroy them, and make them an astonishment, and an hissing, and perpetual desolations.

Moreover I will take from them the voice of mirth, and the voice of gladness, the voice of the bridegroom, and the voice of the bride, the sound of the millstones, and the light of the candle. And this whole land shall be a desolation, and an astonishment; and these nations shall serve the king of Babylon seventy years.

The prediction of seventy years' captivity in Babylon was a remarkably good guess on Jeremiah's part, for Jerusalem fell in 597 B.C. and Cyrus captured the city in 538 B.C. and sent the Jews back to Jerusalem shortly afterward, so they were in Babylon about sixty years. If Jeremiah's prophecy of seventy years were an insertion by a later editor, that person would have made it sixty years, to correspond with the known facts.

Jeremiah, Author

It was during this very year 605 B.C., the fourth year of Jehoiakim, that Jeremiah began to dictate for publication the principal sermons and addresses he had made in his twenty years' career. Baruch, a young nobleman, served as secretary to the prophet and the two men worked together on the book for a year, evidently, as it was in the ninth month of the fifth year of Jehoiakim that the book was first read in the temple.

Why Jeremiah wrote the book is a question. Perhaps he felt that the imminent coming of Nebuchadrezzar would mean his own death and wished to have his words preserved so that posterity might appreciate what his contemporaries had rejected. Perhaps he had been ordered not to preach in public after his open condemnation of the king, or Pashur may have ordered him to keep away from the temple because of the disturbances he generally made there. This seems very likely, for when Jeremiah sent Baruch to read the roll of the book in the temple he said, "I am shut up; I cannot go into the house of the Lord." There is, however, another reason which may explain why the prophet wrote the book.

Jeremiah, Publicity Expert

Jeremiah was one of the greatest publicity experts religion has ever known. He was constantly devising novelties to attract the attention of the people to his message. He knew how to "make news." He connected his sermons with the politics of the day, not only by bringing politics into the pulpit but even by taking his pulpit into the political arena. He hesitated at no personal discomfort or embarrassment, if he might only gain an audience.

We find him doing startling things, breaking an earthenware jar at a dramatic moment, burdening his neck with a wooden yoke, wearing a conspicuously soiled girdle, and drowning a book with a stone attached to it. He seems to have invented the idea of securing publicity by getting arrested, for he was apprehended so many times that it is a wonder the officers did not get suspicious. If there had only been newspapers in his day, he would have "made" the front page frequently.

In the light of this known characteristic of Jeremiah, we are inclined to suspect that the book which the prophet wrote was more than a book: it was a publicity device. He had seen what attention the Book of Deuteronomy had attracted when it was read in the temple. Why should he not write his message in a book and have it read there? Possibly people would pay more attention to the messages if they came in that form. They were tired of his voice, perhaps. Well, let them hear the words proclaimed by another voice.

The plans for launching the new book upon the public were laid and carried out with such skill and success that modern publishers might well read the thirty-sixth chapter of Jeremiah. Jeremiah and Baruch waited until the people of all the towns of Judah were gathered in Jerusalem at the temple for a special fast day.

Upon that day Baruch went to the temple and read the book aloud "in the chamber of Gemariah." Yet he read it "in the ears of all the people." The two circumstances appear hard to reconcile, for it would have been impossible to get any large number in such a small room. But Professor Bennett has explained the situation clearly—namely, that Baruch "betook himself to the 'chamber' of the scribe, or secretary of state, Gemariah ben Shaphan, the brother of Jeremiah's protector, Ahikam. This chamber would be one of the cells built around the upper court, from which the 'new gate' led into an inner court of the temple. Thus Baruch placed himself formally under the protection of the owner of the apartment, and any violence offered to him would have been resented and avenged by this powerful noble with his kinsmen and allies. Jeremiah's disciple and representative took his seat at the door of the chamber, and, in full view of the crowds who passed and repassed through the new gate, opened his roll and began to read aloud from its contents."[19]

The people were predisposed to listen because of the religio-political character of the occasion. The fast day itself may have been set because of the fear of the probable invasion of Nebuchadrezzar. As the reading went on and drew to a close, the importance of the document became more evident. The people recognized many of Jeremiah's ideas often set forth hitherto in their presence, but his words took on new significance in the light of Carchemish. He had revamped his old prophecies of the time of the Scythian invasion twenty years before when he had told of the coming of the evil from the north. Now the northern menace was Babylon. The people listened and wondered if perchance crazy Jeremiah might not be right after all. He had a way of saying things. . . .

Gemariah himself was not present, because there was a council of the nobles and princes taking place that December day in one of the rooms of the royal palace, probably discussing the ominous

[19] Expositor's Bible on Jeremiah, 36.

likelihood of a visit from Nebuchadrezzar the next spring "at the
return of the year at the time that kings go out to battle." Into the
council room came an urgent messenger. It was Gemariah's son,
Micaiah, who was evidently a young man of some insight and initiative. Recognizing the political importance of the public reading
of Jeremiah's book, he had hurried to report the matter to his
father. He had not been able to leave the chamber until the reading
was over, because of his duties as host in his father's absence.

Baruch must have smiled when a messenger from the nobles commanded him to come to them at once and bring the book with him.
The plans were working out very well. "So Baruch the son of Neriah
took the roll in his hand and came unto them. And they said unto
him, 'Sit down now, and read it in our ears.' "

When they heard the bold predictions in the book, they were
much alarmed and whispered to each other that they would have
to report this to the king. But they warned Baruch to go to Jeremiah immediately and hide with him where they could not be
found. Their fears were well founded, for when the book was read
to the king he slashed it into pieces with his penknife and burned
it in the brazier which warmed his room. Then he sent three men
to find Baruch and Jeremiah. "But the Lord hid them."

The Second Edition

The book was now well launched. It had had three readings in
three prominent places. It had been condemned by the highest
authority. It would soon be in great demand. "Then took Jeremiah
another roll, and gave it to Baruch the scribe, the son of Neriah;
who wrote therein from the mouth of Jeremiah all the words of the
book which Jehoiakim, king of Judah, had burned in the fire; and
there were added besides unto them many like words."

The second edition contained the story of the reception of the
first edition and was therefore widely read. For over twenty-five
hundred years the book has had a steady sale, especially since printing was invented. Our Book of Jeremiah in the Bible is based on
that second edition but has also Baruch's additions made as events
occurred for the next twenty years. The fact that Baruch wrote no
account of the death of Jeremiah may confirm the legend that the
secretary was killed at the same time as the old prophet.

Nebuchadrezzar, God's Agent

When the second edition was completed, Jeremiah came forth from hiding and continued his prophesying. He was firmly convinced now that Nebuchadrezzar was the chosen ruler of all nations, sent to punish them all for their sins, and that those who opposed the Babylonian king were opposing the will of Yahweh. Some of the Jerusalemites were still expecting help from Egypt. But Jeremiah asserted that it was a vain hope, as Egypt herself would be controlled by Babylon. The prophet's apostrophe to the land of the Nile has been translated by Dr. Moffatt as follows,

> *You may get balsam from Gilead,*
> *My lady Egypt,*
> *but all your salves are vain,*
> *for you there is no healing.*
> *The whole world hears you wailing,*
> *Your crying rings around,*
> *for one brave falls over another,*
> *and both drop to the ground.*[20]

In spite of Jeremiah's warnings, Jehoiakim revolted from Babylon's rule. Nebuchadrezzar, before coming himself to punish Jerusalem, got the northern neighbors of the Hebrews to harass them. Because of the movements of these peoples, smaller tribes were driven on toward Jerusalem through the cities of Judah. One of these tribes was the Rechabites, Bedouin descendants of those Kenites who were prominent in Moses' day.

Prohibition That Prohibited

These Rechabites were faithful Yahweh worshipers and had been, even before Moses had made Yahweh the god of the Hebrews. One of their strictest tenets was abstinence from wine, for one of their former leaders, Jonadab, had established prohibition which really prohibited.

When Jeremiah saw these tribesmen wandering about the streets of Jerusalem, he seized the opportunity for another "publicity stunt." He led some of them into the temple and set before them

20 Moffatt's Old Testament, Jeremiah, 46:11–12.

great pots of wine, gave them cups and bade them help themselves. But they refused to drink, even when commanded by the prophet. Then Jeremiah turned on the watching crowd and compared the faithfulness of the Rechabites with the unfaithfulness of the Jeru-salemites.

Nebuchadrezzar at Jerusalem

Nebuchadrezzar was on his way to Jerusalem, but three months before he got there Jehoiakim died. He may have been given "the burial of an ass" as Jeremiah had prophesied, but the account in Second Kings (24:6) says that he "slept with his fathers." His eighteen-year-old son Coniah became king and took the name Je-hoiakin, but reigned only three months. The great king of Babylon found no real opposition when he appeared before the gates of Jerusalem in 597 B.C. Now that Jehoiakim was dead, the advice of Jeremiah evidently prevailed, and the nobles and their king sur-rendered unconditionally.

The youthful Jehoiakin was taken to Babylon and lay in prison there for thirty-seven years until he was released by Nebuchad-rezzar's successor. With Jehoiakin there went a long train of cap-tives, the flower of Judah. Seven thousand warriors and one thou-sand workmen, together with many of their families, began the long melancholy march. The treasures of the temple and the king's pal-ace were packed on beasts of burden and taken along too. The riff-raff were left behind under the rule of another son of Josiah, Mat-taniah, better known as Zedekiah, too weak a man to control the unruly remainder.

Jeremiah Left Behind

There have been many conjectures as to why Jeremiah was left behind. The most likely guess is that the captives told their captors that he was a trouble-maker and that they did not want him with them. Perhaps they dreaded his "I told you so." But they misunder-stood Jeremiah. Underneath all his bitter denunciation was a lov-ing heart. He had prophesied against them because his conscience had made him. It hurt him more than it did them. They were his people after all, and there is no sadder picture in history than that of the lonely prophet, who had made his nation his family, standing on the wall of Jerusalem watching them march away into captivity. He loved them and had tried to save them. He had warned them and they had refused to listen. Now they were leaving him and with hate toward him in their hearts. Again, probably, he wished that he had never been born.

The First Epistle of Jeremiah

In a little over a year he sent them a letter. The epistle of Jeremiah to the captives in Babylon, which is found in the twenty-ninth chapter of the Book of Jeremiah, is a wise and beautiful message. Some of the unnamed prophets who were with the exiles were promising them a speedy return to Jerusalem, and many of the young men were idly waiting for that time to come. In the colony of expatriates on the banks of the river Chebar there was an opportunity to build houses, plant gardens, and establish homes, but many refused to do any of these things. Jeremiah wrote them that there would be a return but not until seventy years had passed, as he had told them before.

Build ye houses, and dwell in them, and plant gardens, and eat the fruit of them; Take ye wives, and beget sons and daughters; and take wives for your sons, and give your daughters to husbands, that they may bear sons and daughters; that ye may be increased there, and not diminished. And seek the peace of the city whither I (Yahweh) have caused you to be carried away captives, and pray unto the Lord for it: for in the peace thereof shall ye have peace. . . . For thus saith the Lord, That after seventy years be accomplished at Babylon I will visit you, and perform my good word toward you, in causing you to return to this place. . . .

Then shall ye call upon me, and ye shall go and pray unto me, and I will hearken to you. And ye shall seek me, and find me, when ye shall search for me with all your heart. And I will be found of you, saith the Lord: and I will turn away your captivity, and I will gather you from all the nations, and from all the places whither I have driven you, saith the Lord; and I will bring you again into the place whence I caused you to be carried away captive.

One of the prophets by the Chebar, named Shemaiah, answered Jeremiah by sending a letter to the assistant high priest Zephaniah in Jerusalem demanding that Jeremiah be put in the stocks for sending such an unpatriotic letter. Zephaniah simply showed the letter to Jeremiah, who promptly sent another letter to the exiles condemning Shemaiah for "rebellion against the Lord." Meanwhile in Jerusalem matters were not going well at all.

The Wicked Figs

The people left behind in Jerusalem and the towns round about were convinced that Yahweh had deserted them. They lost faith in him and returned to the worship of other gods. According to Ezekiel (chapters 8 and 9) an *asherah* or sacred tree was set up in the temple itself for the worship of Ashtoreth. Women worshiped the Syrian god Tammuz, and twenty-five men deliberately turned their backs on the temple and their faces toward the rising sun to worship it.

These apostates particularly enraged Jeremiah by claiming that they were better than the exiled people in Babylon, so one day Jeremiah brought before them another of his famous object lessons. He set two baskets of figs in a conspicuous place at the entrance to the temple where all would see them. One basket contained very good figs, the other, "very naughty figs, which could not be eaten, they were so bad." When a sufficiently large crowd had gathered, he explained that the good figs represented the exiles and the bad ones the people left behind—namely, themselves. Jeremiah never was one to hesitate in stating unwelcome truths where they were most unwelcome.

Nebuchadrezzar had not been back in Babylon long before revolt broke out behind him. Judah was only one of the little nations of the eastern Mediterranean coast lands. From the vassal kings of Tyre, Sidon, Edom, Ammon and Moab there came secret messengers to Zedekiah in the fourth year of his reign, urging a coalition against their common Babylonian overlord. Pharaoh Necho of Egypt had just died (594 B.C.) and there was a chance that Psammetichus II, his son and successor, might break his father's treaty of peace with Nebuchadrezzar and come to the aid of the rebels.

The Yoke

Jeremiah, knowing that the rebellion was ill-advised, managed to get hold of the messengers from the five kings. He appeared in their presence wearing a yoke made of thongs and wooden bars.

Then to the startled envoys he gave a message to take back home with them, " 'The nation and kingdom that will not put their neck under the yoke of the king of Babylon, that nation will I punish,' saith the Lord, 'with the sword and with the famine, and with the pestilence, until I have consumed them by his hand.' "

When the messengers had departed, Jeremiah continued to wear the symbolic yoke as a constant reminder to the people of Jerusalem. One Hananiah, however, stepped up to Jeremiah, seized and broke the wooden yoke, and said, "Thus saith the Lord, 'Even so will I break the yoke of Nebuchadrezzar, king of Babylon, from the neck of all nations within the space of two full years.' "

Jeremiah was nonplused for a while but soon appeared with a yoke made of iron bars. Moreover, he prophesied Hananiah's death within the year. When Hananiah did die seven months later, the prophet's prestige was enhanced. It may have been Hananiah's death which broke up the proposed rebellion. At any rate, Zedekiah, king of Judah by grace of Nebuchadrezzar, made a hurried trip to Babylon about this time, probably to assure his overlord of his unimpeachable loyalty.

The Siege of Jerusalem

Five years later, however, in 588 B.C., Ammon and Tyre and Judah joined in a rebellion and sent to Egypt for assistance. Before they could get it, the watchful Nebuchadrezzar was at the walls of Jerusalem.

There was terror within the walls. In an eleventh-hour repentance the inhabitants sought to gain Yahweh's help by freeing those of their slaves who were their fellow countrymen, a law of Deuteronomy which they had neglected. They may also have had in mind the securing of additional defenders to man the walls of the city. With great joy they woke one morning to find the besieging army departing. The help which the rebels had sought from Egypt was on the way. Psammetichus II had been succeeded three years before by Hophra, who was now advancing with the army.

The shortsighted Jerusalemites thought they were to be freed from the overlordship of Babylon. With singular duplicity they enslaved again the men and women they had freed. Jeremiah protested vigorously and said that Nebuchadrezzar would soon be back, would burn the city, and would leave all the towns of Judah round about "a desolation without an inhabitant."

The people of Jerusalem judged this to be nothing less than open treason. Jeremiah was arrested as he was leaving the city on his way to Anathoth. The charge was that he was deserting to the enemy. He was cast into a filthy prison, where he remained for a long time until Zedekiah became worried by reports of the probable return of Nebuchadrezzar. The king sent for the prophet to see if there were any message from Yahweh regarding the new situation. Jeremiah calmly told the king that there was no hope, that he would without a doubt fall into the hands of his great enemy. He took the occasion to make a request for the alleviation of his personal sufferings, and the king had him released from his vile quarters. He was put into the court of the guard and given each day his daily bread as long as there was any bread.

One would think that under the circumstances Jeremiah would have been content to remain quiet, but he continued in season and out of season to proclaim that those who remained in the city would all die either by sword, famine or pestilence, and that those only would live who left the city and deserted to the Chaldeans. Several of the nobles heard these prophecies of Jeremiah and immediately demanded of the king that the prophet be put to death for treason, saying, "Pray, have this fellow put to death; he takes the heart out of all the citizens and soldiers left within the city, by talking like this! The fellow is out to ruin the city, not to help it!"[21] Zedekiah acceded to their requests, and the princes chose a particularly dreadful form of death for the prophet. They let him down by cords into a miry cistern and left him there to die.

A Negro Saves Jeremiah

In spite of the secrecy which probably veiled the putting away of Jeremiah, the deed of the princes was discovered by one of the palace attendants named Ebed-melech, a huge Negro eunuch from Ethiopia. This slave is one of the most interesting characters in the Bible, and we wish we knew more about him. He showed initiative and ability. As soon as he discovered the predicament of the prophet he left the palace and went to one of the gates of the city where the king was holding court. Since the case required emergency meas-

21 Moffatt, Jeremiah 38:4.

ures, if the prophet were to be saved, the slave braved the wrath of the king and interrupted the proceedings of the court, pleading so eloquently that the king ordered that three men follow the Negro back to the palace to help rescue the prophet.

Ebedmelek took the men with him and went to the palace, where he got some torn, tattered rags out of a lumber-room below the treasury; these he lowered by ropes to Jeremiah in the cistern, saying, "Put them between your armpits and the ropes." Jeremiah did so. And they pulled him up by the ropes out of the cistern.[22]

A Secret Conference

Before long King Zedekiah went to the guardhouse where Jeremiah had again been confined and led him into a secluded passageway where an interesting conference followed. The king said, "I am going to ask you a question which you must answer truthfully." "And if I do answer truthfully," said Jeremiah, "you will undoubtedly put me to death." The king swore by the living God and his own soul that he would neither put Jeremiah to death nor give him into the hands of the nobles. Without waiting for the question, which he could easily surmise, Jeremiah said to the king,

If you surrender to the king of Babylon's officers, then you save your life, and this city shall not be burned in flames; you and your household will be spared. But if you will not surrender to the king of Babylon's officers, then this city shall be handed over to the Chaldeans to be burned in flames, and you cannot escape from their hands.[23]

Zedekiah betrayed his weak character by replying that if he surrendered to the Chaldeans he would be reviled by the Jews who had already deserted to the Chaldeans. Jeremiah reassured him on that point, and the conference ended with a strict injunction from the king to Jeremiah that he keep this interview to himself if he wished to save his life. The king said that if people heard of the conference and asked Jeremiah what had transpired, he was to reply that he was simply asking the king not to be sent back to the vile prison. Jeremiah was questioned later and replied exactly as the king had advised him.

[22] Moffatt, Jeremiah 38:11–13.
[23] Moffatt, Jeremiah 38:17–18.

The prophet did not forget the kindness of the Ethiopian eunuch and promised him that when the city was taken he would not be slain but would escape with his life. This reward did not seem to later Jewish commentators commensurate with the value of the service which Ebed-melech had rendered to Jeremiah. Consequently we find an interesting legend in which Ebed-melech takes the laurels away from Rip van Winkle.

It seems that just as the city was about to fall Jeremiah sent Ebed-melech on a pretended errand with a basket of figs. When the Ethiopian got outside the city, the warmth of the day affected him so that he sat down to rest in the shade of a tree. There he fell asleep and slept for sixty-six years. Upon awakening he was naturally much surprised at finding the surroundings changed, especially when he went back into the city and asked for Jeremiah. He could find no one whom he knew. The people told him how the temple had been deserted and the people taken into captivity many years before. Then Ebed-melech realized that he had been rewarded for his kindness to Jeremiah by being spared the sorrow of seeing his friends led into captivity.

Another Hebrew legend says that Ebed-melech was not really an Ethiopian but by that peculiar figure of speech known as antiphrasis had been called "the black" to indicate how "white" he really was. The Hebrew commentators were really very versatile casuists: such a little matter as proving that black was white did not trouble them at all. This version of the story of the reward of Ebed-melech states further that he was allowed the privilege of entering Paradise without tasting death.

The Fall of Jerusalem

The siege of Jerusalem was so strictly maintained by Nebuchadrezzar when he returned from his expedition against Pharaoh Hophra that no food was permitted to enter the city. The horrors of the famine toward the end of the eighteen months during which the Babylonians were besieging the city may be indicated by the fact that the Hebrew mothers finally ate their own children. Reflections of the suffering of the time may be seen in the Bible Book of Lamentations.

On July 9, 586 B.C., in spite of the courage of the weakened defenders, a breach was made in the wall. This time Nebuchadrezzar was not as lenient as he had been eleven years before. He murdered all Zedekiah's children and that dreadful sight was the last which the king saw on earth, for Nebuchadrezzar then put out Zedekiah's eyes and led him captive.

The few remaining treasures of the temple were taken, the city itself was plundered, and then the temple and city were burned and completely destroyed. Even in the outlying towns only a few of the poor people were left to carry on husbandry. These few were given as their ruler a man named Gedaliah, a grandson of Shaphan, the scribe, and a new capital was set up at Mizpeh, not far from the ruins of Jerusalem.

Again Jeremiah was left behind, but this time it was of his own free will. As a reward for his well-known advocacy of submission to Babylonian sovereignty he was given his freedom at Ramah, a place five miles on the road north from Jerusalem, whither the captives were taken for sorting before the long trek to Babylon began. If he had gone to Babylon he would doubtless have been shown great honors and might have ended his life in comparative peace, but quixotic Jeremiah chose to remain with the handful of shepherds and vine-dressers who had been left, that the land might not become a desert. There is little doubt that Jeremiah was influenced in his decision by the fact that Gedaliah, the appointed Governor of Judah, was a man after his own heart.

Gedaliah was the son of that Ahikam who had long ago befriended the prophet. He was evidently a wholehearted convert to Jeremiah's teachings, an ardent disciple, and from him Jeremiah expected much. For a few weeks it seemed as if a fresh start were being made. High hopes rose in the hearts of the remnant of the people. Gedaliah was wise and gentle. But his kindness was misinterpreted as weakness by the surrounding nations. The king of Ammon planned, by a treacherous stroke, to gain control of Judah. He secured the services of one Ishmael, a blackguard.

Gedaliah had been warned against Ishmael but refused to believe evil of him, entertained him hospitably, and was treacherously killed by him, together with a number of Jews and some Chaldean soldiers who had been left behind by Nebuchadrezzar. On his way back to his employer, however, Ishmael was overtaken by a Jewish captain named Johanan and was glad to escape with his life. Johanan turned to Jeremiah for advice as to what should be done in the emergency. An assembly of the survivors was held, and Jeremiah advised that they stay in Judah, remain loyal to Nebuchadrezzar, and build up the waste places as well as they could.

His audience did not receive his advice kindly. They had been left behind in the deportation of 597 B.C.; they had endured the horrors of the recent siege and had survived the massacre by Ishmael. They were quite convinced that Judah was an unlucky place in which to live, and they wanted to get away from it as quickly as they could. Disregarding Jeremiah's advice, they proceeded under Johanan's leadership to Egypt and took the prophet along with them.

In this Egyptian colony Jeremiah spent the remainder of his life. We have no information as to how long that was, nor as to the manner of his death. We know that he continued to prophesy in Egypt, for the forty-fourth chapter of the Book of Jeremiah tells of his protesting against the revived worship of the Queen of Heaven. We also know that Jeremiah gave his recalcitrant flock at least one more of his famous object lessons. At the very entry of the Pharaoh's house in Tahpanhes (Daphne) he buried stones just beneath the pavement. He was careful to do this at a time when his people were watching him. When they asked him why he did it he said that upon that very spot would the king of Babylon spread his state carpet and set up his throne when he had conquered Egypt. Even to the last he must protest and maintain his consistent policy of the necessity of recognizing Nebuchadrezzar as the agent of Yahweh.

The Death of Jeremiah

A tradition which reaches us through the Christian "Fathers," Tertullian and Jerome, asserts that Jeremiah was stoned to death by his fellow countrymen, who were enraged by his irritating words. The tradition sounds as if it were based on truth because it is quite consistent with Jeremiah's character and with the general attitude of his people toward him. A Jewish Midrash states that when the Jews in Egypt stoned Jeremiah, the Egyptians reverently buried the body because of their gratitude to him for having, by prayers, caused the crocodiles to disappear from the Nile. This incident reminds the student of religious legends of the similar ones in which St. Patrick and St. Columba are alleged to have driven dangerous reptiles from Ireland and Iona.

Jeremiah's Writings

There are persistent traditions that Jeremiah's writings are not all included in our present Book of Jeremiah. That is probably true, but various alleged writings of Jeremiah which have come down to us are obviously pseudepigraphic—that is, signed with Jeremiah's name by very much later authors. These include "the Epistle of Jeremy" in the Apocrypha and "The Paralipomena of Jeremiah."

Another line of tradition finds evidence of Jeremian authorship in several of the books of our Old Testament. The book most frequently associated with Jeremiah is Lamentations. Just as the editors who are responsible for the present form of the Bible put all the anonymous psalms under the Psalms of David, so those who translated the Hebrew Old Testament into Greek (the Septuagint version) ascribed the authorship of Lamentations to Jeremiah, a mistake perpetuated in our common English versions. Most modern scholars admit that Jeremiah wrote some lamentations but deny that he wrote the so-called "Lamentations of Jeremiah."[24]

Several scholars believe that Jeremiah wrote the twenty-third, twenty-sixth, twenty-seventh, and twenty-eighth Psalms. To the pen of the prophet has also been assigned the authorship of the Book of Job. It is true that when these writings are reread with Jeremiah's possible authorship in mind they take on new meaning, but a careful examination will reveal many reasons why Jeremiah could not have written them.

The Importance of Jeremiah to Religion

Jeremiah's resemblance to Moses was early noted by Jewish commentators. They were fond of pointing out certain superficial similarities such as the fact that both Moses and Jeremiah prophesied for forty years, that Moses was thrown into the water and Jeremiah into a pit, and that Moses was drawn out of the water by a bondmaid and Jeremiah by a slave. But the resemblance of Jeremiah to Moses was much deeper. The connecting link is rather to be found in the Book of Deuteronomy which represents the ethical ideal which Moses had been striving for and which advocates the re-

24 A. S. Peake, *New Century Bible*, Jeremiah, Vol. II, pp. 292–296.

forms which Jeremiah urged so vehemently. In other words, the torch which Moses laid down and which for a time smoldered, was caught up by a group of prophets of which Jeremiah was the greatest.

We cannot agree with Renan[25] that three fourths of the rays of glory which encircle Moses should be credited to Jeremiah, but we must admit that "rarely has a moral tendency so seized upon a human conscience and filled it with concentrated passion. . . . The religious genius of Jeremiah was without a parallel."

Jeremiah's defects, including his almost constant pessimism and his irritating persistence in stating unwelcome ideas at too opportune times, are very obvious. Sometimes in his fear of being a hypocrite he became a nuisance. Considering the usual reaction of people in that stage of civilization it is almost a miracle that he escaped martyrdom so long.

But recognition of his defects should not blind us to his most unusual qualities. The difference between Jeremiah and the prophets who came before him, which raises him to a position among the world's greatest leaders of religion, is the complete merging of his personality with his problem. The value of such a man to his race and to the world is in his almost unconscious summing up in his own life of the problems facing his people and all people. Jeremiah identified himself not only with the God he worshiped but with the people he condemned.

He might begin every message with "Thus saith the Lord," but there were times when he expressed the wish "Oh, that my head were waters and mine eyes a fountain of tears that I might weep day and night for the slain of the daughter of my people!" In other words, Jeremiah had occasional flashes of that sublime consciousness of identification with God which seems to have been so frequent and sustained in Jesus that he could say, "He that hath seen me hath seen the Father."

Jeremiah's consciousness of the presence of God with him is revealed by his very vivid conception of the Word of God. He believed that there was some peculiar, living power in the Word itself. It was alive and carried with it a certain energy which made sure the fulfillment of the promises and threats which it proclaimed. Jeremiah was convinced that when a message came to him from God the very uttering of it made its accomplishment inevitable. He

25 *History of the People of Israel,* Vol. 3, p. 126.

was in his own eyes not only the announcer of Yahweh's plans but the instrument by which they would be achieved.

One of the most revolutionary proclamations of Jeremiah which definitely separated him from Moses was his announcement that the Ark of the Covenant would no longer be needed and would even be forgotten. The Mosaic Covenant would be superseded by the New Covenant,

> Behold, the days come, saith the Lord, that I will make a new covenant with the house of Israel, and with the house of Judah: Not according to the covenant that I made with their fathers in the day that I took them by the hand to bring them out of the land of Egypt; which my covenant they brake, although I was an husband unto them, saith the Lord: But this shall be the covenant that I will make with the house of Israel; After those days, saith the Lord, I will put my law in their inward parts, and write it in their hearts; and will be their God, and they shall be my people.

> And they shall teach no more every man his neighbor, and every man his brother, saying, Know the Lord; for they shall all know me, from the least of them unto the greatest of them, saith the Lord: for I will forgive their iniquity, and I will remember their sin no more.[26]

Jeremiah's New Covenant, or New Testament, was later taken as the name for the whole body of writings having to do with the beginnings of Christianity. The Old Testament prophet's idea of a future religion in which the individual stood in direct relation to God was so literally fulfilled in the religion of Jesus that we find constant references in the New Testament by Jesus, Paul, and the author of the Book of Hebrews, to Jeremiah's New Covenant.

Renan, indeed, says that without Jeremiah, "the religious history of humanity would have taken another course; there would not have been any Christianity."[27] It is not a mere figure of speech that this passage we have just quoted from the thirty-first chapter of Jeremiah has been called "the gospel before Christ." Jeremiah was the pioneer of personal religion, and the reason for it lay in his own intimate, personal experience with God.

The three great literary links between Jeremiah and the New Testament are to be found in the books of Ezekiel and Deutero-Isaiah, two great prophets who were apparently disciples of Jere-

[26] Jeremiah 31:31–34.
[27] *History of the People of Israel,* Vol. 3, p. 124.

miah and who did their prophesying in Babylon during the exile, and in the very similar Enochan literature of the Essenes, manuscript fragments of which were recently found in the Qumran caves.

Ezekiel's bizarre visions have somewhat obscured the importance of his messages to the exiles. There is no doubt, however, that his buoyant spirit was one of the major forces in preserving among the Jews in Babylon the memory of their former greatness and the hope of returning to their old city. He was ably seconded by another and unknown disciple of Jeremiah. The book of Isaiah in the Bible is the work of several authors. It is recognized now by scholars that chapters forty to fifty-five are the work of this so-called "Unknown Prophet of the Exile." Here some of the most beautiful passages of the Bible are found, instinct with the spirit of his great teacher Jeremiah.

Jeremiah and Jesus

The Enochan books certainly reflect the attitude, message, and personality of Jeremiah just as they anticipate those of Jesus, especially in the famous "Son of Man" passages in Enoch's Book of Similitudes. As will be more fully set forth hereafter in Chapter VII, the "Teacher of Righteousness" was spiritual kin to both Jesus and Jeremiah.

In Jeremiah's own personality was fought the eternal conflict between the lower and the higher natures of man. Because he tore aside the veil and let us look deep within his own burdened heart, he contributed more to a solution of the age-old problem of religion than any other man the Hebrew race has produced, with one exception. The people around him were concerned almost entirely with their own immediate troubles. He sought causes and cures, and from his own experience derived the great thought that after all religion is an inward personal matter between the individual and his God. Dr. J. A. Bewer wrote recently,[28] "Jeremiah's greatest contribution was his personality." In that respect too he resembled Jesus.

With the insight of a true prophet he looked forward to the time when there would be no need of teacher, priest, preacher or book. No man would then need to urge his brother to "know the Lord," for even the least of men would know God directly. This doctrine

28 *The Prophets,* 1955, p. 170.

is spiritually high above that which teaches that the individual needs a mediator between himself and God; therefore it is higher than most historic Christianity. A parallel for it can only be found on the high level where Jesus of Nazareth lived.

NOTE: Doubtless there are both Jews and Christians who would have chosen another prophet—Isaiah, Ezekiel, Amos, Hosea—as a better representative of his time and faith. We have given space to Jeremiah because he was not only great, and representative, but also because his book reveals so frankly the atavisms, common elements and parallel customs of all religions.

BUDDHA

[563–483 B.C.]

WHO FOUND SALVATION IN PSYCHOLOGY

IF SCRIPTURAL ACCOUNTS of the working of miracles are proofs of deity, Gautama the Buddha was a god indeed. Compared with the colorful stories of his marvelous deeds, the sacred books of all other religions appear pale and tame. Modest seem the Christian legends of the angel annunciation, the shepherds, the wise men, and the star over the stable, when placed alongside such an infancy narrative as the following, compiled from the Buddhist scriptures.

The Birth of Buddha

King Suddhodana, who ruled the Sakya tribe of India in the sixth century B.C., decided to choose a wife, and married Maya, the fairest maid in the kingdom, although he had to take her six sisters too in order to get her. The queen bride, resting one summer afternoon on the couch in the state bedchamber, dreamed that four kings carried her, bed and all, to the Himalaya mountains and placed the bed under a tree seven leagues high. Four queens bathed, dressed, and anointed her, and escorted her to a holy bed in a golden mansion on a mountain of silver. A white elephant descended from a golden mountain to the silver one. Bearing a lotus in his trunk, he entered the mansion, circled the bed three times, struck Queen Maya's right side and entered her womb.

When the queen told this dream to her husband, he called sixty-four wise men, fed them well, gave them gifts, and then asked their interpretation of the dream. They rose to the occasion and said, "Be not anxious, O king, the queen has conceived, a male not a female, and thou shalt have a son, and if he dwells in a house he will become a king, a universal monarch; if he leaves his house and goes forth from the world, he will become a Buddha, a remover in the world of the veil [of ignorance]."[1]

Then, according to the Buddhist scriptures, there was an earthquake, and thirty-two miracles occurred, including the curing of the blind, deaf, dumb, and lame in the kingdom, and the putting out of the fires in all hells!

When the queen's time had come, she was walking in the Lumbini grove. As she stood at the foot of a blossoming saltree, she reached up for a branch. It was too high, but obligingly bent down to her hand. Then, still standing, she gave birth to her son, who was received in a golden net by four Brahmas. Although the babe was clean, "two streams of water fell from the sky, one of cold and one of hot water, wherewith they performed the washing of the Bodhisatta and his mother." The Brahmas then passed him to four kings, who accepted him on a robe of antelope skins and transferred him to a silken cushion held by ordinary mortals. The newborn infant then stood up and was worshiped by gods and men. He looked in all directions to see if anyone like himself existed, and finding none took seven steps toward the north. And then, the quaint account relates, "While Mahabrahma held a white parasol over him, and Suyama a fan, and other divinities followed with the other symbols of royalty in their hands, he stopped at the seventh step, and raising his lordly voice, 'I am the chief in the world,' he roared his lion-roar."[2]

This same day was, according to legend, the birthday of his wife, his elephant, his horse, his charioteer, and the tree under which he later discovered the secrets of life. On this day also, a certain wise

[1] From the Nidana-Katha, quoted by E. J. Thomas, *The Life of Buddha*, page 32. This biography will serve as an excellent source book on Buddha for the general reader as it gives copious quotations from sources not easily available.

[2] *Ibid.*, p. 33.

man named Asita saw in the sky above his home in the Himalayas certain gods holding a celebration which they said was because of the birth of a Buddha among the Sakyas. Asita journeyed thither and when he saw the child, rejoiced with exceeding great joy. He pointed out that the boy bore the requisite thirty-two marks of a great man, such as long fingers, projecting heels, prominent ankles, forty even white teeth, black eyes and a large tongue!

The astounding precocity, which the infant so early exhibited, continued. It was decided to take the baby to the temple, and his aunt was given the privilege of conducting him. Indeed, she practically took the place of his mother (who died seven days after his birth), and was already his father's wife. The child asked her, this time in a sweet voice, where she was taking him. Upon learning, he recited three verses to remind her that there was no god in any temple equal to himself, but said, obligingly, that he would go along to be agreeable to custom. As soon as he arrived, all the temple idols fell down at his feet.

When this remarkable child was taken to the writing-school to learn his alphabet, he innocently asked which alphabet the school master was going to teach him, nonchalantly mentioning sixty-four, including the Chinese! With a start like that, one can imagine what miracles he worked when he got his growth. The stories which the canonical scriptures assert that Buddha calmly narrated of his own adventures make not only other religious leaders but even Marco Polo and Baron Munchausen seem mere amateurs in wonder-telling.

Did Buddha Ever Live?

If the historical existence of Moses and Zoroaster has been questioned, it is no wonder that some higher critics have looked askance at Buddha and have considered him a focus for popular legends rather than a real historical character. But archaeologists discovered in 1896 a stone pillar erected in the year 250 B.C. by King Asoka at the birthplace of Buddha, bearing this inscription,

When Devanampriya Priyadarsin [whom we know as Asoka] had been anointed twenty years, he came himself and worshiped [this spot], because the Buddha Sakyamuni was born here. He both caused to be made a stone bearing a horse [?]; and caused a stone pillar to be set up [in order to show] that the Blessed One was born here. [He] made the village of Lummini free of taxes, and paying [only] an eighth part [of the produce].[3]

Other corroborative discoveries since made harmonize with the accounts of two Chinese pilgrims who visited these very places many centuries ago—Fa Hien between 399 and 414 A.D., and Hiuen Tsiang between 629 and 645 A.D. The latter's account even mentions the horse on the pillar at Lummini (or Lumbini). So we have actual historical evidence of the highest value, with an inscription made by a disciple within 230 years after the death of Buddha, which is too short a time for a myth to have been made out of whole cloth. The burden of proof is therefore most decidedly on those who deny Buddha's historical existence.

Granted his historicity, however, what sort of man was he? Surely we cannot believe these preposterous legends. They are of value chiefly in informing us that he seemed to his disciples a marvelous person. Some remarkable traits, at least, must have existed in a personality whose followers today, twenty-four centuries after his death, number, according to one authority, five hundred millions, nearly a fourth of the human race!

The Real Buddha

Scholars have sifted the ancient scriptures, comparing versions, weighed the conflicting items of evidence, and evaluated the truth content of the legends, until the probable man has appeared, a winsome figure of pathetic appeal in his simplicity, and yet a man of mighty intellect and indomitable will. His personality had just those contradictions which we find in every world figure and leader of men. At one time you would call Buddha a dreamy mystic; at another, a hard, relentless mechanist. He appears almost feminine in some of his characteristics, such as an uncanny intuitive perception, yet his system of philosophy is relentlessly logical. His human sufferings are often unpleasantly prominent, only to be followed by periods of godlike calm when he showed great intellectual insight and farsight.

The unusual life story of this man has been revealed by careful

[3] This is Dr. Hultzsch's translation, quoted by Thomas, p. 18. For a different version of this remarkable inscription, which is still well preserved in spite of its great age, see *Encyclopedia of Religion and Ethics*, Vol. II, p. 881.

research, especially of late by those patient workers who have compared the recently translated Buddhist scriptures in the Pali language (the Indian dialect which Buddha himself used) with the
longer-known Sanskrit sources.

Born an Indian prince he doubtless was, of the Sakya tribe and
the Gautama clan, which flourished some miles to the north of the
present Benares; hence he is called sometimes Sakyamuni, the wise
man of the Sakyas, and more frequently Gautama (Sanskrit) or
Gotama (Pali). After his "enlightenment" he was called Gautama
the Buddha, i.e., "the enlightened." Before that, he was called the
Bodhisattva, which means "one destined for enlightenment." His
own personal name was supposed to be Siddhartha, which means
"He whose aim is accomplished," but that seems more likely to have
been given him later by his disciples. He has been called Gautama
Buddha, or simply Buddha, for so long in English-speaking countries that we shall use that form.

A "Delicate" Youth

Save that he was brought up in luxury, we know few details of his
boyhood. In the canonical scriptures Buddha is reported to have
said, "I was delicate, O monks, extremely delicate, excessively delicate. In my father's dwelling lotus-pools had been made, in one blue
lotuses, in another red, in another white, all for my sake. I used no
sandal-wood that was not of Benares, my dress was of Benares cloth,
my tunic, my under-robe, and cloak. Night and day a white parasol
was held over me so that I should not be touched by cold or heat,
by dust or weeds or dew. I had three palaces, one for the cold season,
one for the hot, and one for the season of rains. Through the four
rainy months, in the palace for the rainy season, entertained by
female minstrels I did not come down from the palace."[4]

Contrasted with this effeminate existence are the stories that in
his youth he shot an arrow ten miles and threw an elephant over
the city moat! When he was sixteen, his father built these three
palaces and then looked around for a wife for his son. But neighboring kings were loth to let their daughters marry such a pampered
youth, lest he could not support a wife. So the young man took a
mighty bow requiring the strength of a thousand men and strung
it with his great toe. Thereupon the girls arrived by thousands.

4 Quoted by Thomas, p. 47.

Whether he was married at sixteen, or nineteen, or twenty-nine, we do not know certainly, as accounts vary widely, but the most generally accepted version states that he was married at nineteen to a princess named Yasodhara and lived with her in these three palaces for ten years before their son Rahula was born.

It was an idyllic life. The world was new, the fertile plains of India were rich, and the princes of India, of the old Aryan stock, were evidently men of parts. They built themselves palaces, sang sagas, made love, played games, and jousted in tournaments, much as did the princelings and knights of King Arthur's day many centuries later in Merrie England. And just as Galahad went forth to seek the Holy Grail, so did the twenty-nine-year-old Prince Siddhartha, the Buddha-to-be, set out on his horse Kanthaka, accompanied by his squire Chandaka, to find the deeper meaning of life.

The Great Renunciation

In all religious history we find no more appealing renunciation than that of the young prince. We are told that his father had kept from him all knowledge of sorrow and trouble, that he had lived in palaces without knowing that outside the walls were poverty, misery, and death. Even when the young man determined to take a ride outside, his father sent those ahead who should remove from the wayside all save the happy and contented. But the plans miscarried, and the prince saw four sights new to him, an old man, a very sick man, a corpse, and a religious ascetic. These sights moved him deeply. He wondered why suffering existed. All that his father and his wife could do did not distract his mind from thinking on these things.

The four sights may have been the immediate cause of his determining to leave home, but there were other motives of which even the prince himself may have been unaware. All young men have at times a desire to leave home and see the world. They usually leave their parents at marriage, if not before, but ten years after marriage Buddha was still under his father's jurisdiction, a loving superintendency, but still a restriction on a spirited fellow.

Again, he was nearly thirty. Frequently it happens that something comes over a man then, a sudden spurt of mind growth, just as the body develops rapidly in adolescence. Especially, if anything of the prophet is in the man's nature, at thirty is the time he wishes to save

the world. That was the age of Zoroaster when he set forth just a
century before in Persia. That was the age of Mahavira, the founder
of the Jain religion in India, when he renounced the world less than
forty years before Buddha, and Jesus was thirty when he began his
ministry.

The part that seems hard to understand is that Buddha should
have left home just the very week that his wife, after ten years of
happy married life, presented him with their first child, his little
son Rahula. Two things need to be said in this connection, however, neither of them to the great credit of Buddha.

First, every social worker knows that just before or just after a
man's child is born is a time when he is very apt to desert his wife.
You can verify this inglorious fact by reference to the records of
desertion cases in any charity organization. And it is not among the
poor alone that this happens. Among some savage tribes, it is the
custom to keep the husband in bed during his wife's childbirth
period. Anthropologists say it is an instance of sympathetic magic,
but there may be a canny notion in savage heads that it is just as
well to keep track of the husband at such times.

Second, when Buddha "opened the door of the chamber" and saw
by the light of the "lamp of scented oil" his wife and infant son
sleeping "on the bed strewn with heaps of jessamine and other
flowers," he knew that this little life would soon be so entwined
with his that it would be another bond to keep him at home. One
scripture, with forced etymology, interprets Rahula as meaning
"bond." Silently through the palace Buddha fled past the rows of
female musicians, asleep in attitudes which disgusted his super-
esthetic soul, out into the June full moonlight, and mounted his
horse and away. We will leave to the wiser moralists of tomorrow
the decision as to which is the greater and abler prophet, he who
abandons his family for the religious life or he who never marries at
all.

Prince Becomes Pauper

The young man traveled until dawn and then dismounted, cut
off his hair with his sword, removed his royal garments and sent
them and the horse back with Chandaka. Assuming the yellow robe,
which later was to be the badge of the Buddhists, he became a

traveling monk with begging bowl, razor, needle, girdle, and water strainer.

To the east he set his face. After traveling through three kingdoms, he found two teachers, but they failed to help him in his search for truth. For six years he fasted frequently and inflicted self-tortures. Five disciples accompanied him and he was looked upon as very holy because of his austerities. Buddha's description of his painful strivings to discover through asceticism the secrets of life has been preserved to us in both the Pali and Sanskrit versions, and is therefore very old and probably authentic. It is most interesting to the student of the psychology of religion. He said,

Then I thought, what if I now set my teeth, press my tongue to my palate, and restrain, crush, and burn out my mind with my mind. [I did so] and sweat flowed from my armpits. Just as if a strong man were to seize a weaker man by the head or shoulders—so did I set my teeth. I undertook resolute effort, unconfused mindfulness was set up, but my body was unquiet and uncalmed, even through the painful striving that overwhelmed me. Nevertheless such painful feeling as arose did not overpower my mind.

Then I thought, what if I now practice trance without breathing. So I restrained breathing in and out from mouth and nose. And as I did so, there was a violent sound of winds issuing from my ears. Just as there is a violent sound from the blowing of a blacksmith's bellows, even so as I did so there was a violent sound.

Thereupon he wondered what would happen if he abstained from all food, and decided not to try such a decisive experiment. Better cut it down gradually.

Then I thought, what if I were to take food only in small amounts, as much as my hollowed palm would hold, juice of beans, vetches, chickpeas, or pulse. My body became extremely lean. The mark of my seat was like a camel's footprint through the little food. The bones of my spine when bent and straightened were like a row of spindles through the little food. As the beams of an old shed stick out, so did my ribs stick out through the little food. And as in a deep well the deep low-lying sparkling of the waters is seen, so in my eye-sockets was seen the deep low-lying sparkling of my eyes through the little food. When I thought I would touch the skin of my stomach, I actually took hold of my spine. When I thought I would ease myself, I thereupon fell prone through the little food. To relieve my body I stroked my limbs with my hand, and as I did so the decayed hairs fell from my body through the little food.[5]

He found that "by this severe mortification" he did not "attain superhuman truly noble knowledge and insight." "Perhaps," he said, "there is another way to enlightenment." He decided wisely that he would be more likely to find the truth if he kept a sound mind in a sound body, avoiding both sensual indulgence and super-asceticism, and choosing what he called the Middle Way of temperance. He afterward referred to his years of self-torture as "time spent in endeavoring to tie the air in knots."

When he began to give his body proper nourishment—rice and sour milk—he was deserted by his five horrified disciples. One version has their horror caused not so much by his eating a full meal as by his doing so in the presence of a woman! Still another account increases the sin and excitement of the situation by revealing that Nanda, the herdsman's daughter who had found him dying of starvation, saved his life by slowly feeding him milk from her own breasts.

Either the desertion by his disciples, or the strength derived from the food, or both, seemed to arouse in Buddha a fresh determination to discover the explanation of the sorrows of life. He sat down under a Bo-tree (a species of fig) and determined to sit right there until he knew the truth. He said, "Skin, sinew and bone may dry up as it will, my flesh and my blood may dry in my body, but without attaining complete enlightenment I will not leave this seat." Evidently he had not wholly surrendered his asceticism.

The Indian devil, Mara, "came also" and tempted him, but failed, although assisted by his armies and even by his daughters. Finally the devil departed, saying, "For seven years have I followed the Lord step by step. I can find no entrance to the All-enlightened, the watchful one. As a crow went after a stone that looked like a lump of fat, thinking, surely here I shall find a tender morsel, here perchance is something sweet, and finding no sweetness there, the crow departed thence; so like a crow attacking a rock, in disgust I leave Gotama."[6] For four weeks (some say seven) Buddha remained

5 Quoted by Thomas, pp. 64–66.
6 Quoted by Thomas, p. 73.

under the tree. Others say that he stayed a week under each of four trees, and then, one night, the enlightenment came.

The Enlightenment

This great revelation was exceedingly simple—namely, that all pain is caused by desire and therefore peace comes when one ceases to crave anything. This thought was new to him and to the world, and it struck him with blinding force and exalted him for the rest of his life. He said afterward, "In me emancipated arose the knowledge of my emancipation. Ignorance was dispelled, knowledge arose. Darkness was dispelled, light arose." Emancipation or enlightenment came to him, he says, "in the last watch of the night." As the dawn brightened, his soul was illumined by the effulgence of his newly discovered truth.

Two passing merchants fed him with rice and honey cakes and became the first lay disciples. Buddha started out immediately to preach his new-found truth. He went first to Benares to find the five monks, his former companions, and won them again.

Buddha's famous first sermon, the Sutta of Turning the Wheel of the Doctrine, may have really been his first, or may be a concentrated compilation of several sermons, like Jesus' Sermon on the Mount. At any rate, it contains the central truths of Buddhism and is a clear and simple exposition of his discoveries under the Bo-tree. He summed it up under Four Noble Truths. Abbreviated, they are:

1. All living is painful.
2. Suffering is due to craving or desire.
3. Release from suffering comes when desire ceases.
4. The way to cessation of suffering is by the Eight-fold Path of "right views, right intention, right speech, right action, right livelihood, right effort, right mindfulness, right concentration."

And for nearly twenty-five centuries, millions have found this an acceptable path to peace.

Salvation by Psychology

It is essentially salvation by psychology, and Buddha was the first "practical psychologist." It is to be noted that there is no mention of prayer or ceremony or God or the devil or any supernatural

beings. It is a philosophical psychology or a psychological philosophy. Buddha was the first man on this planet to assert that man's
salvation and peace come not from outside gods but from the control of his own mind.

He was now thirty-five or thirty-six years of age, and went forth
preaching this message until his death at the age of eighty. The five
monks became ardent disciples and the band soon increased to
sixty. He sent them out with this great commission, "Go ye now,
out of compassion for the world, for the welfare of gods and men.
Let not two of you go the same way. Preach the doctrine which is
glorious. Proclaim a consummate, perfect and pure life of holiness."[7]

Buddha showed a certain astuteness in directing the propagation
of the faith. He kept retreat, like Zoroaster, during the rainy season,
when he probably meditated, wrote, and planned the summer
preaching tours. When difficulties arose and explanations were
necessary, he found great assistance in the doctrine of transmigra-
tion, the rebirth theory.

The Doctrine of Transmigration

According to this doctrine, which did not originate with him but
which he developed considerably, men have lived before and will
live again in an almost infinite series of rebirths. If a man walks in
the Eight-fold Path he will gradually improve until in some final
life he will attain the extinction of all desire, which will be the
blessed peace of Nirvana. When evil comes to good men, it is because of sin in some previous life. When bad men are not punished
in this life they will be punished in a later incarnation. This explanation of the existence of evil is far more satisfactory to the
average man, if he can believe it, than the theories of evil held in
other religions. Buddha fell back on it frequently, as for example,
when two recent converts were given preference above other early
disciples, he solved the seeming favoritism by saying that in their
previous lives these two had made a wish to become in later lives
the leading disciples of a Buddha. His wanderings eventually took
him back home, and it is recorded that his wife and son became
converts.

[7] Sacred Books of the East, 13:112.

Buddha's Death

Finally, the end came in a small "wattel-and-daub town, in a branch village" with 500 disciples around him. The old man suffered intensely from overeating pork. In the third watch of the night his sufferings ended, his last words being, "Now then, monks, I address you; subject to decay are compound things: strive with earnestness." The body was cremated and the bones preserved for sacred relics. Around each little bit a holy place of worship grew up later. The Buddha's poor bones were venerated, then worshiped, and temples were raised to one who had warned against worship. The atheist became a god!

The Appeal of Buddha to the East

To the people of the East the new religion made a great appeal. Buddha resolutely attacked and exposed the falsities of the religion of his day, which was largely ritualistic, and not far removed from animism, or spirit worship. He seems to have been a great preacher and an effective missionary. He had the good habit of illustrating his sermons with stories and parables, some of which have come down to us.

To a woman who came to him asking for medicine for her dead child, which she carried on her hip, he said, "You have done well to come here for medicine. Go into the city and get a mustard seed from a house where no one has died." She had not visited many homes before she saw the point. Going to a cemetery, she laid the body down and, taking the little hand in hers, said, "Little son, I thought that death had happened to you alone; but it is not to you alone, it is common to all people." Then she went back to Buddha and became his disciple.

Much of Buddha's attractiveness was due to his democratic appreciation of the common people. Himself of noble birth and wealthy parentage, he nevertheless adopted the life of the poor as his own and denounced the rich who oppressed them. Naturally the lowly flocked to him as they did later to Jesus. Yet he rebuked the poor who were living wrongly, and he placed character above wealth, position, or even ritualistic religion. That was rather advanced doctrine for his time. He also strengthened the appeal of his religion by spiritualizing many current practices and giving moral meaning to already accepted customs.

The Spread of Buddhism

During his long service of over forty years he reached many hearers with his spoken words and trained a group of preaching monks who spread the new gospel far. The Constantine of the new religion was King Asoka, who lived two centuries after Buddha's death. He is reported to have founded 80,000 monasteries and to have driven out many heretics. His son carried Buddhism to Ceylon, where it soon flourished. It also spread rapidly in Burma, Siam, and even Tibet. Later it attained its largest growth in China and Japan. It is at present found almost exclusively in Mongolian countries, having died out in India.

On Wesak Day, Buddha's birthday, at the full moon of April-May, Japanese children in California sing,

In fair Lumbini's Garden
The royal babe was born,
The Bringer of Salvation
Unto a world forlorn.

There are two main groups of Buddhists, called the "Lesser Vehicle" and the "Greater Vehicle." It is the tragedy of Buddhism that the greater group in numbers as well as name consists of those who have so far departed from the teachings of the gentle monk as to worship him as a god. Gautama the good has become an image, a "Bloomin' idol made o' mud, Wot they called the Great gawd Budd." Theologically he has developed into a divine saviour and even a member of a Buddhist trinity! This larger section of Buddhism is the northern one, in China and Japan. The south Asian section, the Lesser Vehicle, regards Buddha as a teacher of a way of living, and avoids theological discussions.

The Buddhist Bible

The Bible of Buddhism has three "Testaments," called baskets or "pitaka," hence the whole is known as the "Tripitaka." The first is called the Sermon Basket, the second the Discipline Basket, containing rules for the higher order of Buddhists, and the third is a dreary maze of metaphysics known as the Doctrinal Basket. One writer says that the pages of this third basket are very dry but "like the Desert of Sahara they are to be respected for their very immensity." Not all of the Buddhist Bible has been published in English or even in Pali, but when it is published it will be the largest book of scripture in the world, containing about ten thousand pages. All parts are not held to be of equal value, however; only the reported words of the Lord Buddha are considered to be divinely revealed.

The Appeal of Buddha to the West

The teachings of Buddha have lately excited more interest in Europe and America as they have become better known. This is partly because of their resemblance to Christianity. Both Buddhism and orthodox Christianity look somewhat pessimistically upon the present world as an unsatisfactory place. Both Buddha and Jesus were partly reformers of existing religions and partly originators of new teachings. Both were outdoor preachers—the scene of Jesus' great Sermon is given as "on the Mount" and that of Buddha's Sermon of the Wheel of the Law as in a deer park. Buddha's "beloved disciple" Ananda has been compared rightly to John, and Devadatta to Judas; while the aged Asita rejoiced over the infant Buddha as did old Simeon over the Christ-child.

Many other comparisons might be made,[8] such as the fondness of both for parables, but it must be said that their outlooks on life were decidedly different. Jesus believed in God and prayer and Buddha did not. Jesus taught that individual life was full of meaning, and Buddha that each person should seek to lose his seeming individuality. And Jesus' heaven of many mansions contrasts vividly with Buddha's Nirvana, or extinction of individuality. But the appeal of Buddhism to the occidental mind is not confined to its relation to Christianity. There is a peculiar resemblance of Buddha's philosophy of life to that of some modern scientists. Not only do his recurring cycles of life remind one of evolution, but his emphasis on *dharma*, which can hardly be translated into English save roughly by "natural and social law," is very similar to the recognition of universal inevitable law in nature and human life which

[8] E. J. Thomas in Chapter XVII of *The Life of Buddha* gives sixteen parallels alleged by other scholars.

characterizes much philosophy today. Many scientists would agree with Buddha that man is but a drop in the river of life.

It may be that Buddhism will have a new lease of life by transplantation to America in some modified form. This is not so impossible as it might seem at first, for several of the newer American cults, with their emphasis on the control of the body by the mind and the importance of meditation and of getting in tune with cosmic law, show strange affinity with Buddhism.

The Faults of Buddha's Teaching

There is much, however, in Buddha's teaching which is not in line with Western thought. For one thing, Buddhism is blighting to that individual initiative upon which progress depends. It is negative and pessimistic. It places a low value on human life and despises the human body. We do not agree with Buddha's bitter characterization of it as, "This nine-holed frame, This body foul, this charnel-house."

Buddha's estimate of family life, especially his low valuation of woman, is far beneath ours. When his old aunt and nurse, Mahapajapati, applied for discipleship, he refused three times and then reluctantly admitted her to a low position in his order, saying, "Now the religious system will not last long—for just as houses, when there are many women and few men, are easily broken into by robbers, even so in the doctrine and discipline in which a woman goes forth, the religious system will not last long."

On his deathbed Buddha was asked by Ananda, "How are we to act, Lord, with regard to women?"

"Not seeing them, Ananda."

But Ananda knew that that was impossible and continued, "If we see them, how are we to act?"

"Not speaking, Ananda."

But his beloved disciple persisted, "What must be done by one who speaks?"

"Mindfulness must be exercised, Ananda."

Social progress has not been fostered by Buddhism, and history bears eloquent witness to that fact. But we must recognize that many of the faults of Buddha's outlook were due to his time and environment and that his contribution to human thinking has been almost incalculable. He taught men to seek peace by controlling their minds and he gave cosmic sweep to man's consciousness of his relation to the universe.

Note on Mahavira (599–527 B.C.)
The Founder of Jainism

In India, forty years before Buddha, there branched off from Hinduism a sect known as Jainism (pronounced Jine-ism). The founder, Mahavira, was, like Buddha, brought up in luxury, but became an ascetic at the age of thirty. He wandered about naked, meditating and seeming to court suffering. He neither prayed nor worshiped and told his disciples, "Man, thou art thine own friend!"[9]

His religion was a sort of humanism which included pacifism, nudism, and vegetarianism. He was especially against killing any form of life, and his present-day followers (who pray to him and worship him) go so far as to frown on the sex act, holding that in sexual intercourse nearly a million minute beings of human shape, but mindless, are generated and destroyed.

But Jainism does teach self-reliance, and urges the conquest of anger, greed, pride, and deceit, the four deadly sins. One of the central teachings from the Jain Bible is, "Difficult to conquer is oneself. But when that is conquered, everything is conquered."

[9] Sacred Books of the East, 22:33.

VI

ornament

CONFUCIUS

[551–478 B.C.]

THE APOSTLE OF MORALITY

(Including Lao-tse of the Divine Way)

IT IS A STRIKING THING that every history of the religions of the world includes Confucianism, but protests at the same time that it is not a religion but merely a system of morality or ethics. Even those who admit that modern Confucianism is a religion insist that the original teachings of Confucius were not at all religious.

But Confucianism is now and always has been a religion. Confucius was religious himself. He assembled the religious literature of the Chinese. His disciples were religious, and have grown more and more religious through the centuries.

Whatever Confucianism may be called—philosophy, ethical system, or religion—it has certainly fulfilled the functions which religion has ordinarily been expected to exercise. The reason why some people do not see how Confucianism can be called a religion is because they have too narrow a definition of religion. They have confused religion with *their* religion or with the general type of religion of which theirs is an example. It is true that Confucius ignored many things commonly thought essential to religion. It was not that he was opposed to these practices, but that he did not consider them essential. He did not encourage prayer, nor assemblies for worship. He did not believe in an anthropomorphic God, nor in immortality.

The First "Humanist"

The type of religion which Confucius taught and practiced is akin to a new type of religion now rapidly spreading in liberal Christian circles, which has sometimes been called Humanism. In fact, Confucius was the first Humanist. He advised men not to depend upon supernatural beings for their progress but to practice self-culture. He was constantly urging men to extend their knowledge of the world and of themselves. From this cultivation of individual excellence would derive, he was confident, better families, better states, and a better world.

Anyone who says that Confucianism is not religion and that Confucius was not religious is going directly contrary to certain plain statements in the Christian New Testament. For instance, in the Book of James it is stated, "If any man among you seem to be religious and bridleth not his tongue, but deceiveth his own heart, this man's religion is vain. Pure religion and undefiled before God and the Father is this, To visit the fatherless and widows in their affliction, and to keep himself unspotted from the world."

These injunctions are quite Confucian. The great sage of China particularly emphasized the bridling of one's tongue, the importance of family ties, and the need of a pure and upright life. And when Paul said, "Let every soul be subject unto the higher powers. For there is no power but of God: the powers that be are ordained of God," he might have been quoting from Confucius. And if one turns to the Old Testament he will find Confucian doctrine in the Ten Commandments, especially, "Honor thy father and thy mother that thy days may be long in the land which the Lord thy God giveth thee."

Perhaps there is an unconscious trend toward the religion of Confucius in America today because the four things which he did not consider important, prayer, worship, belief in a personal God and immortality, are being increasingly questioned and revised by the left wing of Christianity today. Many a man who considers himself a Christian is proclaiming that the Golden Rule is all the religion he needs. Which was what Confucius taught twenty-four centuries ago. Six times in the Confucian scriptures occur the words "What you do not want done to yourself, do not do to others."

The Father of Confucius

In the year 552 B.C., in the province of Shantung, China, an old soldier over seventy years of age began to worry about his funeral. It would be necessary, in order for the proper celebration of the religious rites and the later maintenance of family worship, that he should have a son. His wife had borne him nine daughters. There were two sons by a concubine, but they did not count. So he determined to get another wife. Probably he divorced the one he had. There were ample grounds in the fact that she had borne him no son.

This old gentleman belonged to the ancient and honorable family of Kung and wished to marry into a family of equal rank. He approached a man of the House of Yen who had three daughters and proposed to marry any one of them. The father called the three girls into the conference and pointed out the merits and defects of the old man and asked which one of them wished to be his wife. The two elder ones maintained a discreet silence, but the youngest, Ching-tsai, stepped forward, bowed deeply, and said, "Father, why do you ask us? That is for you to determine." The father replied, "Very well, you will do."

And a year later the eighteen-year-old girl brought great peace to her elderly husband when she presented him with an infant son. The descendants of that son, in the seventy-sixth and seventy-seventh generations, are now living in the very same locality in the province of Shantung. They are honored and greatly respected because of their relationship to the great Confucius.

The Boy's Name

The boy was not named Confucius; indeed, he never heard that name throughout his life. "Confucius" is the Latin transliteration of his name which was made by the Jesuit priests of the sixteenth century who had been living in China and who recommended to the Pope of Rome that Confucius be placed on the list of saints of the Roman Catholic Church. "Confucius" was as near as the Jesuits could get to Kung-fu-tse.

Kung-fu-tse meant "Kung the Master" or "Kung the Teacher," but that name, of course, was not given him at birth. He was first called "Kin" or "Little Hill." Whether this was because of some small eminence in the vicinity in which he was born, or because of the peculiar shape of his head, we do not know. He was given another name at the same time, "Chung-Ni," which means "Second Mount Ni." The "First Mount Ni" was his step-brother, the son of his father's concubine. So the boy's name was really Chung-Ni.

He early showed considerable ability, a fact which is reflected in the inevitable infancy narratives which later disciples told. There are interesting parallels to the legends concerning Jesus' birth. Just as the angel appeared to Mary and announced that she should bring forth a son of whose kingdom there should be no end, a spirit appeared to Ching-tsai and said, "You shall have a son wise beyond other men."

A peculiar animal also appeared, the sacred kilin, somewhat like a unicorn, somewhat like a deer, and somewhat like a dragon, which placed before Ching-tsai a precious stone inscribed with the words "The son shall be a throneless king." And tradition also maintains that the child's birth (in the autumn of 551 B.C.) took place according to prophecy in a cave called "The Hollow Mulberry Tree." One of the several versions of the birth of Jesus states that the stable in which he was born was really a cave.

China at Confucius' Birth

Conditions in China at the time of the birth of Confucius were chaotic. The great dynasty of Chou was degenerating. The nobles were the real rulers and the actual form of government was feudal. The barons were fighting each other, and the people were suffering from continual war and from the exactions of the tax collectors. These conditions obtained generally throughout the lifetime of Confucius, and one of the incidents told of him illustrates the sufferings of the people. He was traveling at one time with his disciples slowly along a country road near Mount Tai when he heard at a little distance from the road the crying of a woman. When Confucius asked why she was lamenting in this desert place, she answered, "The father of my husband was slain here by a tiger, so was my husband, and just now my son has also been killed in the same way."

"Why, then," asked Confucius, "do you dwell in so terrible a place?"

"Because," she answered, "here there is no oppressive ruler."

Turning to his disciples, Confucius said, "Take note, students, oppressive rule is worse than a tiger."

Boyhood and Education

We know as little of the boyhood of Confucius as we do of that of Jesus. There are legends which testify to the boy's eagerness for knowledge. We are told that when he was fourteen he was assisting in the teaching of the other boys because he had already learned all that the teacher could give. That legend is evidently based on fact, for we have Confucius' own statement that "at fifteen I had my mind bent on learning."[1]

We are not to infer, however, that the youth was a pale, anemic scholar. We know that in later life he was a skillful hunter, an expert charioteer, and an accomplished musician. He had to labor after school hours to contribute his part in the support of the family,[2] for his father had died; some say before the boy's birth, and some say three years afterward. His hunting and fishing helped to vary the scanty menu of the little home, and he evidently turned his hand to anything which might help out the family income.

A Government Official

At the age of seventeen he was given a government position in the state of Lu, where he lived. It was not a particularly important position, but it was honorable. He was responsible for the storage of grain and supervised a certain section of the public lands. His scrupulous devotion to duty soon won him a place in the community. He seems to have exercised more intelligence than ordinarily was found among the state supervisors. In his adjudication of the claims made by rival herdsmen he made his first public pronouncement of his philosophy of life. He gathered the disputants together and lectured them on the absurdity of quarreling.

1 *Analects*, 2:4. 1.
2 *Analects*, 9:6. 3.

The Golden Rule

The future sage of China then revealed his famous penchant for making simple rules for conduct. The rough herdsmen could not understand the subtle philosophies and ethical niceties of the ancient classics of China which Confucius had been studying. It was necessary for him to simplify. Under the urgent need of the moment he invented a simple sentence-statement, a sort of rule of thumb for the shepherds. The task he faced was much like that which confronted Moses seven centuries before, but the solution which Confucius adopted was the one given by Jesus nearly six centuries afterward. Instead of ten commandments, Confucius gave the herdsmen one inclusive principle. He said to them, "Do not do to others what you would not want them to do to you."

It may have been poor pedagogy to put the statement in the negative form, but it is to the eternal credit of the youth of seventeen or eighteen that he was able to go directly to the heart of the problem and find the central principle of proper social conduct. He was later to call attention to this principle of action many times in his more mature teaching. When we think of the boy, still in his teens, announcing the principle which was the center of his later philosophy we are reminded of the youth of twelve who, in the temple of Jerusalem, revealed that he was already conscious of his life mission.

Confucius' scrupulous attention to duty not only won him a place in the community but increased his income sufficiently so that he was able to marry at the age of nineteen.

The Children of Confucius

We know nothing about his wife. The only reference to her in the Confucian scriptures occurs many years later when Confucius rebuked his son for mourning her death. This son was born in 531 B.C., a year after the marriage. We have an evidence of the esteem in which Confucius was already held, in the story that the duke who ruled the little principality of Lu sent to the proud young father, with his congratulations, two sacred carp for the birth banquet. Confucius, who was never to be outdone in ceremonial courtesy, responded to the duke's gift by naming his son "Li," which is the Chinese word for carp.

Now, at the very time that Confucius was rejoicing in the birth of his son, Buddha was naming his newborn son "Rahula." Tradition also has it that two daughters were born to Confucius before something came up to disturb his marital happiness. Chinese history is very vague on the subject. It appears that the separation occurred about four years after the marriage. No one knows the cause of it. It may have been due, however, to Confucius' long mourning of his mother.

He Mourns His Mother Many Months

It was then the custom in China that a young man should retire from active life for a long time at the death of a parent. Confucius, always punctilious in the observing of traditional ceremonies, actually meditated for twenty-seven months at his mother's grave. We know that he was twenty-four years of age at the time that he lost his mother. Her death evidently made a great impression upon him. Ching-tsai had been both father and mother to him because his father had died when he was an infant. She seemed a very part of himself, and when she went it disturbed his whole inner life.

Perhaps he had somewhat neglected his mother in his interest in his marriage and the coming of the children, and, at the death of his mother, felt conscience-stricken. The revulsion of feeling may have led him to act in such a manner that his wife felt hurt. During the more than two years that he spent in meditation by his mother's grave, the estrangement evidently became complete. From that time on, so far as we know, he had no relations with her or with any other woman. Our sources are so meager that we do not know whether he made financial provision for her and his children.

The Teacher

Upon the completion of the prescribed months of mourning Confucius returned to his work. Shortly after his marriage he had begun to teach. Evidently he was an itinerant pedagogue followed by a growing number of disciples. Why Confucius abandoned his government position and embarked upon such a precarious profession as that of a traveling teacher we have no information. A logical assumption would be that in his settling of the disputes between the herdsmen he developed an audience-consciousness and acquired a taste for that which later proved to be his lifework—namely, the reduction of the philosophic wisdom of the ancients to simple, easily understood precepts and proverbs.

Confucius was essentially a popularizer. Every eminent religious leader has filled that role to a greater or lesser degree, but if we measure by the number of people who have been affected by the popularized sayings of the leader we must by all means give the palm to Confucius. His maxims have for many centuries been the daily guide of millions of Chinese. Buddhism and Taoism have claimed the allegiance of many, but whatever a man's religion in China, he is still, it has been said, an "ex-officio Confucianist."

Confucius was twenty-one or twenty-two when he began to teach. It may have been this rather than his mother's death which was the cause of his separation from his wife. She may have objected to his continued absence which would throw the burden of the family entirely upon her, or her objections may have been to the reduced income which would make life harder. On the other hand, it may well have been that he realized that a family was a burden to a traveling teacher. At any rate, the beginning of his preaching mission, his separation from his wife, and the mourning of his mother's death, all occurred within a comparatively brief period of time and evidently marked a crisis in his life.

There are no records of any theophany—that is, any special vision —which came to Confucius, which he interpreted as a call to preach. But there must have been something of the sort to lead him to make such momentous changes in his method of living as to abandon a government position and divorce his wife. The period of mourning for his mother corresponds to the usual period of retirement which is noticeable in the career of every great religious leader and which immediately follows the decision to devote oneself to a public career. After his mourning for his mother had ended, he resumed his itinerant teaching. The meditations of the mourning period had enriched the content of his teaching, and the number of his pupils grew until he had three thousand.

Confucius' method of teaching resembles somewhat that employed by Aristotle in Greece two centuries later. He walked about from "place to place accompanied by those who were absorbing his views of life." Whenever the journey took them any distance he rode in an ox cart. The slow pace of the animal enabled his pupils to follow on foot, and it is evident that the subject of his lectures was frequently suggested by events occurring on the road. Modern pedagogues, who urge that children be taken out of the school room and brought into contact with the actual conditions of life, are really returning to the method of Confucius.

The curriculum of the "traveling university" included music, poetry, history, literature, civics, and ethics. What little science was known at the time was also taught. We are given a little more insight into the mind of Confucius when we note that the four subjects of conversation which he particularly avoided were feats of strength, marvels, revolutions, and the supernatural. He seems to have had no particular objection to the performance of religious ceremonies, and in fact was quite scrupulous in following the religious customs of the time, but he did object to any prolonged discussion of supernatural beings.

Another indication of Confucius' instinctive recognition of the principles of good pedagogy lies in the fact that he seems to have maintained close personal relations with all his pupils. Although he had in his school many sons of the well-to-do, he was never known to turn away a poor boy who really wished to learn. What he insisted upon was a studious and virtuous spirit. Of the subjects which he taught he was inclined to favor civics. His life concern was the science of government. Any pupil, therefore, who showed signs of administrative ability or oratorical talent was apt to receive special recognition from the master.

The personal example of Confucius was, of course, a great factor in the education of his pupils. When they asked him why he wore linen instead of silk he confessed to a sentimental repugnance toward killing even the silkworm. When they asked him why he did not drink milk he explained that the custom of taking a calf away from its mother, so that man might enjoy the milk, was unfair. He took pride in the fact that he never used a net to catch fish and never discharged an arrow at a bird unless it was in flight. He wished them to have a fair chance to escape. That which seemed a novel compunction to his contemporaries has now become a part of the ethics of good sportsmanship.

Although Confucius was very successful as a teacher he was not convinced that it was his lifework. His interest in the theory and philosophy of government was so great that he was constantly looking for an opportunity to secure a high governmental position in order to try out some of his own ideas. When we think of him as an office-seeker he is apt to fall in our estimation, but it should be remembered that the reason for his seeking office was not to obtain personal power or financial remuneration. What he was interested in was to secure better living conditions for the average man through the correct administration of the affairs of the state. One of his teaching trips was made to a neighboring state in order to visit an old man who had a great reputation for wisdom.

Confucius and Lao-tse

One reason why Confucius wished to visit this old man, Lao-tse (pronounced *Lowdzuh*), was doubtless because he had heard that Lao-tse was also not much interested in gods or in supernatural religion. Only one book of Lao-tse's has come down to us, *The Tao-Teh-King*. This title is difficult of translation but has been rendered *The Book of the Path of Virtue* and *The Canon of Reason and Virtue*. Consistent with its title, the book is a purely ethical treatise and contains neither supernatural religion nor superstition.

Confucius did find himself somewhat in harmony with some of the older man's principles, but, although he did not realize it at the time, his philosophy and that of Lao-tse were fundamentally opposed in certain important particulars. "Lao-tse" means "Lao the Teacher," just as "Kung-fu-tse" means "Kung the Teacher." At the time of the visit, Confucius was thirty-four and Lao-tse eighty-four. It is worth noting, in order to point out what a remarkable period this was in the development of religion in the world, that Lao-tse was a contemporary of Zoroaster, Buddha, Mahavira, Jeremiah, Ezekiel, and the Unknown Prophet of the Exile. Anyone inclined to believe in the occult influence of the stars upon the life of this planet would look for some particular combination in the heavens to account for this most singular period of religious activity on earth.

Whether Lao-tse and Confucius actually had a debate at the time of their meeting is not known. It appears from the most reliable records that the old man gave the young man some good advice and that Confucius went away from the presence of the great sage with a very humble impression of his own ability and a profound admiration and envy for Lao-tse, who seemed to dwell on a higher plane philosophically than he did himself. But whether or not there was an actual debate in the year 517 B.C. between the founders of two of the great religions of China, there was a conflict between their teachings.

Lao-tse's message is read with surprise by modern Christians who have been accustomed to think that Jesus' famous injunction to return good for evil is original with Christianity. In the writings of Lao-tse we find the following statements: "To those who are good to me, I am good. And to those who are not good to me, I am also good. And thus all together come to be good.[3] Recompense injury with kindness."[4]

But Confucius did not agree with that principle. He believed in reciprocity and said, "Recompense injury with justice, and recompense kindness with kindness."[5]

It will be noticed then that we must class Lao-tse and Jesus together, and that Confucius preached a doctrine resembling the "eye for eye and tooth for tooth" dictum of Moses. Let it be clearly understood, however, that Confucius' idea of recompense had in it nothing of retaliation. It lacked the stern quality which seems to characterize the Mosaic code. Confucius believed in returning kindness for kindness, and his reason for recompensing injury with justice was based upon another cardinal tenet of his faith. He believed that private morals should not be higher than the policy of the government, and he knew that in the then troubled state of affairs in China it would be simply inviting chaos if the state forgave all those who offended it. Confucius' theory was much better adapted to the conditions of the day than was Lao-tse's.

Taoism and Christianity

It may then be asked if Lao-tse is not to be ranked as greater than Jesus because he taught the principles of Jesus although surrounded by the conditions of the time of Moses. The answer is that Confucius and Jesus are both respected more than Lao-tse because the latter simply announced a theory and did not try to bring it into practice among men as did the other two.

We shall understand this better when we consider what Lao-tse

3 *Tao-Teh-King*, 49:2.
4 Ibid., 63:2.
5 *Analects*, 14:36.

meant by the "Tao" (pronounced Dow). This word is almost impossible to translate into English. Various suggestions have been made by different scholars, such as *reason, word, path, road,* and *way.* Christians will be able to understand it better if they are reminded that when the New Testament was translated into Chinese the first verse of the first chapter of the fourth gospel was rendered by the missionaries: "In the beginning was the Tao, and the Tao was with God and the Tao was God." And Christian scholars will thereupon recognize that by the word *Tao,* Lao-tse anticipated the Christian doctrine of the Logos.

But Lao-tse was not particularly anxious that the word *Tao* should be understood. In fact, the first verse of his one book, the *Tao-Teh-King,* is "The Tao that can be understood cannot be the real Tao." In other words, the difference between Confucius and Lao-tse is the eternal difference between the popularizer and the scholar-theorist, between the teacher and the theologian. Confucius would never have said, as did Lao-tse, "To withdraw into obscurity is the way of Heaven."[6]

These two Chinese leaders reacted characteristically to the conditions of the time. Confucius was trying to find a practical working method of government to reduce the disorders of the day. The older sage also deplored the general break-up of society, which included robbery, greed in high places, and poverty among the people, but he did not attempt any practical solution of the difficulties. When things became too much for him he resigned from the government position and retired into that "obscurity" which he called "the way of Heaven."

The Taoist Scriptures

Just as Lao-tse in a little cart was crossing the boundary of the state, he was recognized by an official, who suspected the old man's plans and begged him to write down his well-known wisdom before he departed from the world of men. Lao-tse tarried long enough in the little border town to comply with this reasonable request, and the result was the *Tao-Teh-King.* This book consists of eighty-one short chapters, not very well arranged, and contains mostly words of advice. It is not particularly interesting reading, and it is said that an emperor of China who lived in the third century A.D.,

6 *Tao-Teh-King,* 9:2.

who used to lecture on the *Tao-Teh-King,* was obliged to promise
a reprimand to any of his audience who "either stretched, or
yawned, or expectorated during the discourse."[7] Nevertheless, the
book represented a remarkable philosophy for so early a time.

Taoism, as the religion of the followers of Lao-tse was called,
underwent a process of degeneration after his death until it bore
little resemblance to its original high quality. The book which Taoists consider next in importance to the *Tao-Teh-King* comes from a
later period and indicates that at the time of its composition there
had already been incorporated in Taoism features which would
have been especially repugnant to its founder. For instance, we read
in this later scripture such injunctions as the command not to sin
or dance on the last day of the month or of the year. Taoists were
forbidden to weep or expectorate toward the north, and it was considered a sin to point at a rainbow. The process of degeneration proceeded rapidly. One Chinese emperor, who was a confirmed Taoist,
actually sent out vessels to find the "fairy isles where the herb of
immortality grew."

The Taoist Pope

In the year 1 A.D. a Taoist pope was established, and in the same
year one of the Taoist leaders tried to manufacture a pill of immortality. The practice of magic grew rapidly. In the eighth Christian century "gold stone" medicine was used even by the emperor,
and in the next century the Taoist doctors became so corrupt that
they were banished from southern China.

Of late years the fanaticism, witchcraft, and generally degraded
practices of the Taoists have made the name Taoism a word of reproach, until H. C. DeBose has said, "There is little hope for China,
religiously, morally, or politically, until Taoism is swept away from
the face of the land."[8] The Boxer uprising was partly due to the
misinterpretation by Taoists of certain words of Lao-tse. In the
Tao-Teh-King[9] Lao-tse wrote of the ideal Taoist, "When coming
among soldiers, he need not fear arms and weapons." Certain fanatical Taoists were actually convinced that because of these words of

[7] H. A. Giles, *Confucianism and Its Rivals,* p. 181, quoted in R. E. Hume, *The World's Living Religions,* p. 135.
[8] *Religion of Mission Fields,* p. 181.
[9] 50:4.

their founder they were invulnerable and could not be hurt by the lead bullets of foreigners. In their fanatic zeal they attempted to drive out of China the exponents of Christianity.

Anyone, however, who is tempted to make comparisons between Christianity and Taoism, to the detriment of the latter, by pointing out the great difference between the actual teachings of Lao-tse and the superstitions of modern Taoism, should be reminded that he is living in a glass house. There are forms of Christianity today which harbor superstitions not found in the teachings of Jesus, to put it rather mildly.

If there is one thing that impresses itself upon the student, it is the fact that the teachings of any founder of a religion become so obliterated by the admixture of atavistic survivals of former and lower religions that in the course of time his followers are religiously practicing the direct opposite of the precepts of the founder.

Deification

Buddha, Confucius, and Lao-tse were all practically atheists, yet all three are now worshiped as gods. As early as the second century A.D. sacrifices were offered to Lao-tse; in the fourth century A.D. Taoists developed the doctrine of the supernatural conception. They went far beyond the Christian doctrine, declaring that Lao-tse was "born an old man with white hair, having been in his mother's womb for either seventy-two or eighty-one years."[10] He was therefore called "the venerable philosopher" or "the old boy."[11] This latter term has not the connotation of impudence that it would have in America. Finally he was made a member of the Taoist trinity along with Chaos or the Demiurge and Yu Huang Shang Ti, "the Pearly Emperor."[12]

Lao-tse Rebukes Confucius

It is reported that at the time of Confucius' visit to Lao-tse, the venerable man rebuked his young visitor. Confucius was very much interested in the exact procedure in certain ceremonials which had

[10] Sacred Books of the East, 39:35, Note 1.
[11] Hume, *World's Living Religions*, p. 132.
[12] Soothill, *Three Religions of China*, p. 82, 83; Hume, p. 132, 133.

come down from ancient sages. He hoped to restore order in China by the revival of the strict observance of these ceremonials and social customs. Naturally he expected to secure information concerning these customs from such a man of wisdom as Lao-tse, but the old philosopher said to him, "The men about whom you talk are dead and their bones are melted to dust. Put away your proud aims and desires."[13]

This was like a dash of cold water to the enthusiastic young reformer. His rising popularity as a teacher had enabled him to clothe himself as he thought a great teacher should. He had unconsciously assumed an air of importance which was offensive to Lao-tse, who lived much more simply. The old man suggested that as a rule great men of wisdom allowed no one to suspect their importance from their appearance, but even assumed an appearance of stupidity.

He seized the opportunity to counsel Confucius to study in order to discover the central principle of all things, the Tao. Confucius replied that he had been studying for twenty years. Lao-tse answered that the Tao was not something which could be handed out like a gift, or left as a legacy to one's children. The only way to obtain it, he said, was to "give it room in one's heart."

Confucius turned away pondering deeply the old man's words. On the way home he remarked to his disciples, "I know how birds fly, how the fishes swim, and how animals run. But there is the dragon. I cannot tell how it mounts on the wind through the clouds and flies through heaven. I have seen Lao-tse and I can only compare him to the dragon."[14] This may have been intended as a compliment for Lao-tse or it may have been an ironical remark, gently ridiculing the ethereal character of Lao-tse's philosophy.

Dr. Hume very aptly characterizes and contrasts the two philosophers, "Lao-tse must have appeared to Confucius like an otherworldly dreamer soaring among the clouds of his own speculations, and Confucius must have seemed to Lao-tse like a busybody meddling in everybody's affairs. The two most influential men of China were indeed different from one another in their interests, aims and methods and general systems."[15]

13 Sacred Books of the East, 39:34.
14 Sacred Books of the East, 39:34, 35.
15 World's Living Religions, p. 130.

The Magistrate

For seventeen years more Confucius continued his itinerant teaching. At the age of fifty-one he finally had the opportunity for which he had been seeking all his life. In the year 500 B.C., when he was asked to serve as magistrate in his own state of Lu, his methods were so successful that he was promoted first to the office of Minister of Works and then to the position of Minister of Justice.

As soon as he was given office, it became evident that his ideas were very practical. His methods worked well, both in the state itself and, later, in the negotiations with other states. Law and order appeared as if by magic. Before his time, the main business of the government had been the collection of taxes. Confucius changed the entire point of view and insisted that the thing to be sought was the adequate performance of his proper duties by each officer in the state. To use modern language, Confucius was an efficiency engineer.

At one time he was talking to the Duke of Chi, a neighboring province, whose state was notably maladministered. The Duke had discovered that he was being managed by his own ministers and was in doubt as to the wisdom of letting his eldest son succeed him. He appealed to Confucius and asked the question "What is kingcraft?"

"Confucius answered, 'When the king is king and the minister is minister; when the father is father and the son is son.'

" 'True, indeed,' said the duke. 'Were the king no king, and the minister no minister; were the father no father, and the son no son, could I get aught to eat, though the grain were there?' "[16]

At another time when he was asked the same question, he replied, "To be tireless of spirit and faithful at work."[17] But Confucius had only four years in which to demonstrate the truth of his theories. The rulers of the state of Chi grew envious of the growth of the state of Lu and plotted to overthrow it. They knew well that the only way of succeeding would be by creating dissension between the Duke of Lu and his Minister of Justice, Confucius.

Eighty girls, beautiful in face and form, and well-trained in music, dancing, and the other arts of their profession, were sent as

16 *Analects*, 12:11.
17 *Analects*, 14.

a gift to the Duke of Lu. His enemies knew his weakness. He turned with joy from the severe regulations of Confucius to the delightful relaxations supplied by his enemies. Confucius was unable to secure an audience with his sovereign for three whole days. The dancing girls demolished the structure which Confucius had been building up by four years of intensive work.

When Confucius saw that the important ceremony of the Sacrifice to Heaven was performed hurriedly and perfunctorily, his heart was broken, and he resigned. He determined to find some place where the ruler was a virtuous man and where he would secure intelligent co-operation in the carrying out of his plans. Although he searched for thirteen long years, he was unsuccessful. He still felt that good government was the basis of all reform, and even looked forward to the abolition of capital punishment, could good government be established but for one hundred years.[18] From town to town he went searching for a virtuous ruler, sometimes in danger of his life[19] but still persisting in his hope. At last he was called home, not to govern, but to spend his remaining years in scholarly pursuits. This last period of his life, from the time he was sixty-eight until he died at the age of seventy-two, was occupied with the completion of his work on the classics, begun long before.

The Editor of the Classics

There are nine Chinese classical books with which the name of Confucius is closely associated. Five of these are called "*king*," the remainder, "*shu*." Sometimes the word "classical" is applied to the five *king*, and the other four are called simply "The Books."

The five *king* are:

The *Shu King*, or, Canon of History,
The *Shi King*, or, Canon of Poetry,
The *I King*, or, Canon of Changes,
The *Li Ki King*, or, Book of Rights,
The *Chun Chiu King*, or, Spring and Autumn.

Sometimes a sixth one is added, the "*Hsiao King*," or, Book of Filial Piety.

Of these books Confucius probably wrote only one, "Spring and Autumn," which is a very uninteresting history of his own state.

18 *Analects*, 13:11.
19 *Analects*, 9:5.

The other *king*, however, he seems to have collected and edited, although even that much connection is, by some scholars, denied. The four *shu* came from a later time and were written by the disciples of Confucius. In a certain sense the five *king* books represent the Old Testament of Chinese sacred literature, and the four *shu* resemble the New Testament.

The *shu* consist of reports of conversations between Confucius and his contemporaries, together with various maxims and doctrines on both ethical and political subjects. These four books are called:

The *Ta Hsio*, or, Great Learning,
The *Chung Yung*, or, Doctrine of the Mean,
Lun Yu, or, The Analects,
Meng-tsze, or, Mencius.

"Great Learning" is a discourse on virtue. "Doctrine of the Mean" counsels temperance and moderation. "The Analects" is a collection of the maxims of Confucius, and is the most popular book, especially among foreigners. "Mencius" is the collected works of the greatest commentator on the works of Confucius.

It is interesting to note that although these nine books have been, for many centuries, of the greatest influence in the life of China, and although applicants for government positions were obliged to pass civil service tests in these books in the famous Chinese examination halls, nevertheless there has not developed a theory of infallibility or literal accuracy. An educated Chinese can afford to smile at some hotly defended Christian doctrines.

Although Confucius can be credited with the actual composition of only one of these nine books, nevertheless he must be given credit for selecting from the vast mass of literature before his time those sayings which have come down to us.

An editor is frequently responsible for the real value of a book, especially if the book be of the sort that these were. It requires considerable perspicacity to recognize a valuable bit of literature and to sift the wheat from the chaff. The turn of a verse sometimes redeems a trite saying and makes it live forever. There is no doubt that Confucius had a genius in this direction. He took the vast mass of knowledge of the time and put it in outline form. His time was remarkably similar to the period through which we are now passing. Previously, most of the knowledge had been held by scholars and was not available to the common people because of the style and language in which it was written. It must have taken a great deal of labor to read all the extant literature and then simplify it for the consumption of the people. The *Shu King* was really an outline of history; the *Shi King,* an outline of poetry; the *I King,* an outline of prophecy and augury, and the *Li Ki King,* an outline of etiquette.

The "Humanizer"

Confucius is responsible for the diffusion of knowledge among the people of China. He was really the father of Chinese education. He humanized what was previously abstruse and difficult to comprehend, and the books which he edited have been the handbooks of China. There is a striking similarity between Confucius and Benjamin Franklin. Both were political reformers, and both published books of maxims. Confucius' "Analects" constantly reminds one of "Poor Richard's Almanac." A very keen sense of worldly wisdom pervades the maxims of the book, a few of which may be quoted,

I do not speak of what is ended, chide what is settled, or find fault with what is past.[20]

Rank without bounty, ceremony without respect, mourning without grief, why should I cause them a glance![21]

Neglect of what is in me, want of thoroughness in learning, failure to do right when told me, lack of strength to overcome faults, these are my sorrows.[22]

To listen much, pick out the good and follow it; to see much and think over it: this comes next to wisdom.[23]

Give the old folk peace; be true to friends, and have a heart for the young.[24]

Poetry rouses, courtesy upholds us, music is our crown.[25]

A gentleman looks within; the small man looks unto others.[26]

[20] *Analects,* 3:21 (Lyall's Translation).
[21] *Analects,* 3:26.
[22] *Analects,* 7:3.
[23] *Analects,* 7:27.
[24] *Analects,* 5:25.
[25] *Analects,* 8:8.
[26] *Analects,* 15:20.

Cunning words confound the mind; petty impatience confounds great projects.[27]

Hatred of the many must be looked into; the friendship of the many must be looked into.[28]

The fault is to cleave to a fault.[29]

Learning knows no rank.[30]

The whole end of speech is to be understood.[31]

A gentleman has nine aims: To see clearly, to understand what he hears, to be warm in manner, dignified in bearing, faithful of speech, keen at work, to ask when in doubt, in anger to think of difficulties, and in sight of gain to think of right.[32]

Besides his maxims, Confucius made other contributions of help to the self-culture of the ordinary man. To him self-culture was the important thing because he recognized that the strength of the state lay in the culture of the citizens and that there was nothing more important to good government than the education of the people in self-culture. For this he did not recommend religion, but he did lay great stress on poetry, ceremonials, music, and archery. He believed that poetry was of value because it aroused the individual to attempt what he might not otherwise try to do. He advised the maintenance of ceremonials, even those connected with religion, because they taught careful attention to detail.

The contribution of music to self-culture he found in the fact that it seemed to lead the mind to higher thoughts. He himself had a lute which he was accustomed to play for a period before he began to write or to teach, as it enabled him, he thought, to concentrate his mind upon his work. In the *Li Ki* we find the statement, "When one has mastered music completely, and regulates his heart and mind accordingly, the naturally great, gentle and sincere heart is easily developed, and joy attends its development. This joy proceeds into a feeling of calm; this calm continues on. In this unbroken calm, the man is heaven within himself."[33]

The inclusion of archery with poetry, ceremonials and music as

[27] *Analects*, 15:26.
[28] *Analects*, 15:27.
[29] *Analects*, 15:29.
[30] *Analects*, 15:38.
[31] *Analects*, 15:40.
[32] *Analects*, 16:10.
[33] Book 17: Sec. 3, Verse 23.

one of the four main methods of self-culture seems somewhat surprising to us, but Confucius had a real reason for including it. The virtue of archery was that it cultivated aim and precision rather than strength. "To pierce through the target does not score in shooting, for men are not alike in strength."[34]

Confucius and Occidentals

There is much in Confucius that appeals to the Western mind. We like his humanism, his common sense, and his emphasis on self-culture. We also appreciate his emphasis upon improving conditions of this present life rather than spending one's time preparing for the next.

Certain elements of his philosophy of life, however, do not appeal to us as moral. The only book of the five classics which is attributed to his pen, "Spring and Autumn," or the Annals of the State of Lu, is quite immoral from our point of view. We cannot, today, forgive a historian who concealed and twisted facts in order to please his patron. He suppressed the truth about certain nobles and about some of his own relatives. In spite of the fact that Confucius advised his followers to have little to do with the gods and the spirits, there was evidently a great deal of underlying superstition in his nature. He was careful not to say anything against the gods or spirits. We are told that he was much disturbed by a sound of thunder or by coming upon a person clad in mourning garb.

His Personality

Those who had to associate with him probably found him very fussy, extremely conservative, and very punctilious in small matters. He was cautious to the point of timidity, and self-conscious to the point of absurdity. "He wore an awed look and dragged his feet as though they were fettered."[35]

His extreme reverence for high officials made him obsequious. It is said that "at court he talked frankly to men of low rank, winningly to men of high rank, while in the king's presence he looked intent and solemn." He does not impress one as being a brave man,

34 *Analects*, 3:16.
35 *Analects*, 10:5.

and one gets the impression from reading his collected sayings and the various legends about him that he was over-given to complaint. A very interesting picture of his personal appearance and habits is presented in the tenth book of the Analects,

This gentleman was never arrayed in violet or mauve; even at home he would not don red or purple. In hot weather he wore unlined linen clothes, but always over other garments. With lamb-skin he wore black, with fawn he wore white, with fox-skin he wore yellow. At home he wore a long fur robe, with the right sleeve short. He always had his nightgown half as long again as his body. In the house he wore fox or badger skin for warmth.

When out of mourning there was nothing wanting from his girdle. Except for court dress, he was sparing of stuff. He did not wear lamb's fur, or a black cap, on a visit of condolence. At the new moon he always went to court in court dress. On fast days he always donned clothes of pale hue, changed his food, and moved from his wonted seat.

He did not dislike his rice cleaned with care, nor his hash chopped small. He did not eat sour or mouldly rice, putrid fish, or tainted meat. Aught discoloured, or high, badly cooked, or out of season, he would not eat. He would not eat what was badly cut, or a dish with the wrong sauce. A choice of meats could not tempt him to eat more than he had a relish for. To wine alone he set no limit, but he did not drink till he got fuddled. He did not drink bought wine, or eat ready-dried market meat. Ginger was never missing at table. He did not eat much.

After sacrifice at the palace he would not keep the meat over night, at home not more than three days. If kept longer it was not eaten. He did not talk at meals, nor speak when in bed. Though there were but coarse rice and vegetable soup, he made his offering with all reverence. If his mat were not straight, he would not sit down.

The impressions presented by these items of interest, set down by some disciple of Confucius, are rather baffling when one attempts to reconcile them and unite them in a single consistent portrait. If the descriptions are accurate he could not have been a particularly comfortable person to get along with. Nevertheless, none of his disciples deserted him during his lifetime, and a growing tradition of reverence persisted until Confucianism dominated the entire country and its literature.

He appears to have been peculiarly attractive to the Chinese mind; probably because he represented in his own person and his books the problems of that temperament. In spite of the distinctly different mode of thought of the Occident there is much of help that may be derived from the literature of Confucianism.

Mencius

About one hundred years after the death of Confucius, "a second sage," Mencius, was born, whose name has been given to one of the four *shu*. He is generally recognized as Confucius' greatest disciple. Mencius carried somewhat further the doctrines of Confucius, reiterating and emphasizing the belief that man is naturally good rather than evil. He also was more democratic than Confucius, and openly asserted that the king was not to be compared with the people in importance. His statement, "Heaven hears as the people hear," is the Chinese of *"vox populi, vox dei."*

Mencius anticipated modern social doctrine when he asserted that it was impossible for starving people to be good people. To him it seemed that the problem of education would be largely solved when the people's hunger was satisfied. Then they would educate themselves.

Chucius

In point of view of popularity, however, Mencius was surpassed by Chu Hsi, or Chucius, who lived in the twelfth century A.D. and wrote commentaries on the classics. His particular contribution to Confucianism was an attempt to solve the problem of evil, but the general influence of his writings has been so wide that some have said that Confucianism should be called "Chucianism."[36]

Confucianism Today

Confucianism has changed from the simple ethical culture advocated by Confucius. In its ceremonials today a student of religion will recognize a thinly veiled animism, worshiping many gods and many demons. The highest of these gods is Heaven. It is important for a Christian studying Confucianism to bear in mind that in Chinese theology Heaven has absolutely no connotation of a place of residence for the just after death. When a Confucianist speaks of

36 *Encyclopedia of Religion and Ethics*, Vol. 4, p. 18.

Heaven he means very much what Christians mean when they use the word Providence; although to a Confucianist there is no connotation of personality. The great defect of Confucianism is the fact that it looks to the past for its golden age rather than to the future.

That backward look is now, in the mid-twentieth century, in the crucial process of being abruptly reversed (whether for the better or not remains to be seen), by the sudden political domination of the ideology of Communism, which promises a rosy utopian future for China under the so-termed dictatorship of the proletariat, the People's Republic. This ideology of state socialism is quite in opposition to the family-based mores so characteristic of Confucianism, but it is sympathetic with the non-theistic teachings of Confucius himself.

Confucianism, however, is by now pretty deep in the Chinese racial unconscious and already has a record of a remarkable capacity for absorbing and digesting invading alien religions and philosophies, and will probably eventually treat Communism as it has Buddhism and Christianity.

VII

THE TEACHER OF RIGHTEOUSNESS

[170 B.C.?–100 B.C.?]

WHO PREPARED THE WAY IN THE WILDERNESS

THE DRAMATIC DISCOVERY and identification a dozen years ago of ancient manuscripts in caves near the Dead Sea has given the world another great religious leader. The continuation of the explorations in that region, with the consequent discovery of more caves and more manuscripts, has enabled us to fill the gap between the Old and New Testaments of the Christian Bible, by restoring to us books which belong there, books which greatly illuminate and supplement the gospels, acts, epistles, and apocalypses that Christians later added to the Jewish Bible.

The rich finds in the caves and crevices of the marly cliffs in and near the gorge or wady named Qumran, or Goomran, long ago by the Arabs (because they thought it was the site of the ancient sin-city of Gomorrah) led archaeologists to explore the khirbet, or mound, of Qumran, which had always been considered the unimportant ruins of some old Roman fort.

The work of excavation, now practically complete, has revealed a great Essene community center, comprising several connected buildings, with remarkably complete facilities for the service, comfort, and activities of many people.

As the desert dust raised by the archaeologists settles, we can estimate the extent and character of the operations of the remarkable Qumran Community, with its great audience hall, refectory, kitchens, dormitory, cemetery, pottery, swimming pools or baptisteries, scriptorium or publishing house, and the vast library of thousands of religious books, hastily hidden in nearby caves when the tenth Roman legion was reported to be approaching, in A.D. 68.

For this library of an Essene semimonastic community predates Christianity, having been established in and with the settlement at its founding by the anonymous "Teacher of Righteousness" or "Righteous Master" two centuries or more before the imperial eagles of the Roman standards appeared on the horizon.

What that library's complete contents were, in its most flourishing period, we shall never know, but enough of its very precious treasures remained after two thousand years of pillage by ignorant nomads and detrition by the teeth of time to make the discovery the most important in the annals of Biblical archaeology. Its pre-Christian dating is verified by the agreement of the most exacting tests—archaeologic, numismatic, paleographic, and even Carbon 14 radiation.

Yet the remains of the library still contain scrolls and fragments of all the books (save Esther) of the Hebrew Bible which Christians call the Old Testament, in manuscripts a thousand years older than any we have hitherto had, plus samples and sections of twice as many so-called "apocryphal" scriptures not now in the "authorized" Bibles, and including a number of hitherto unknown books giving the rules, rituals, practices and beliefs of the Qumran Community itself, which so strangely resembled the earliest Christian churches in all these respects and even called itself the Community of the New Testament, or New Covenant!

These recently excavated non-Biblical scriptures so neatly dovetail with, corroborate, elucidate, and anticipate the sayings of Jesus and the writings of Paul and John that it is becoming increasingly difficult every year, as more fragments of these priceless manuscripts are deciphered, to deny that some of the Christian disciples and their beloved Master were very familiar with these Essene scroll-books and may even have lived and studied for a while at Qumran.

The resemblances were so obvious that some students of the newly found scrolls who were also familiar with the New Testament books thought at first that the anonymous "Teacher of Righteousness," adored and followed by the communitarians of Qumran, may have really been Jesus himself. But further study, with access to fragments of manuscripts found in later-opened caves, made the identification impossible to maintain, as it became increasingly evident that the life spans of the two great Jewish religious leaders could not have coincided historically, or even overlapped.

Gradually, after scholarly exponents of theories placing the great unknown Essene teacher in various historical situations from the third century B.C. to A.D. 65 have had their say and exchanged their arguments, it is becoming apparent that the weight of expert opinion in the United States, at least, is swinging toward the middle of the second century B.C. as being the most likely dating for the Teacher. But Dr. H. H. Rowley, of Manchester College, England, places his death in 171 B.C. and the migration of his followers about 131 B.C. to Damascus, then to Qumran, "a few years later."

Personally, I am inclined at present to believe, judging from the evidence now available, that this great leader of men led his followers into the Judean desert, to make there a highway for his God —i.e., to prepare a pure place for the coming of God's Kingdom; for the Teacher and his students were disgusted with the wickedness of the Jerusalem hierarchy. And I think this hegira to the desert retreat, definitely obeying the command of their favorite prophet Isaiah (chapter 40, verses 3 to 8) to make a godly place in the wilderness, where they could be delivered from the Evil One (the Wicked Priest ruling in Jerusalem) and where they could not only pray "Thy Kingdom Come" but also labor and live purely as God's Elect to make that prayer come true—this decisive and historic step must have been taken about the year 130 B.C. The oldest of the many coins found in the Qumran ruins were three silver ones of the reign of Antiochus Sidetes, which we would date as of 136, 130, and 129 B.C., and fourteen coins variously allotted to dates during the reign of John Hyrcanus, who held power from 135 to 104 B.C.

There on a limestone plateau overlooking the Dead Sea, only a few miles from Jerusalem, the fugitives from a corrupt religious center set up a new and holier habitation, to follow more strictly the laws (Torah) given by Yahweh through Moses. And the marvel is that this self-sufficient community of self-exiled saints maintained itself for two full centuries, until the Romans wiped out both Jerusalem and Qumran.

The greater wonder is, however, that after the fall of Qumran in A.D. 68, it seemingly passed from the memory of men, at least of Western Christendom, until its accidental discovery nineteen centuries later, when a Bedouin teen-ager, chasing a stray goat, found in 1945 in a cave "some leather with scrawling on it," which he thought might do for sandal straps. Two years later, his uncle took some of the leather to the Bethlehem black market "to see if it might be of any value." His whole tribe is now rich from the sale of many other scrawlings to "dealers in antiquities."

The whole world knows now (America rather belatedly) about the scrolls and their significance for all Christendom and all Jewry, and to some extent for Islam. The Bedouin followers of the Arabian Prophet, however, are busy digging for and selling to the crazy Christians the precious scraps of leather and papyrus in the floor dirt of the hundreds of Dead Sea caves, scraps which sell now for four or five English pounds per square inch. Business is much better now for them than when they sold the rich guano from the caves to the Israeli for fertilizing the new peach and almond orchards. If it weren't for the war and so many guards with guns, the Bedouin would be infiltrating the orchards and sifting the soil for more pieces of Isaiah and Habakkuk and Enoch.

How was it, though, that this treasure remained hidden for so many centuries? Some simple souls think that God kept them hidden till today because of the apocalyptic, end-of-the-world, kingdom-come character of the writings of the Teacher of Righteousness and his disciples, who believed, as did Jesus and his disciples a little later, that national and world conditions were so bad that the end of the world, the Day of Judgment, when the Son of Man would come on the clouds of heaven, was very imminent, perhaps coming before that generation passed away.

Now, again, these modern believers in the Second Coming maintain, has come an apocalyptic period, with atom bombs and H bombs and cobalt bombs likely at any moment to blow us all to Kingdom Come. Millions now living are likely to die, with only the elect, the 144,000 saints, saved, as both Qumranites and Christians believed and their apocalypses show. Only the righteous, the "just, shall live by faith." The Essenes of Qumran interpreted that fourth verse of the second chapter of the prophecies of Habakkuk to mean that in the Last Judgment, soon to come, they, the elect, would be saved from the dreadful punishment of sinners by their faith in the Teacher of Righteousness. The Qumran *pesher* or commentary on Habakkuk, found in the first cave, plainly says so. What a Great Soul that leader of theirs must have been that they pinned their hope of their own souls' salvation on him!

Paul's interpretation, of course, as given in the first chapter of his letter to the Christians of Rome, was that Habakkuk meant that "the gospel of Christ" was "the power of God unto salvation to every one that believeth." And Luther's belief that Habakkuk and Paul both meant that salvation comes not by works but only by faith in Christ was what launched the Protestant Reformation. And careful reading of that chapter of Paul's letter by anyone who has read the Qumran books, especially their favorite apocalypses of Enoch, will reveal that Paul was familiar with the Qumran point of view and was trying to improve on it by implying that Jesus Christ was a greater Teacher of Righteousness, offering a better hope of salvation.

But, returning to Qumran and the Essene colony there for a closer look at how that community lived and to get some idea of what they thought were the basic values of life, we wonder again at the power and beauty and righteousness that has so long been hidden from us. The more we contemplate the buildings, the communion dishes (if that is what those two thousand bowls were, so neatly stacked), the tall jars, the pottery and kiln where they were made, the beautifully written scrolls in some of them, and the one buried under the floor with 500 coins in it, the "scriptorium" or writing room with desks, seats, and even inkwells with the dried ink still there, the more the wonder grows that such a great religious experimenter's monument should have so long been unknown to us.

Down through the ages Moslem invaders, Christian Crusaders, pilgrims from every land, humble Bible students visiting the Holy Land, and great scholars from afar in the eighteenth and nineteenth centuries of exploration, World War soldiers, Lawrence of Arabia, and Fulton Oursler of New York collecting material for his book *A Skeptic in the Holy Land,* and more recently still Arab and Israeli skirmishers and border guards—all these men, every century for at least a millennium and a half, have marched, trudged or scouted within a few rods of Qumran's vast treasures, without hitherto managing to stumble upon them!

And all the time, this heap of "Roman ruins" and the adjacent rock caves and crevices, within a dozen miles or so of Jericho, Jerusalem and Bethlehem, have concealed since the time of Christ the answers to so many questions the world has been asking about him for centuries!

A romantic French savant has, by stretching Arabic a little, derived "Qumran" from "qamira" (be white); hence he thinks Khirbet Qumran may be freely translated *"la ruine des veilleurs au clair de lune,"* and so we presume that tourist guides will soon be pointing it out as "The Ruin Which Kept Watch in the Moonlight." Already, according to Dr. Geza Vermes (the learned Roman Catholic scholar of Louvain and Paris whose book *Les Manuscrits du Desert de Juda* is the most beautifully written of all scrolliana), the guides are calling the first-discovered cave, near the ruins, *"The* Grotto of the Manuscripts."

It is a solemn but emotionally warming thought that at the most flourishing period of the Essene community's life, when those white walls of Qumran and the great square watchtower were still standing, "in the silent midnight centuries ago," there was born in the cave stable, the Grotto of the Nativity, not very far away, a boy baby, from whose birth date our calendar is roughly reckoned today; and from that birth date we reckon backward to the time "Before Christ" when the Teacher of Righteousness lived, whose teachings and written literature so influenced that baby and his followers a little later. Born in a cave stable, buried in the cave tomb of Joseph of Arimathea; and now, so long afterward, it is in other caves nearby that the precious revealing scrolls have been discovered.

To know and appreciate the personality and character of the Teacher of Righteousness one should read, in the several translations now available, the Essene books found in the caves, such as The Rule of the Community, sometimes called (from Dr. Millar Burrows' early and not too happy suggestion) "The Manual of Discipline," The Damascus Document, originally named "Fragments of a Zadokite Work," The Pesher or Commentary on Habakkuk, The Psalms of Thanksgiving, The Peshers on Micah, Nahum, and Psalm 37, The War of the Sons of Light and the Sons of Darkness, and The Genesis Apocryphon, formerly called "The Lamech Scroll."

In addition, and importantly, you should read the non-Biblical books now known to have been produced by the Essenes, in part at least, and probably edited at Qumran. These books are usually called Apocrypha by Roman Catholics and Pseudepigrapha by Protestant scholars. Neither name is very satisfactory. Apocrypha once meant "hidden" or "secret" writings, the meaning of which was known only to favored initiates or adepts; but because these books were, for reasons not always deemed valid today, excluded from the canon or official list of approved holy scripture, the word "apocryphal" came to mean "spurious" or even "false."

In the Greek translation of the Hebrew Bible (Old Testament) made in Alexandria in the third century B.C. and later, and called the Septuagint (LXX) because supposedly made by seventy scholars, there are fourteen books not accepted by the Jews as canonical. Eleven of them are included in the Roman Catholic canon, but Protestants do not consider them official for determining doctrine (which is one reason why Catholic and Protestant Christian doctrines differ on some points). But Protestant Bibles once (in Elizabethan times) included them as inspirational and moral reading, and they seem to be coming back into favor, possibly because of the rising curiosity regarding the scrolls, but partly, too, from their blood, thunder, murder, and sex chapters, frowned upon by Victorians.

The books called Pseudepigrapha by Protestants are called Apocrypha by Catholics, but are not canonical for them any more than among the Protestants. The Pseudepigrapha are simply scriptural books the authors of which have used as a pseudonym the name of an ancient well-known holy man. By so doing, the writer could say things which needed to be said, but which would endanger the life of the writer if he were found out. After the time of Ezra, no scripture was reckoned as canonical by the Jews, and it was a crime punishable by death for a writer to presume to be a prophet and speak for God.

But great and good men did write, under the "byline" of the ancients and patriarchs, Abraham, Moses, Solomon, Baruch, Ezra, Isaiah, Adam and Eve, the Twelve Patriarchs, and especially Enoch. There is a whole series of books by different authors and editors, writing under the Enochan nom de plume, all once called The Book of Enoch but now known as the Enochan Books or the Enochan Literature. We had "Ethiopic Enoch" brought back from Ethiopia by James Bruce in the late eighteenth century after having been "lost" since it was suppressed by certain theologians about the fourth century A.D. Ethiopic Enoch has proved to be five books, including a lost Book of Noah, combined by some editor. "Slavonic Enoch" was deemed, when it first came to the attention of Western scholars about 1890, to be merely a Slavonic translation of part of Ethiopic Enoch and was called Second Enoch, but it is now known to be a separate pseudepigraph, although dealing, like the other Enoch books, with the trip of that ancient patriarch, the seventh from Adam, to the seven heavens.

The Books of Enoch, it is belatedly admitted now, were of Essene origin, perhaps some of them proto-Essene, but all apparently edited and copied at Qumran. One or more of them may very likely have been composed by the Teacher of Righteousness himself. The Enochan literature resembles the newly discovered Essene documents. In fact, parts of ten Enoch books were found in one cave, Cave Four, as well as fragments in other caves, and they were in the original Aramaic, in which Canon R. H. Charles said a half century ago the Ethiopic Enoch must originally have been written.

Moreover, it should be here noted, as another link between the Qumran Teacher and Jesus, that the Enochan books, as well as the other Essene pseudepigrapha, such as the Book of Jubilees, resemble parts of the New Testament not only in vocabulary, doctrine, and emphasis, but also in what we have lately learned to call thought-forms and frames of reference.

You soon notice that the expectation of a Messiah, the emphasis on brotherhood and sharing, the community of goods, the practice of baptism, the ritual meal of bread and wine, the frequent reference to the new covenant, the giving up of animal sacrifice in the Temple, the mention often of the spirit of truth and the holy spirit, the supervisor, overseer, or bishop and the Council of Twelve, and many other ideas are common to both the Essene community and the early Christian Brotherhood.

Among the words of Jesus, you will recognize that much of the "Sermon on the Mount," especially the fifth chapter of Matthew, also the thirteenth of Mark and its parallels in the other gospels, sometimes called "The Little Apocalypse," seem almost verbatim quotations from the Books of Enoch, the Book of Jubilees, and the

Testament of the Twelve Patriarchs. If Jesus was quoting from book passages he had memorized at Qumran, his hearers probably knew it. Our New Testament manuscripts were guiltless of quotation marks, not then yet invented.

The Teacher of Righteousness, or his Essene successors, apparently influenced the writer of the fourth gospel, called the Gospel According to John, and of the three Johannine epistles, for this "John" (or these Johns) is so much like the Qumranians in his thought and words that some scholars think he must have lived for a time among them. The Gnosticism (mystical religious philosophy of Greek and Oriental origin) in John's thinking, such as his metaphysical emphasis on the Logos or Word, a semi-personal entity which was with God at or before the beginning or creation of the world—in fact, "without him [the Logos] was not any thing made that was made"—that Gnosticism or metaphysical secret wisdom was what led some scholars to date the fourth gospel much later than the others, even in the second century A.D., as having been influenced by the Hellenism of Alexandria.

But that Gnosticism is now seen to have been current at Qumran in Essene circles, in an early form at least, even before Mark's gospel was written, so that some parts of John's gospel, or the sources from which he compiled it, may be older than the synoptic gospels (Matthew, Mark, and Luke). And John's account of Passion Week, which differs so much chronologically from the synoptic accounts, is supported by the Essene calendar of the Enochan books and the Book of Jubilees. If Jesus partook of the ritual supper with his disciples, a simple meal foreshadowing the Messianic supper he expected to share with them in Kingdom Come, on Tuesday evening according to the Essene calendar and as John intimates and some of the early church fathers openly state, it allows a more reasonable timing for the dramatic events of Passion Week than does the overcrowded schedule demanded by a Thursday night Passover with a Friday noon crucifixion and, rushed in between, Gethsemane, Betrayal, and two trials.

This Gnosticism, by the way, is important to note in any study of the Teacher of Righteousness, the founder of the Qumran Brotherhood, for it was an indication and a testimony to the synthesis, the blending of several strands of religious inspiration and teaching. Persia, Greece, Alexandrine Egypt, and even yogic, vedic

India made their contributions to the remarkable blend which was the Essenism taught at Qumran.

Saluting the sun as it rose in the east was one of the Persian customs the Qumran Essenes followed. Then they worked at their various tasks until eleven o'clock, when they bathed or baptized themselves and put on white robes, another Persian custom still religiously observed by the Parsees (Persians) in India today. Then they took their places for their simple meal, and each member was given that day his daily bread, but did not touch it until the leading priest had said grace and reached for his allotted loaf. After this they went back to their work, gardening, weaving, pottery-making, cooking, mending the common store of garments, for, like the early Christians, "neither said any of them that ought of the things possessed was his own; but they had all things common" (Acts 4:32). Many of them must have been scribes, and labored long hours in the scriptorium copying manuscripts old and new.

The late Dr. Ralph Marcus of Chicago rather aptly compared the various Jewish parties and sects of the time of the later Essenes and the earliest Jesus-followers to the American political and social groups. Without forcing the parallels too far, he compared the Sadducees to our Republicans, the Shammaite (strict) Pharisees to the Conservative Democrats, the liberal Hillellite Pharisees to the New Deal Democrats, the Apocalyptic Pharisees to the Radical Democrats and Progressives, the Essenes to Socialists, the Gnostics to those Teddy Roosevelt dubbed the "lunatic fringe," and the Zealots to the Communists.

Of these seven groups, both Jesus and Paul would probably fit best in the Essene category; John the Baptist, between the Essenes and the Zealots; and John the Disciple would perhaps be at home with the Gnostics, who were, however, hardly to be fairly called lunatic fringers. Perhaps the current term "egghead" is more nearly accurate, now that the stigma has been somewhat removed, to describe John, and possibly T. Roosevelt himself.

Dr. Marcus may have been reading Josephus (A.D. 37–95) on the Essenes, for that voluminous Jewish historian much admired their economic system, and said: "They despise wealth, and their socialism is remarkable. None among them can be found richer than another. . . . There is never seen among them either abject poverty nor great wealth."

Philo (?B.C.–A.D. 50) tells how the Essenes' Lawgiver "trained in community living thousands of disciples. . . . Their organization is not based on family kinship, in which a man has no choice, but on zeal for virtue and love of all men." Pliny (A.D. 23–79) called them "a race by themselves and remarkably different from all other men in the whole wide world."

But Philo, in another book, *Every Virtuous Man Is Free,* paid them the highest tribute:

There are still God-guided men today who live naturally and reasonably, men who are themselves so free that they inspire their neighbors also with the spirit of freedom. There are not many of them, it is true, but that is not to be wondered at, for high nobility of that degree is always rare. These men have attained to it by separating themselves from the common crowd that they may dedicate their lives to the study of the great truths of nature. . . . We beg them, however, to come out to us and pacify our too turbulent and troubled lives, preaching to us to substitute for our wars and slavery and unspeakable evils their gospel of peace and freedom, and an abundance of their other rich blessings.

Recalling that it was when Jesus was a young man that Philo wrote this direct plea for these self-immolated saints to come out from their desert retreat to the busy haunts of men and bring with them their blessed gospel, and since Jesus did preach his message in the market place to publicans, harlots, and other sinners, one wonders if he listened to Philo and his own conscience and gave up the quiet of the monastery to proclaim his gospel.

Probably, however, the Essenes were not quite such ascetics and retiring cenobites as Philo and Josephus represent them. We know that they had settlements in Damascus, En-gedi, and Alexandria, besides cells and house groups in Galilee.

The Teacher of Righteousness, as he appears reflected in his writings, is no hermit, but a wise and experienced man of far travels and deep thoughts.

He is gradually emerging from the mists, as the fragments of the library he established and the books he wrote, edited, and published are being cleaned of the dirt and stains of centuries, deciphered and fitted into place, like jigsaw puzzles.

One section of the Zadokite work, the Damascus Document, gratefully testifies to the greatness of this man divinely sent in times of apostasy and wickedness. God "remembered the covenant of the forefathers and caused a remnant to remain to Israel . . . but they, like blind men, had been groping for the way for twenty years. And God considered their works, for they sought Him with a perfect heart; and He raised up for them a Teacher of Righteousness to lead them in the way of His heart."

This heaven-sent leader was not afraid to do an original and surprising thing, for his new co-operative brotherhood, with a new priesthood modeled on the old righteous Zadokite type of Solomon's day, not only met and supplied the need of the period, but it was far-reaching and forward-looking in advance of its time. For it was the first religious community to establish and maintain the ritual of baptism and the sacrament of the eucharistic meal. Moreover, and in this it was in advance of the Christianity of many centuries later, it was the first society to condemn and abolish within its domain the age-old institution of human slavery.

The Teacher of Righteousness was not the first pacifist, for before his time there were many advocates of peace, from Akhenaten on down, but he was the first to implement his peace theories with a comprehensive realistic regulation which, if generally adopted, even today, would actually eliminate war. We are today struggling to get the nations to disarm: this unknown strategist went deeper. Philo testifies:

You would not find among them [the Essenes] any maker of arrows, spears, swords, helmets, breast plates or shields, nor any manufacturer of arms or engines of war, nor any man occupied with a military avocation, or even the peaceful practices which might easily be converted to mischief.

The great Teacher of Righteousness actually created a new form of social order, an experimental co-operative commonwealth, a democracy of dedicated men, trying to make a little heaven on earth, a place where God's will should be "done on earth as it is in heaven." And it proved to be an intermediate step between Judaism and Christianity.

The subtle and sensitive nature of this leader of men and of the mystic and spiritual brotherhood of his followers may be noted in some of their writings, such as these Essene Enochan beatitudes:

Blessed is the man who renders a just judgment, not for remuneration, but for justice's sake, and does not wait around for something in return: he will himself receive afterward an impartial judgment.

Blessed is he who clothes the naked with his own robe and gives his own bread to the hungry.

Blessed is he who is so possessed of truth that he speaks the truth to his neighbor.

Blessed is he on whose lips are both truth and gentleness.

Among the good resolutions in the Manual of Discipline are the following:

I will return to no man evil for evil: rather I will pursue him with good. . . . I will not entertain any envy of mischievous spirits, and my soul shall not long for goods acquired by violence. . . . I intend to practice truth and righteousness, and loving consideration for those who are tired out, and to strengthen the hands of the timid of heart, and to teach understanding to bewildered souls . . . and to reply quietly to the haughty in spirit.

Has any religion produced a finer benediction than the one in the Manual of Discipline, Column II, lines 1b to 4a, probably composed and taught by the Teacher of Righteousness at Qumran!

And when they bless all the men who are on God's side, those, that is, who walk uprightly in all His ways, the priests shall say:
"May He bless you with all that is good,
 And deliver you from every evil.
 May He clarify your mind to understand life,
 And permit you to experience Eternity,
 And there turn to you His loving face
 For your happiness forever."

VIII

✿

JESUS

[8–6 B.C.?—A.D. 29–33?]

WHO SAID HE WAS A SON OF GOD

AMONG ANCIENT LEGENDS there is one told of a little boy who once amused himself at play by modeling clay images of sparrows. Delighted with his creations, he clapped his hands, whereupon the little clay birds took flight in alarm. This story of the child Jesus was one of the most popular of the many infancy narratives which the early Christians told about their leader. When the books of the New Testament were finally (in the fourth century A.D.) more or less officially selected from among the gospels, acts, epistles and apocalypses of early Christian literature, several "gospels" were omitted, partly because they contained stories of the infancy of Jesus which were too marvelous altogether, like this one about the sparrows. Other stories, like the one which tells that in anger he struck a playmate dead with a word, dropped out because they were not considered consonant with the character of Jesus.

The earliest accepted gospel, Mark, does not give us any childhood stories at all, but Luke enriches Christian tradition with several. His colorful account includes narratives of the angelic annunciation to Mary, her visit to Elizabeth, her virgin motherhood, the beautiful story of the angels and the shepherds, and the account of the presentation of the baby Jesus in the temple when Simeon prophesied the child's marvelous future, just as on a remarkably similar occasion Asita predicted the future greatness of the baby Buddha. Matthew, too, has given us infancy narratives—the story of the angelic annunciation to Joseph, the visit of the Zoroastrian priests, the plotting of wicked Herod, and the flight into Egypt.

The Visit to Jerusalem

Of all the stories of Jesus' early days, however, the one for which we are most grateful is Luke's account of the boy's visit to Jerusalem at the age of twelve. It is rightly the most popular by Christian firesides, in Sunday schools, and in the art of Christendom, because it is so humanly natural and yet clearly reveals the divine fire already in the heart of the youth.

The whole life purpose of the greatest religious genius of mankind is evident in his first recorded sentence. His parents had taken him from the home in Nazareth among the Galilean hills to the holy city, Jerusalem, for the springtime religious feast of the Passover, a week of religious ritual and pilgrim picnicking. At the end of the first day's journey homeward they missed him. He was not to be found in the caravan as they had supposed, so they returned to the city anxiously searching. On the third day they found him in the temple discussing theology with the learned doctors, amazing them with his wisdom and comprehension.

But Mary, who in the gospel records is always the anxious, misunderstanding mother, whatever later Christian theologians did in the way of idealization, said just the wrong thing at this critical time. It was the hour of triumph for the young student. He was engaged in theological debate with the leading scholars of the nation. He had matched his knowledge and his wit with theirs and was tasting the fruits of the first of his many victories over the scribes and Pharisees. But his mother failed utterly to understand. He had just proved his manhood and she treated him as a small boy. Complainingly, almost querulously, she scolded him publicly before his opponents, "Son, why have you treated us this way? You have brought sorrow to your father and me. We have been hunting everywhere for you." By that speech she unwittingly built a barrier between her boy and herself which grew with the years, as the records plainly indicate.

Her complaint in the temple caused him to lose patience with her because of her failure to recognize the important feature of that occasion. The fact that his parents had missed him and had hunted for him seemed to him comparatively unimportant. To be considered lost when he was in the temple, his heavenly Father's house, appeared absurd. He was exasperated that his mother should be anxious about a minor matter and indifferent to the important fact that her son had just won a great intellectual victory. In his exasperation he answered her question with other questions, reflecting her mental attitude of reproof with reproof in turn, "How is it that you sought me? Didn't you know where to find me? Where else would I be but in my Father's house, about my Father's business?"

The key to his life, his death, and his eternal influence in the religious life of mankind is in that phrase, "about my Father's business." Moses had discovered the personality of God: many Hebrew prophets and teachers had spoken of God as Father, Father of the nation and even of the individual; but here was one who actually took it for granted that he really was a child of God. Later he was to recognize the deeper truth that if God was his Father, then all men were his brothers, and they were, or could be, sons of God too, but here he was, at the age of twelve, assuming that his paramount duty in life was to attend to his heavenly Father's concerns. His spiritual stature is seen already towering above that of the confused doctors of theology and the surprised parents.

Nazareth

But he went back to Nazareth with them and was "subject unto them." He had rebelled against their absorption in his physical needs and their apparent ignorance of his spiritual urge. Now, however, he outwardly acquiesced in apparent acceptance of the routine of daily living. We are told that Mary "kept all these sayings in her heart." Perhaps that was the trouble. If she had talked them over with her growing boy she might have come to understand him. But we are told that his parents "understood not." Their loss, however, was the world's gain. The lack of parental comprehension and sympathy drove the boy more and more to seek the companionship of the unseen Supreme Being he called his heavenly Father, and the fruits of that inner communion have enriched the human race ever since.

The naturalness with which he prayed in later crises indicates that the Nazarene hills must have witnessed many an hour of secret devotion when the young carpenter fled from the noisy houseful of uncomprehending relatives to the quiet of some solitary place where he could talk with God.

Biographers of Jesus write of "the eighteen silent years," referring to the time between the incident in the temple and his baptism by John at the supposed age of thirty. To this important period of his life the gospel sources devote but one sentence, Luke's statement that he "increased in wisdom and stature and in favor with God and man," which is only to say that he was a normal youth and young man. A little more light on this period is given us indirectly by the gospel writers later, upon the occasion of Jesus' speech in the synagogue at Nazareth. The narrators say that his townspeople "wondered at the gracious words which proceeded out of his mouth," and that they said, "Is not this the carpenter's son? Is not his mother called Mary? His brethren, James, and Joses, and Simon, and Judas? And his sisters, are they not all with us? Whence then hath this man these things?"

This testimony of those among whom he was presumed to have passed these eighteen years, going in and out among them daily, would certainly justify the inference that he was a normal boy, an inconspicuous member of a large family of young people. Evidently if the people of Nazareth had ever heard about what happened in Jerusalem eighteen years before, or the wonderful events at his birth, they had forgotten it.

The supposition that Jesus himself was a carpenter has become accepted as fact, but the only basis for it is one doubtful passage, Mark 6:3. Here the Matthew verse just quoted has been changed to "Is this not the carpenter, the son of Mary?" This looks suspiciously like an attempt "under the influence of the doctrine of the Virgin Birth" to get rid of Joseph as parent. Many early manuscripts have Mark the same as Matthew, and "Origen, the greatest biblical scholar of his time (early third century), says that he never saw a Gospel that described Jesus as a carpenter" (The Interpreter's Bible 7:727).

Carpenter's son or not, the discovery of the Qumran Scrolls and the comparison of them with the teachings of Jesus lead us to infer he may have spent part, at least, of the "Silent Years" at Qumran.

Brothers and Sisters

Opinion is sharply divided in Christendom about Jesus' brothers and sisters. Some hold that he was the eldest of the children and that they were all the children of Mary. Others maintain that all save Jesus were children of Joseph by a former marriage. It undoubtedly made considerable difference in the effect of family life on Jesus whether he was the oldest son with many own brothers and sisters looking up to him or the youngest with many older step-brothers and -sisters.

The genealogical lists in Luke 3 and Matthew 1, especially the latter, are obviously artificial and carelessly edited. They disagree with each other and with the Old Testament. In spite of the fact that Jewish genealogies rarely include women, Matthew mentions four, and what a quartet! Tamar, Rahab, Ruth, and Bathsheba were hardly samples of virtue. Was Matthew clumsily attempting to defend "love children"?

Whether Jesus' brothers and sisters were full kin to him or not, we know that he was not very happy with them. The author of the fourth gospel tells us of an interesting conversation which Jesus had with these brothers of his. They taunted him with sly innuendo, and dared him, if he thought he was so great, to go to Jerusalem and proclaim himself openly. "For," says the account (John 7:1–9), "neither did his brethren believe in him." Anyone who thinks that Jesus was always meek and lowly should read his subtle and cutting retort on this occasion. He said, in effect, to his taunting brothers, "You go up to the feast. I'm not going up. You see, they hate me up there and want to kill me, but it isn't time for me to die yet. They hate me in Jerusalem because I tell them the truth about their evil works; but you go up: there will be no danger for you. The world cannot hate you."

Another indication of the probability that Jesus' family life was not happy is the number of scripture passages revealing that, after his ministry began, family ties meant little to him. He ignored, renounced, and rebuffed his mother and brethren when they sent a message to him as he was preaching. When he was told that they were without, seeking to speak to him, he said, "Who is my mother and who are my brethren? Whosoever shall do the will of my Father who is in heaven, he is my brother and sister and mother." Again he said, "A prophet is not without honor, save in his own country, and among his own kin, and in his own house."

On another occasion he went so far as to say, "If any man cometh unto me and hateth not his own father and mother and wife and children and brethren and sisters, yea, and his own life also, he cannot be my disciple." Even when we make due allowance for the enthusiasm of a prophet demanding singlehearted devotion to a great cause, we must see that family loyalty was unimportant to this man. Very likely we have here reflected his own personal experience with parents who did not understand spiritual things and brothers who not only refused to believe in him but openly jeered at his mission.

In Acts 1:14, however, we are told that Mary, the mother of Jesus, and his brethren were in the upper room among the 120 disciples, the group which was eventually to form the Christian church. Today scholars are wondering if the "brethren" were relatives or perhaps "lodge-brothers," and whether the mother of Jesus may not have been confused with Mary, the mother of John Mark, in whose home the group gathered. (See the late Dr. A. Powell Davies' recent (1958) book *The First Christian*, pp. 176–177.)

What Jesus Read

A youth who was inclined to studiousness would naturally find in further study a refuge from uncongenial home contacts. That the eighteen silent years, whether spent in Nazareth, Qumran, Alexandria or Persia and India, were years of study and reading of his national literature his later utterances reveal. He had a thorough acquaintance not only with those parts of Hebrew literature known to Christians as the Old Testament and the Apocrypha: he knew also the other writings—the various commentaries, and the books now known to scholars as the Pseudepigrapha. These "falsely signed" books, like First and Second Enoch, Jubilees, the Psalms of Solomon, and the Testament of the Twelve Patriarchs, were evidently the best sellers of Jesus' day, and he read and remembered them.

In his words in the New Testament we find quotations from Deuteronomy and Isaiah, his favorite Old Testament books, and from Genesis, Exodus, Leviticus, Numbers, First Samuel, the

Psalms, Jeremiah, Hosea, Daniel, Zechariah, and Malachi, but we also find many quotations from the pseudepigraphical books, which evidently influenced him greatly.

It has been correctly said that practically all the recorded utterances of Jesus can be duplicated in Jewish literature written before the New Testament was written. But it should also be said that he took these sayings of his people and made them live anew by reinterpretation. When, for instance, he spoke of "many mansions" in heaven, he was using a concept already familiar to his hearers even to the very words. In Second Enoch, chapter 62, verse 2, he had read, "in the great time to come are many mansions prepared for men, good for the good, bad for the bad, without number many." But Jesus said that the "many mansions" (literally, "abiding places") were in his Father's house, and that he was going there to get them ready for his disciples.

Jesus evidently loved this book of Second Enoch, or the Book of the Secrets of Enoch, as it was probably called in his day, for he quoted from it several times. He said to his disciples, "Swear not at all; neither by heaven; for it is God's throne: Nor by the earth; for it is his footstool: . . . But let your communication be, Yea, yea; Nay, nay: for whatsoever is more than these cometh of evil," which is remarkably like Second Enoch, chapter 49, verse 1, where we read, "I swear not by any oath, neither by heaven nor by earth, . . . If there is no truth in men, let them swear by the words, Yea, Yea, or else, Nay, nay."

The Beatitudes, especially as given by Luke, are evidently modeled on the Beatitudes in Second Enoch, chapters 42 and 52, but Jesus' version of the Beatitudes is an improvement. It seems as if all the images which his boyhood reading of his national literature had fixed in his mind came forth in his preaching later, more beautiful than before because of their remaining a while in his memory.

As he read these books and pondered their meaning, he became more than ever convinced that God was his Father. He found many references to the coming of the Messiah who should usher in a new day, the day of God's reign upon earth, the coming of the kingdom. The phrase impressed him, and he prayed, "Thy kingdom come." In fact, the entire "Lord's Prayer," recited today all over Christendom, closely reflects the Essene Messianic literature we have found in the caves.

Just how far Jesus accepted the description of the Messiah as applying to himself, it is impossible for us to determine from the confused records. At times the sources indicate that Jesus verily believed that he was to return alive after his death and while his generation was still alive—return triumphantly in bodily form on the clouds of heaven. That he said he would do so is one of the best attested of all his sayings, and that his disciples expected him to do so cannot be gainsaid. But he also spoke of the kingdom of God as coming gradually and quietly, and seemed sometimes to conceive of his own role as not so much that of the conquering Messiah as that of the "Suffering Servant" depicted in Deutero-Isaiah. And he said again that the kingdom was already among them.

At any rate, during the eighteen years he had been strengthened in his earlier conviction that not only was God his Father, but that he had a mission—to be about his Father's business.

The Baptism

All the gospel writers agree that what started him out on his public ministry was the preaching of John the Baptizer. It was A.D. 27, as nearly as we can determine, that the baptism of Jesus took place. Through an error of later calendar-makers, Jesus' birth was set several years too late. The B.C.–A.D. division of historical time was not made until A.D. 533, by the monk Dionysius Exiguus, who did rather well, considering. But by his reckoning Herod died in 4 B.C., and if the story of the massacre of the infants is true, Jesus was born before that, probably in 5 or 6 B.C. So 1958 is really the Year of Our Lord 1963, or 1964.

And Jesus was well over thirty years old when he was baptized, if we allow three years' ministry before his death A.D. 30.

Rightly has Christian tradition and art considered Jesus' baptism an important event in his life. It was a psychological crisis with him. Surely he had been subject to his parents long enough. His studies had been prosecuted to their practical completion. He was now prepared for his work, and when the clarion call of John rang out upon the startled Jordan side announcing that the kingdom of heaven was at hand, there was only one thing for Jesus to do.

Brushing aside John's protest that he had no sins to repent of, Jesus underwent John's baptism "to fulfill all righteousness." Or did Jesus mean, perhaps, "to carry out our Essene principle of righteousness"?

Baptism is the most significant religious ceremony known to man, especially in its primitive form, immersion. He is a hard soul indeed who can be solemnly plunged beneath the cleansing waters and raised again, without opening his spiritual eyes to a new life. The physical shock gives a thrilling emotional reaction. The moment was to the sensitive soul of Jesus almost overwhelming. He felt that the very heavens opened and that a voice said, "Thou art my beloved son, in thee I am well pleased."

He had long been calling God "Father": now he felt that God had called him "Son." It set the seal upon his mission. He believed that now the very spirit of God was in him, that it had descended upon his baptized head as gently as a dove.

The Temptation

And straightway that spirit drove him into the wilderness. How normal his "call" was! It would seem that every great religious leader "finds himself" and his God in the wilderness and sees his theophany there. All of them speak of a bright light shining—Moses and the burning bush, Zoroaster and the bright angel of Ahuramazda by the river Daiti, Buddha and the morning light through the Bo-tree branches, Paul dazed on the Damascus Road, Jesus and the opening heavens by the river Jordan.

Deeper into the wilderness Jesus must go, apart into a solitary place to think this thing through. The high point of the theophany must be succeeded by depressing days of doubt and temptation. Again, how normal and human! As to what actually happened in the wilderness, the gospel accounts do not agree. The oldest one, Mark's, says simply that he was there forty days with the wild beasts and that angels ministered unto him. Matthew and Luke have the devil appear in person presenting three temptations, but they differ as to the order and details. Recurring like a refrain, however, are the words of the tempter, "If thou *art* the son of God—"

That, then, was the temptation. At the moment of baptism he was sure he was the son of God, but when the ecstasy was over, he doubted. Nevertheless, assurance returned, and after the six weeks of deep meditation in the wilderness, the man who came out and began to preach, repeated John's message with an urgency and power that John never knew, "and they were all astonished at his teaching; for his word was with authority."

During his wilderness sojourn, Jesus evidently planned his public career, definitely deciding to cut loose altogether from his family and to follow John's example of proclaiming the Essene *Kerygma* of the coming of the kingdom. He would set out on a preaching tour of Galilee with a few chosen disciple-companions, train them, and then send them out to live and preach the gospel of the coming kingdom of the heavenly Father. As he came out of the unsettled country to the towns, he found news which must have tested his new resolve. John Baptist had been seized and put in prison for his fearless preaching. But Jesus never faltered in his purpose. Straight into the danger zone he went and proclaimed the gospel openly in the Galilean synagogues. Almost immediately he called four fishermen to leave their nets and follow him. Such was the power of his personality and his consciousness of divine guidance that they went after him unquestioningly.

The Day in Capernaum

Into the synagogue of Capernaum they followed him and heard him preach with electrifying power. They were accustomed to hearing the scribes discuss authorities, but here was one who seemed to be his own authority. A partly demented man, of the sort that seems to gravitate toward religious assemblies, sensed the difference from the usual type of service and cried out with an almost uncanny appreciation of the situation, "What have we to do with thee, Jesus thou Nazarene? art thou come to destroy us? I know thee who thou art, the Holy One of God!" Jesus immediately rebuked the interrupter, and his sharp tones of authority shocked the man into silence, if not into sanity. Eager for sensation, the excited audience hailed the occurrence as a miracle, and the news spread rapidly.

To escape the sudden unwelcome notoriety, Jesus went directly from the synagogue to the home of Simon Peter, one of his new disciples, only to meet the very thing he was fleeing from. Another event occurred which strengthened his new reputation as a healer. There was no miracle required to make a sick mother rise and minister to the needs of her sons and their new teacher who was honoring the home with a visit. But the synagogue incident had just occurred and miracle was in the air. At this fresh fuel the flame of excitement mounted higher, and by sunset the sick of the city were at the door.

Jesus, who would be a preacher, found himself unwillingly forced into the role of healer. Their pitiful condition and their insistence led him to lay hands on them. Mark says that many were cured. By the time Matthew wrote, the story had become that "he healed all that were sick." It is worth noting that all three mention that many of those treated were possessed with demons, by which may have been meant a form of mental or nervous disease, yielding to the commanding presence of a dominant personality. This is not to say that Jesus had no power to heal the sick. It is very evident that he did cure many. But we need not postulate miracles.

He was an unwilling healer, however. At daybreak, when the crowd, augmented by the spreading news of the coming of a new healer, returned to seek his aid, he was not there. Long before dawn he had stolen away into a desert place, to escape the crowds and to talk with his heavenly Father about this unexpected problem.

The Preacher

By the time Simon Peter had followed and found him and told him that everybody was seeking him, he had his decision ready, saying, "Let us go elsewhere into the next towns, that I may preach there also; for to this end came I forth." That is, he had decided that preaching rather than healing was his Father's business. Nevertheless, as he went out upon his lifework of preaching, Mark notes that he also cast out many demons.

It is quite possible that Jesus' preaching ministry lasted only a year before he too was arrested and killed as John Baptist had been. All the events recorded by Mark can be easily included in one year. The accounts of Matthew and Luke, if harmonized into one narrative, no easy task, would require about three years. The fourth gospel, which is a tract rather than a chronological biography, might take ten. Christian tradition has generally counted three years, which, if he was baptized A.D. 27, would make A.D. 30 the year of his death, at the age of thirty-six.

It was a brief public life at longest, and it is one of the most noteworthy things in the history of religion that such a short ministry should have so impressed the world that in three centuries Chris-

tianity overcame its rivals and became the official religion of the
Roman Empire and has for sixteen centuries since been the dominant religion of the civilized world.

The Message

What dynamic spiritual message did this man have? When we
examine his words and life, we find them puzzlingly simple. The
essence of his teaching is in the few pages of the so-called Sermon
on the Mount, which Matthew evidently compiled from the best-
known of his utterances, for we find parts of that sermon scattered
all through the other sources. And the Sermon on the Mount can
be summed up in six words, "Act like a child of God."

He taught his disciples not to retaliate for injuries received, but
to forgive as their loving Father would forgive them. When they
prayed, they were to say, "Our Father—" They were not to worry
about food, clothing, and shelter, for if God provided for even the
flowers and birds, he would care for his own children. They were
to seek first the kingdom of God. If they were sons of God, they
should ask for what they wanted, and God would give it to them.
In short, he let his followers know that he wanted them to act as if
they were children of God and live a perfect life. That was his whole
message, and in the inspiring fact that Jesus really expected them
so to act and believed them capable of doing so lay the secret of his
power with them.

When we look at his life, we find that he actually practiced so
faithfully what he preached, and really lived so nearly like his own
exalted conception of what God would do if God were a man, that
the opinion early arose among his followers and still persists among
the most of them that he was in reality God himself come down
upon earth for a little while among men. Other religionists have
deified their leaders, but Christians have been most successful because they have had a better leader to admire. Given such a life, it
was inevitable that his followers should early exhaust their vocabulary of praise and attribute godhood to him as the only adequate
explanation of his goodness. He lived like a son of God, and Christian theology has made him the unique and only Son of God, completely equal to his Father.

But certain of Jesus' own words are hard to reconcile with that
theology. If believing that Jesus was the only Son of the Father is

true Christianity, then there is a serious question as to whether or not Jesus himself was a Christian. For he was ever trying to get others to recognize themselves as children of the heavenly Father. He was more concerned with the idea of man becoming godlike than with the idea that he was God become manlike. When they called him Lord, he turned them from himself and urged them to do the will of the Father. When they called him good, he said plainly, "Why call ye me good; there is but one who is good, that is God." And he foretold that his followers would do greater things than he.

So Christendom has ever been divided, and probably will be for centuries yet, into a majority which believes Jesus to have been really God himself and a minority which believes him to have been a man who lived as if God were his Father and taught others to live that way. Those of the party of the majority have frequently said that those of the minority are not real Christians. The members of the minority have usually retorted that they hold to the religion of Jesus rather than the religion about Jesus. And there the matter hangs at present.

This same controversy exists in Buddhism, which is still divided into the Greater and the Lesser Vehicles.

Approaching Death

The path to Calvary and death can be traced back to the early ministry of Jesus. The black shadow of the castle of Machaerus where John Baptist languished lay athwart the very opening of the preaching campaign of Jesus. He worked feverishly, incessantly, to gather about himself a few disciples to whom his message might be transmitted before the inevitable end came.

A dozen men rallied around him at his call. Very quickly he instructed them in his teaching by taking them around with him as he preached. "Follow me," he said, "and I will make you fishers of men." As soon as he dared, he asked the group two questions and eagerly awaited the answers, to see if they had learned the great truth. Deliberately he centered their attention on himself. "Who do men say that I am?" And they answered, variously, John Baptist, Elijah, Jeremiah. Then with great trepidation he tested them and thereby his own teaching. "But who say ye that I am?"

And when Simon Peter thrilled him by replying, "Thou art the

Christ, the son of the living God," Jesus was so pleased and relieved that, according to one source, he praised Peter extravagantly and promised him the keys of heaven and said that upon this Peter, this *petra,* this rock, he would build his church. Then, as all three gospels, Mark, Matthew and Luke, agree in saying, from that time he began to get his disciples ready for his own coming death.

There is tremendous appeal in the picture of this man Jesus preparing his followers for his approaching death. One is reminded of Socrates. Jesus knew that he had won, though death was immediately before him. To him that death was incidental. He did not succeed at once in getting the disciples to understand that though he died, still he would live in them. The gates of hell could not prevent that.

They misunderstood. Even Peter, and especially Peter, protested vehemently that death should not claim the loved teacher. Jesus had to rebuke him. Later they understood, after his death, partly, but enough. Jesus knew that he would live again, after his death, in all those who would dare, as Peter did, to believe that a man could be a son of God—in all those who would deny themselves and take up their crosses and follow him. He who lost his life for the gospel, saved it. But the disciples made out of it later that at Cesarea Philippi, when Peter made his famous confession, Jesus was predicting his own bodily resurrection. Even so, they got enough of his great idea to pass it on to others.

The Last Week

With face set steadfastly toward Jerusalem, Jesus trod the path which led to the last week of his life. Yet he was so happy about it all that his disciples noticed that his countenance seemed transfigured with unearthly glory. Again he heard God saying to him as at his baptism, "This is my beloved son in whom I am well pleased." Passion week needs no retelling here. But it is well to point out that through his last days, like the dominant chord of a great symphony, runs Jesus' continual consciousness of God as his Father, sustaining him in his hours of trial.

When he cleansed the temple that last week, he did it because they had made his Father's house a house of merchandise. When he was agonizing in Gethsemane, he cried, "My Father, if it be possible, let this cup pass away from me: nevertheless, not as I will, but as Thou wilt."

When, however, Caiaphas asked him at his trial, "Art thou *the* son of God?" Jesus apparently disliked the form of the question, as implying "the *only* Son of God," and replied, in effect, "That is the way you say it, but what I say is that you will see the Son of Man seated at the right hand of Power, and coming on the clouds of heaven." This was a direct quotation from the heretical Book of Enoch, the 62nd chapter, so the High Priest said, "What more evidence do we need? This is blasphemy," and the council declared, "He deserves death."

And on the cross, in his last hours, this is what stood out against the blackness of the thing, that a man was dying, put to death for daring to call himself a son of God, and still, with all his last strength maintained it firmly. When he prayed, it was, "Father, forgive them, for they know not what they do."

They taunted him with it, saying, "He trusted on God; let Him deliver him now, if He desireth him: for he said, 'I am the son of God.'"

For a moment, doubt crept into his tortured spirit and he cried, "My God, my God, why hast Thou forsaken me?" But soon came triumph and peace and the great soul went out with the victorious prayer, "Father, into Thy hands I commend my spirit."

The epilogue was spoken by the Roman centurion, who voiced the verdict of history, "Truly this man was a son of God."

The Significance of Jesus to Religion

The new approach to the problems of religion and theology is the personal one. We study our personalities with the aid of all the sciences, especially psychology, and we discover certain elements, processes and laws. We examine the great prophets and leaders who have had a real religious experience and find in them a higher development of the same qualities and tendencies which we ourselves possess. In Jesus the religious consciousness was developed until it permeated his entire personality and he could say in moments of exaltation, "I and my Father are one." That was not a statement to be interpreted theologically but psychologically.

He had also his moments of depression, in the garden and on the cross. The transcendence of one's lower self by the higher is never to be accomplished without struggle, and Jesus was no exception. His will had a real, a mighty task. Quarantania and Gethsemane are no myths. As we come to understand him better, we shall find that these two records of how his personality grew will be more and more valuable to us. The crucifixion and resurrection stories appealed to the early Christian centuries because they were more spectacular. From the point of view of the achieving of character, the forty days of struggle in the wilderness and the short, keen agony in the garden are bound to rise in the esteem of the new Christian consciousness. He was a man, fighting a man's battles; with each victory his character grew stronger.

Jesus was more fully developed than we in many elements of his personality. He entered farther into the vast continent of the human soul than any other man. Like all early explorers, he made some mistakes. But he did know what was in man, because he had collected experimental data from within himself and had studied it carefully. His remarkably developed personality is compellingly attractive and inspiring. Even at this distance, when time and differing thought forms tend to separate him from modern folk, the memory of him saves them from the sin of the lesser good. He challenges men to live up to their possibilities: he calls them to their higher selves.

Was He Unique?

A great deal has been made of the uniqueness of Jesus. Today the word is the last entrenchment of those whose intellectual honesty has compelled them to give up the doctrine of his deity. But mere uniqueness is not a highly desirable quality. And if the records of Jesus' life tell us anything plainly, it is that uniqueness was the very thing he desired to avoid.

He would not have the crown at Galilee; when attention was drawn to himself, he quickly directed the attention toward God; he classed himself with repentant converts at John's baptism; he claimed that anyone who did the will of God was his own closest kin; and he rebuked those who emphasized his lordship while they neglected his message. He tried his best to proclaim his oneness with humanity. In fact, his message was plainly that he was not to be taken as unique, but rather as an example of what other men could be if they wished. His greatest concern was to convey to men the good news that they could have just that same intimacy with the Father that he had.

The Future Evaluation of Jesus

The next great "Life of Jesus" will forever dispose of the myth that the Man of Galilee was a god who came down to earth, a deity incarnate, bringing an absolutely new revelation to mankind.

Jesus will be seen by the men of tomorrow as a student of his national literature, possessed of its quaint superstitions and all its lore of demons and angels and seven heavens and the millennium, but possessed of its treasures as well. He will be known to have made few original additions to the ethics of his countrymen, but to have been so steeped in the literature of his own godly people that he remolded it into mosaics of sermons and explanatory parables so artistically and ethically beautiful that they will last as long as the race of men endures. Even more than that, he will be thought of, by the Jew and Gentile of tomorrow, as a man who really lived the best truth he knew, who took what he had read and thought, and interpreted it to humanity by embodying it in his own life. He successfully demonstrated truth by incarnating righteousness.

When men hereafter bow to him it will not be in homage to a deity but in recognition of a superior craftsman in the art of living.

IX

PAUL

[?–A.D. 62]

WHO INTERNATIONALIZED CHRISTIANITY

C HRISTIAN TRADITION, preserved in a book which was not included in the New Testament, gives us a word picture of Paul's
personal appearance which is not particularly flattering but certainly vivid. "The Acts of Paul and Thecla"[1] relates that on Paul's
first missionary journey in Galatia, when he fled from Antioch to
Iconium, he was met at Iconium by Onesiphorus, who was expecting the traveling preacher to stay at his house. There is a very
realistic description of the bustle and preparation of Onesiphorus
and his wife, Lectra. Their two children go with them to the
King's Highway, that Roman road through the provinces along
which Paul must come.

Titus, who was a sort of advance agent for Paul and preceded
him into most cities in order to arrange accommodations, had told
them the sort of man to expect, so Onesiphorus looked eagerly at
every stranger who came along the road,

And he saw Paul coming, a man little of stature, thin-haired upon
the head, crooked in the legs, of good state of body, with eyebrows join-
ing, and nose somewhat hooked, full of grace: for sometimes he appeared like a man, and sometimes he had the face of an angel. And
when Paul saw Onesiphorus he smiled, and Onesiphorus said: "Hail,

1 See the Apocryphal N.T., translated by M. R. James, pp. 270–281.

thou servant of the blessed God." And he [Paul] said: "Grace be with thee and with thine house."

There were, however, two traveling companions with Paul whose jealousy spoiled the good fellowship of the arrival. Demas and Hermogenes were "full of hypocrisy and flattered Paul as though they loved him." He knew their character but had endeavored to improve their dispositions by preaching to them all along the road from Antioch. Their small souls, however, were stirred to envy by the fact that Onesiphorus did not call them also "servants of the blessed God." He had been looking for Paul and evidently knew nothing about any traveling companions. In the surprise of finding Paul accompanied he may have seemed inhospitable. When they said, "Are we not servants of the blessed God that thou didst not salute us so?" he replied dryly, "I see not in you any fruit of righteousness, but if ye be such, come ye also into my house and rest yourself."

To the home of Onesiphorus the little party went, and "there was great joy and bowing of knees and breaking of bread." After the meal, Paul preached in the house at intervals for several days. The people crowded around, and among those who listened was a young woman named Thecla, with whose adventures as Paul's traveling companion, the rest of the book is concerned.

The authenticity of this book is questioned, partly because it contains many incredible miracles. Besides, the Bible account of Paul's visit to Iconium says nothing of Demas and Hermogenes, giving Barnabas as Paul's companion. But the description of the meeting of Paul and his host is so veridical that it is possible we have here the preservation of a tradition based upon an eyewitness account.

"The Acts of Paul and Thecla" is but one section of "The Acts of Paul," a popular Christian storybook of the second century, much longer than the Bible storybook mostly about Paul named "The Acts of the Apostles." Several new manuscript fragments of the very interesting "Acts of Paul," one of eleven pages in Greek, filling in gaps in the Coptic version used by Dr. M. R. James, have lately been discovered, and these additions are included by Dr. J. W. B. Barns in the new revised 1955 version of Dr. James's book.

These newly discovered pages (in the Hamburg papyrus codex) give us further details of the charming legend (elsewhere tantalizingly referred to by the Church Fathers) of the lion with which Paul made friends in the mountains and even baptized at the digni- fied beast's request. The lion later, in the arena, refused, of course, to harm Paul, his pal, and conversed casually with him, as follows,

"Are you the lion I baptized?"

"Yes, Paul."

"Well, how did you get caught?"

"Same way you did, Paul."

Then a terrible hailstorm drives the arena crowd home, one sharp hailstone slicing off the ear of Hieronymus, the Governor of Ephe- sus, who had condemned Paul to the lions because the governor's wife had shown too much interest in the captive. Paul escapes to Macedonia after saying goodbye to the lion, which stalks sedately home to his mountains.

Tertullian (160–220) asserts that a church official of Asia com- posed "The Acts of Paul" and was on that account deposed from office as an impostor. But the book is very early and was written probably about A.D. 160, which was not long after the composition of the last books of the New Testament.

Even if parts of it are made up out of whole cloth the talented author may have had access to and made a copy of some trustworthy document which has otherwise perished. At any rate, this descrip- tion of Paul in "The Acts of Paul and Thecla" has been generally accepted by Christian tradition. It cannot be contradicted, for there is in the New Testament no description of Paul. The scanty refer- ences we have corroborate rather than contradict it. We know, for instance, that when Paul and Barnabas went on from Iconium to Lystra the people of that place said, "The gods are come down to us in the likeness of men." They called Barnabas, Jupiter, and Paul, Mercury. Now, Mercury was traditionally pictured as noticeably smaller than the rest of the gods, which corroborates the book's phrase, "little of stature."

Abnormal or Genius?

When we turn from the description of Paul's physical appearance to a study of his character we find ourselves in the presence of one of the great men of history. Paul's personality was rich and com- plex, difficult to analyze or classify. He would have been a most in- teresting subject for a modern psychiatrist or psychoanalyst, for in the accounts we have of his words and actions, especially in his own confessions in his intimate letters to his little groups of disciples, there are traces of sadism, masochism, dual personality, recurrent trance states and other pathological conditions. There were times when his spirit seemed to hover on the borderland between insanity and genius. Sometimes we are reminded of Akhenaten, whose abnormal body housed an extremely sensitive soul, and again, when Paul is reciting his sufferings, we notice his similarity to Jeremiah.

Paul's internal conflicts, which produced these various evidences of a disturbed mind, were due to the fact that in his own person, as on a miniature battlefield, the great religious and philosophical forces of his time struggled for supremacy. It was Paul's ability to make the transition from narrow Judaism to a world-wide religion that made Christianity possible. He was a Jew of the Jews, a Pharisee of the Pharisees, and yet he was a Roman citizen, which meant at that time a citizen of the world.

Paul's Idea of Jesus

Paul had his own ideas about Jesus which differed quite radically from those of the disciples of Jesus. He was therefore in continual conflict with the Jewish Christians, and they were responsible for much of his persecution. Where did Paul get his own peculiar concept and knowledge of Jesus? He claimed it was from Jesus himself. But although Paul was probably born about the same time as Jesus and lived in Jerusalem for some time during the Galilean's lifetime, there is no record of his ever having met him.

Paul was very insistent that he did not get his impression of Jesus from the twelve disciples. He claimed that a special disclosure was made to him: that Jesus appeared to him in a "heavenly vision" sometime after the crucifixion and that therefore he had the highest authority for his interpretation of Jesus' mission to the world. It was a "revelation," outranking the mere stories about Jesus—what he did and what he said.

Paul was even responsible for the name "Christ" being attached to Jesus. That is not to say that the name had not been applied to Jesus by others than Paul, for the word "Christos" is simply the Greek form of "Messiah." But it was Paul's work in the Roman world which was responsible for the fact that we today refer to the

Galilean as Jesus Christ, an Anglicized Greek form of his name which Yeshuah bar Yosef never heard.

Although Jesus and Paul were contemporaries and were brought up in Jewish homes, there was a great difference in their early environment, the difference between a country town and a metropolitan center.

Tarsus "No Mean City"

Tarsus was a city of half a million inhabitants in the province of Cilicia, which is now included in Armenia. It was important, not only as a trade center, ten miles from the coast at the entrance to the passes northward into Asia Minor, but also as the seat of a great university, not as large as those in Alexandria and Athens, but known throughout the Roman world. Besides being a commercial and educational center, Tarsus was a free city. For more than a century it had not been subject to the Roman land tax. It did not have a Roman garrison and was thus raised above the rank of the colonial city. It even had the control of its own financial system, and its citizens were responsible to no one outside the city.

The effect of this freedom can hardly be appreciated today by those who take the autonomy of cities for granted. Not to feel any subjection to an outside authority, not to have the soldiers of a foreign power walking the streets as in Jerusalem, had produced an atmosphere of independence. The *esprit de corps* of the citizens was excellent. Because they were free and masters of their own destiny they were naturally anxious to make their city progressively better. Tarsus in the first century of our era was a good place in which to live. Paul might well say boastingly, "I am a man which am a Jew of Tarsus, a city in Cilicia, a citizen of no mean city."

Paul's Boyhood

Since the fact that Paul spent his boyhood in Tarsus has a direct bearing upon the character of Christianity, even down to the present day, it is regrettable that we do not have the records of his youth, but since we know what Tarsus was like, and since we know what Paul's disposition and characteristics were, we are able to construct an imaginative picture of the young Jewish boy in the free Cilician city. Paul, like Jeremiah, was conscious of having been

dedicated to his lifework from his mother's womb.[2] Without postu-
lating any providential prearrangement we can still appreciate the
four ways in which the boy's early environment was remarkably
calculated to prepare him for the great work he had to do in the
world.

He was brought up in the traditions of the Jews, as was necessary
for one who was to preach salvation through Jesus, the Jew. He
was trained to manual labor which enabled him to appreciate the
problems of the artisan class among whom Christianity was most
likely to spread rapidly. The city in which he grew up was a center
for the dissemination of those philosophies which were current in
the world where he was to work. And fourth, and perhaps most
importantly, it was also a gathering place of devotees of certain
mystic cults and mystery religions, which afforded Paul a pattern
for the religion he was to organize.

Paul was proud of the fact that he was "circumcised the eighth
day, of the stock of Israel, of the tribe of Benjamin, an Hebrew of
the Hebrews; as touching the law, a Pharisee." When he was at
home he spoke Aramaic, a sort of dialect of Hebrew, but widely
known; probably the first "Yiddish." This prepared him to make
public speeches to the Jews in their synagogues as he later had occasion to do many times. He learned also the ancient Hebrew in
which the Scriptures were written.

His quotations from the Old Testament, however, are mostly
made from the Septuagint, or Greek version. This was not inconsistent with his Jewish training because the Septuagint supplemented the Hebrew version among the Jews of the Diaspora—that
is, the Jews who had been dispersed from Palestine and were residing in other parts of the Roman world. Since Greek was the *lingua
franca,* or *koine,* the common language of commerce and literature,
the Jews had been obliged to learn it for trade purposes. Many of
them had been long away from Jerusalem and had associated with
the Gentiles so much that they were unable to read Hebrew, so this
Septuagint version had been made for them in Alexandria about
250 B.C.

Paul's letters are sprinkled with sentences which prove how much
he appreciated his Jewish home and kindred. He was indoctrinated
in their legends and lore and was brought up according to the
strictest sort of Judaism. The Pharisees were meticulous in their

2 Compare Galatians, 1:15, 16: Jeremiah, 1:4, 6.

observance of the minute points of the law. They were deeply concerned over the depth of the fringe of their garments, and held
long debates over minor matters of the law. He said later, "Where-
fore the law was our schoolmaster to bring us unto Christ."

Tarsus was famous for its manufacture of cilicium, a very dura-
ble coarse fabric woven from goat's hair. It was used not only for
making tents but for mats and even clothing. The making of tents
from this rough cloth was hard work, but it assured a workman em-
ployment in almost any town in that part of the world. We know
that it later afforded Paul his means of livelihood during his missionary wanderings. He was, in a sense, a journeyman member of
the then unorganized international tent and garment workers'
union. When he said, "Ye, yourselves, know that these hands have
ministered unto my necessities," he probably held out his hands to
them, roughened and stained as they were from his work upon the
coarse cloth. The democracy of Christianity was assured by the fact
that its first great missionary was the horny-handed laborer, Paul.

It is not necessary to infer that Paul's parents were laboring
people. They may have been, but the fact that Paul was born a
Roman citizen points in the other direction. If he was born a Roman citizen, his father must have been a Roman citizen, and
citizenship was not often held by the artisan class. But the Jewish
people of the day had an excellent custom which required that all
boys, no matter what rank their parents held, and no matter for
what professions the boys might be intended, were required to learn
some useful trade. As an apprentice in some workshop in Tarsus,
the boy learned other things besides tent-making. He came in contact with the teeming life of the city and was exposed to educative
influences which were not Jewish.

The philosophy of the first century A.D. included more than
what is technically known as philosophy today. It was not purely
metaphysical but was largely concerned with physics and ethics.
What few simple facts were known about the properties of matter
were used to illustrate principles of conduct. Great discussions were
held. It appears that the Stoic and Cynic philosophies were the
topic of conversation, not only in the university, but even in the
barbershops and on the street corners.

Tarsus was full of famous teachers of Stoic philosophy.[3] Strabo
placed it above Athens and Alexandria for the quality of its philo-

3 Strabo, 14:10. 13–15.

sophic teaching. Many graduates of the University of Tarsus were
teaching the Stoic philosophy in Rome. The Stoics were named
from the "Stoa" or porch, the roofed colonnade surrounding the
market place of Greek cities and sometimes extending into the
principal streets. In the shelter of this porch the teachers of philosophy walked around, surrounded by groups of their pupils. A bright
Jewish boy like Paul would naturally be attracted by these groups
of men and would draw near to listen to their discussions.

Besides, a subtler and greater influence was the very spirit of the
city itself. There seems to have been no great antagonism between
town and gown, and most of the pupils at the University of Tarsus
were natives of the city. Consequently the whole city was a university. However exclusive the Jews might hold themselves in such
a community, its atmosphere was bound to seep into their lives.

It is quite possible that Paul attended the University of Tarsus
for a period, for he later showed himself familiar with the various
philosophies of his time. When he made his famous speech on Mars
Hill he revealed his acquaintance with the works of the poet Aratus
who had lived in Tarsus in the third century B.C., and in his letter
to Titus (1:12) he may have referred to Epimenides. It is possible
also to find similarities between Paul's teachings and the teachings
of the Stoics.[4] Furthermore, the arguments in Paul's letters resemble much more in form and expression the rhetoric of the Stoics
and Cynics than they do the forms of exposition used by the rabbis.

The Roman world of the time of Paul was eager to try out new
religions. When Paul spoke on Mars Hill he is reported in the
Authorized Version to have said, "Ye men of Athens, I perceive that
in all things ye are too superstitious." That is a poor translation.
Paul was too wise a public speaker to antagonize his audience at
the outset of a speech. A much better translation of his words is "I
perceive that in all things you are very religious." An editorial note
by the author of the Book of Acts states in explanation that "all
the Athenians and strangers which were there spent their time in
nothing else, but either to tell, or to hear some new thing." That
spirit was not confined to Athens. Tarsus, as a university center full
of eager seekers for knowledge, would be especially hospitable to
new religions.

Among the most popular of the cults of the day were the various
mystery religions, so-called because their rites could not be under-

[4] Bishop Lightfoot, *Commentary on the Philippians.*

stood by outsiders. Their mysterious ceremonies were only for initiates. A common element in such religions was the processions and ceremonials dramatizing the death and rebirth of some god; the most popular in Tarsus was allegedly Sandan. Processions gathered in the city and marched mournfully to some place in the country bewailing the death of their god. After a period they would return rejoicing because of the resurrection of their deity.

Very few boys can resist the attraction of a public procession. There can be little doubt that the Jewish boy, even if he did not witness the actual rites performed outside the city, must have been impressed by the difference between the attitude of the mourners who went out of the city and that of the devotees who returned rejoicing. Considering the various influences of the great city upon the growing boy, it is doubtful that he could have lived in any environment better calculated to prepare him for his great task of welding into one conquering faith the various religions and philosophies of his time.

Paul and Gamaliel

Many ambitious Jewish parents in the provinces who desired to prepare their sons to be rabbis sent them to Jerusalem to study under the various famous teachers in the city. Paul was evidently sent earlier than the usual age. Doubtless the brilliancy of learning which he later displayed was already appearing in his early teens. The natural reluctance of the parents at sending so young a boy more than five hundred miles away from home was probably somewhat diminished by the fact that he was to live with his sister. We know that he was very young when he went to Jerusalem because in a speech there many years later he said that he had been "brought up in this city at the feet of Gamaliel." And we know that he had a sister in Jerusalem because he was saved from assassination later by a message carried to an important official by that sister's son.

Paul, the Persecutor

There is a gap in our information about the life of Paul. At one moment we see him, a brilliant young student, sitting at the feet of Gamaliel studying the law of Moses. The next, he is breathing out threatenings and slaughter against the heretical new sect of

"Followers of the Way," disciples of the recently crucified Galilean. What caused the change? Was the reason for his persecuting them intellectual or emotional? Probably it was really emotional but he thought it intellectual—that is, he rationalized his emotions.

Paul was ever one to be enthusiastic about the thing in which he was immediately engaged. His study of the law in the temple at Jerusalem at the feet of Gamaliel had inflamed him with a holy zeal for a punctilious observance of the minutest requirements of it. When he came in contact with a sect whose leader had said, "Ye have heard that it was said to them of old time, but I say unto you . . ." and who had warned men to beware of the "leaven of the Pharisees," it was something not to be endured, for the leaven of the Pharisees was Paul's daily bread.

Just when or how he came into conflict with the followers of Jesus is not known. If he studied under Gamaliel from the time he was thirteen until he began persecuting the followers of Jesus he must have been in Jerusalem when Jesus was tried and crucified. But we know from his letters that he never saw Jesus in the flesh, so he probably was absent from the city, perhaps visiting his home in Tarsus, when the drama of Passion Week was enacted. It may have been upon his return to the city of Jerusalem after such a visit that he first became aware of the new sect. In other words, the crucifixion advertised the fact that there existed such a sect. Most of the Nazarene's preaching was in Galilee, Samaria, and Perea, and probably the circle of zealous students of the law in the Jerusalem temple had not been aware of important events that were taking place to the northward, or perhaps considered them of no great consequence.

It was a very few weeks after the crucifixion that Peter preached his famous sermon which resulted in the conversion of three thousand. The account in Acts says,

They then that received his word were baptized: and there were added unto them in that day about three thousand souls. And they continued steadfastly in the apostles' teaching and fellowship, in the breaking of bread and the prayers. And fear came upon every soul: and many wonders and signs were done through the apostles. And all that believed were together, and had all things common; and they sold their possessions and goods, and parted them to all, according as any man had need. And day by day, continuing steadfastly with one accord in the temple.

and breaking bread at home, they took their food with gladness and singleness of heart, praising God and having favor with all people. And the Lord added to them day by day those that were saved.

It was evidently during the period of the rapid expansion of the little group of disciples that Paul returned to Jerusalem and discovered what was going on. He was tremendously disturbed by what he found. It seemed to him the rankest heresy. His intense nature demanded action and he was evidently the leader of the younger and more violent group of Pharisees who set about a systematic persecution of the new sect. Very likely if Paul had been in Jerusalem at the time of the trial and crucifixion of Jesus his voice would have been the loudest of those crying, "Crucify him, Crucify him."

Matters came to a crisis when one of the young followers of Jesus, named Stephen, debated successfully against those who were persecuting him. The account includes among those who disputed with Stephen, "they of Cilicia and of Asia," so it is quite possible that Paul and Stephen may have engaged in debate. But Stephen won. We read that "they were not able to resist the wisdom and spirit by which he spake."

That was the last straw. It was bad enough for these heretics to be preaching their new faith among the common people and winning them by thousands, but to have one of their representatives, probably in front of a large assembly, defeat in debate the defenders of the law, was something which required desperate measures at once. Stephen, at least, must be put out of the way. Men were hired to assert that they had heard Stephen blaspheme. He was arrested and brought before the council. The false witnesses openly accused him of speaking blasphemy against the temple and the law. The accusation was completed by the statement, "We have heard him say that this Jesus of Nazareth shall destroy this place and shall change the customs which Moses delivered to us."

The eyes of all turned toward Stephen "and all that sat in the council looking steadfastly on him saw his face as it had been the face of an angel." When Stephen was asked if the charge were true, he made a learned and convincing speech. At the very end, however, with an almost foolhardy bravery, he turned upon the council, calling them stiff-necked and resisters of the Holy Spirit, and asked dramatically, "Which of the prophets have not your fathers persecuted? and they have slain them which shewed before the coming of the Just One; of whom ye have been now the betrayers and murderers."

At this accusation his persecutors were so angry that they "gnashed on him with their teeth," but before they could stop him he got in his final dramatic climax. Gazing skyward, he said, "Behold, I see the heavens opened, and the Son of Man standing at the right hand of God."

This was not a mere rhetorical flourish: it was a cue, a signal, almost a war cry. In the light of the Qumran Library contents, we understand better why this particular statement by Stephen should have sent the council members into such a frenzy that they stoned Stephen forthwith. For we see now that it was the same key sentence of the Essene sect, a mantra repeatedly found in their Book of Enoch (62:1–14, 69:26–29, 71:14–17), uttered by Jesus himself before the same council (Matthew 26:59–68) which led to his crucifixion.

As the brave Stephen expired, he cried out, "Lord Jesus, receive my spirit. Lord, lay not this sin to their charge." "And the witnesses laid down their clothes at a young man's feet, whose name was Saul."[5]

"As for Saul, he made havoc of the church, entering into every house, and haling men and women committed them to prison." If a modern psychiatrist were presented with a case for analysis of a young man "breathing out threatenings and slaughter," going from house to house haling men and women to prison because of his opposition to their religion, the psychiatrist would be apt to say that the actions were not due so much to theological conviction as to psychopathic inclination.

We are not told in the scriptures that Paul killed anyone with his own hands. Nor are we told the contrary. We do know that he was guilty of murder when he stood by at the stoning of Stephen. There may have been some mental satisfaction to the young rabbinical student in seeing these blasphemers and heretics done to death, but he probably interpreted it as a righteous vindication of the truth and a defense of the revealed law of God. He could point to Deuteronomy 13:6–11, where it was commanded that heretics should be stoned to death. His defeat, or the defeat of his friends, in the debate with Stephen may have been the immediate cause of the arous-

[5] Saul or Shaul was Paul's Hebrew name.

ing of his anger to the point where he was ready to act. When once he had consented to Stephen's death, the die was cast, and he threw himself into the persecution with characteristic enthusiasm. It appears that his crusade received the sanction of the authorities and was soon carried on outside Jerusalem.

Paul's Conversion

On the road to Damascus, whither he was riding posthaste upon this mission, an event occurred which changed his whole life and, indeed, greatly affected the history of Christendom. There are three accounts of this single event in the Book of Acts (9:1–31, 22:3–21, 26:9–20). They differ in rather important details, and a comparison of the King James and Revised Standard versions of Acts 9:5 and 6 reveals how the new version eliminates the clumsy attempts of pious editors to reconcile the three accounts by inserting parts of the second and third in the first. These details may not matter so much, except to the literalists (and the psychiatrists); what matters most is the effect of the experience on Paul. From his own comments concerning it in his letters to the Corinthians (I Cor. 9:1, 15:8) and Galatians (1:15–16) it appears that he was thereafter forever convinced that he had actually seen Jesus, the Jesus whose followers he was then persecuting and who had been crucified months before.

It is evident to the student of comparative religion that we have here a typical theophany. Paul says that he saw a great light and that he heard Jesus saying to him, "Saul, Saul, why persecutest thou me? . . . It is hard for thee to kick against the pricks."

Some of the circumstances are important. Paul had evidently been working very zealously in his work of persecution. He was hurrying to Damascus and, unwisely, was traveling at noontime, contrary to the custom in Palestine. There may have been physical conditions conducive to a mental and emotional upset. Zealous as Paul was for persecuting the followers of Jesus, he must have been impressed by the calm manner in which they met their death. The serene beauty of the face of the dying Stephen doubtless haunted the emotional Paul. The cogent arguments by which Stephen had defended his new-found faith must also have impressed the logical Paul.

The cataclysmic experience as he neared Damascus was probably the eruption of pent-up, subconscious doubts as to the wisdom of his course and the sudden realization that the truth was on the side of his victims. Whether he saw an actual light or not is hard to tell. One account says that those with him heard the voice but saw no light. Another account turns it about and relates that they saw the light but heard no voice. The shock of the experience weakened him, and they had to lead him into the city. The young man who had left Jerusalem to bring back with him the bound victims of his wrath entered Damascus a changed man.

Any modern interpretation of this experience of Paul's must discount the appraisal which Paul and his contemporaries made of it. Their knowledge of psychology was exceedingly limited. "Greek and Roman, as well as Jew, then firmly believed that the spirit of the departed could become visible to the human eye and exert a powerful influence in the affairs of men. They also believed the gods could enter and dwell in men and direct their thoughts and words and acts."[6] Paul was convinced not only that he had seen the spirit of Jesus but that that spirit had entered into him. Throughout the rest of his life he felt that the spirit of Jesus was really abiding in his body in conflict with the spirit of sin and death, which, alas, also abode there. Another gap occurs here in our knowledge of the life of Paul. Very little information has been preserved for us concerning the next fifteen years. Paul says that for the first three years of the fifteen he remained in the neighborhood of Damascus. In Acts it is stated he joined the church there.

There is some discrepancy as to the cause of his leaving Damascus. In Acts 9:23–28 it is stated that the Jews of Damascus tried to kill Paul, but that his friends let him down from the city wall in a basket and that he went to Jerusalem, where he was received with suspicion on account of his former activities, until Barnabas championed his cause. Then he was welcomed at Jerusalem and preached there. But Paul himself, in his second letter to the Corinthians, says that it was the Governor of Damascus who tried to seize him and from whom he escaped in the basket let down by the wall. It is quite possible that Paul's manner had made him enemies in more than one quarter and that he was fleeing from both Jews and Syrian officials.

From Luke's account one would infer that he went to Jerusalem

[6] Kent, *The Work and Teachings of the Apostles*, p. 76.

very shortly after his conversion and stayed for some years, but Paul himself, in his letter to the Galatians, says distinctly that immediately after his conversion he did not go up to Jerusalem but went into Arabia and then returned to Damascus, and that it was two or three years after his return to Damascus before he went up to Jerusalem to see Peter, with whom he stayed for fifteen days. He specifically states also that he saw no other of the Apostles except James. After the fortnight visit in Jerusalem he says he went into the regions of Syria and Cilicia and preached the faith which once he destroyed.

Of this period of twelve years that he spent in Syria and Cilicia we know little save that he was preaching and that it was a time of great trial. In the second letter to the Corinthians he refers to some of those experiences, "Of the Jews five times received I forty stripes save one. Thrice was I beaten with rods, once was I stoned, thrice I suffered shipwreck, a night and a day I have been in the deep; In journeyings often, in perils of waters, in perils of robbers, in perils by mine own countrymen, in perils by the heathen, in perils in the city, in perils in the wilderness, in perils in the sea, in perils among false brethren; In weariness and painfulness, in watchings often, in hunger and thirst, in fastings often, in cold and nakedness." These twelve years were Paul's training for his later work. It was a rigorous school.

One other glimpse he gives us of something which happened during that period. He wrote the second letter to the Corinthians sometime between 52 and 54 A.D. In the twelfth chapter of that letter he speaks of a peculiar experience he had had fourteen years previously, which would bring it into the middle of this twelve-year period. He says,

It is not expedient for me doubtless to glory. I will come to visions and revelations of the Lord. I knew a man in Christ above fourteen years ago (whether in the body I cannot tell; or whether out of the body I cannot tell: God knoweth); such an one caught up to the third heaven. And I knew such a man (whether in the body, or out of the body, I cannot tell: God knoweth); How that he was caught up into paradise, and heard unspeakable words, which it is not lawful for a man to utter. Of such an one will I glory: yet of myself I will not glory, but in mine infirmities. For though I would desire to glory, I shall not be a fool; for I will say the truth: but now I forbear, lest any man should think of me above that which he seeth me to be, or that he heareth of me.

And lest I should be exalted above measure, through the abundance of the revelations, there was given to me a thorn in the flesh, the messenger of Satan to buffet me, lest I should be exalted above measure. For this thing I besought the Lord thrice, that it might depart from me. And he said unto me, My grace is sufficient for thee: for my strength is made perfect in weakness. Most gladly therefore will I rather glory in my infirmities, that the power of Christ may rest upon me.

Paul's Trip to Heaven

The "man in Christ" we know was himself. He speaks of that man in the third person for several verses, but by the time we reach the "thorn in the flesh" we discover it is himself that he is talking about. This passage is one of several seemingly obscure sections in the New Testament which are illuminated by a knowledge of certain books which once were considered scripture but are not now in our Bible.

When one reads these first verses of the twelfth chapter of Second Corinthians, he seems to be moving in the midst of different thought forms. The "third heaven" and "paradise" appear to have been familiar concepts to Paul and his fellow Christians. It is when we read the Essene "Book of Enoch," which Dr. R. H. Charles, of Oxford and Westminster, called Paul's *"vade mecum"* (constant companion), that we really understand Paul's phraseology and ideology.

This circle of ideas was not distinctly Jewish nor distinctly Christian, but was an importation from Zoroastrianism into Christianity, by way of the Essene teachings. Zoroaster made several visits to the heavens and attempted to describe the unutterable mysteries which he beheld there. The "principalities and powers" who intervened between Zoroaster and his Lord Mazda were what Paul referred to in Romans 8:38 as unable to separate him from his Lord Christ. But between Zoroaster and Paul were the Essene writers of the Enochan books in which these "principalities and powers" and other celestial, semidivine "angels," spirits, influences, and intermediate beings are fully described, especially in chapter 61 of I Enoch and chapter 20 of II Enoch.

From Zoroaster's time to the present there has been a long series of alleged visits to heaven. The last book of the Bible is a record of such an experience. One coming to a reading of the Book of Revelation from a perusal of ancient Zoroastrian scriptures finds himself still in the same world.

We are somewhat confused by the fact that Paul seems to use the "third heaven" and "paradise" as synonymous terms for the same place. A little knowledge of the geography of the heavens, as pictured by the people of Paul's day, enables us to understand this circumstance. There were supposed to be a number of heavens above the earth, arranged like a great layer cake. The plural form "heavens" appears nearly ninety times in the New Testament. When Paul used "third heaven" and "paradise" synonymously he was presuming among the Corinthians the knowledge that paradise was in the third heaven. Strangely enough, hell was there too, and the inhabitants of paradise might converse with the suffering sinners in hell, as we learn from the account of Dives and Lazarus in the sixteenth chapter of Luke. And it was to the paradise in the third heaven that Jesus was confident he and the penitent thief would go.

Some authors said there were three; some maintained there were seven; and the most elaborate geography of the interstellar spaces describes ten heavens. (Three, seven and ten have always been sacred numbers. Nearly every religion of the world speaks in terms of these numbers or their combination.) Seven, however, appears to have been the favorite number of heavens.

Paul was widely read in the apocalyptic literature, of which the Book of the Secrets of Enoch is a good example. We know this from the many quotations in his letters which parallel passages in this literature.[7] It is quite likely that he had been studying the eighth, ninth and tenth chapters of this book just before he had this vision, and that his dream was made vivid by that imagery. He seems to have been quite confident that this vision of paradise came to him from God. He admits feeling rather elated over it, and it doubtless made a great impression upon him. He recognized it as a divine seal upon his work—a sort of assurance from God that His blessing would attend him.

[7] Compare the last part of the eighth chapter of Romans with the twentieth chapter of the Secrets of Enoch, in the various editions, translations, interpretations, and commentaries by Charles and Morfill, 1893, Charles and Forbes, 1913, Bonwetsch, 1896, 1922, Vaillant, 1952, Bonsirven, 1953, and Potter, 1958.

The Thorn in the Flesh

Paul had some physical difficulty which troubled him greatly, and he really believed that it was sent to him lest he should glory too much over his having been permitted to see the heavens. He says, "Lest I should be exalted above measure through the abundance of revelations there was given to me a thorn in the flesh, the messenger of Satan to buffet me." Just what this thorn or stake in the flesh was, has been discussed for centuries, but as Paul himself did not choose to tell, it is useless to speculate.

It is vastly more significant to note Paul's attitude toward this physical infirmity. He grew to glory in it. Whatever its nature, it was something which caused him intense suffering. His words convey the idea that he was impaled upon a stake of torture, but he actually grew to derive pleasure from this as from all his sufferings. The fifth, ninth and tenth verses of II Cor.: 12 are very important for an interpretation of Paul's temperament. It is evident to a person at all familiar with modern psychiatric theories that Paul's pleasure in his sufferings indicated masochistic tendencies.

The fierce, almost sadistic pleasure he had taken in the persecutions of the followers of "The Way" had, by this time, become inverted, and he was taking pleasure in his own sufferings. It is an abnormal state of mind, but one which is comparatively common. We are all familiar with certain self-made martyrs who glory in their sufferings, and Paul simply had this eccentricity to an exaggerated degree. Consequently, when we are inclined to admire Paul for "glorying in his infirmities" we must qualify our admiration by recognizing the semi-pathological nature of his state of mind. Furthermore, we become suspicious of a theology, based on Paul's personal pains, which tells us that the more we suffer, the better purified we are, and therefore the likelier we are to reach his paradise in the third heaven.[8]

8 But we must admit that Paul's dogma has a modern parallel, or vindication, or at least a good sermonic analogy, in that at present any man who would essay the ionosphere must suffer quite a bit first in very uncomfortable quarters.

The third heaven analogy could easily be extended, for modern research recognizes at least three layers in the ionosphere, already named D, E, and F, roughly 50, 75, and 100 miles up, formed by the sun's electromagnetic radiation. But no golden heaven space platform has yet been found in Layer F. We do hear music from the ionosphere, but it is of earthly origin, the bounced waves from our radio stations, bent back by the free electrons in the E and F layers.

Preparing to Preach

During this period of a dozen years or more, when Paul went about Syria and Cilicia, it is probable that he spent some time in Tarsus, and in other cities, studying everything which seemed important in connection with his lifework.

Gradually there was forming within him the consciousness that he was to be a great missionary to the Gentiles. With such feverish activity did he devote himself to his studies that his abnormal condition was aggravated. Later on, a Roman official who was examining him stated it was his opinion that "much learning" had made Paul mad. While the judgment was indignantly repudiated by Paul, it is, nevertheless, pertinent as an indication of the opinion of a contemporary.

While Paul was at his studies in Tarsus he was sought out by Barnabas, who asked him to go with him to Antioch and assist in a new project there.

Up to this time, almost all of the preaching about Jesus had been done among the Jews themselves. When Peter delivered his famous sermon at Pentecost there were in his audience Jews from all parts of the eastern Mediterranean area. When they returned to their homes they carried the new gospel with them. Besides, many other Jews fled abroad from the persecution which Paul superintended.

The persecution of this new heresy had really extended it. In an attempt to stamp out the fire, Paul had only scattered the sparks, and each spark started up a new fire.

Antioch

The new gospel spread only in the Jewish quarters of the Gentile cities until certain men from Cyprus and Cyrene went to Antioch and tried the experiment of preaching to the Greeks there. "And the hand of the Lord was with them, and a great number believed and turned unto the Lord."

Antioch was another great free city. It was the third or fourth largest in the Roman Empire at the time and had probably nearly a million inhabitants. Attached to the large Jewish synagogue there, were a number of Greeks who had adopted Judaism. It was probably among these Greeks and their friends that the new gospel received its first Gentile hearing. In the liberal atmosphere of Antioch the new faith made rapid progress, but that progress raised a great question which later caused considerable trouble to Paul. Should the Gentiles who became followers of Jesus be obliged to become converts to Judaism first?

It seemed to be taken for granted at first that they should, and it was only after a long and bitter controversy that Paul succeeded later in eliminating that requirement. When the news first reached Jerusalem that the gospel was being preached among the Greeks, great interest was aroused, and Barnabas was sent to investigate the situation. He was so impressed that he went to Tarsus to get Paul to aid him. Barnabas remembered how boldly Paul had preached at Damascus and knew that this was just the type of person needed at Antioch. And Paul was glad to see Barnabas because the latter had befriended him on his first visit to Jerusalem. The two were soon hard at work at Antioch. For a year they labored with gratifying results. "And the disciples were called Christians first at Antioch."

Who Named the "Christians"?

Commentators have asserted that the word *Christian* was a nickname given to the followers of Jesus by outsiders (just as ostentatiously pious and goody-goody boys in college are termed "Christers"), but perhaps Paul was the one to apply this name to them. Paul was not so much interested in Jesus as he was in Christ. He appears to have been little concerned with the life and teachings of Jesus. His faith was built upon the vision he had had on the Damascus road: the vision of the risen and glorified anointed one, the *Christos*. Since he knew that Jesus had died on the cross in Jerusalem, there was only one inference to be drawn—namely, that in spite of the crucifixion, Jesus was now alive in heaven; therefore the man Jesus had become the God, Christ.

It was Christ and Him crucified and resurrected that Paul preached for the rest of his life: not the Galilean carpenter-teacher but the supernatural being who had come from God and had returned to God. Doubtless, during that year at Antioch, his preaching rang the changes on that theme. He pointed out to the little band of disciples that they were followers of the Christ. This new way of life was the Christian way, and they were therefore Christians. The fact that Paul's year of preaching in Antioch is coupled in Acts 11:26 with the fact that the disciples were there first called Christians certainly suggests strongly that Paul was the one who so named them.

It is to be noted that Paul was not quite the first to preach to the Gentiles, but it is because of his labors that the scattered little groups who were the followers of "The Way" became the widespread and important Christian church. As a graceful and grateful recognition of the bond of fellowship between the Gentile Christians in Antioch and the Jewish Christians in Jerusalem, an embassy of friendship was sent from the former to the latter. There was a famine in Jerusalem and the Christians in Antioch took up a collection and sent it by Paul and Barnabas to relieve the sufferers. When Paul and Barnabas returned from Jerusalem after having discharged their mission, they had with them a young man named John, who is better known by his surname, Mark.

The Missionary

The chief characters in the coming great missionary campaign were assembling. A simple little ceremony was held in the church at Antioch which was of great significance for the future history of the world. With fasting and prayer, as behooved so momentous an occasion, the Christians at Antioch selected Paul and Barnabas and commissioned them to carry the new message to the Gentile world. It was the Antioch Christians who sent Paul out, but the initiative probably came from him. The success of his year's preaching there had convinced him that his period of preparation was over and the time for his great lifework had begun. It was ten years now since his conversion—ten years of careful study and perfecting of methods. But when he and Barnabas went out into the cities of Asia Minor on their first missionary expedition his immediate success was somewhat mixed with chagrin because, in the cities which he visited, the Jews started up trouble. The militant Paul spoke out boldly and said that inasmuch as the Jews had refused to receive the gospel of Jesus and had thereby proved themselves unworthy of everlasting life, therefore the Christian preachers had turned to the Gentiles. But the Jews were powerful and succeeded in having the missionaries expelled from Antioch in Pisidia. They went on to Iconium, Lystra and Derbe, Perga, and thence back to their home base in Syrian Antioch.

The expedition had been generally successful, but they had been harassed from city to city by the Jews. The trip had occupied three years, and when Paul and Barnabas returned to Antioch they found a controversy in full swing. Paul must have been exasperated. It was bad enough that the orthodox Jews in the cities of Asia Minor should oppose his work. He was learning to succeed in spite of their dog-in-the-manger attitude. But to find that the Christian Jews were opposing the preaching of the gospel to the Gentiles was the last straw.

The Circumcision Controversy

In Antioch he found Jews from Jerusalem telling the Antioch Gentile Christians that unless they were circumcised, as Moses had commanded, they could not be saved. A long discussion in Antioch on the subject had no results, and it was determined that Paul and Barnabas should lead a delegation to Jerusalem to have the matter out there. On the way to Jerusalem, Paul took the opportunity to preach in several places and to point out the success he had had in his mission to the Gentiles. The debate in Jerusalem was bitter. There seemed to be good arguments on both sides. The Jews pointed out that Jesus had never permitted his disciples to neglect the Law of Moses. He had even seemed to advocate its complete observance. The issue, therefore, seemed to be between the Law and the Gospel. It was not simply whether or not Gentile Christians should be circumcised. The larger question was whether the old Law was to be a part of the new Gospel.

Peter made a wonderful speech in which he pleaded with his friends not to "put a yoke upon the neck of the disciples" and pointed out that the Law was irksome, not only to the Gentiles but to the Jews themselves. Paul and Barnabas both spoke, reciting the great success of the three-year missionary journey. And we may be sure that Paul was most politic in the presentation of his side of the matter because, as an astute organizer, he recognized the importance of securing the approval of the leaders of the mother church of Jerusalem. Then James "the Just" spoke and proposed that the circumcision issue be dropped, but that a letter be sent to the Antioch Gentile Christians urging the keeping of certain important sections of the Mosaic Law, such as abstaining from meats offered to idols, and from fornication.[9]

The Beginning of the Internationalization of Christianity

This first Christian council was of immeasurable importance. It decided whether Christianity would be simply an obscure Jewish sect or whether it would be a world religion. In a few decades the Jewish Christians were an inconsiderable fraction of the great church.

Paul's great work of internationalizing Christianity was accomplished not only by the sufferings of his missionary journeys but even more by his labors of conciliation in that council. He won what he wanted—namely, the freeing of the young church from the needless handicap of what, after all, was the survival of a barbaric custom of primitive phallic religion. As a matter of fact, he won more than that because, although there were other controversies later concerning certain matters of Jewish customs, nevertheless Paul's victory at Jerusalem encouraged him to disregard the Mosaic Law whenever it hindered the acceptance of Christianity by his Gentile audience.

Paul remained with Barnabas in Antioch for some time teaching and preaching, but the fever of the road was in his veins and he wanted to be off. He proposed to Barnabas that they make a visit to the little churches they had established on their first missionary trip. Barnabas was willing to go but wished to include John Mark in the company. The friendship between Paul and Barnabas was marred by a sharp contention which resulted in Barnabas and Mark sailing without Paul to Cyprus. Paul chose Silas, who had come

9 James the Just was James the Righteous and was also called "the brother of the Lord." He probably wrote the Epistle of James, and because that book is so Essenic, some modern scholars think James may have been among the Essenic "brethren" of Jesus, for the Jerusalem followers of Jesus, before they formed a Christian Church, may have been a splinter group of the Essene Covenanters of Qumran. James was later called the first Bishop of Jerusalem and may have been one of the "overseers" mentioned in the Scrolls as Essene officers, or his traditional cognomen of "James the Just" or "James the Righteous" may reflect his possible earlier title as a successor of the Essene Teacher of Righteousness.

back from Jerusalem with him, and they went into Syria and Cilicia. On this second missionary tour, Paul not only visited the churches which he and Barnabas had established but also strengthened the faith of the Christians whose conversion had been the result of his individual efforts in the twelve-year period after his own conversion.

In Lystra he added Timothy to his staff, a companion who was to be a joy and inspiration to him the rest of his life. Perhaps part of Paul's great love for Timothy was due to the fact that the young man was the son of a Jewish mother and a Greek father, and thus in his own person symbolized Paul's mission. To the farthest western limits of Asia Minor he journeyed, and at Troas on the Aegean Sea had a vision in which a man appeared and begged Paul to "come over into Macedonia and help us." He took this dream as a divine call and crossed the sea carrying on his work in Philippi, Thessalonica, Berea, and even in Athens and Corinth. He was not received as enthusiastically as he had been in Asia Minor. By the time he got to Corinth he was quite cast down, but his success there greatly encouraged him and he remained for a year and a half in that vicinity.

The First Books of the New Testament

While in Corinth his mind turned toward the little church which he had established at Thessalonica, and to them, in his anxiety, he sent two letters. In our Bible these are the well-known Epistles to the Thessalonians and have been deemed the earliest of all the New Testament books—that is, if the New Testament were arranged chronologically, First and Second Thessalonians would be placed before any of the gospels. Mark, the earliest of the four gospels, was not written until fifteen or twenty years later.

The discovery and examination of the Qumran Scrolls, however, has led some experts to suggest that the Fourth Gospel (John's), usually hitherto dated later than the others on account of its Gnostic sections, may be the earliest because of its Essenic phrases, and especially because some of the cave manuscripts contain enough typically Gnostic words and ideas to enable us to date Gnosticism much earlier than before. Also the fact that the Epistle of James is so very Essenic, even quoting the Manual of Discipline, has raised the question of its dating, previously put by many as in the second century. The Scrolls' discovery, however, greatly strengthens the case for James's authorship and a date as early as A.D. 45, thus, before even the Epistles to the Thessalonians. But, at any rate, these letters are the earliest we have of Paul's.

In the fall of the year A.D. 51 Paul returned by sea from Corinth to Antioch, going by way of Ephesus and Caesarea. While at Caesarea he took the opportunity to go up to Jerusalem to exchange friendly greetings with the church leaders there. After a short rest he started out on his third missionary tour, which took him to the churches of the southern part of Asia Minor and then on to Ephesus. He remained in Ephesus for three years and evangelized the whole vicinity. During this period he wrote his famous epistles to the church in Corinth, where some members had taken his gospel of freedom too literally and were indulging in unseemly excesses. In fact, the radicals there were so rebellious that he had to visit Corinth in an attempt to settle the matter, but he was unsuccessful.

He was obliged to leave Ephesus because of the growing opposition to his work. He went into Macedonia to strengthen the churches there, and from Macedonia sent a letter to the churches in Galatia, our Epistle to the Galatians. His heart was cheered by news brought him by Titus that matters were all right again in Corinth, and he hurried there and stayed three months. During this period he composed his Letter to the Romans. He had never been in Rome but was looking forward eagerly to a visit there.

For some time he had been collecting a free-will offering from his various churches for the mother church in Jerusalem, and at the end of his three months' stay in Corinth he sailed thither. He was welcomed by the Jerusalem church but found a strong opposition to him personally because of his continued disregard of Jewish ceremonial laws. His hosts proposed that he prove his loyalty to the Law by going into the temple and participating in a seven days' ceremony as the sponsor for four men who were under a religious vow. Strange as it may seem, Paul acquiesced willingly, and the suspicions against him would have been allayed, but the series of events which led to his martyrdom in Rome was begun by an incident which occurred in the temple during the last day of the ceremony. Certain Jews from Asia Minor recognized him and cried out that this was the man whom they had heard preach against the Law. They accused him of having brought a Greek into the holy place, and a great tumult arose.

The Arrest

As a result of the brawl, the Roman garrison of the city was called out and rescued Paul from the mob who were beating him. For safety's sake the captain commanding the soldiers escorted Paul toward the castle, but as he was leading him away, Paul spoke to him. Surprised at being addressed in Greek, the captain listened to Paul's statement and allowed him to address the crowd. It is significant that even in this moment of great personal danger, Paul should so far have forgotten his own safety as to take the opportunity to preach a sermon. His defense, as he "stood on the stairs," is a magnificent apology for his life and works, and it may be read in the twenty-second chapter of Acts.

Before Paul had finished, however, the audience howled him down and called for his death. The captain prepared to scourge him, when Paul claimed immunity on account of his Roman citizenship. That made it necessary that he be examined by higher authorities. Determined to go to the bottom of the matter, the captain, Claudius Lysias, summoned the Jewish leaders of the council of the Sanhedrin and asked them to examine him.

Paul had hardly begun his defense before the Sanhedrin when the high priest commanded him to be struck upon the mouth. Paul promptly retorted with biting words, for which he quickly apologized. Noticing that part of the Sanhedrin was Sadducees and part Pharisees, he determined to provoke a dissension between them. He announced that he was a Pharisee, whereupon the Pharisees promptly championed him, and so great a quarrel immediately arose that to save Paul's life the captain cast him into prison.

During the night Paul had a vision in which, he said, Christ appeared to him and promised that he should preach in Rome. The next day the captain learned through Paul's sister's son that a conspiracy had been formed among a number of Jews to kill Paul upon his next appearance before the council. In order to avoid further dissension the captain determined to send Paul secretly to Caesarea to be examined by Felix, the governor. Paul was safely transferred to the coast, but the high priest heard of it and immediately secured audience with Felix and accused Paul of being "a pestilent fellow and a mover of sedition among all the Jews throughout the world, and a ringleader of the sect of the Nazarenes."

When Paul was summoned to answer this charge he confessed that he was a heretic but denied that he was the cause of the disturbances. Felix postponed decision in the matter, and meanwhile allowed Paul considerable liberty. The Roman governor had been impressed by the bearing of his prisoner and sent for him to explain his faith further to himself and to his wife Drusilla. He was much influenced by Paul's statements but did not release him because he expected to receive bribe money to let him go.

After Paul had been in Caesarea two years, Felix was succeeded by Festus. Immediately the high priest, whose anger against Paul still rankled because of Paul's plain words to him, headed a delegation and asked Festus to send Paul to Jerusalem. Meanwhile, the high priest laid plans to have Paul killed on the road. Festus refused to send the prisoner to Jerusalem and asked the Jews to meet and face him in person. This they were willing to do and "laid many and grievous complaints against Paul which they could not prove."

The Appeal to Caesar

Festus asked Paul if he was willing to go up to Jerusalem and be judged there. Paul answered, "I stand at Caesar's judgment seat, where I ought to be judged: to the Jews have I done no wrong, as thou very well knowest. For if I be an offender, or have committed anything worthy of death, I refuse not to die: but if there be none of these things whereof these accuse me, no man may deliver me unto them. I appeal unto Caesar." Since Paul had appealed unto Caesar, he must, by Roman law, be allowed to state his case in Rome. But before he was sent there he was called upon once more to make a statement of his faith.

Drusilla, Felix's wife, was entertaining company. It was really quite an intimate party because her brother Agrippa had come with his wife to congratulate Felix on his accession to the governorship. Now Agrippa had brought with him his wife Bernice, who was his own sister, and therefore the sister of Drusilla. As a part of the entertainment Paul was brought out and made a most moving speech, at the conclusion of which Agrippa said laughingly, "Almost thou persuadest me to be a Christian." And after Paul had been taken back to prison, Agrippa remarked to Festus that Paul might have been set at liberty if he had not appealed unto Caesar.

Paul Goes to Rome

The journey to Rome in the fall of 57 or 58 was interrupted by the wrecking of the ship on the Island of Malta. The description of the storm and shipwreck in the twenty-seventh chapter of Acts is one of the most vivid accounts of marine disaster in the world's literature. The company remained on the island during the winter, and sometime in the spring of 58 or 59 arrived at Rome. Paul was met by a delegation from the Christian church of Rome and was treated with consideration by Roman officials. For two years he lived under guard, but in his "own hired house." During the two years he accomplished a great deal of work, for he not only preached frequently but wrote letters to the Philippians, Colossians, and Ephesians, as well as a short one to Philemon.

Concerning Onesimus, a Runaway Slave

Onesimus had stolen some of the property belonging to Philemon, his master, and had fled from Colossae to Rome. There Paul had come in contact with him and had converted him to Christianity. Then Paul sent him back to his master with a letter asking Philemon to forgive Onesimus and receive him, not as a returned slave, but as a brother in Christ. The incident is indicative of Paul's personal interest in his converts and of his active concern for their welfare, even when he himself was in chains. This letter and the others written during the time of imprisonment in Rome are full of wise counsel and spiritual inspiration and have been a source of strength to the Christian church ever since. Some think that at the end of two years Paul was tried and executed, but there is a strong opinion among some scholars that he was freed by Nero because of the lack of any weighty evidence against him.

Paul in Spain

It is thought that he went back to his missionary work and that possibly he traveled to the west as far as Spain on an evangelistic tour. When he had previously written to the church in Rome he had promised to stop at Rome on his way to Spain, and his release may have given him an opportunity to carry out his former plan.

It is thought also that he visited some of the churches which he had founded in parts of Greece and that he was arrested in one of these cities and taken again to Rome.

The Last Letters

The theory is that he then was condemned to death about A.D. 65. According to this hypothesis, his letter to Titus and his first letter to Timothy were written between his first and second Roman imprisonments, and his second letter to Timothy was written just before his death while in a prison in Rome. There is a touching personal item in the concluding chapter in the second letter to Timothy. We find among the many personal greetings which he asks Timothy to give to his dear friends, a request that when Timothy comes he should bring his books, which request he couched in the following language, "The cloke that I left at Troas with Carpus, when thou comest, bring with thee, and the books, but especially the parchments." Paul was still the scholar to the end and wanted his beloved books to solace him in his last imprisonment. Whether or not the books reached him before his death we do not know. We hope Timothy arrived in time to wrap the "cloke" around the great apostle to the Gentiles before he breathed his last.

Paul's Place in the History of Religion

Even in his own day Paul was recognized as the foremost agent in the extension of Christianity to other lands. In the centuries since, his figure has assumed constantly greater importance, until today there are many who are inclined to consider him as of more importance than Jesus himself in the actual establishing of Christianity in the world. This view, of course, seems like blasphemy to orthodox Christians, who labor under the impression that the religion *of* Jesus and the religion *about* Jesus are one and the same.

No discriminating student of the history of early Christianity will deny that without Paul, or someone like Paul, Christianity would probably have remained an insignificant Essenic Jewish cult, only one among the many religions that were striving for power in the vast and complex Roman life of the day. The Jews had rejected Jesus as their Messiah and considered him as only one of several scores of messiahs who had claimed to be the fulfillment of prophecy. The Jews who did accept Jesus as the Messiah were too much constricted by their legalism and national narrowness to have been able to win the Gentile world to their faith.

Paul's peculiar preparation and almost ideal equipment for the particularly exacting work of the one who would internationalize Christianity seem almost providential. Not only did he understand thoroughly the Jewish life and literature which formed the background of the early church, but he was an expert in the higher subtleties of Phariseeism, and therefore was able to meet and vanquish any arguments of the best men of his own nation. To this intimate knowledge of the Jewish background and temper, he added what was equally necessary—namely, a knowledge of the life, philosophy, customs, literature, and religion of the Gentile world. He was aware of the narrowness of nationalistic Judaism. He knew that Christianity must be broadened before it would be accepted by Gentiles. He knew also that from the ceremonials and practices of the Jews must be eliminated those items which would be offensive to the Gentiles and that there must also be incorporated in the Christian churches certain ideas which were common to some of the other religions of the time.

One need not be a great scholar to discern in Christianity traces of Greek philosophy, especially of the Stoic school, nor to see evidences of close affinity to some of the mystery religions of the eastern Mediterranean world. But the sum of these three things—the Jewish religion, Greek philosophy, and the mystery religions—would not make Christianity. There was another element, perhaps the most important of all. These three were synthesized by Paul and then transmuted by being passed through the crucible of his own vivid personal experience. His vision on the road to Damascus, his other visions, his terrible sufferings on his journeys, his agonizings over the foes within and without the church, his own confident hope in Christ, were all mighty factors in the integration of all the elements into a unified Christian faith.

Of course we must not credit Paul with having incorporated into Christianity all the elements of its later complexity, or blame him either. The Alexandrian school contributed a great deal. Other great Christian leaders from different backgrounds brought from their own experiences and environment rich contributions to the growing Christian religion. It was several centuries before Christianity assumed its well-known outlines. Lively church councils and bitter controversies with strong heretical minorities left their mark on the creeds of Christendom. It was not until the time of Augustine that the synthesis was finally made, and without Augustine, Paul's work would largely have been lost.

To Paul, however, belongs the eternal glory of having taken a narrow Jewish sect, whose members were filled with prejudices and superstitions, but who were aflame with loyalty to the remarkable personality of their crucified leader, and to have so broadened that sect as to set it on its triumphant march toward world domination.

X

AUGUSTINE

[A.D. 354–430]

ARCHITECT OF THE CITY OF GOD

THE GREATEST NAME in Christian theology, both Catholic and
Protestant, is that of Augustine. The reason for this is three-
fold: he was the first to explain the difficulties and contradictions
of the Bible to the satisfaction of the average Christian; he was the
first to build a coherent and complete system of theology for the
rapidly growing Christian church; he was in his own personal life
the first great example of the power of Christian salvation to redeem the blackest sinner and heretic and make of him the brightest
saint.

The Bible is a difficult book to understand, especially when it is
viewed as a consistent unit. Much explaining is necessary to reconcile the Old Testament with the New, and the letters of Paul with
other New Testament books. In the days of Augustine clever people
were asking Christians embarrassing questions, such as where Cain
got enough men to build the first city and why a city was needed
when there were only three men on earth, Cain, his father Adam,
and his son Enoch.

Such questions Augustine answered so capably that his writings
are even today the refuge of ministers hard beset by infidels. In fact,

the works of Augustine form a complete commentary on the Scriptures and are to Christianity very nearly what the Talmud is to Judaism.

Not only did his prolific pen explain the Bible: it also built up the first consistent Christian theology, which reconciled the warring parties within the church and strengthened its defenses against hostile critics without. Augustine's statement of Christian doctrine was rapidly and widely accepted and soon became what it still is, the cornerstone of the official orthodoxy of Christendom. It is an astounding fact that the Christianity of the last 1,500 years has been largely shaped by this one man.

He was able to do this great thing not only by reason of his intellectual power and dialectical ability but even more because he had experienced in his own sensitive soul all the warfare of faith against doubt, of spirit against sense, which harassed the church of Christ. Christian doctrines reflect Augustine's personal experience and are therefore much more easily comprehended if one is familiar with the dramatic life of the libertine and heretic of Carthage who was changed by Christian conversion into the saintly Bishop of Hippo.

Thus he justified Christianity not only by his eloquent defense of it but also by his remarkably changed life. His conversion gave double strength to his words. Augustine himself was the miracle that proved the claims of the Christianity he promulgated. He was at once both preacher and illustration. Very cleverly but very humbly he used his own life story as a warning and inspiration to others by doing a thing then unheard of. He wrote a book about himself!

His Turbulent Youth

In the famous *Confessions* or memoirs Augustine describes interestingly his turbulent youth. He was a Roman colonial, born at Tagaste in Numidia in North Africa in A.D. 354 of a pagan freeman named Patricius and a devout Christian mother, Monica. We get hints of a divided home, his meek but persistent Christian mother yielding temporarily to the rough will of his unbelieving father, only to have her own way in the end. Augustine's turmoil of soul in later years was in part a reflection of the family conflict between pagan and Christian which he unconsciously felt as an infant, and in part a product of the wider world struggle at that time between the same forces.

The man's memory was unusual, for in middle age he recalled how he had first learned to talk. In a passage which except for its phraseology might have been written by a recent psychologist, he tells us of his early struggles for self-expression,

This I remember; and have since observed how I learned to speak. It was not that my elders taught me words—in any set method; but I, longing by cries and broken accents and various motions of my limbs to express my thoughts, that so I might have my will, and yet unable to express all I willed, or to whom I willed, did myself, by the understanding which Thou, my God, gavest me, practise the sounds in my memory. When they named anything, and as they spoke turned towards it, I saw and remembered that they called what they would point out, by the name they uttered.—And thus by constantly hearing words, as they occurred in various sentences, I collected gradually for what they stood; and having broken in my mouth to these signs, I thereby gave utterance to my will. Thus I exchanged with those about me these current signs of our wills, and so launched deeper into the stormy intercourse of human life.[1]

Although young Aurelius Augustinus became in time a teacher and a great scholar, schooldays seem to have been to the lad a period of "miseries and mockeries." He confesses how weary he found the paths of learning and that his sole delight was to play. Ball games prevented his making proper progress in his studies, and he was evidently frequently punished by beating. His first quaint prayers arose from his desire to avoid these punishments,

For so I began, as a boy, to pray to Thee, my aid and refuge; and broke the fetters of my tongue to call on Thee, praying Thee, though small, with no small earnestness, that I might not be beaten at school. And when Thou heardest me not (not thereby giving me over to folly), my elders, yea, my very parents, who yet wished me no ill, mocked my stripes, my then great and grievous ill.[2]

Latin he liked, but Greek and the three R's he looked on as a great "burden and penalty." He wondered why, and decided that it was because he had picked up the Latin from those around him in the nursery, smiling and encouraging him, while the other studies had been forced on him by stern discipline. From his own

[1] *Confessions,* Book I:13 (Pusey's translation, Everyman Edition, p. 8).
[2] Ibid., I:14, p. 9.

experience he therefore deduced an axiom of pedagogy, a "new idea" in education, "No doubt, then, that a free curiosity has more force in our learning these things, than a frightful enforcement."[3]

One of his worst sins, in his own eyes, was thieving, but at its worst it was very petty larceny. He "stole" from his parents' table and cellar. He laments most the theft of some pears from a neighbor's orchard, fruit "tempting neither for color or taste" which with other "lewd young fellows" he stole and then flung to the hogs. It was an unsocial act surely, but we are hardly prepared to condemn a boy's orchard prank in the terms which he uses of himself on this occasion—"Foul soul, falling from Thy firmament to utter destruction."[4]

Upon the Latin authors he lays much of the blame for his introduction to the lewdness and debauchery in which he confesses he indulged from adolescence to his early thirties. In the classics the gods were represented as engaged in amorous pursuits, and these passages Augustine "learnt willingly with great delight, and for this was pronounced a hopeful boy."[5]

His years in the local school at Tagaste were followed by the study of grammar and rhetoric at a nearby city, Madaura. In his sixteenth year he was at home for a time while his parents were arranging to finance his further studies. During this year Satan found much mischief for the youth's idle hands to do, or, as he put it, "The briers of unclean desires grew rank over my head, and there was no hand to root them out."[6] He complains that while his father went beyond his means to provide for his son's higher education, his paternal care did not include the chastity of his son, and that even his mother was so concerned with his scholastic advancement that she discouraged the early marriage which he thinks would have solved his great personal problem.

His Mistress

About this time the boy took to himself a mistress, evidently without strenuous objection from his parents. He kept her for about fifteen years. It appears that much of his self-condemnation in his *Confessions* is on account of this relationship. It was reprehensible

3 Ibid., I:23, p. 15.   5 Ibid., I:26, p. 17.
4 Ibid., II:9, p. 26.   6 Ibid., II:6, p. 23.

enough in the light of this later Christian consciousness, but it was not particularly wicked from the point of view of most of his contemporaries. He appears to have loved the girl and she, him; but the feeling of guilt during so long a period worked so deeply into his consciousness that his later remorse was correspondingly great, and much affected his theology.

In Carthage

In his eighteenth year this passionate youth was sent to Carthage to continue his studies. To one of his age the opulence of the pagan city made a tremendous appeal. Its great temples, beautiful theaters, magnificent palaces, and luxurious public baths all impressed him, and the lively cosmopolitan atmosphere stimulated him strangely. To a boy brought up as a Christian, it seemed all very wicked, and very interesting.

To Carthage I came, where there sang all around me in my ears a cauldron of unholy loves. I loved not yet, yet I loved to love, and out of a deep-seated want, I hated myself for wanting not. I sought what I might love, in love with loving, and safety I hated, and a way without snares.[7]

For two years he stayed in Carthage studying, carousing, and much given to attending stage plays. Tragedies he doted on, and recorded wonderingly the pleasure he experienced in being made to feel sorrowful. The religious pageants and dramas in honor of the fertility goddess Cybele attracted him. He says in *De Civitate Dei*,[8]

I myself, when I was a young man, used sometimes to go to the sacrilegious entertainments and spectacles; I saw the priests raving in religious excitement, and heard the choristers; I took pleasure in the shameful games which were celebrated in honor of gods and goddesses, of the virgin Collestis, and Berecynthia (Cybele), the mother of all the gods. And on the holy day consecrated to her purification, there were sung before her couch productions so obscene and filthy for the ear . . . so impure that not even the mother of the foul-mouthed players themselves could have formed one of the audience.

[7] Ibid., III:1, p. 32.   [8] Book II, Ch. 4.

His wild revelry seems not to have hindered his scholastic progress, for he became "chief in the rhetoric school," which corresponded roughly to our college of liberal arts. He was becoming expert in logic, philosophy and public speaking, but was more concerned with style and clever casuistry than with the pursuit of truth. But an intellectual awakening suddenly came to him when he read Cicero's discourse on the value of philosophy, the book called *Hortensius*. For once, not the style of the writer but the message itself appealed to the youth. He says, "Every vain hope at once became worthless to me; and I longed with an incredibly burning desire for an immortality of wisdom."[9]

He even turned to the Bible with a new interest, but the Scriptures were a disappointment. They seemed to him then "unworthy to be compared to the stateliness of Tully." He was still prejudiced against a simple style, for he had been trained to appreciate magnificent sentences and well-rounded periods.

The Manichean

In the late fourth century those who loved philosophy and could not accept the Christian Scriptures sometimes joined the Manicheans, a semi-religious, semi-philosophical company. Their belief had elements in common with Buddhism, Zoroastrianism, and Christianity and they especially emphasized the doctrine of two principles at work in the world, one good and one evil. They abhorred idolatry, magic, and superstitions, and laid much stress on reason as the guide to truth. In this respect they were much like the Unitarians of the present day. Augustine was attracted to them and for many years was one of them. Indeed, the influence of their doctrines upon his thinking continued long after he had become a Christian.

Manicheism was not a heretical Christian sect, as was long supposed, but a very important and powerful religion itself, a real rival of Christianity. Neo-Platonism was the third of the three great world systems which were struggling for supremacy in Augustine's day. He tried that religion also before he finally embraced Christianity. It is only lately that historians have realized how strong these rivals of Christianity were. When we consider how important

9 *Confessions*, Book III:7, p. 36.

Augustine's work was to Christianity, we wonder what would have happened if he had remained a Manichean, or a Neo-Platonist. Possibly Christianity's final overwhelming triumph was partly due to the fact that Augustine incorporated in it the desirable elements of its rivals, avoided their evident mistakes, and eliminated the weak points in Christianity which its rivals criticized. One of the Manichean daily prayers which has come down to us does not seem particularly heretical,

> I prostrate myself and adore, with a pure heart and a truth-speaking tongue, the great God, the Father of Lights, the Essence of Lights, adored and blessed art Thou, all Thy majesty and Thy blessed worlds which Thou hast called into existence; he adoreth Thee who adoreth Thy hosts, Thy holy ones, Thy word, Thy majesty, and that which seemeth good to Thee, because Thou art the God who is all truth, life, and holiness.[10]

Augustine had the great advantage of knowing all three religions from the inside. Traces of both Manicheism and Neo-Platonism, especially the former, are to be found in his theology. Moreover, it was on these two religions as anvils that Christianity was pounded into shape by Augustine's hammers of logic. As we read his treatises against his former faiths we can still feel the heat of the long-ago conflicts.

Manicheans were divided into two classes, the *auditores* or hearers and the *perfecti* or initiates. Augustine was never fully initiated, remaining in the larger group of beginners. That may have been because he did not fully approve the Manichean tenets, the reason his admirers would have us accept, or it may have been because he did not think he was "good enough" to live up to the strict ascetic standards of the *perfecti*. Their triple seal of mouth, hands, and bosom was far stricter than Christian prohibitions, for it required the initiate not only to abstain from animal food and evil speech but also to avoid all contacts with matter that were not absolutely necessary. They abstained not only from marriage but from concubinage and prostitution as well, and that was quite remarkable heroism in Carthage in the latter half of the fourth century.

Augustine was not quite ready for such perfection, although he

---

[10] *Encyclopedia of Religion and Ethics*, VIII, p. 399.

wished he were. One of his prayers of that period is preserved for us in his very frank *Confessions,* " 'O Lord, make me pure and chaste, but not quite yet.' For," he confesses, "I feared lest Thou shouldest hear me soon, and soon cure me of the disease of concupiscence, which I wished to have satisfied, rather than extinguished."[11]

In spite of Augustine's later contemptuous references to Manicheism as a "sacrilegious superstition," we can see that his long contact with it prepared him for Christianity, for the followers of Mani, like those of Christ, had bishops, elders, baptism, the eucharist, fasting, services of prayer and song, and an annual commemoration of the death of the founder of the faith.

His Son

But Augustine did not spend all his time in Carthage in attending school classes and Manichean meetings. He evidently explored the life of the city much as college students have from his day till now. During this undergraduate period in Carthage his mistress was living with him and, before he was nineteen, presented him with a son whom he promptly named Adeodatus, the gift of God. Whether the name was given in a moment of facetiousness we do not know, but the child became very dear to the young father, who seems to have kept the boy with him until the latter's untimely death at the age of sixteen.

How did the young student-father meet his financial obligations as head of a family? His own father had died, a Christian at last, just before Augustine had started for school in Carthage, and his mother could spare but little from her scanty income. But a generous friend and fellow townsman of his father's, named Romanianus, supplied the student with tuition money and, as nearly as we can determine from the sources, actually paid all the bills until Augustine began to earn money as a teacher. For many years thereafter Romanianus was ready to help in financial difficulties.

The two crowded years of study in Carthage, during which Augustine not only passed his courses with honor but also read widely outside his prescribed lessons, were succeeded by a year of teaching in his home town, Tagaste.

[11] *Confessions,* Book VIII:17, p. 163.

The Rhetor

But Tagaste was very tame and quiet, and Augustine was soon back in Carthage, this time for a stay of nearly ten years. He opened a school of his own, a school of expression, where literature, public-speaking, and argumentation were taught. Not content with merely teaching others, he contended for the prizes given in rhetorical contests. He kept at it until he had been crowned victor in a poetry competition in the theater of Carthage by the proconsul himself.

Vivid pictures of that decade in Carthage are given us in the *Confessions*. The man in the forties looking back on himself as a wild young man in the twenties recalls with regrets his wasted youth. As one reads between the pious lines, however, one notes a sort of middle-age pride in schoolday pranks. The confessing approaches boasting at times, like an old man in prayer meeting thanking God for having saved the young hellion he once was.

Glimpses are given of the godly mother Monica, sorrowing at home over her wayward son, weeping not so much that he was maintaining a mistress as that he was embracing Manicheism. He wonders that his mother on his visits home permitted him to sit at the same table with her, since she so abhorred and detested his blasphemies, but she had been helped by a good Christian Bishop whom she had pestered with her trouble until, rather testily, he had told her that he had been a Manichee himself and had got over it, and that it was "not possible that the son of these tears should perish."

Another fad of the day claimed the young rhetor's attention. It is rather startling to read, "Those impostors, then, whom they call Mathematicians, I consulted without scruple," until we discover that he is talking about astrologers, who used many figures in their computations. This infatuation was short-lived, for another interest soon crowded it out.

On to Rome

Toward the end of his twenties, Augustine's eyes naturally began to turn toward Rome, the haven of orators. He had heard of a brilliant Syrian rhetor there named Hierius who had come from Antioch with a reputation for eloquence in the Greek tongue and had so rapidly mastered Latin as to gain instant fame as a Roman orator.

"That orator," says Augustine candidly, "was of that sort whom I loved, as wishing myself to be such." With such a model of learning and eloquence before him, the teacher of Carthage turned to his studies with redoubled energy. He had already mastered the Ten Categories of Aristotle easily and without a teacher and was writing a book of his own entitled De Pulchro et Apto, or On the Fair and Fit. This he dedicated to Hierius and sent a copy to him in Rome, preparing the way for his own appearance there.

He had grown tired of teaching unruly students in Carthage. In Rome, he heard, classrooms were orderly. Monica was bitterly opposed to his going, but her opposition evidently brought him to the point of decision and he sailed without her knowledge, taking his books, his family, and his friend Alypius with him. But in Rome he found a greater difficulty than noisy classrooms. Students attended courses decorously until almost the end of the semester and then decamped before paying the fees. And nothing is said about a warm welcome from Hierius.

Milan

Within a few months, however, a wonderful opportunity for promotion came to him through Manichean influence. A municipal rhetor was needed for the great city of Milan, and on New Year's Day, A.D. 385, the thirty-year-old rhetor who made the oration of thanks to the consul for the appointment was Aurelius Augustinus, late of Rome and Carthage, who spoke fluent Latin with a slight Punic accent. Augustine now found himself in a position of considerable prominence where he met many leading citizens.

Ambrose

Ambrose, Christian Bishop of Milan, was a speaker of great eloquence, whom Augustine went to hear as a matter of course and to study his oratorical method. He who came to criticize, however, soon found himself so interested in what the great man said that he was forgetting how he said it. It is quite likely that Ambrose was the first Christian of any great intellectual acumen with whom Augustine had come into contact and the bishop's words, probing deep beneath sophistries and rhetorical arguments, touched Augustine to the heart. Testimonies of others who had been converted to Christianity interested and influenced him also, and he was soon in a torment of indecision. Monica began to rejoice that her prayers were about to be answered. She had followed to Rome and Milan and was already such an assiduous worshiper under and of Ambrose that she was rebuked for bringing "cakes and bread and wine" to church and distributing it to those near her.

The Conversion

The conversion of Augustine to Christianity was by no means as simple and sudden a matter as those think who believe it all occurred like a flash of lightning when he was in a garden under a tree. Many influences had been working on him both ways for a long time. Keeping him back from a decision to embrace Christianity were powerful forces, chief of which were gratitude to the Manicheans, who had got him his present fine position, and a real affection for the mistress who had been his faithful companion for many years.

Some scholars think his mother's prayers brought about his conversion. Others credit it to Bishop Ambrose, or to Paul's Epistles. All these affected him, to be sure, but the Neo-Platonic writings of Plotinus which he was reading in Milan at the time, and which afforded a good philosophic transition from Manicheism to Christianity, probably influenced him as much as Paul's Epistles. His distaste for the childish elements in Manicheism had been growing for some time, ever since he had met Faustus, their renowned leader, and found him a comparatively ignorant man.

Even the profession of teaching elocution began to seem futile, like selling "loquacity to overcome by." Again he was more and more disturbed in conscience about his illicit relation with the mother of Adeodatus. And a physical difficulty, some disease of the throat and chest, worried him greatly. Sometimes it is a little incident which turns the tide. The municipal orator, outwardly prosperous and successful but inwardly very much troubled, was walking with his distinguished friends through a street of Milan when he noticed a poor but happy beggar "with a full belly, joking and joyous." Augustine says,

I sighed, and spoke to the friends around me, of the many sorrows of our phrenzies; for that by all such efforts of ours as those wherein I then toiled—we yet looked to arrive only at that very joyousness, whither that beggar-man had arrived before us, who should never perchance attain it. For what he had attained by means of a few begged pence, the same was I plotting for by many a toilsome turning and winding; the joy of a temporary felicity.[12]

So it may not have been Monica, or Ambrose, or Paul, but the merry mendicant of Milan who should have the credit of Augustine's conversion.

Meanwhile Monica was very busy preparing for her son's baptism. He had been accepted as a catechumen, or candidate for baptism, but could not be baptized while in his present sinful relation with the mother of his son. His own energetic mother arranged everything, however. Her son should marry a woman of his station in life. Augustine says, "I wooed, I was promised, chiefly through my mother's pains, that so once married, the health-giving baptism might cleanse me."[13]

His "concubine" was torn from his side and packed off to Africa, although his "heart which clave unto her was torn and wounded and bleeding" and although the girl vowed "never to know any other man," and left their son with him. Augustine promptly procured another mistress, as his promised bride could not marry for two years. Neither he who became Saint Augustine nor she who became Saint Monica appears in this incident in as favorable a light as the nameless girl they both wronged.

One summer afternoon in a garden with his friend Alypius Augustine burst into tears of shame for his sins and threw himself down under a fig tree in an utter abandon of emotion. Suddenly he heard from a nearby house a child's voice chanting in the singsong of a game, "Tolle, lege. Tolle, lege." (Take up and read). He received it as a divine command, and, opening Paul's letter to the Romans, read the 13th and 14th verses of the 13th chapter, "Not in rioting and drunkenness, not in chambering and wantonness, not in strife and envying, but put ye on the Lord Jesus Christ, and make no provision for the flesh, to fulfil the lusts thereof." At the reading of that verse, the struggle was at an end. "No further would I read;

12 Ibid., VI:9, p. 103.　　　　　13 Ibid., VI:23, p. 114.

nor needed I: for instantly at the end of this sentence, by a light as it were of serenity infused into my heart, all the darkness of doubt vanished away."[14]

The Baptism

Augustine celebrated his conversion by a perfect orgy of composition. That was his profession and he consecrated it to God. In spite of his sickness he wrote five treatises in the winter of 386 before his baptism, beginning promptly that long series of theological books for which he is noted.

If you visit Milan you will be shown in the public square the place where Saint Ambrose baptized Saint Augustine while Saint Monica looked on. It was a touching ceremony that Easter Day A.D. 387, for Adeodatus and Alypius were baptized, too, and the assembly did a novel thing for those days: they sang hymns, newly written by Ambrose himself. Probably this circumstance gave rise to the old tradition that Ambrose and Augustine by a simultaneous inspiration composed and sang the Te Deum in unison at the moment of baptism.

Soon after Monica had seen her fondest hopes realized by her son's admission to full Christian church membership, she passed away at Ostia as they were about to set sail for Africa. Their last days together were very precious and are immortalized in a passage of beautiful prose in the Confessions, the best part of the book.[15]

The next year Augustine went to his father's old farm in Tagaste and established a sort of country retreat where he and his friends delighted in discussing theology and philosophy. In 391 he was made a presbyter and in 395 Bishop of Hippo, an office which he held until his death in 430. Hippo was not an important bishopric, but Augustine's influence went out from it to all Christendom through his almost incredibly voluminous writings, numbering, small and large, over a thousand treatises. Most of these were sermons, doctrinal essays, and controversial pamphlets against various heresies, but there were two of such importance and wide appeal that they have been printed almost countless times, his Confessions and his City of God.

14 Ibid., VIII:29, p. 171.   15 Ibid., IX:17-37, pp. 189-203.

The City of God

When Augustine died in 430, the Vandals were at the gates of the city of Hippo and it soon fell, as Rome had fallen before Alaric just twenty years before. Though earthly cities pass away, the City of God would abide forever. That was the thesis of Augustine's great book, begun in 412 and finished in 427, the greatest defense of Christianity ever written.

Paganism had been abolished and Christianity made the official Roman religion a century before. But when the Gothic invasion brought disaster throughout the empire, pagan ceremonies were revived, for the people said that the old gods had abandoned the city for forsaking the deities who had always protected it and who had brought it great prosperity. It was a time of sore trial for the Christian church, for the establishment of Christianity was to have brought in the Golden Age. Instead, here was imminent ruin. What could Christians say to the jeers and insults and mocking questions of the pagans?

Augustine told them what to say! With masterly learning he wrote twenty-two books in one, his great "apology" which was an attack. The first ten books showed that when Rome had worshiped the gods faithfully she had had troubles enough. Cleverly the great rhetorician held the pagan gods and their worship up to devastating ridicule. Then in the last twelve sections he contrasted human cities with the divine city and pagan faiths with Christianity. The book answered the leading questions of the time and was actually an outline of history written in pungent style and popular form. It was very human and elemental. For a student of comparative religion it is invaluable even today, although rather prolix and sophistical.

The City of God which Augustine conceived was really the Catholic Church in the Holy Roman Empire. The old bishop's dream became in later centuries a historical reality. We are not surprised to learn that Charlemagne read the *City of God* carefully and that the Catholic church today holds it as second only to the Bible.

There were harsh elements in Augustine's character, it is true. In his later years he sanctioned intolerance and persecution, and his doctrine of infant damnation seems horrible to us today. But those who cannot accept Augustine's doctrines of The Fall and the Depravity of Man, The Atonement, Saving Grace, and Predestination can still have their faith in God kindled anew by the "fire of the love of God" still burning in the old books of the Bishop of Hippo. Without Augustine it is doubtful that Christianity would have weathered the Fall of Rome and the darkness of the Middle Ages. Catholicism acknowledges him the greatest of the Church Fathers, and Protestant theologians call him "the Paul after Paul and the Luther before Luther."

The Early Church Fathers

Augustine is the first outstanding name after Paul in the history of Christianity. But in the interval between the two there were many leaders who helped to shape the growing thought of the early church. The most prominent of these were:

69–155	Polycarp
130–202	Irenaeus
160–220	Tertullian
185–254	Origen
256–336	Arius
260–340	Eusebius
293–373	Athanasius
329–389	Gregory Nazianzen
330–379	Basil
335–394	Gregory of Nyssa
340–397	Ambrose
345–407	Chrysostom
340–420	Jerome

These men make a living chain from the apostles to Augustine. Their lives are chronicles of self-denial and great bravery, and their writings, many of which have come down to us, form an appendix to the New Testament which ought to be required reading for all who take their Christianity seriously. In the letters, tracts and books composed by these fathers of the early church are anticipated all the sects and schisms of later Christendom. As these doughty warriors of the faith splintered lances with the leaders of powerful heresies, and as they clashed with each other over certain interpretations of Christian doctrine, they gradually whipped into shape the beliefs of Christianity. It was Augustine who finally summarized, de-

limited, and formulated Christian doctrine, but he was vastly indebted to his predecessors.

It was not primarily through the books of the New Testament
that Christianity was transmitted; it was rather through such living
documents as these early fathers and their fellow Christians. This
fact has been more appreciated by Greek and Roman Catholics
than by Protestants.

Polycarp

When we note that Polycarp, for instance, sat as a learner at the
feet of the apostle John and other disciples who had seen Jesus, we
realize what the Christian world has missed in not having Polycarp's
beautiful Epistle to the Philippians included in the New Testament. Irenaeus, in a letter to a friend, tells how he, in his turn, sat
at the feet of Polycarp, "who was not only instructed by the apostles
and had intercourse with many who had seen Christ, but was also
appointed for Asia by the apostles in the church that is in Smyrna,
an overseer." In another part of the same letter Irenaeus says that
Polycarp "related his familiar intercourse with John and the rest
who had seen the Lord, and how he rehearsed their sayings, and
what things they were which he had heard from them with regard to
the Lord and his miracles and teaching."

The intimate fellowship of the early Christians and their habit
of counseling one another to stand firm in the midst of persecution
is charmingly illustrated by a verse from the tenth chapter of Polycarp's Epistle to the Philippians, "Stand therefore in these things
and follow the example of the Lord, being firm and immutable in
the faith, lovers of the brotherhood, lovers of one another, companions together in the truth, exhibiting toward each other the
sweet reasonableness of the Lord, despising none."

Polycarp himself was "firm and immutable in the faith" unto the
end. Christian history has no scene surpassing the martyrdom of
this early saint. In the very city where for forty years or more he had
lovingly performed his duties as bishop, a great persecution arose
against him and his flock. Mobs surged through the streets demanding the death of the Christians and shouting "away with the
atheists." It seems strange to us today that the early Christians were
the original "atheists," so-called because they would not worship
the Roman gods and emperors.

Into the arena they dragged Polycarp and other Christians. Around the aged bishop they piled the faggots. The proconsul promised him release if he would but blaspheme the name of the Christ. Down through the ages come ringing his dying words, "Eighty and six years have I served him and he has done me no evil. How can I blaspheme my king, my redeemer?"

Irenaeus

At the time of Polycarp's martyrdom Irenaeus, a young man of twenty-five, was teaching in Rome. Shortly thereafter he went west into Gaul and became an assistant to the Bishop of Lyons. When the bishop was martyred A.D. 177, at the time of the persecution of the Christians by Marcus Aurelius, Irenaeus was elected bishop and occupied that office for twenty-five years, until, according to tradition, he was also martyred in the persecution under Septimius Severus. Irenaeus' contribution to the faith of the church was in the line of scholarship. His most famous work was one entitled *Against Heresies.*

Tertullian

But Irenaeus' scholarship was far surpassed by that of Tertullian, a young lawyer from Carthage, who was converted to Christianity in Rome at the end of the second century, when he was about forty years old. Back in Carthage, he served as presbyter in the church for the rest of his life. His tracts and books were numerous and are characterized by vigor of language and by strong satire, and although he wrote a book against heretics he was suspected of heresy himself.

Origen

The greatest of all the third-century teachers was Origen, born in Alexandria, Egypt, A.D. 185 of Christian parents. The same persecution under Septimius Severus which martyred Irenaeus in the west reached as far as Egypt and deprived the seventeen-year-old Origen of his beloved father. The boy was already so devoted a Christian that he decided to die with his father, but his wise mother, feeling that her boy was destined for a great career and could do more for Christianity by living than by dying, hid his clothes, a ruse which proved adequately deterrent.

At the age of eighteen he had progressed so far in his knowledge of the scriptures and his general education that he was chosen as head of a school. In his young manhood he was much impressed by the words of Jesus in Matthew 19:12, and made himself a eunuch "for the kingdom of heaven's sake."

Another persecution arose when he was about thirty years old, so he left Alexandria and traveled a while in Palestine. Upon his return he began to compose many theological treatises, for a wealthy man, impressed by the learning of the young teacher, paid the salaries of stenographers and manuscript writers. By this aid Origen was able greatly to increase his output of books, many of which have come down to us. Just how many he wrote will probably never be known. A writer of the next century credits him with six thousand works, but those probably included many by Origen's followers.

His great contribution to the Christian life of the third century was as a textual critic and commentator. One monumental piece of work which he did was the *Hexapla*, a six-volume edition of the Old Testament in as many versions. His residence in Egypt had made him familiar with the Alexandrian philosophy, and from it he incorporated into Christianity the famous Logos doctrine, according to which the Word of God became incarnate in Jesus. It was also in Origen's time, and largely due to his influence, that the allegorical interpretation of the Bible became increasingly popular.

Arius, Athanasius, and Eusebius

Alexandria continued to be the center of the Christian stage. The greatest controversy that ever raged in all Christendom was between two Africans: Arius, who was born in Libya and became minister of the church in Alexandria, and Athanasius, who was born in Alexandria and was bishop of that city for nearly half a century.

Since apostolic times there had been many opinions as to the relation of Jesus Christ and God. In the early period of missionary propaganda, and later when the great persecutions arose under the emperors Decius, 249–251, and Diocletian, 284–305, there had been little time to debate on theological questions. It became evident, however, early in the fourth century, as Christianity grew in strength, that some theological agreement must be reached by those who called themselves Christians.

Gradually the various opinions simmered down to two great opposing schools: one maintaining that Jesus Christ was equal in every way with God; the other maintaining that Christ, although great, was in some ways less than God. In 318 Arius stated that if Christ were really the Son of God then there must have been a time when there was a Father but no Son; therefore, the Father was greater than the Son. In a council held in 321 Arius and his friends were expelled from the church for this opinion. But Arius had powerful support on his side, and the bishops divided into two great groups. Bishop Alexander of Alexandria led one, and Arius the other.

The clash came in the year 325, when a great general church council was held in Nicaea. Besides lesser ecclesiastical officers there were over three hundred bishops present. The issue involved was really the question of the deity of Jesus. If Jesus were in any way inferior to God the Father, then, obviously, he could not be God. The great defender of the deity of Jesus was a young writer named Athanasius, a deacon of Alexandria who spoke for his bishop, Alexander.

A third party in the controversy was led by Eusebius, Bishop of Caesarea, who opened the Council of Nicaea and proposed a mediating view. His party avoided discussion of the nature of the Trinity and advocated using scripture language instead of the metaphysical terms which the two major parties were introducing. But the Athanasians were clever enough to see that although Eusebius offered a way whereby the two opposing parties could retire with dignity from the controversy, nevertheless, a vote for Eusebius was really a vote for Arius, for the Bible itself contained no clear statement of the doctrine of the Trinity. Consequently, the Eusebian compromise was rejected and it soon became evident that the Athanasians controlled the council. Arius and his friends were banished and his books were burned publicly.

Inside of six years, however, Arius was recalled by the emperor Constantine, through the influence of friends at court. Constantine did not know much about theology, and Arius succeeded in persuading him, in the interview, that he was not so heretical as Athanasius insisted. Consequently, Constantine ordered Athanasius to take Arius back into the church. When the Bishop of Alexandria refused, there was a great deal of trouble. In 335 Constantine deposed Athanasius and sent him into Gaul, and another gathering was held at Jerusalem which restored Arius and his party to church communion. In 336, however, Arius died, but the controversy continued, and by the middle of the century the two parties were fighting over one Greek letter.

The Athanasians held that Jesus was of the *same* essence as God, while the Arians maintained that he was of *like* essence. The two words, identity and similarity, were represented in Greek by *homoousion* and *homoiousion*. Two synods, one in 353 and another in 355, decided in favor of the Arian side, but by the end of the century the emperors allowed the bishops to fight it out themselves. Athanasianism triumphed and has been the orthodox doctrine of Christianity ever since. Arianism has continued to be represented in Christian history by small groups such as the Socinians and, more recently, the Unitarians, Universalists, and liberal wings of other denominations.

Eusebius was prominent not only for his attempt at mediation between the Arians and Athanasians but, because of his many historical writings, became known as the Father of Church History.

The Three Cappadocians

While the great Arian-Athanasian controversy was agitating the church, six great church leaders were born in the dozen years between 329 and 340. In 329, Gregory Nazianzen; in 330, Basil; probably about 335, Gregory of Nyssa; in 340, Ambrose and Jerome; in 345, Chrysostom. Gregory Nazianzen and Basil were two of the famous Three Cappadocians who, toward the end of the fourth century, after the death of Athanasius, were the real leaders of Christian orthodoxy.

Gregory Nazianzen was so named for the town of which his father was bishop. He himself became Bishop of Constantinople. Basil became Bishop of Caesarea in Cappadocia and gave his younger brother Gregory, the third Cappadocian, the bishopric of Nyssa, a small town in Cappadocia. This latter Gregory of Nyssa is the one who had so much to do with the final shaping of the doctrine of the Trinity, but, although admittedly a deeper thinker and better writer, he is not regarded as highly in orthodox circles as the other two Cappadocians because he was one of the first advocates of the Universalist heresy that all men will finally be restored to harmony with God. He taught that even all the angels and devils would eventually be saved.

Gregory Nazianzen is sometimes called the Theologian. No young man of his time had a better education. He assisted his father at Nazianzus for a time. When about forty years of age he was made bishop of a small town but was soon called to Constantinople to preach. This city had remained Arian in spite of the decisions of councils, but it contained a group of orthodox Christians. This fact was the making of the Nazianzen Gregory, for the challenge of the situation developed him as a leader and preacher. About 381 he was made Bishop of Constantinople, but, tiring of the quarrels of ecclesiastics, he went back to Cappadocia to write in peace. He assisted in the formulation of the doctrine of the Trinity, contributing particularly the theory that although God is of one essence, nevertheless he exists as three persons.

Basil, the third Cappadocian, was addicted to asceticism, and from his twenty-seventh to his thirty-fourth year lived as a monk, establishing the system which still prevails in the Eastern church. In 364 he was made presbyter in Caesarea in Cappadocia, and became very active in works of mercy. His interest was in practicing Christianity rather than debating about it, but he gradually swung to the orthodox side of the controversy. In 370 he was elected Bishop of Caesarea, a position of great responsibility. He endeavored to heal the growing split between eastern and western Christianity but was unable to do so because he refused to grant that Rome was supreme.

Ambrose

Ambrose's chief claim to fame was the fact that Augustine was converted to Christianity under his preaching. As Bishop of Milan from 374 to his death in 397 Ambrose was much loved and was noted for his effective sermonizing. His eloquence was attributed by some to the fact that when, as a child, he lay in his cradle, a swarm of bees settled upon his lips. He introduced into Italy the practice of weekly sermons, composed Christian hymns, did much to raise the professional standards of the clergy, and seems to have been one of the first to dream of what Augustine later initiated—namely, the conquest of the Holy Roman Empire for Christianity.

Chrysostom

Greater than Ambrose, as a preacher, was Chrysostom. His real name was John of Antioch, but he is always known as Chrysostom (golden mouth) because of his preaching ability. Like Augustine, he was taught by a very religious Christian mother. But Antioch had been Christian longer than Carthage, and young John was less tempted by the customs of paganism. He intended to become a lawyer but soon turned toward religion.

At the age of thirty he went into the desert and for six years lived the life of an ascetic. By the time he was forty he was attracting attention by his preaching and was soon known as the greatest public speaker in the church of the East. He was made Bishop of Constantinople at the age of fifty-three and took his duties seriously. He was so severe with the under clergy and so outspoken in his condemnation of the evil lives around him that he was twice banished. In his banishment he continued to write letters and treatises, so the emperor finally sent him on a long journey on foot to the north Caucasus mountains. On the way Chrysostom died at the age of sixty-two.

His greatness as a preacher consisted in his interpretation of scripture by a rational rather than an allegorical method. He was, in a way, an early Biblical critic and pointed out the contradictions and human side of the Bible. His rationalism, however, did not cool the fire of his ardor, and his sermons and writings appear to us today to represent the best type of early Christianity.

Jerome

The greatest scholar of the early church was Sophronius Eusebius Hieronymus, better known as Jerome. Born of wealthy parents in Dalmatia, he was educated in Rome. Always of an inquiring nature, he explored the Catacombs and became much interested in the history of Christianity. He could not be called a moral youth. In him, as in Augustine, there was a great conflict between paganism and Christianity. In his early twenties he was nominally converted to Christianity and thereafter traveled widely both west and east from Rome.

While traveling in Syria he passed one miserable winter. When a combination of accidents and sickness brought on a spiritual crisis he resolved to devote himself absolutely to the Christian life, which he interpreted as asceticism. He appears to have had a theophany, or at least a dream which had the same effect upon him. He says, "Suddenly I was caught up in the spirit and dragged before the judgment seat of the Judge; and here the light was so bright, and those who stood around were so radiant that I cast myself upon the ground and did not dare to look up. Asked who and what I was I replied, 'I am a Christian.' But he who presided said, 'Thou liest. Thou art a follower of Cicero and not of Christ, for "where thy treasure is, there will thy heart be also." ' "16

This message he interpreted as a condemnation of his habit of carrying around with him a library of manuscripts of the classics which he himself had copied in Rome. Like Paul, he went into the desert after the theophany, but memories of his former lascivious life pursued him, and as a refuge from his passions he turned to the study of Hebrew.

After some years in the desert he came back to civilization, met Gregory of Nazianzus in Constantinople and there studied the Greek Fathers. As an avocation he translated Eusebius' and some of Origen's works. Later he went to Rome, and Pope Damasus requested that he translate the entire Bible into Latin. Fortunately, several wealthy women made his work financially possible. So, for peace, quiet, and proper atmosphere, he went to the Holy Land and spent the rest of his life, from 386 to 420, in Bethlehem.

There one of the wealthy women, named Paula, built a nunnery for women over which she presided, and a monastery for men, of which Jerome was the head. A third building was for the accommodation of pilgrims. In this quiet retreat Jerome composed his monumental treatises, commentaries, and translations. It is upon his Latin translation of the Bible that the famous Vulgate version is founded. His works, even today, are interesting reading because of his vivid imagination, his wide vocabulary, and his fascinating literary style.

No one can really understand the Christianity of that day without reading Jerome. Appreciating the biographical approach to

16 Letter xxii, Sec. 30.

religion, he wrote a book, *Illustrious Men,* containing the history
of Christianity by the lives of its leaders beginning with Paul and
ending with himself, which included one hundred and thirty-five
biographies. His letters have been famous ever since they were
written. The best known of them is the famous Letter XXII, which
is a treatise on virginity, addressed to Eustochium, the daughter of
his patroness, Paula. His correspondence with Augustine, his
younger contemporary, throws an interesting light upon the Christianity of the very beginning of the fifth century.

Jerome has been a favorite subject of the artists. Correggio, with
a sublime disregard of chronology, but with a deep appreciation of
Jerome's place in Christendom, depicts him standing by the manger
of the Babe of Bethlehem reading reverently Isaiah's prophecy,
"Unto us a child is born; unto us a Son is given; the Wonderful,
the Mighty God, the everlasting Father, the Prince of Peace."

XI

❦

PATRICK

[A.D. 389-461]

WHO CHRISTIANIZED IRELAND

T HE COMMON IMPRESSION is that Patrick was an Irish Roman
Catholic saint born on the seventeenth of March who drove
all the frogs and snakes out of Ireland.

The only inaccuracies in that statement are the facts that he was
not Irish, that he was not a saint, that his name was not originally
Patrick, that he was not born on the seventeenth of March, and that
he did not drive the frogs and snakes out of Ireland. Even the statement that he was a Roman Catholic is a point that has been very
extensively debated for centuries, for there is interesting evidence
that early Irish Christianity may have come from Alexandria, which
would account for its Greek, Gnostic, and Essene survivals.

Nevertheless, all these inaccurate popular impressions concerning Patrick have some justification for their existence. Although he
was not born in Ireland, he spent many years on the Emerald Isle
and is closely identified with its history. Seumas MacManus, in his
Story of the Irish Race,[1] referring to Patrick's escape after seven
years' slavery in Ireland, says with characteristic Irish reasoning,
"Be it noted that the Irish land which he had entered as a foreigner

1 p. 111.

he now left as an Irishman . . . for it is not where a man is born or spends the careless years of childhood, but where and among whom he spends the plastic and absorbing years of youth that determines his nationality. So the Irishman Patrick now sailed away from his own land where he had arrived several years before, an alien Patrick."

Although he would have protested vigorously if anyone had called him a saint during his lifetime, and although his canonization did not come until centuries after his death, nevertheless, it is evident from the records of his life that he was of an unusually saintlike character. And although his real name was Succat, he had another name, Cothrigge, which was Latinized as "Patricius" and from which his later popular name, Patrick, was derived.

Although he was not born on the seventeenth of March, he died on that date, and it was the custom in early Christian centuries to celebrate the date of a good man's death rather than the date of his birth because it was reckoned that the time of his entry into the world of bliss was more to be celebrated than his advent into this vale of tears. And although Patrick did not drive out reptiles and batrachians from the island, he did expel a superstitious religion of necromancy and magic. Evil spirits are popularly associated with, and supposed to reside in, frogs and snakes.

Sources: the Confession

The sources of our knowledge concerning Patrick are mainly three of his own writings. We have, first, his famous *Confession*, so-called because it ends with the words, "This is my confession before I die." There is no valid reason for doubting the authenticity of this document of twenty-five short chapters. It is written in crude Latin and abounds in Biblical quotations. Careful study of these quotations by textual critics has practically established the genuineness of the composition. Bible quotations in the *Confession* are not identical with the wording of the versions which we have today, nor even with those of the Middle Ages, but are quoted from versions which were in circulation at the time when Patrick lived.

"The Letter to Coroticus"

The second of the writings of Patrick which have come down to us is called "The Letter to Coroticus," although it was really addressed to the soldiers of Coroticus, the robber baron who made a raid on Ireland about the middle of the fifth century and carried off a few of Patrick's recently baptized converts. Some have supposed that Coroticus came from Wales, but recent opinion is inclined to locate his baronry in Scotland, at Strathclyde.

Patrick, by that time Bishop of Ireland, determined to appeal to the Christians who were known to be among the soldiers of Coroticus. He requested that the letter be read "in the presence of all the people, yea, in the presence of Coroticus himself: if so be that God may inspire them to amend their life to God sometime; so that even, though late, they may repent of their impious doings—murderer of the brethren of the Lord!—and may liberate the baptized women captives whom they had taken, so that they may deserve to live to God, and be made whole both here and in eternity."

The "Lorica"

The third surviving document from Patrick's pen is the "Lorica," an Irish hymn or verbal charm. This was really a prayer in rhyme which invoked the protection of God against the forces of evil. It is obviously very old, and probably genuine. It was still being used as a charm in Ireland a century ago, and is commonly known as "The Breastplate of St. Patrick."

Early Biographies

Besides these three compositions of Patrick himself, there are two ancient biographies. The later of these is a sort of diary kept by Bishop Tirechan probably about A.D. 670. The other biography is by Muirchu and is, properly speaking, the first real life of Patrick now known. It must have been written during the seventh century A.D., for the bishop to whom it was dedicated died at the end of that century. Tirechan's diary and Muirchu's life are both found in the famous Book of Armagh, now in Dublin, which was composed in the early ninth century.

A more delightful document to read than Muirchu's *Life of St. Patrick* would be hard to find. In the preface he confesses that his qualification for writing the book is not so much literary ability as an admiration for the great missionary. He concludes his preface with these words, "My skill is small, my authorities are uncertain, my memory is treacherous, my intelligence is worn out, my style is poor, yet the feeling of my love is most pious." As the centuries pass, the books contain an increasing number of fables. The gaps in the life of Patrick are filled in by pious legend. The process has gone on until comparatively recent times. Only very lately has there been a serious scientific attempt to discover the actual Patrick.

The Real Patrick

Brushing aside the cobwebby traditions, and returning to the compositions of Patrick himself, we discover a sincere man of a generally sweet character. He was, upon provocation, however, capable of great wrath. His oaths were certainly powerful and mouth-filling. He manifested great organizing ability and was able to carry a line of action through to its finish. His persistence was rendered effective by a dignified and dynamic personality. When from the scanty references we reconstruct the environment of his boyhood, we are impressed by its apostolic simplicity.

It is true that in the fifth century A.D. Christianity had, in the lands of its origin, developed quite a complex organization. But the Christianity of Bannavem Tabernae, the little town on the English coast where Patrick was born, still reflected the earlier and simpler forms of Christianity. Later Catholic tradition naturally interpreted that Christianity in terms of its own highly developed ecclesiastical organization. But an unprejudiced perusal of Patrick's own writings, where no mention is made of Rome or the Pope, forces one to recognize that Patrick, like Augustine, belongs neither to Roman Catholicism nor to Protestantism, but to the whole Christian church.

He tells us that his father, Calphurnius, was a deacon, and that his grandfather, Potitus, was a presbyter. Like Paul, Calphurnius, although engaged in Christian work, earned his living in another way. He had a small farm. It is comparatively easy for a person with any imagination to reconstruct the home life of the boy. The land had for some centuries been developing in civilization under the administration of Roman colonial governors, and Calphurnius appears to have held a civil office as well as a religious one, for he is spoken of as a "decurion." As the son, then, of a respectable citizen who was an officer in both state and church, the boy's position in the community would be one of some importance.

The labors on the farm were not heavy enough to occupy the boy's whole time. The family was well-enough-to-do so that the boy had sufficient leisure for mischief. We must not take too seriously his description of his condition at the age of sixteen. He says of himself later that at that time, "he knew not the true God, and kept not His commandments and was not obedient to his spiritual advisers." It is not unusual for pious confessors to tell of the heinous crimes of their youth, which, upon examination, often prove to be innocent peccadilloes. It is likely that he was a normal boy of his time. If he was not particularly amenable to the discipline of the church, it may have been because of the perverseness traditional in sons of the clergy.

The Raid by the Wild Irish

At the beginning of the fifth century A.D., the coast of England was raided several times by wild Irish tribes, under the lead of their chieftains. The civilization of Ireland was considerably behind that of Britain, and as has happened many times in history, the barbarians profited materially by the industry of their civilized neighbors. In one of these raids, some Irish chieftain, perhaps Niall of the Nine Hostages, took a number of captives in Bannavem Tabernae and vicinity. Among them was the sixteen-year-old Patrick, then known as Succat. The prisoners were sold as slaves upon the return of the marauding band to Ireland.

The Slave

From a life of comparative ease and comfort in Britain the boy found himself suddenly transferred to the life of a shepherd slave. For six years he toiled somewhere "nigh to the western sea." The location of the place of his servitude is difficult to determine and is identified by some as the kingdom of Connaught, and by others as County Antrim. During the six years of slavery the youth had plenty of time to meditate. He recalled the wasted opportunities of his boyhood, and during the long watches when he was alone on the mountainside with his sheep, he gradually had an awakening of conscience. A real religious experience developed. His own account of this experience is found in his *Confession*,

Now, after I came to Ireland, tending flocks was my daily occupation; and constantly I used to pray in the day time. Love of God and the fear of him increased more and more, and faith grew, and the spirit was moved, so that in one day [I would say] as many as a hundred prayers, and at night nearly as many, so that I used to stay even in the woods and on the mountain [to this end]. And before daybreak I used to be roused to prayer, in snow, in frost, in rain; and I felt no hurt; nor was there any sluggishness in me—as I now see, because then the spirit was fervent within me.[2]

This record of his conversion or spiritual awakening is not as complete as the student of the psychology of religion would wish. The usual catastrophic change of heart is absent. There is no record of any burning bush or shining light appearing to him at this period. He particularly emphasizes a gradual growth in his faith. Many other men have found God in the quiet solitudes of nature. It is astonishing how many great religious leaders have been shepherds. There seems to be something salutary for religious growth in a long period of separation from one's fellows. The distractions of daily converse disappear, and slowly the majesty and beauty of nature are reflected in one's own soul. But at the end of this period of prayer and fasting, he began to have visions. One night he heard a voice saying to him, "Blessed youth, thou art soon to go to thy fatherland."

The Escape

It is quite likely that the voice he thought he heard reflected a long-cherished wish. It was six years since he had left home. A short time later he heard the voice say, "Lo, thy ship is ready." He took this voice as a divine message to him and proceeded to search for the ship. He says in his *Confession* that he fled from his master and walked two hundred miles before he found the ship.[3] If he lived "nigh to the western sea," he must have walked along the coast for some distance before he covered two hundred miles, but he may have gone back and forth over the same route several times.

Just as he arrived in one of the coast towns he learned that a ship

2 Ch. VI.   3 Chs. VI and VII.

PATRICK   [253

was about to sail. He approached the shipmaster and begged him to take him aboard. But the shipmaster was annoyed and replied roughly and angrily, "On no account seek to go with us." The youth turned away dismayed and took refuge in prayer, from which he was roused shortly afterward by a messenger, bidding him come quickly. Something had occurred to change the shipmaster's mind, and the boy was taken aboard.

The captain was engaged in the business of purchasing Irish wolf-hounds in the various towns along the coast and carrying them to southern Europe, where they were much in demand. His crew were rough fellows, and during the many days the homesick young man was with them, he must have suffered greatly. Muirchu says that they were "strange, barbarous and heathen men who worshiped many false gods." Patrick himself says that he held himself aloof from them, although he nourished a hope that some of them would become Christians.

Patrick in Gaul

The voyage lasted three days and terminated disastrously with a wreck on the coast of Gaul. For twenty-eight days the little band of mariners tramped through a desert country. There is reason for supposing that this may have been that part of southwestern Gaul through which the Vandals had lately passed on their way to Spain, leaving the countryside devastated. Their supply of food gave out, and they were reduced to desperate straits. The captain turned on the young man and reproached him in these words:

What, Christian, do you say now—that your God is still great and all-powerful? Why, then, don't you pray for us, that we may not perish here of hunger? For hardly shall we see a single human being again.[4]

Patrick says that he advised the captain to do his own praying. But he does not tell us whether or not the captain took his advice. At any rate, Patrick gives God the credit for the fact that a herd of swine soon appeared. The famished men fell upon the animals, slaughtered many of them and gorged both themselves and the dogs which they still had with them.

[4] *Confession*, VIII.

Nightmare or Theophany?

Now on that same night, when I was sleeping [wrote Patrick], Satan assailed me mightily, in such sort as I shall remember as long as I am in this body. And he fell upon me as it were a huge rock, and I had no power over my limbs. But whence did it occur to me—to my ignorant mind—to call upon Helias? And on this I saw the sun rise in the heaven, and while I was shouting "Helias" with all my might, lo, the splendour of that sun fell upon me, and straightway shook all weight from off me. And I believe that I was helped by Christ my Lord, and that his Spirit was even then calling aloud on my behalf.[5]

The fact that Patrick interpreted this obvious nightmare, due to his overeating of half-cooked pork, as a spiritual vision from Christ, raises the question as to how many of the visions of the world's saints have been due to physical causes.

It is interesting also to note the exclamation used by Patrick. A devout Christian would say that Patrick was calling upon God as Jesus did when he cried, "Eloi, Eloi," which some of those around the cross interpreted as "Elias, Elias." In fact, Dr. Todd, in his *Life of St. Patrick*, in commenting upon this incident, maintains as much. But the worship of the sun was prevalent in Europe in those days, and even in Ireland. There were notable affinities between the Druid sun worship and the eastern worship of solar deities. Consequently, a scholar, upon reading the *Confession*, would at once surmise that possibly Patrick was calling upon the sun, the Greek word for which is *Helios*. That suspicion would be strengthened by the fact that immediately after Patrick shouted the word, "the splendor of that sun fell upon" him, according to his own account. Students of theophanies will recognize the appearance of the bright light seen during the vision as characteristic of such experiences.

Wanderings in Gaul

The sailors deemed that the food had come from Patrick's God and thereafter they were respectful to him. It was two weeks more before they reached a town, just as their food had given out again.

5 Chs. VIII and IX.

For a period of some years after this our knowledge of Patrick's movements is very unsatisfactory. His *Confession* is disappointingly ambiguous in its statement. Reference[6] is made to another captivity of two months. He says that after a few years he was back in Britain with his parents, who urged him not to travel any more.

What happened between the time he reached the town in Gaul and his return to his parents is a matter of some dispute among his biographers. Some say that he became a monk and studied for some years in two monasteries, one at Lerins, an island off the coast of Provence, and another at Tours. Legends assert that he studied there with the well-known Martin of Tours, who later became the patron saint of France. It is even stated that this Martin was his uncle, but inasmuch as Martin of Tours died in the year 400, when Patrick was about eleven years old according to our best knowledge, it is quite unlikely that the two ever met.

There is no reference whatever in his *Confession* to any period passed in any monastery anywhere, nor does he mention any visit to the Pope, although one later account has it that he visited Rome in the year 431 and was commissioned by Pope Celestine to preach in Ireland; and another, that he went there between 441 and 443 and was given the approval of Pope Leo the Great. Since his *Confession* was written toward the close of his life and subsequent to these alleged visits, it is difficult to see why he omitted reference to such an expedition which would doubtless have seemed to him one of the most important events of his life.

Home in Britain

While he was visiting his parents he had another vision, the most significant of all that came to him. "In a vision in the night" he saw a man arriving, as if from Ireland, with a great many letters in his hand, one of which he gave to Patrick. Patrick thought he opened it and that it was entitled, "The Voice of the Hibernians." When he had read the major part of the letter, it suddenly seemed to him that he heard many voices speaking in unison. The people, who lived beside a forest near the western sea, in accents which he recognized as those of former companions in the days of his slavery, were calling to him, "We entreat you, holy youth, that you come here and walk among us."

[6] *Confession,* Ch. X.

Extremely moved by this appeal, Patrick awoke. It was evidently some time before he answered the call, however. The stories are too meager for us to know assuredly why he did not respond immediately. The fact that in his dream he was called a youth leads us to infer, contrary to common tradition, that the period of his stay on the continent had not been long and that he was still a young man. He speaks in his *Confession*[7] of a "few years" ("*paucos annos*") as the period of time before he returned to Britain from the continent. Allowing six years for his captivity in Ireland, and even six more for his experiences in Gaul, he would have been barely more than twenty-eight when the call came to him to return to Ireland. Somewhere around thirty is a common age for religious leaders to feel called to their lifework.

It may have been this consciousness of youth which hindered him from starting at once for Ireland. It may have been a consciousness of his lack of preparation for missionary work, for in his writings he is constantly referring to himself as "unlearned." A third reason for his remaining could have been the solicitude of relatives,[8] from whom he had been separated for so long. They probably looked upon his going to Ireland again, if he mentioned it, as a crazy adventure, and did everything possible to dissuade him.

The Missionary to Ireland

In chapter twelve of his *Confession* he states that he did not proceed to Ireland until he was "nearly worn out." What the phrase may mean it is hard to conjecture. It may signify that he was worn out by the studies which he undertook to prepare himself for his mission. The succeeding sentences indicate that he made such preparation, for he speaks of "God preparing him for what he should be." The phrase may mean, however, that he was worn out by the conflict in his own mind between the urgings of conscience and the arguments for remaining with his family. But go he did at last and, once on the island, set to work with great vigor and considerable ingenuity.

Legend says that he had not long been in Ireland before he came in conflict with the reigning ruler, Loiguire MacNeill, who may have been the son of that Niall who had taken the youth into cap-

---

7 Ch. X.   8 See *Confession*, Ch. X.

tivity. There is no mythology anywhere comparable in human interest and vivid imagery with the cycle of stories which soon grew up among the disciples of Patrick and their descendants. The Irish have always been an imaginative folk and have outdone themselves in describing the incidents of Patrick's conquest of Ireland for Christianity.

The story of his encounter with the king of the Irish, as told in Muirchu's book, reads very much like the experiences of Zoroaster at the Court of King Vishtaspa, or of Moses at the Court of Pharaoh. The Irish of Patrick's day were at the same stage of religion as the Persians in the time of Zoroaster, or the Egyptians in the days of Moses. That is, their religion was full of superstition and magic. All three accounts tell of tournaments of magic in which the advocate of the new religion overcame, by his enchantments, the mightiest magicians which the reigning king could bring against him.

The Contest of Magic

Just as Moses had to overcome the magic of Jannes and Jambres, so Patrick was opposed by Lothroch and Lucetmael. But by the power of God he was enabled to overcome them and all their schemes. In Muirchu's biography of Patrick, another parallel between him and Zoroaster is presented. Patrick came into conflict with a chieftain named Daire, from whom he at last secured a little plot of ground on which to build a church, but Daire commanded his groom to take his horse and put it to pasture on this holy ground. Next morning the horse was found dead, and when Daire commanded that Patrick be slain, a sudden disease fell upon the chieftain, from which he was cured only when his wife asked Patrick's blessing. The forgiving missionary blessed some water and gave it to the messengers, which, when they sprinkled it upon Daire and his horse, restored them both to life. One is reminded of the story of Zoroaster[9] and King Vishtaspa's favorite horse, by the cure of which the Masdean prophet won his way to power.

When Daire had been restored to life by Patrick's holy water, he "came to pay his respects to St. Patrick, bringing with him a wonderful bronze pot holding three gallons that had come from beyond the seas. And Daire said to the saint, 'Lo, this bronze pot is for thee.' And St. Patrick said, 'Grazacham.' And when Daire returned

[9] See chapter on Zoroaster, *supra*, pp. 74, 75.

to his own house, he said, 'That is a stupid man, who said nothing more civil than "Grazacham" in return for a wonderful bronze three-gallon pot.' And Daire then proceeded to say to his servants, 'Go, and bring us back our pot.' So they went and said to Patrick, 'We are going to take away the pot.' Nevertheless, St. Patrick that time too said, 'Grazacham. Take it away.' And they took it away. And Daire questioned his companions and said, 'What did the Christian say when ye took back the pot?' And they answered, 'He just said "Grazacham." ' Daire answered and said, ' "Grazacham," when it is given! "Grazacham," when it is taken away! His expression is so good that his pot must be brought back again to him with his "Grazacham." ' And Daire came himself this time, and brought the pot to Patrick, saying, 'Thy pot must remain with thee; for thou art a steadfast and unchangeable man; moreover, as for that parcel of ground which thou didst once desire, I give it thee now, in so far as I possess it; and do thou dwell there.' "

Evidently Daire did not know that *"Gratias agam"* was simply Patrick's polite and pious Latin for "I give thanks."

The Facts behind the Myths

A sober account of the actual facts of Patrick's mission to the Irish would credit his success rather less to miracle than to the statesmanship exhibited in his approach to the problem. He seems to have recognized the proper point of contact with the life of the people. During his previous stay upon the island he had observed their clannishness. They were as tribal in their loyalties as the ancient Israelites, and clan fought clan with enthusiasm and great joy upon every possible occasion, as their descendants continued to do and as their close relatives have done in Scotland, until comparatively recent times.

Patrick took advantage of this clannishness and sought first of all to win the chiefs, for he knew that if once the head of a clan were converted to Christianity, his loyal people would quickly follow in his train. Instead of combating the spirit of clanship he endeavored to improve it. With the wisdom of a great leader of men, he sought to recognize as far as possible the ancient customs to which the Irish were attached, and incorporated them in the Christian ceremonies which he established. He traveled widely, evidently in an early model of the Irish jaunting car, and seems to have met with almost uniform success. Later biographers state that he himself baptized twelve thousand people and that he founded a church for every day in the year.

King Loiguire still clung to the old Druid religion, but his brother Conall was converted, and thus Patrick gained a strategic position in the kingdom. His course seems to have been from County Down, where he began his work, through County Meath into Ulster, and then into Connaught. He made Armagh the Rome of Ireland. Most of his work was done in the northern half of Ireland: there are very few references to the southern counties.

The Druid Religion

Patrick's missionary work naturally encountered its greatest opposition from the religion already held by the Irish. That religion was almost pure magic and is an interesting example of that stage in the evolution of religion. We speak of its priests today as Druids. The *Drui* was not only a priest but a philosopher (wise man) and a wizard (physician and amateur scientist) as well, so by the ignorant people of the time he was believed to have almost unlimited supernatural power. All the mystery and magic of the forest was associated with the Druids, and as the oak tree was particularly sacred, their rituals were performed frequently in oak groves, and their highest reverence was reserved for its parasite, the mistletoe, the "Golden Bough" of Sir James Frazer.

When it is understood that the Druids were all-powerful for many centuries, not only in Ireland, but in England and Gaul, it is easy to understand why there are several Druidic survivals among Christians—such customs, for instance, as the winding of the Maypole, the use of holly at Christmas, and the custom of kissing beneath the mistletoe. Of course, in the modern revised version of the rites around the Maypole and under the mistletoe, the original phallic emphasis has been considerably sublimated.

"Knocking on wood" to avert a "cold," a deeply fixed superstition which two millennia of Christian teaching has been unable to eradicate, is allegedly a survival of Druidic and perhaps older appeals to the tree spirits for protection. And "Eeny, meeny, miny, mo," the apparently innocent children's "counting-out rhyme," especially in its earlier versions beginning "Eena, mena, mona, my," has been traced to the *filid* death chants used to select victims to be ferried across the *Menai* Strait and burned alive in wicker cages as human sacrifices in the Beltane spring festival on the sacred Isle of *Mona* (now Anglesey), the great Druid sanctuary, where prehistoric stone cromlechs still bear mute and mysterious testimony to the old-time religion.[10]

Druidism versus Christianity

The conflict of Christianity with Druidism had begun before Patrick and lasted for many centuries afterward. Thirteen hundred years later we find the early Christian settlers of New England protesting against the license and immorality of the Mayday merriment on Merrymount, where some of the gayer settlers were continuing a custom which they had brought with them from England.

In the year 1627 Thomas Morton, an English adventurer, erected in the village of Merrymount, now Quincy, Massachusetts, a Maypole, eighty feet high, and the orgies in connection with the Mayday celebration, which lasted for some days, were so faithful in their reproduction of the ancient Druid fertility cult, that the colonists of nearby Plymouth were scandalized. Captain Myles Standish arrested the enthusiastic Druid in 1628 and sent him back to England. Gay-colored streamers wound by Sunday-school children around a Maypole erected in a church yard are abiding evidence that although Christianity overcame Druidism, it did it by adopting some of its practices.

Wizardry

The Druids are supposed to have had power to bring sun or rain at will, and to cast out insanity by throwing a bewitched bit of straw in the face of their victim. They were believed to be able to forecast future events from dreams and visions and from the casting of lots and the interpretation of the chirpings of birds. Ravens were their favorite birds, and evidently they tamed them and kept them available for purposes of necromancy. When anyone consulted a Druid, the priest would pretend to receive an oracle from the croakings of the bird.

[10] See *Standard Dictionary of Folklore*, Vol. I, 1951, articles on "Counting-out Rimes" and "Eny, meny, miny, mo," by C. F. P.

The superstitions concerning ravens and their occult powers have persisted, and today there are many people in America who believe that it is a bad sign when a crow flies over their road as they start on a journey. If one wishes to have a sympathetic understanding of the fear in the heart of a follower of the Druid religion he has to but read Edgar Allan Poe's "The Raven."

Sneezing was an event of considerable importance, a trace of which survives today, when, after a sneeze, one sometimes hears the phrase "God bless you." The wizards seem to have been amateur psychiatrists, too, for, realizing the value of atmosphere in their incantations and rites, they wore white robes which were supposed, in themselves, to have magic power. Like the Hebrews and the magicians in the Court of Pharaoh, they had sacred rods. Those of the Druids were made of yew, inscribed with holy runes.

"Tara's Halls"

There is an incident of interest to readers of comparative religion in a section of Muirchu's life of Patrick, entitled, "Of the Heathen Feast at Temoria." It was an old custom of the Druids to have a springtime festival of great magnitude, during which all fires in the land were extinguished until the priests kindled a sacred fire in the palace of King Loiguire at Temoria. (Temoria is better known as Tara, familiar in the old song, "The Harp That Once Through Tara's Halls.") There were dire penalties for anyone lighting a fire during the period of darkness, but on Easter eve Patrick appeared on the Hill of Slane, on the north bank of the Boyne, and in sight of the people assembled for the Druid feast at Tara, nine miles off, lighted a great fire on the top of Slane. It was a challenge and was recognized as such. King Loiguire's magicians said to him,

Oh, king, live forever. As for this fire which we behold and which has been lighted up this night before one was lighted in thy house, that is, in the Palace of Temoria, unless it be put out on this night on which it has been lighted up, it will not be put out forever. Moreover, it will overcome all the fires of our religion.

This circumstantial account from the oral tradition about Patrick preserved for us by Muirchu represents not so much any particular historical event as the entire conflict between Patrick's Christianity and the Druidism of the reigning house. The story is a dramatization of the process whereby the springtime Beltane fire festival was absorbed by the Christian Easter.

Patrick was astute enough to recognize that such a formal fixed custom as the kindling of a springtime fire could not easily be eradicated, and therefore should be assimilated. Consequently, the very ancient springtime feast, which was old when Moses adapted it to Yahwehism in the wilderness and which was adopted from Judaism by early Christianity and connected with the death and resurrection of Jesus, continued its career in Ireland by amalgamating with the Beltane feast. Tradition says that the king set forth with nine chariots to investigate this impudent invasion. He had a conference with Patrick at which very wonderful things happened, but the result was that the king summoned Patrick to appear at the palace the next day.

The Magic Hymn

On his nine-mile journey to the palace, Patrick feared an ambuscade, and legend says that he protected himself and his companions by chanting a hymn. This hymn magically changed him and his companions to deer, so that those waiting in ambush saw only a herd of deer passing by. From this incident, the hymn which he chanted is known as "Faeth Fiada," or, "Deer's Cry." It is possible, however, that the words *Faeth Fiada* did not originally mean "Deer's Cry" for, as Professor Atkinson had suggested,[11] the very similar words *Feth Fiadha* mean a spell peculiar to Druids and poets who by pronouncing certain words made themselves invisible.

Now, this magic hymn is believed by some to have been the "Lorica," and it may be that the "Lorica" includes both what Patrick said upon that occasion and the later explanations of it. It shows that in the time of Patrick the religion of Christianity itself was closely related to magic. When he chanted his "Lorica" against the evil incantations of the Druids he represented that element in Christianity which still makes the sign of the cross to ward off the evil eye. After invoking the aid of the angels, archangels, patriarchs, and apostles, as well as of all the forces of nature, he concluded his hymn as follows,

11 *Liber Hymnorum*, Vol. II, p. 209.

I invoke therefore all these forces:

> against every fierce merciless force that may come upon my body and my soul;
>
> against incantations of false prophets;
>
> against black laws of paganism;
>
> against false laws of heresy;
>
> against encompassment of idolatry;
>
> against spells of women and smiths and druids;
>
> against all knowledge that is forbidden the human soul.

Christ for my guardianship today:

> against poison, against burning,
>
> against drowning, against wounding,
>
> that there may come to me a multitude of rewards;

Christ with me, Christ before me,
Christ behind me, Christ in me,
Christ under me, Christ over me,
Christ to right of me, Christ to left of me,
Christ in lying down, Christ in sitting, Christ in rising up,
Christ in the heart of every person who may think of me!
Christ in the mouth of every one who may speak to me!
Christ in every eye which may look on me!
Christ in every ear which may hear me!

I arise today:

> in vast might, invocation of the Trinity,
>
> belief in a Threeness;
>
> confession of Oneness;
>
> meeting in the Creator;

Domini est salus, Domini est salus, Christi est salus;
Salus tua, Domine, sit semper nobiscum.

Patrick as Lawmaker

The strange likeness of Patrick to Moses is emphasized by the fact that just as the latter is credited with having collected and codified the laws of his people, so Patrick is given the honor of the authorship of the famous Brehon laws. And similarly, as Moses is alleged to have set up many other laws which really came into being much later, so Patrick is popularly supposed to be the author of *all* these Brehon laws, although they were not written down in their present form until about the tenth century.

The section of the Brehon law known as the *Senchus Mor* or "Great Book of the Ancient Law" is primitive in form and partly expressed in verse. Scholars say that it was written sometime between the introduction of Christianity into Ireland and the end of the sixth century. Since that would include Patrick's period, there is no reason to deny that this part at least of the Brehon laws comes from Patrick himself, although the accompanying commentaries come from the *Brehon* or lawyers of later centuries.

The Miracles of Patrick

As early as the time of Muirchu a great cycle of miracle stories had clustered around Patrick, many of them similar to those told in the Christian Bible. It would appear that many of the Bible miracles which Patrick related were vaguely connected with him in the oral tradition, and in process of time were told as having occurred to him rather than to Bible characters. Muirchu is constantly pointing out how very much Patrick resembled Bible characters like Jonah, Moses, John the Baptist, and Jesus himself. We read of an angel appearing to Patrick in a burning bush which was not consumed;[12] of his conversing with a dead man in a tomb, as Jesus talked with Lazarus;[13] of the angels comforting and counseling him as they were wont to help saints of old;[14] and of how he saw the heavens open.[15]

The legend of Jesus turning water into wine becomes strangely changed in Patrick's ministry: he turns wine into ice. Once when he was eating with a certain Druid who desired his death, the priest put poison into Patrick's cup of wine. Patrick noticed it and blessed the wine, which immediately turned into ice "as when he had turned the vessel upside down, that drop only, fell out which the magician had put into it. And he blessed his cup again, and the liquor was restored to its own nature; and all marveled."[16]

12 Muirchu's *Life of Patrick*, Bk. II, Ch. 5.   15 Bk. I, Ch. 28.
13 Bk. II, Ch. 2.   16 Bk. I, Ch. 20.
14 Bk. II, Ch. 15.

The Snakes and Frogs

But the miracle most commonly associated with the name of Patrick is that of the expulsion of all snakes, frogs and toads out of Ireland. The story has been carried to all parts of the world by the migrating Irish and has become part of the common folklore of the race. In fact, it is practically all that the average person knows about Patrick. In Ireland today the legend is not confined simply to the statement that Patrick drove the reptiles from the land. The people of Connaught say that Patrick gathered all the snakes from the entire island into the western part of Connaught and drove them into the sea from the summit of *Cruachan Aicle,* or Eagle Hill (since known as Croagh Pat).

Whenever the snakes seemed disinclined to travel farther, he would ring his bell *Finn-Foya,* meaning "sweet voice." Then the snakes would hurry along rapidly enough. He was obliged to hurl the bell among them at the very last before they would leap from the rocks into the waves. In a museum in Dublin the visitor today is shown the very bell by which the snakes were driven. And if anyone doubts the legend, there is the bell to prove it. Furthermore, it is believed by many Irishmen that snakes and toads cannot live in Ireland, and if they should be brought there they would perish. This belief is a very ancient one.

In the latter part of the twelfth century A.D., Garaldus Cambrensis visited Ireland and wrote a book called the *Topography of Ireland,* introducing into it some of the legends he found in circulation among the natives. It is evident that even at that early date the story had been believed for some time. Garaldus himself did not believe that Patrick had driven the snakes out of Ireland. He thought that there was something about the soil which prevented their living there. But Garaldus did believe that no snakes could live in Ireland, and that imported ones died. He records that some English mariners brought snakes to Ireland which died even on shipboard before they reached land and states that in any country snakes and toads can be kept out of a garden by sprinkling over the surface soil brought from Ireland. Garaldus even believed that if a toad were put in a circle, the circumference of which was formed by a strip of leather made from the skin of any Irish animal, the toad would be unable to get out of the circle.

A Belgian monk named Jocelin, who lived in the same century as Garaldus, wrote a *Life of Patrick* in which he asserts that "until Patrick came to Ireland the place was cursed with the triple plague of reptiles, demons, and magicians." The *Tripartite Life of Patrick* was written in the tenth century or before by some Irish author. It is even more embroidered with legend than the accounts of Garaldus the Englishman, and Jocelin the Belgian, and is not trustworthy as an historical account, but it contains a version of Patrick's campaign of purification which may give a clue to the source of the legend about his driving out the snakes.

The author relates that when Patrick was proceeding triumphantly through Connaught, having great success on his mission, he celebrated Lent, going into the wilderness on the slopes of Cruachan Aicle. Like Moses on Sinai, he spent forty days there. As Easter Sunday approached, he was visited there by many demons, just as Christ was visited by the devil in the wilderness of Quarantania. To Patrick, the devils appeared in the form of huge black birds which came in great numbers and could not be driven away by his prayers. But when he rang his bell and flung it among them the birds left, and an angel came and ministered unto him.

This legend of the demon-possessed black birds may have suggested the legend of the demon-possessed reptiles of two centuries later. There are many parallels between the snake story and the folklore of other nations. Ophiolatry, or serpent-worship, was widespread among primitive peoples and was evidently a part of Druidism. Druids and other Celts believed that in the springtime of the year snakes gathered together in groups, especially on the eve of Mayday.[17] Now, it is a well-known fact among biologists and boys that snakes do appear in the springtime in groups and colonies. They may be found in large numbers on many a sunny ledge in the mountains. Besides, they are equally abundant in popular pictures of the torments of Hell.

In brief, the story of St. Patrick driving the snakes out of Ireland arose from the fact that he did drive from the island the Druids, whose connection in the popular mind with snakes is revealed by the twelfth-century Jocelin's phrase, "reptiles, demons, and magicians." As for the absence of snakes, frogs, and toads in Ireland, that was probably due to geological rather than theological causes.

17 Frazer, *The Golden Bough,* Vol. 10, p. 15.

The Death of Patrick

Of course, the death of Patrick is the occasion for many legends. Muirchu tells us that he died on the seventeenth of March at the age of one hundred and twenty (perhaps a pious parallel to the Deuteronomy 34:7 statement of Moses' age at death). The best scholarship is inclined to deduct fifty years from that estimate; and considers Patrick to have been born in 389 and to have died in 461.

Legend says that for twelve nights after his death there was no darkness and that for the rest of the year the nights were not as dark as usual. We are told of angels keeping watch over his body and singing songs, and that after they returned to heaven "they left behind them a most sweet odor, as of honey, and a delicious fragrance, as of wine."

His body was placed upon a wagon to which were attached two unbroken bullocks who were allowed to go their own way. Where they stopped, at Dun-Lethglaisse, known now as Downpatrick, there he was buried. Later, when a church was built above his body, a flame was seen bursting from his tomb. A great controversy arose afterward between two groups of disciples concerning the disposition of his relics and came to an end only "when the sea arose and forbade the people to fight."

For a period before the old man died he was unjustly criticized. It is alleged that he was supplanted as head of the Irish church, although that fact is not assuredly known. Tradition asserts that Patrick found no Christians in Ireland and left no heathen there, but the statement is an exaggeration. Nevertheless what Seumas Mac-Manus says in *The Story of the Irish Race*[18] is true: "What Confucius was to the Orient, Moses to the Israelite, Mohammed to the Arab, Patrick was to the Gaelic race."

Bridget

The work of evangelizing the island went on after Patrick's death. One of the most active persons in the years immediately following was a young woman variously known as Bridget, Bridgid, or Bride. She was born in the year 450 or 453 of a nobleman named Dubetach and one of his concubines. She was only eight years of

18 p. 124.

age, possibly eleven, at the time of Patrick's death, but popular legend says that she helped to sew his shroud. Another legend reports that she fell asleep during Patrick's preaching at one time and had a dream in which was foretold the part she was to play in later history.

On a farm little Bridget was a dairymaid, and upon occasions attended the sheep. The stories of her girlhood picture her as like St. Francis in her love for animals and birds, and miracles are related of her youth. Many suitors came seeking the hand of the beautiful maiden. But she had no use for them and found her greatest delight in giving away to the poor much of her father's wealth, exactly as Thomas Aquinas is reported to have done later. Her penchant for giving away other people's property developed to such an extent that she was soon left without a home. But her admirers gave her a house near which she built a church and founded a missionary school. Kildare, as she called her religious center, soon became almost as popular as Armagh itself. Bridget traveled about on missionary journeys, her fame spread to the continent, and she was a great influence in continuing the spread of Christianity. Legends grew up about this holy woman, and the Irish people today reverence her memory and call her the "Mary of the Gael."

She was buried at Kildare in a wonderful tomb which was plundered three centuries later by the Danes. Some say that her bones were interred in the same tomb with those of Patrick. When Garaldus visited Ireland he found at Kildare an eternal flame called the "fire of St. Brigit," kept burning by the nuns in her memory, which was not put out until the sixteenth century, when Henry the VIII closed the monasteries.

Columba

Four years before she died, Columba was born, known to the Irish as Colm Cille. As Bridget resembled in some ways the Virgin Mary, so Columba is comparable to Paul. His resemblance to the first Christian missionary is found, not only in his many evangelizing tours, but in the fact that he was a learned man. He founded churches throughout Ireland and went on a missionary tour to Scotland with twelve disciples when he was forty-two years old. As Patrick had made Armagh the center of the work, and as Bridget had chosen Kildare, so Columba selected the Island of Iona. Up and down the hills of Scotland he traveled founding churches and monasteries. Iona became the burial place of Scottish kings and nobles for many centuries.

Columba's love of scholarship showed itself in his avocation of preserving and copying the manuscripts of the Bible which came to his hand. He is credited with having made three hundred copies of the Christian Scriptures. He also wrote hymns and poems. Death came to him when he was copying one of the Psalms.[19]

The Irish people consider Patrick, Bridget, and Columba their three patron saints, and rightly so, for the pioneer work of Patrick was supplemented and strengthened by the heroic and self-sacrificing labors of the other two. They were responsible for having freed Ireland from its slavery to superstitious Druidism, which they supplanted with a higher conception of religion. Christianity suffered some changes in the process, of course, and Irish country people still retain, underneath the Christian religion, a deep-rooted love of fairies and other little folk whose origin can be found in ancient Celtic Druidism.

[19] NOTE: Columba's biography, largely a collection of miracle stories, was written in the latter half of the seventh century by his seventh successor as Abbot of Iona, Adamnan, another scholarly monk. The book reveals that Columba and his biographer were both concerned with maintaining, through the rules in their *Manual of Discipline,* a community monastery on Iona which strangely resembled in many aspects the Essene Covenanters of Qumran. Furthermore, Adamnan's other great but little-known masterpiece, *Fis Adamnain,* Vision of Adamnan, recounting a dream visit to the Seven Heavens and Hell, remarkably reflects one of the "lost" Books of Enoch and bridges the literary gap between that Essene classic and the *Divina Commedia* of Durante Alighieri, which appeared five centuries *after* the beautiful Irish Apocalypse of Adamnan.

XII

MUHAMMAD

[A.D. 570–632]

THE STRANGE PROPHET OF ISLAM

N<small>O ONE KNOWS</small> when the Black Stone fell from the sky upon the Arabian desert. Diodorus Siculus the Greek mentions it in his universal history written during the century before Christ. It may have been a very primitive race of men that heard its meteoric rush and saw its flaming arc through the heavens.

Many people came to gaze upon the wonder, and around it a town grew up. The town became a sacred city which waxed wealthy from the gifts and purchases of pilgrims from all Arabia. So precious did the stone become, both religiously and financially, that its reverent and prudent custodians decided to protect it. Just as Americans long afterward built a shelter for their revered Plymouth Rock, so the citizens of Mecca built a house for the Black Stone. To the mathematically minded early Arabians perfection was represented by the cube. The house they built near an ancient sacred spring for their heaven-sent stone, they called the Kaaba, or Cube.

There is an Arabian tradition which gives a different explanation of the origin of the Kaaba. It relates that when the Hebrew patriarch Abraham, at the behest of his jealous wife Sarah, banished into the desert his concubine Hagar and their child Ishmael, the exiles wandered far until they came into the valley of Mecca, where as they were perishing from thirst an angel revealed to them the spring

Zem Zem. As Hagar and the boy lay by the spring, the Black Stone fell from heaven at Ishmael's feet, and he was promised that his children should finally become more powerful than those of Isaac, the son of Sarah. Abraham himself, so the tradition says, came along later and helped Ishmael build at Kaaba. Christian scholars note with interest that the oldest name of Mecca was Bakkah, and some see a reference to this legend in the familiar Bible words of the 84th Psalm, "Who passing through the valley of Baca make it a well." As to the prophecy that the children of Ishmael would eventually surpass in strength the children of Isaac, the latest world census figures give the Moslems 416 million and the Jews twelve.

Enter Kutam

At the beginning of the seventh century of the Christian era a great flood damaged the Kaaba. In the reconstruction, when the point was reached for the restoring of the sacred Black Stone to its place in the eastern corner of the Kaaba, there was much rivalry among the various families of the Koreish tribe as to which should have the ineffable privilege. It was finally decided that the honor of replacing it or choosing someone to do it should fall upon the first man who chanced to enter the sacred court within which they were then disputing. All eyes turned eagerly to the gate.

The situation was dramatic in the extreme. The Koreish knew that he who would enter would thereby become a marked man among them, one designated by the gods for special favor, but they little knew that he would change the map of the world and the religion of continents. As they watched, there appeared outlined in the gateway a short but dignified man of thirty-five or forty, black of beard and piercing of eye, dressed in the garb of a rich merchant. They recognized him as one of their own tribesmen, Kutam, son of Abdallah and husband of Khadijah, the wealthy woman merchant of Mecca, whose caravans traveled far. Kutam was her agent and was also engaged in business in the city on his own account. He was known as a man of good judgment, and all the waiting Koreish hailed his appearance with sighs of relief that chance had made such an excellent choice.

Kutam had evidently heard the commotion in the Kaaba enclosure and had left his shop to see what his tribesmen were about. He was doubtless surprised to find himself the center of attention as he advanced through the gate but calmly listened to their excited explanations and agreed to their proposition. He proceeded to his delicate task with a full appreciation of its dramatic and political possibilities. Taking off his burnoose, he spread it upon the ground and, with all eyes upon him, reverently placed the stone upon the middle of the cloak. Then, calling the leaders of the several factions, he bade them take hold of the edges of the garment and lift it to the level of the stone's proper location in the wall. When it was at the desired height, he put the sacred relic in place himself and turned to receive the praises of his fellows.

It was probably at this time that men began to call Kutam by another name, "Muhammad," the praised one. The appellation was accepted and replaced his earlier name so completely that only a tradition remains to tell of it. Perhaps the new name changed the man. He went in and out among his associates as usual for a while, but he was preoccupied and thinking of other matters than buying and selling agricultural produce. After a time he was occasionally missed from the market place and it was noticed that his business was neglected. He was not praised so much but he was still the topic of conversation. They wondered what he was about.

In a cave among the foothills of Mount Hira not far from Mecca, Muhammad was meditating on religion. There is little doubt that his selection as restorer of the Black Stone turned his thoughts toward divine matters and was the beginning of a deep religious experience. Something was happening to the merchant of Mecca. Thoughts too big for him were struggling for expression in the days following the affair of the Kaaba. He had to get away from the bazaars into the quiet of the wilderness. Like all great religious leaders, he sought solitude to marshal his tumultuous thoughts and surging emotions.

The Orphan

Muhammad's life up to this time had not exhibited any remarkable traits. He was born in the latter half of the sixth century A.D. in Mecca. The year is usually given as 570, figuring from the report that he was 62 years of age at the known time of his death, 632. But if he was born "in the year of the elephant," and tradition on that point is ancient and persistent, that would place his birth in 562 at the latest. The year of the elephant was named from the invasion of Arabia by Abraha the Abyssinian, who had a war elephant among his forces, which much impressed the Arabians. This invasion occurred during the war between the Byzantine emperor Justinian and Khosrau I of Persia, which raged from 539–562. Muhammad's parents both died in his infancy, and the orphan spent his youth in the desert among the Bedouins, cared for by a foster-mother, Halima.

The Caravan Conductor

When the boy reached adolescence, he made long journeys by camel caravan with his uncle, Abu Talib, as far as Syria and perhaps into Abyssinia. The bright-eyed lad saw much on these trips and learned the hazardous business of conducting caravans. He became proficient at it and when only in his twenties secured a fine position in the employ of the wealthy widow Khadijah. Tradition says he married her when he was twenty-five and she was forty. He was older than that, however, if he was born in 562, and she was probably younger than forty, for she bore him seven children.

Upon the caravan journeys and even at home he came into contact with Jews and Christians and learned from their mouths the stories in their sacred books. He admired Abraham, Moses, and Jesus, although he did not understand the theology of Judaism or Christianity, nor the difference between them. He supposed that Miriam, the sister of Moses, was the same person as Mary, the mother of Jesus, and that the Christian trinity was composed of Jehovah, Mary, and Jesus. It is very doubtful that he read any of the Bible: indeed, it has not been proved that he ever read anything, or wrote anything. He called himself "the illiterate prophet." But he had a retentive memory and remembered the oral traditions of Jew, Christian, and Arab pagan with delightful impartiality and little discrimination. Dr. R. H. Charles, the great authority on the noncanonical books called the Apocrypha and the Pseudepigrapha, said that Muhammad must have had access to one of the Essenic Books of Enoch, since there are at least six *suras* (chapters) of the Koran (3, 6, 18, 23, 41, 47) in which "every detail is borrowed" from the Essenic descriptions of the seven heavens.[1]

Eight fragmentary manuscripts of various Books of Enoch in

[1] *The Book of the Secrets of Enoch,* Morfill and Charles, Oxford, 1896, p. xlvii.

Aramaic were found in Qumran Cave IV in 1952,[2] but are not yet available for study.

Animism in Arabia

Arabia in the early seventh century A.D. was ripe for a religion which would unite the scattered warring tribes. They had religion but not a religion. Indeed, the student of the evolution of religion can see in the beliefs of pre-Muhammadan Arabia an interesting stage of development. Animism was in the process of becoming polytheism. The worship of sacred springs, stones, trees and mountains naturally led to the conception of guardian spirits in charge of each holy spot. These patron saints were soon personified and became gods and goddesses. As pilgrims passed from shrine to shrine they became polytheists with a growing pantheon. Allah was dimly recognized as the greatest but not the only deity. Some scholars think Allah was a common name for any god. In Mecca three goddesses were worshiped, Allat, Aluzza, and Manat, and they were called the daughters of Allah, although Allat was sometimes looked on as his consort.

The Prophet in the Cave

Even at this distance it is not difficult to follow Muhammad's probable line of reasoning as he meditated in his cave. Here was his homeland Arabia bound and circumscribed spiritually and morally by strong but senseless superstitions and a crude paganism. He had come into contact with a Semitic monotheism that was refreshing and inspiring. Why could not his people have a better religion, a monotheism of their own? Who would bring a worthy religion to Arabia?

The sources are too obscure for us to be able to determine when or exactly how Muhammad's theophany took place. Most prophets and mystics relate the shining of a bright light when God appeared to them. This was true of Moses, Zoroaster, Buddha, Jesus, and Paul. But Muhammad's experience was different. We are told nothing of any light, but of uncanny noises, resounding like bells, of vague voices speaking and of trancelike fits. Evidently these disturbing spiritualistic phenomena occurred over a considerable period of

2 *Revue Biblique*, Jan. 1956, pp. 50, 60.

time. Somebody seemed to be desiring to communicate with him and tell him to tell others something.

One night the urgency of his spiritual disturbance broke through into his consciousness and became clearly vocal in what Muhammad took for a divine command. The voice was that of "a faithful spirit" ordering him to repeat to men the words which would be dictated to him. This first revelation has been identified as Sura (or chapter) 96 of the Koran, beginning, "Recite in the name of thy Lord, who hath created all things; who hath created man of congealed blood." Here was a clear "call" for him to prophesy. Other revelations came, and he became convinced that there was a heavenly book, the contents of which were being revealed to him gradually, a chapter at a time.

He did not begin public preaching at once. He told his wife Khadijah about these manifestations. Very naturally she decided to visit the cave and observe for herself what was going on there. She saw enough to cause her to decide to seek advice from a friend of the family's who was wise in religious matters. Waraka the mystic had himself become dissatisfied with the religions of Arabia and was experimenting with monotheism and studying Christianity. Evidently Muhammad was not the only seeker for the light in Mecca at that time. Waraka became convinced of the genuineness of Muhammad's experiences and probably confirmed the new prophet's growing conviction that he was in the direct line of the accredited prophets Abraham, Moses, and Jesus, and destined to bring their work to completion.

When Muhammad found that besides Khadijah and Waraka he had ardent supporters in his cousin Ali, his slave Zeid and his old friend and business chum, the cloth merchant Abu Bekr, his confidence increased. Meetings were arranged in the house of an early convert, Arkam, and there the former produce merchant and caravan leader assumed his new role of prophet and repeated the divine communications which he had memorized in his cave.

Muhammad's Message

Under the stimulus of the intimate and friendly atmosphere of the little group of disciples he developed his message, which he summed up in the phrase, "There is no god but Allah; and Muhammad is his prophet." Thus was first delivered to Arabia its needed monotheistic religion. But long years of struggle awaited the prophet before his message would be accepted by his country-men.

When Muhammad set out to preach in the streets of Mecca he was received with mockery or indifference. But as he grew bolder and, aroused by opposition, denounced his hearers bitterly for not accepting him, he met angry looks and heard muttered threats. To all who would listen he spoke of Allah, the great and only God, "Fly therefore unto God; verily I am a public warner unto you from him."

He seems to have identified Allah with Jehovah and to have echoed the Mosaic commandment, "Thou shalt have no other Gods before me." Boldly he declared that all other gods and goddesses were false. Into the idolatrous nature worship of Mecca his message cut like a sword of truth. He pointed out that the idols were noth-ing. The only reality was Allah; the only duty, submission to Allah.

Now the Arabic word for submission was *islam,* and Muhammad so drilled that word into the minds of his hearers that the whole re-ligion he founded is named Islam. The common Western interpre-tation of the philosophy of Islam is incorrect: it does not mean mere submission to necessity, a fatalistic bowing to the inevitable. The doctrine is that whatever happens, happens according to Al-lah's will. Therefore all is well. The value of Muhammad's theology was that it brought peace of mind: the danger was that it tended to inhibit progress.

The Enemy of the People

When Muhammad openly announced that the religious customs which had gathered around the Kaaba were superstitions, even the religiously indifferent pricked up their ears. For four months every year hostilities had long been suspended in Arabia that pil-grims might visit Mecca unmolested by brigands. The only robbers then were the merchants in the Meccan bazaars and the purveyors of the sacred waters of Zem Zem.

The "praised one" found himself the cursed one after he de-clared the falsity of the Meccan religion. If the sacred places of the city were only objects of deluded superstition, then people would no longer come to Mecca to worship, and the prosperity of the city would be ruined. Did not the wealth of his own tribe, the Koreish, depend upon the reputation of the Kaaba? Was this fellow to be permitted to utter such heresies? Surely he was an enemy of the people. It was as if a resident of an old New England town, which depended for its income upon the summer tourists who came to see its historical sites, should persistently proclaim in public that all the profitable history of the town was mere myth.

Muhammad recoiled from the fury of his enraged fellow citizens and sought to compromise with them as he saw his mission endangered at the very outset. He even revised one of the Suras which he had been reciting, in which he had condemned the three favorite goddesses of the city. In conciliating his opponents he inserted after the rhetorical question, "Have you seen Allat and Aluzza and that other, Manat the third idol?" the new line, "These are the sublime princesses and truly their intercession may be looked for." Upon this recantation the listening Meccans forgivingly prostrated themselves with Muhammad before Allah.

But the prophet's conscience troubled him, and his faithful followers reproached him. Filled with remorse and throwing policy to the winds, he said that the devil had whispered the false line in his ear and that it was preposterous to suppose that God had daughters. That was as blasphemous as the Christian teaching that God had a son! To make amends for his cowardly compromise with idolatry he launched into a preaching campaign in which he denounced those who refused to believe that he was the messenger of God and predicted for them the same terrible fate which had fallen on those who had persecuted the prophets which were before him. We learn that, "When he talked of the Day of Judgment, his cheeks blazed, and his voice rose and his manner was fiery."

Certainly his words were fiery enough in the fourth Sura, "Verily those who disbelieve our signs, we will surely cast to be broiled in hell fire; so often as their skins shall be well burned, we will give them other skins to exchange, that they may taste the sharper torment." Such torture rivals that in Isaiah's description of hell, "where their worm shall not die nor their fire be quenched" (Isaiah 66:24), which Mark says (9:48) was accepted by Jesus.

There was a stern moral note also in Muhammad's preaching. He condemned many of the social conditions in Mecca and urged reforms. Licentiousness prevailed, much of it with a religious sanction in the phallic worship of the fertility goddesses. Adultery was common and women were treated cruelly. Female children were frequently killed. In business, dishonesty of the most flagrant sort and excessive usury were common practice. The poor were oppressed, and the rich lived in gluttony and drunkenness. Murder and theft went unpunished unless the victim belonged to a powerful tribe. Against all these social abuses Muhammad directed his denunciations.

His career would have been very brief had he not belonged to the strong Koreish tribe. The people of Mecca endured him for months, knowing that to deal harshly with him would bring on an intertribal war. When Muhammad found few converts, only forty in the first three years, he grew more extravagant in his condemnations, and it was decided that something must be done to hush him up. Abu Talib was the head of the family to which Muhammad belonged, and it was intimated that if he did not muzzle his troublesome nephew, others would, even if war resulted. When his uncle advised the fiery prophet to moderate his words. Muhammad replied, "Though they gave me the sun in my right hand and the moon in my left, to bring me back from my undertaking, yet will I not pause till the Lord carry my course to victory, or till I die for it."

He is a brave man who can persist in a lonely and unpopular course when family pressure is brought to bear. That this bold decision cost him much is indicated by the fact that he burst into tears at its close. His uncle was much affected and promised to stand by him.

The Prophet's Trials

War did not break out, but persecutions and insults increased daily. Then came a rapid succession of events whose precise order of happening we do not know, but all were calamitous for Muhammad. A number of converts to the new faith were obliged to flee for safety to Abyssinia. Muhammad himself went to Taif, seventy miles away, to make more converts, but was driven out with insults and missiles. An edict exiling most of his followers from Mecca to a rocky valley east of the city made life very difficult. Then his faithful wife Khadijah and his protecting uncle Abu Talib both died. It was a hard time for the prophet and his followers. Still he preached Islam to them, submission to the will of Allah.

The Sword

Nevertheless, it was probably during this discouraging period, when blow after blow fell upon him, that a new policy was shaping itself in his mind. To put it briefly, when the iron entered into Muhammad's soul, he forged it into a sword.

Preaching, exhortation, denunciation, the reciting of the Suras—this method of bringing men to the worship of the one God had failed. At least the results were few and slow to arrive. The humiliations and insults to which his proud soul had been subjected forced him to fight for his most precious faith. If it were not to perish from earth, this new religion must have the benefit of temporal power. Force had been employed to humiliate and defeat the prophet of Allah. The prophet would even use force to place the religion of Allah in power. But as Carlyle has said in *Heroes and Hero Worship,* where he glorifies Muhammad in the chapter on the hero as prophet, "First get your sword!"

The organizing genius of Muhammad is best appreciated when one realizes that a decade from the time when he was a discouraged exile in a rocky glen with a hundred half-starved followers, he had so engineered affairs that he was the religious, political and military head of all Arabia. How did he do it?

Yathrib

He found his sword in Yathrib.

More than two hundred miles north of Mecca lay Yathrib, inhabited by Jews and two tribes of Arabs. To Mecca to the annual religious festival of the year 620 came some of the latter, and Muhammad saw them there. The edict of the exile against him and his followers had recently been lifted. Some say that the document of banishment had been eaten by mice; others that Muhammad had promised not to try to divert Meccans from their own religion.

At any rate Muhammad had not given his word to desist from preaching to those who came to Mecca from other towns, and he much impressed the men of Yathrib. Their reception of his message encouraged him to ask what chance there would be for him in their city. They promised to investigate and to report in a year. A deputation of twelve waited on him a year later, reported progress and swore loyalty to him, pledging themselves to worship only Allah, to eschew slander, adultery, theft and infanticide, and to obey Muhammad "as far as was right." The twelve returned to Yathrib as missionaries and worked so enthusiastically that a year later, March of 622, seventy-three men journeyed to Mecca, met Muhammad secretly, struck his hand in fealty and invited him earnestly to come to Yathrib. He would come if they would vow to take the sword to defend him. They did, and he promised to come soon.

The Hegira

The careful prophet, however, sent his Meccan adherents to Yathrib ahead of him and followed in June with only one disciple, Abu Bekr, stealing secretly away at night. From that year, 622, Moslems date their era. The year which Christians call A.D. 622–623 is for them year one A.H., *Anno Hegirae,* the Year of the Flight.

A warm welcome awaited the prophet in Yathrib. Instead of giving him the keys of the city, they renamed it for him. *Medinat al nabi,* the city of the prophet, shortened to Medina. For eight years Muhammad was very busy training a city in a new religion, a new code of morals, and a new method of warfare. Whenever a decision was to be made, Muhammad would go into a trance and his utterance would be taken as an oracle to decide the matter.

There were many Jews in Medina, and at first the prophet endeavored to win them to his religion by prescribing that in prayer his followers should face Jerusalem. But he found the Jews remarkably tenacious of their ancient religion. Many of his Suras included interesting stories of the lives of Jewish heroes, but the garbled versions which Muhammad had picked up in his youthful travels and which had filtered through his memory irritated the Jews, who pointed him to the correct stories in their scriptures. These, with sublime aplomb, he declared to be forgeries and perversions, since what Allah had revealed to him must be the correct version.

The refusal of the Jews to accept what Muhammad considered the pure religion of Abraham led him to change the *kiblah,* or direction in prayer, from Jerusalem to Mecca. The change meant more than a reversal of policy toward the Jews. It was a challenge to all Arabia. Muhammad was appropriating for the holy place of his new religion the most sacred spot in the whole country. At the same time it was a clever appeal to the Kaaba worshipers to join his ranks.

In Medina Muhammad's religion grew in strength every day. The energetic prophet had come into his own and was making the most of his opportunity. In a brief time he had built up a city-state. Where had been discord and turmoil, order prevailed. He built a mosque and instituted daily worship and religious education. He was practically dictator, like Calvin in Geneva later, but insisted that he was only the agent of Allah, reciting his decrees. Any rebellion was heresy, promptly punished.

The Battle of Bedr

The problem of making a living soon faced the Muhammadans who had come from Mecca. It was solved by their turning brigands and robbing caravans. When they attacked pilgrims during the sacred months, thus violating the ancient truce of the desert, the indignant people of Mecca sent an expedition of nine hundred men against Muhammad. He met it with three hundred at Bedr and won a victory, owing to the superior discipline of his troops and their fanatic disregard of death. Muhammad had revealed that the reward of one who died fighting for Islam would be immediate transition to a paradise of unspeakable bliss, where every sensual gratification would be provided. The effect of the victory at Bedr was to increase Muhammad's prestige. His armies did not always win in the campaign which followed, but his power grew rapidly, and Mecca began to prepare for the inevitable. The Koreish decided there was no use fighting any longer against the man who had been divinely chosen to replace the Black Stone in the Kaaba wall.

Muhammad in Mecca

The Muhammad who rode into Mecca victorious in January 630 at the head of an army of ten thousand fighting men was not the same man who had fled from it eight years before, although, histrionically enough, he rode Al Kaswa, the same camel. In Khadijah's place was now a whole harem of wives and concubines. The persecuted prophet had become a pampered prince. His Suras had lost their early fire and were now rambling discourses concerned with such matters as rebukes to his wives for complaining about the unfair distribution of his attentions. The prophet who had denounced the superstitious practices of Kaaba worship now included them in his religion. The pilgrimage to Mecca had been made part of it, even to the kissing of the Black Stone and the quaffing of the brackish waters of Zem Zem.

It has frequently happened in the development of a religion that the followers of a prophet after his death have made compromise with competing cults and have achieved power at the expense of purity, incorporating parts of the rival religion in order to absorb it. But Muhammad achieved the synthesis himself during his lifetime. There was already much of Judaism in his teachings, and even of Christianity as he knew it. Now he included many customs of the old pagan religion. Muhammad gave Mecca the same thorough housecleaning that he had given Medina. He consolidated all the tribes of Arabia into one religious and political unit. Ambassadors came to him from so many tribes and nations that the year after the capture of Mecca was called "the year of the deputations."

No wonder that in two years after the capture of Mecca Islam was supreme throughout Arabia.

The Death of the Prophet

With the keen sense of the dramatic which never forsook him he called his followers together, gave them much good advice, and then said, "Oh, Allah! Have I not completed my mission?" And all the people answered, "Yea, Allah!" Then he returned to Medina to die. The disease was probably pleurisy, but he insisted that his sickness was due to goat's flesh poisoned by an enemy. He lingered but a few days and died in the arms of his favorite young wife, Ayesha.

Muhammad's Character

Ayesha knew him well and summed up his sensualism in a devastating epigram, "The prophet loved three things—women, perfumes, and food; he had his heart's desire of the first two, but not of the last." Of women, his taste ran to widows with a temper; of perfumes, he preferred musk; of food, he especially liked mutton, dates, honey, cucumbers, and pumpkins. For recreation he delighted in cobbling shoes. Perhaps his greatest joy was when he beheld the severed heads of his enemies.

His dislikes were just as varied. He detested silk-lined clothes, interest charges, dogs, others' lies, Jews and Christians. He hated poets, and said, "Every painter will be in hell."

He was inordinately vain. A clever woman poet satirized him. She was slain when asleep with her child at her breast, and the vengeful Muhammad praised her murderer. Once he tortured a Jew to find the location of hidden treasure and then had him killed and added the widow to his harem. Strange indeed was the character of the prophet. How could such a person inspire such reverence and devotion? It is one of the puzzles of history.

It was not that he developed a great theology, either, for what little theology Islam has, worthy of the name, was built up after Muhammad had long been dead.

The Secret of His Success

The only explanation of the remarkable success of his religion is that he knew his people and deliberately planned a religion which would be attractive to them. They loved the dramatic, and he always gave it to them with all the flourishes. They loved their country, and he made patriotism a part of religion. Like all nomads, they coveted the lands and wealth of their more civilized neighbors, and he told them it was their religious duty to conduct "holy wars" of conquest, which brought them rich booty. He knew that men like women, and women like property. So he allowed the men plenty of women on earth and promised them an endless supply of young and beautiful damsels in heaven. And he allowed the women property rights eleven centuries before Christendom dreamed of such a thing. In every way he sought to make religion easy. He even said, in the fourth Sura, "God is minded to make His religion light unto you: for man was created weak."

He did not burden them with prescribed duties but left them simply the ambiguous Koran and the five cardinal duties of the true Moslem,

1. Acceptance of the creed: There is no God but Allah; and Muhammad is His prophet,

2. Prayer, preferably five times a day, but at least three,

3. Almsgiving,

4. Observance of the fast of the month Ramadan,
5. The pilgrimage to Mecca, once at least.

The Spread of the Faith

There was a revolt after the prophet's death. All Arabia fell away save Medina, Mecca, and Taif. But under the leadership of Muhammad's faithful friend, Abu Bekr, all Arabia was won back in eighteen months. The spread of Islam by the sword in the next decade, 634–644, under Omar was incredibly rapid. Damascus fell in 635; Jerusalem in 636. The Euphrates region was won from Persia in 637. Egypt capitulated in 640. When Omar was assassinated in 644, he had carried Moslem power to the very borders of India.

Hardly a check was suffered by the Muhammadan armies until a century after the prophet's death. All northern Africa and even Spain fell into their hands. At the Battle of Tours in France in 732 Charles Martel stopped them. But they held for centuries what they had gained. When Europe suffered the eclipse of learning in the so-called Dark Ages, culture and science were kept alive in Islam. Even today when we write the date we use Arabic figures.

The Koran

The Muhammadan Bible is about the size of the New Testament and consists of 114 Suras or chapters, each comprising a single revelation. Tradition says that Muhammad dictated each Sura during or after a trance and that one of the bystanders wrote down the sacred words upon the nearest available writing surface, bits of leather, ribs of palm leaves, flat stones and even shoulderblades of sheep.

The Koran seems to us an incoherent jumble of legends and laws, but it is much reverenced and constantly read by Moslems. It is read more than any other sacred book in the world. The Christian Bible may be the "best seller" and "the book nobody knows" in America, but the Koran is the book everybody reads in Islam. Rambling and uninspiring as the Suras seem to us, many of those who have followed their precepts have lived beautiful lives. Christian devotional literature has no nobler sentence than this one from the Moslem woman saint, Rabia,

O God, if I worship Thee in fear of Hell, burn me in Hell: if I worship Thee in hope of Paradise, exclude me from Paradise: but if I worship Thee for Thine own sake, withhold not Thine everlasting beauty.

Islam Today

Islam is divided into seventy-two sects or denominations, and there is a great spirit of unrest in the Moslem world. Reform movements seek to make the religion less formal and literal and more ethical and humanistically scientific, but modern science is even harder to reconcile with orthodox Moslemism than with orthodox Christianity. Nevertheless, at the call to prayer from thousands of minarets this very day, over four hundred million followers of the prophet bowed themselves reverently toward Mecca, the city of the Black Stone and the sacred spring Zem Zem, and chanted, "There is no God but Allah; and Muhammad is His prophet."

XIII

❧

AQUINAS

[A.D. 1227–1274]

THE "DUMB OX WHO FILLED
THE EARTH WITH HIS BELLOWING"

I F IT IS TRUE, as modern psychologists assert, that a man's whole
life is colored by the emotional shocks of the first few years,
something very startling must have occurred in the infancy of
Thomas Aquinas, for he was one of the most remarkable religious
geniuses that ever trod this earth, unusual in both his emotional
and intellectual life and the interaction of the two. We shall attempt here no psychological analysis of the greatest of the medieval
scholars, but such a study might reveal valuable data about the
mental life of children, data of importance to our whole educational method.

The Child in the Castle

The boy was born in the year 1227 in the Castle of the Dry Rock
(Roccasecca), the family stronghold of the Counts of Aquino, in
the kingdom of Naples. The infancy narratives which are sooner or
later told of every great religious leader are not wanting in the
biography of Thomas. There is the usual Annunciation, made to

his mother Theodora by a good hermit, Bonus the Solitary, in the classic formula, "Rejoice, O lady, for thou art with child, and thou shalt bring forth a son whom thou shalt call Thomas."

Theodora protests her unworthiness, but in due time bears a son. The pious find it significant that he was born in the year when the sainted Louis the Ninth of crusading fame came to the throne, which was also the year when Francis of Assisi died. They tell, too, of a halo about his baby head and that his infant cries would cease when he was given a book as a plaything. A characteristic legend, in part very credible, relates that his mother once found him with a bit of paper in his hands which she could not account for. When he fought for it as she tried to take it away, she let him have it, because she saw that it was inscribed, "Hail, Mary." The child promptly swallowed it. We know that when he grew to manhood, he preached all one Lent on this text. The pious would see in the sermon series the result of the swallowing of the text, but others might judge the sermons to be the cause of the infancy narrative.

Legend's most significant contribution to the study of the child's psychology, however, has little of the miraculous and is probably true. Roccasecca Castle, whose ruins are still discernible, crowned a great rocky bluff which stood out above the circumjacent plain. In the month of June 1230, many earthquakes occurred in the neighborhood of Naples, and during a severe electrical storm, lightning struck the prominent castle and killed Thomas' little sister by his side. The three-year-old boy was unharmed physically, but the event must have made a deep impression on him.

The delicate adjustments of the human mind are still beyond the analysis of the most skillful psychologist, even when all the circumstances of such emotional shocks are known, but the sense of a Great Power beyond human control may have entered his consciousness even that early and imbedded itself so deeply as to account in some measure for his impregnable and unquestioning adult faith in God. The three-year-old child was of course too young to understand the cause of his sister's death, but the family conversation for months afterward doubtless fixed in his mind the impression that he had been miraculously spared by God for some high destiny.

What the high destiny was his mother Theodora thought she knew. The most conspicuous object upon the horizon as one looked out from the ramparts of Roccasecca was the monastery of Monte

Cassino, a rich and powerful abbey. More than two hundred years before, a fighting Count of Aquino had taken Roccasecca itself by force from the control of the abbey. Theodora wished to have the lands and wealth of Roccasecca and Monte Cassino again united, and schemed to secure that end by preparing her young son Thomas to fill the abbot's seat someday. Her later acts give us ground for believing that she must have frequently turned the eyes and thoughts of the boy toward the abbey on the mountain top six miles away.

The Child in the Monastery

When he was but five years of age, his parents took him to the monastery, dedicated him there to God, and left him to be taught and trained by the monks. So at a most impressionable age the boy found himself in cloistered halls in the company of sober, slow-moving men who talked much and with great reverence of One called God. Every activity of the place centered in the thought of God. In the early morning the still sleepy child found himself one of a solemn company making obeisance before the Holy Presence. Not a meal might be touched without invoking God's blessing.

In the traditions of the Benedictine monks whose most prominent monastery was Monte Cassino, which sheltered the bones of St. Benedict himself, the story is still reverently told that little Thomas of Aquino kept asking the monks, *"Quid est Deus?* What is God?"* The answer which his teachers gave him was not completely satisfying to his inquiring mind. There was then no sufficient answer to that question, nor has there ever been, but in his later writings, Thomas came nearer to making a comprehensive answer for his time than any man has ever come.

Monte Cassino was a great center of learning. There the boy very early laid a firm foundation for the imposing structure of his vast knowledge. The elements of Latin grammar were fixed in his mind by memorizing the Psalms and other Latin texts. He studied Virgil, Cicero, Seneca, Lucian, Ovid, Horace and many other authors, besides the elements of logic and philosophy. The simplicity and clarity of his later style can be better accounted for when one knows what masters he read in early youth. For seven years, from the age of five until he was twelve, Thomas remained in the monastery. We can understand the remarkable saintliness of the man when we know the rigid training to which he was subjected in those seven plastic years. The Benedictine order of monks required of its members certain severe disciplines, holding that the ideal monk is devout, prayerful, sober, silent, given to periods of solitude, and strictly observant of all rules.

No Puritan child in New England was ever trained in as rigorous a school as the little Thomas. His early education was calculated to kill all love of play and destroy any sense of humor, and his masters did their work well. But it seems that they had little difficulty with the boy, who naturally, or perhaps unnaturally, fell into the strict routine of the monastery and felt at home in its atmosphere of quiet piety. He was a "good boy," sweet in spirit, sober in demeanor, and earnest in devotion. He probably never played a rollicking game with other boys in his life.

The peace of the monastery was suddenly and rudely disturbed from without by the warfare between Pope Gregory and the Emperor Frederick. The vicinity of Monte Cassino was the scene of several battles. Even while the abbot was at Frederick's court pledging loyalty to his gracious monarch, the sly sovereign sent soldiers to Monte Cassino to capture and rob the wealthy abbey. Some of the monks were killed and the rest driven out and the rich treasury rifled.

The Boy at Loreto

Thomas, now a boy of twelve, found himself very suddenly in a totally different environment. Forced by the sack of the monastery to seek refuge with his parents, who had removed from Roccasecca to Loreto, another castle of the Aquinos, his routine was interrupted and he entered another world. The medieval castle life was everything which the monastery life was not. In place of quiet was music, song and laughter; in place of meditation was lusty lovemaking; in place of peaceful prayers was tourneying and fighting. The castle life seemed to have no appeal for Thomas. One would think that to a boy of twelve the life and color of Loreto would have been irresistible. But his character had already been molded along other lines. It is characteristic of his whole life that he found opportunity for religious good works wherever he might be. The whole atmosphere of the place was worldly, yet around the youth there seemed to be an odor of sanctity and a halo of goodness.

It was a time of famine among the peasants of the neighborhood, and the usual group of beggars about the castle gate was augmented by the scarcity of food until it became a crowd. To Thomas his father assigned the task of dispensing food to the starving people. He eagerly assented and when he found the assigned supplies insufficient for the need, took more from the storehouse without securing his father's permission. We are told that once when his father caught him with his cloak full of food and spoke sharply to him, the boy in confusion dropped the provisions, but instead of meat and bread, roses showered at his feet! Properly chastened by this divine rebuke, the father said that the boy could give away anything and everything he wished. In discussing the dubious morality of this doubtful story, one pious biographer of St. Thomas remarks ingenuously,

It is a very beautiful legend, and there is no reason to believe it is not founded on fact; anyhow, it leaves upon the mind a pleasing and edifying impression. . . . It may possibly be objected that there could be no virtue in taking food, even for the poor, without permission. But the answer to this is simple. What is a sin in one man is not necessarily a sin in another man. St. Thomas was, I take for granted, divinely guided to carry out the action of a higher law.[1]

The naïveté of the child and the pure casuistry of the commentator are beautifully matched. Thomas' stay at his father's castle was very brief. Perhaps his father sent him away hurriedly lest he should impoverish the family by his unlimited charity. And the fact that he sent him to the University of Naples may reveal another paternal motive.

The Youth in Naples

Naples, under the patronage of the Emperor Frederick, had become by 1240 a magnificent city. A brilliant and sophisticated society and a great university with a faculty of learned and noted men combined to give style and prestige to the beautiful city by the sea. It was a center of fashion, pleasure, and learning. It had also the reputation of being the wickedest city in the world. Perhaps the father of Thomas, having seen and noticed what the monks had

[1] *Life and Labors of St. Thomas of Aquin*, by Archbishop Vaughan, abridged by Dom Jerome Vaughan, pp. 30, 31.

made of his son, desired to counteract such excessive and unnatural piety by plunging the boy into an environment which would make him a man of the world.

In the university the boy soon attracted attention by his scholarship and ability. His ardor for study and his talent for comprehending a problem and its solution almost simultaneously enabled him to make great strides in his education and to shine even in the brilliant company in which he found himself. The time which other students spent in play and in the delights of the city was by Thomas devoted to the study of the precious volumes which the generosity of Frederick had made available. It is related by an early biographer, Malvenda, that when Thomas' turn came, as the custom was, to repeat before his classmates a lecture which they had heard delivered by a professor, the young Aquinas did so with a readiness and completeness which surprised everyone. They said that he much improved upon what he had heard. Consequently he became locally famous, although he was only in his early teens.

At the age of sixteen he joined the Dominican order of friars. The reasons for his doing so were probably not fully understood even by himself. The Dominicans themselves played a considerable part in the matter. Here was a brilliant youth of great promise and they wanted him among them. They worked for him with the ardor and persistence of the "rushing committee" of an American college fraternity, and if we grant this remarkable youth any human feelings whatever, we must presume that he felt flattered that they wanted him in their distinguished and scholarly company.

But Thomas was never one to be persuaded contrary to his own judgment. The attraction which the Order of St. Dominic held for him was due not so much to the friendliness of its members as to the unique character of the institution itself. While the Benedictines were of the older type of cloistered monks, hidden away from the sins of the world, and powerful because of their great wealth, the Dominicans were active preaching friars at work among men, begging their way and owning no property.

During the twelfth century there had come about a revival of learning, due largely to the Crusades, leading to the establishment of two institutions, the municipal universities and the orders of preaching friars, Franciscan and Dominican. Hitherto, all learning had been shut up in the monasteries. When universities were established in the cities, however, the danger to religion was apparent, for they taught not only theology but law, the classical Greek and Latin authors, and even the new science then filtering in from Arabian sources.

The answer to the menace was the educated traveling friar who should preach in university towns and elsewhere the reconciling of Greek philosophy and Arabian science with Christian theology. Thomas had studied some philosophy in Monte Cassino, but when he came in contact in Naples with the subtleties of the followers of Aristotle and the startling facts of the new science, the precocious youth realized the menace to theology and desired to prepare himself to defend the church. He saw clearly where the front line of theological battle was drawn and turned his steps instinctively that way.

The Young Dominican

With no question in his mind, without even notifying his parents (he was singularly modern in some ways), he renounced all his worldly prospects, all his mother's dreams of ecclesiastical preferment, donned the white woolen garment of poverty, and received the badges of penance and subjection. All Naples congratulated the Dominicans, save a few who said the clever friars should be ashamed to have tricked a mere boy into abandoning a future of such brilliant promise.

Theodora felt disgraced and desperate. She was humbled in the sight of her servants who had brought her the news that they had seen her son wearing the garb of the begging friars. That her son, a Count of Aquino, should descend to what seemed to her a low level of society was bad enough, but that her hopes of being the mother of the Abbot of Monte Cassino should be taken away by the rash act of a headstrong boy was too much. To Naples she hurried, but found that the boy was already on the road to Rome. At Rome the Dominicans refused her admittance to the house where they were hiding Thomas, and she went to the pope to tell him she had been robbed of her boy. Meanwhile he was spirited off toward Paris. The energy of the woman is seen in the fact that when she found he had gone, she sent a fast messenger to her two other sons and had them intercept the boy and his Dominican guides before the fugitives had gone eighty miles.

At Acquapendente they caught him and took him to the castle of

St. John, where they kept him prisoner until his mother came. All her threats and tears and arguments were useless: the boy's mind was made up. For a year she kept him imprisoned. Every means was used to change his mind. His two sisters were brought to help in the siege by their gentle persuasions, but he converted them both to religion. His brothers tried rougher methods, using insults and oaths. They even tore the hated robe from his back.

The baffled brothers then in desperation hired the services of a young woman accomplished in the arts of the brothel and hid her in Thomas' cell. She shortly came forth shrieking, pursued by the young friar, who brandished a burning stick. Many years later Thomas told a friend that after he had driven the girl out he drew a cross on the wall with the blackened end of the stick and, kneeling before it, vowed perpetual chastity. He said that during his sleep that night two angels bound him very tightly with a girdle and that never thereafter was he even disturbed by temptation.

How Thomas escaped from his prison we do not surely know. One story is that his sisters acted as messengers for him and carried news of his plight to his brother friars, who told the Pope. The pontiff ordered the emperor to have Thomas set free. Some say that his sisters let him down from the walls in a basket like Paul the Apostle. Still others state that his mother, despairing of changing such a stubborn will, herself liberated him.

If she did free him, it was but to try another method, for she very soon appealed to Pope Innocent to release her boy from his Dominican vows. The Pope called Thomas before him and tried to settle the matter diplomatically by offering to appoint him Abbot of Monte Cassino and still allow him to remain a Dominican friar, thinking thus to satisfy both mother and son. The mother was overjoyed at the prospect, but this Thomas still proved stubborn. A friar he would be, and nothing else, and, as usual, he won.

At Christmastime in the year 1244 the seventeen-year-old student was journeying on foot from Rome to Cologne in the distinguished company of John of Germany, the head of the Dominicans. They traveled by way of Paris and reached Cologne in three months. It was a remarkable initiation into the fraternity, and one wishes that a diary had been kept by either the sturdy old man or the indomitable youth. Only one anecdote of that journey has come down to us. When they were approaching Paris and its grandeur burst upon them, John said to his young companion, "What would you give, Brother Thomas, to be king of that city?"

The boy replied, "I would rather have St. John Chrysostom's treatise on the Gospel of St. Matthew than be king of the whole of France."

Albertus Magnus

In Cologne Thomas met the man whose learning had led the boy to make the long journey, Albertus Magnus, whose influence was to shape his entire life, and whose pioneer work in theology the young disciple was to bring to a brilliant completion. Prodigious in his learning, profound in his thinking, and indefatigable in his scholastic labors was this Albert. In him Thomas found at last a teacher who challenged his admiration and called forth his best efforts.

Albert was in the height of his intellectual power when John of Germany presented Thomas of Aquino to the great scholar. A walking encyclopedia the professor must have seemed to his disciples, for he was master of the learning of his day, both theological and secular. The twenty-one volumes he left to the world testify to that. He is credited with having been familiar with alchemy, anatomy, architecture, geography, and geology, but we must remember that these sciences were then very rudimentary. Besides Albert's various professorial positions, he held the offices of bishop, master of the sacred palace, and papal legate. He lectured almost continually and did thrice the daily work of an ordinary man. And beyond all this, Albert is said to have repeated all the 150 Psalms every day!

To such a man came Thomas and sat reverently and silently at his feet. The young man himself was by this time no mean scholar. Besides his wide reading at Monte Cassino and Naples, he had memorized during his imprisonment, we are told, some of Aristotle's works, the Sentences of Peter Lombard (which was a collection of the sayings of great theologians), and the entire Bible in Latin.

The Dumb Ox

Many young men, attracted as Thomas had been by the reputation of Albert, attended his school for young friars. They were noisy and disputatious, and Thomas must have wished for the quiet of the monastery. These students had not heard of Thomas' Neapolitan reputation and openly ridiculed his reticence. Even the master himself joined his pupils in calling the overgrown boy with his broad forehead and large placid eyes, "the huge dumb ox from Sicily." Thomas seemed not to mind their taunts, but they probably rankled. Once he retorted.

He was studying in his room when they called to him to come to the window and see a great marvel, a flying ox! Unfamiliar with the tricks of collegians, he rose to the bait and appeared at the window. They greeted him with loud laughter and asked him how he could be so gullible. He replied, "I did not believe an ox could fly, nor did I, till now, believe that a friar could tell a falsehood." What an insufferable prig he must have seemed to his fun-loving schoolmates!

Thomas stayed at Cologne but a few months and then accompanied Albert to Paris, but before leaving was able to put himself far above his fellow students and almost in a class with the master himself. From a chance-dropped paper, Albert surmised that there was more in the quiet Thomas' mind than they had suspected. He set a thesis for the boy from the south to defend against the teacher and before the class. Almost no notice had been given him, but Thomas so ably defended the thesis and so thoroughly covered the subject that the teacher and class were amazed, and the master said, "You seem to be occupying the position not of defendant but of judge."

Thomas replied that that was the only way he knew how to treat the question. Albert, somewhat nettled, determined to put the pupil in his proper place by entangling him in subtle arguments. But the clear-minded youth parried every thrust and more than held his own until, compelled to admiration, Albert announced to the openmouthed young theologs, "We call this young man a dumb ox, but he will one day fill the world with his bellowing."

Paris

Paris was a magic name among theological scholars when Thomas journeyed thither with his master in the summer of 1245. The greatest thinkers of the day were there, and their main concern was theological lectures and disputations. Theology was the queen of the sciences. The twelve hundred volumes of the library of King

Louis were there, a magnificent collection when one realizes that every volume in those days was written by hand. Bologna for law, Salerno for medicine, Paris for theology—these were the centers of the learning of the thirteenth century. His three years in Paris with his great teacher Albert probably seemed to Thomas like a pleasant dream. Crowds attended Albert's lectures and at the end of three years he was given his doctor's degree and went back to Cologne to found a school of theology in which the twenty-one-year-old Thomas was to be second professor.

Cologne

Thomas Aquinas now began to come into his own. His four years at Cologne from 1248 to 1252 were years of growing power as he began to find himself. The Dumb Ox was beginning to bellow. Where his pupils looked for reflections of Albert they found a brilliant originality, coupled with a gentle sympathy which made him an ideal teacher. He also tried his hand at writing small treatises. He did some preaching and was well received.

Paris Again

Back to Paris in 1252 Thomas begged his way to take his degrees at the command of the order and to establish a Dominican school. About this time discord was increasing between the university and the teaching friars. The latter would not conform to university customs—did not belong to the union. There had been friction before, but when the secular professors went on strike because of trouble between town and gown, the friars kept on teaching. This brought matters to a head, and the University of Paris refused a teacher's license to any candidate who had taught during the strike. Thomas was sent to the Pope to plead the cause of the Dominicans and in 1255 secured a decision in their favor.

Honors

He received his own degree of Doctor of Divinity in 1256 and remained for five years in Paris teaching ever-growing crowds of students. Indeed, in a short time, the university which had almost refused him his degree found itself growing because of his fame.

In 1261 he was called by Pope Urban IV to Italy to receive high honors. He refused the honors but remained eight years as lecturer in the "University of the Papal Court," a traveling school which went with the Pope on his tours of Italy.

Death

For a period of three years, from 1269 to 1272, he was again in Paris, where he was held in great esteem and his every word treasured. In 1272 his order recalled him to Italy and he lectured in his old school, the University of Naples. In 1273 he started for the great Council of Lyons but took sick on the way and died the next year, March 7, 1274, at the Cistercian abbey of Fossa Nuova. Immediately a quarrel arose over the possession of his body. The Dominicans fought the Cistercians and finally won, after nearly a century of verbal conflict. The body was divided. Most of it was interred in Rome. Parts are in Salerno and Naples and his right arm is in Paris. These relics are greatly reverenced.

Saint Thomas

In 1323 Thomas Aquinas was canonized—that is, recognized officially as a saint, and in 1567 Pius V pronounced him one of the five Doctors of the Church. This meant that he was reckoned equally important with Jerome, Ambrose, Augustine, and Gregory the Great. He is also considered the patron saint of all Roman Catholic educational institutions.

The death of Thomas Aquinas was untimely: he was only forty-seven years old. The eighteen years from his receiving the doctorate until his death were filled with almost incredible labors, and it is apparent that he worked himself to death. He was accustomed to three or even four scribes all working at once and each writing down Thomas' thoughts on a different subject. So broad and clear was his mind that he seemed to have no difficulty in keeping his lines of thought separate. When one realizes his tremendous literary output, thirty-four octavo volumes, and considers the high quality of it, one is amazed at the seeming ease with which it was put forth. But he does admit in beginning some of his letters that he is overwhelmed with work.

Visions

His hard work, with no recreation, and his habit of beating himself in his cell with an iron chain as a penance probably account for his early death and may have had something to do with his ecstasies and visions. He believed that he saw and had conversation with a sister and a friend who had both died. Pious legend has so overlaid these occurrences with miracle that it is difficult to ascertain just what occurred, but his trances increased toward the end and he became so exalted in spirit that he stopped his theological writing. He even left his masterpiece, *Summa Theologica,* unfinished, in spite of the protests of his friends. The failing man said that during a vision which shook him with an ecstasy of rapture while celebrating mass, he had had such a revelation of heavenly truth that what he had previously written seemed nothing but rubbish.

His Works

But the world does not call it rubbish. His two great works, the *Summa Theologica* and the *Summa contra Gentiles,* not only summarized the theological and philosophical knowledge of the day but organized it along new lines. Together with his commentary on the Sentences of Peter Lombard and the theological commentary on the Gospels, called *Catena Aurea,* they have formed the backbone of the teaching of the Roman Catholic Church for nearly seven centuries. These books are too little known by Protestant Christians though they contain many excellent statements of beliefs common to both Catholic and Protestant.

There is much in the scholasticism of Thomas Aquinas, however, which is foreign to modern thought. We do not care how many angels could stand on the point of a needle, and evidently thirteenth-century people were much concerned about it. Arguing about the nature of the angels was the cross-word puzzle game of the time. Page after page of the *Summa Theologica* is occupied with such questions as whether an angel knows himself, whether one angel knows another, and whether an angel can pass from one extreme to another without going through the middle! Some perfectly good Christians today are not even sure that such beings as angels exist.

Our admiration for Thomas Aquinas is not increased when we learn that he carried about with him a relic of St. Agnes which he believed would cure illness. Nor can we agree with his science when he says, "It is not possible for there to be another earth than this one, since every earth would naturally be carried to this central one, wherever it was."[2] And it is certain that one who believes in evolution will find himself disagreeing with the sainted scholar very frequently.

We recognize, however, that Thomas Aquinas lived in the thirteenth century and that knowledge of the world has changed since his day. If some of us cannot accept his reconciliation of science and religion, we can appreciate his magnificent service to historical Christian theology. We can hope also that another learned and devout Thomas Aquinas will arise in our day to make the much-needed synthesis between our science and our religion.

[2] *Summa Theologica* II, p. 260.

XIV

NANAK

[A.D. 1469–1538]

THE REFORMER AND PEACEMAKER OF INDIA

FOURTEEN YEARS before the birth of Luther, the reformer of India was born in a village about thirty miles from Lahore. We are told that it was toward morning of a moonlight spring night in 1469 and that heavenly music greeted the arrival of the infant.[1] The most ancient Sikh scripture tells of those who came to bring him homage. The shepherds and the wise men of the Christian Christmas legend sink into insignificance compared with the scores of saints, heroes, sages and old men who worshiped the newborn founder of the Sikh religion. "Thirty-three crores of gods paid homage."[2] In Indian measure a lakh is one hundred thousand and a crore is one hundred lakhs.

The infant was given the name "Nanak Nirakari," which means, "Nanak, servant of the formless one." His mother, Tripta, was noted for her piety, and his father, Kalu, seems to have been engaged in several occupations at the same time. He was a merchant, a farmer, an accountant, and had charge of the land belonging to the feudal lord of the village, a Muhammadan Rajput. The boy

1 *Adi-Granth*, Trumpp's trans., p. vii.　　2 Ibid.

was from infancy a puzzle to his parents and to his companions. He was exceedingly precocious and was well versed in the Hindu scriptures at the age of five. When he was seven his father entered him in school.[3]

"Sir," said Nanak to his teacher, "what have you learned that you may teach me?" "I have learned all the branches of knowledge," replied the teacher; "I have learned the Sastras and the Vedas—I know arithmetic and bookkeeping—I know everything." "All that kind of learning is utterly useless," said Nanak. "Listen, Sir;

'Burn worldly love, rub the ashes and make ink of it; make of faith the best kind of paper;

Make the heart the pen, the intellect the writer; ask the Guru and write the judgment;

Write the Name and the praise thereof, write that which has no end or limit.

Sir, if you are able to teach me this manner of knowledge, then teach me.' "

The Idle Dreamer

Two years later he learned Persian, and not long after left school. To the despair of his father he took to visiting the various begging friars of the neighborhood. He liked nothing better than to go out into the wilderness and find the solitary cell of a hermit and confer about the matters of life and death. He was never interested in the games of the children of his own age but was an irresponsible young dreamer. His father tried to get him to do some sort of work, but the youth failed in one thing after another from lack of interest. At one time when his father set him to watch a herd of buffalo, he lay down in the corner of the pasture and went to sleep. The herd got into a fine wheatfield belonging to a neighbor and there were disastrous consequences all around.

Later writers maintained that when the owner protested at the trespass, Nanak said that God would bless the field. The owner was rather skeptical about it and complained to the authorities. When the officers questioned Nanak, the boy said that nothing had been hurt, and, lo and behold! when the messengers reached the spot,

[3] *Encyclopedia of Religion and Ethics*, Vol. IX, p. 182-b. See also Trumpp's translation of the *Adi-Granth*.

they found that not a single blade of the growing grain had been injured.[4]

The Janeu

It was the custom among the Hindus to place around the neck of the boys a *janeu* or sacred thread. It was a survival of the ancient rite of initiation into the religion of the tribe. When Nanak was nine his father arranged a great celebration and called all the relatives and neighbors to witness the placing of the thread around the boy's neck. Just as the priest was about to do so, the boy seized the thread from the priest's hand and asked him what use it was to put a thread like that around his neck. The protest was an early indication of his refusal to participate in meaningless ceremonies.

The priest replied that the whole Hindu religion was contained in that thread, without which the boy would only be a low-class person, and that the putting on of the thread meant the putting on of greatness, both for the present and for the future. But Nanak was not to be satisfied with such dogmatic assertions and proceeded to give to the priest a spiritual interpretation of the *janeu*, while the surprised relatives listened. He said,[5]

Make mercy thy cotton, contentment thy thread, continence its knot, truth its twist.

That would make a janeu for the soul; if thou have it, O Brahman, then put it on me.

It will not break, or become soiled, or be burned, or lost.

The Brahman priest rebuked the impudent boy and said he could not be wise because he was only a child. He then made the mistake of stating that unless Nanak wore the thread he would be considered "a person without religion." This gave the earnest boy a chance to call attention to a fact which everyone knew, but which few admitted—namely, that all around were men who had committed theft and adultery and were well known as liars and robbers and that these villains were all wearing the *janeu*.

This made the Brahman priest very angry, and he asked the boy if he thought everybody else was a fool and he alone wise. The boy replied that no string could keep a person from impure acts. In

4 MacAuliffe, *The Sikh Religion*, Vol. I, page 15.
5 Ibid., p. 16.

other words, he set forth that true religion was a matter of the inner life and of man's relation to God rather than a matter of the ritualistic tying of strings.[6] The parable of the *janeu* of the soul must have been the composition of a much more mature mind than that of a boy of nine. It is likely that Nanak uttered it in a much later sermon and that by his admiring disciples, in their zealousness, it was placed at the time of his own investment with the *janeu* at the age of nine.

When he was twelve years old his father, with great sorrow, pointed out to him how useless he was and how unfit to carry on the family business. Yet the father tried again and again, hopefully remembering that when the priest had named the boy he had declared that the fame of the child would be spread like a canopy over the father. When Nanak was seventeen his father sent him on business to a nearby village, after the boy had begged him to trust him once more. But the twenty rupees with which he set out were soon in the possession of a little band of religious beggars whom Nanak happened to meet on his journey. When the boy returned empty-handed and told what had happened, the father slapped him vigorously on both cheeks and gave up hope of making anything out of him.

Literary Excuses

Throughout his teens the boy was the cause of great reproach to his parents, but the replies which he made to their suggestions that he should assume various duties are in themselves religious essays of unusual beauty. When his father begged him to help him cultivate the little farm, as he was big enough to be of help, he said,[7]

Make thy body the field, good works the seed, irrigate with God's name;

Make thy heart the cultivator; God will germinate in thy heart, and thou shalt thus obtain the dignity of nirvan.

When his father then offered to set him up as a shopkeeper, Nanak said,[8]

---

6 Ibid., pp. 15, 16.   7 Ibid., p. 21.
8 Ibid., p. 23.

Make the knowledge that life is frail thy shop, the true Name thy stock-in-trade;

Make meditation and contemplation thy piles of vessels; put the true Name into them.

When he was urged to become a traveling dealer in horses, he replied,[9]

Make truth the horses thou takest to sell;

Tie up virtues as thy traveling expenses.

After all these failures to make the boy work, a family consultation was held and it was decided to call in a physician. When the medical man began to take Nanak's pulse, the boy drew his arm away, and said,[10]

The physician is sent for to prescribe a remedy; he taketh my hand and feeleth my pulse.

The ignorant physician knoweth not that it is in my mind the pain is.

Physician, go home; take not my curse with thee.

I am imbued with my Lord; to whom givest thou medicine?

When there is pain, the physician standeth ready with a store of medicine:

The body is weeping, the soul crieth out, "Physician give none of thy medicine."

Physician, go home, few know my malady.

The Creator who gave me this pain, will remove it.

The Official

It was finally decided to send him to the village where his sister, Nanaki, lived. His brother-in-law thought he would be able to get him into the Government service. When the young man left home there was a very touching scene. By this time he had a wife and two children. On seeing him make preparations for his journey, his wife began to weep, and said,[11]

"My life, even here thou hast not loved me; when thou goest to a foreign country, how shalt thou return?" He answered, "Simple woman,

9 Ibid., p. 23.
10 Ibid., p. 27.
11 Ibid., p. 32; also *Encyclopedia of Religion and Ethics*, Vol. IX, p. 183 a.

what have I been doing here?" Upon this she again entreated him, "When thou satest down at home, I possessed in my estimation the sovereignty of the whole earth; now this world is of no avail to me." Upon this he grew compassionate, and said, "Be not anxious; thy sovereignty shall ever abide." She replied, "My life, I will not remain behind; take me with thee." Then Nanak said, "I am now going away. If I can earn my living, I will send for thee. Obey my order."

To everyone's surprise Nanak was a success in the government position of storekeeper at Sultanpur, which his brother-in-law had secured for him. He seemed to get along better away from home without his father's continual supervision and reproaches. One of his old friends from his native place came to visit him, Mardana by name. After the day's work was done, Nanak would compose verses and sing them, while Mardana accompanied him on the "rebek," a sort of primitive mandolin. They were very happy together. But Nanak soon had a spiritual experience which resulted in a change in his whole life.

The Revelation

It was his custom to bathe in a river very early in the morning before his day's work. One morning after his bath, Nanak disappeared in the forest and was "taken in a vision to God's presence. He was offered a cup of nectar, which he gratefully accepted. God said to him,

"I am with thee. I have made thee happy, and also those who shall take thy name. Go and repeat Mine, and cause others to do likewise. Abide uncontaminated by the world. Practise the repetition of My Name, charity, ablutions, worship and meditation. I have given thee this cup of nectar, a pledge of My regard."

Nanak was so thrilled by this message from God that he composed an ode to God which ended as follows,

Had I hundreds of thousands of tons of paper . . .
Were ink never to fail me, and could I move my pen like the wind,
I should still not be able to express Thy worth.

Then came the great revelation. He thought God spoke to him, saying,[12] "My name is God, the primal Brahm, and thou art the di-

12 Ibid., p. 35.

vine Guru." The word *Guru* means teacher. This was Nanak's great commission, and thereafter he was known as Guru Nanak. One wonders if he was unconsciously paraphrasing Muhammad's famous sentence, "There is no God but Allah; and Muhammad is His prophet."

Three days later the missing man returned from the woods and reappeared at his lodging place, to the relief of his friends, but he stayed with them only long enough to give away absolutely all his possessions. One is reminded of the rich young ruler whom Jesus advised to pursue a similar course, but who failed of the test. There is a remarkable spiritual affinity between Jesus and Nanak. His friends thought he was crazy and brought in a Moslem priest to drive the devil out. But Nanak was not out of his mind. He was thrilled through and through by the theophany in the forest.

In the light of this experience, exorcism by the Moslem priests was the highest mockery. While the priest was writing an amulet which was to be hung around Nanak's neck to exorcise the evil spirit, Nanak indignantly exclaimed, "Cursed are the lives who write God's name and sell it." His friends were soon convinced that Nanak was not only possessed of a devil but insane as well. Whereupon he said,[13] "Simpleton Nanak hath become mad upon the Lord, and knoweth none other than God."

Sitting silent in meditation for a whole day, he then gave utterance to a single sentence which was significant of his whole life's mission. He said, "There is no Hindu and no Musalman." Then he started forth on a missionary journey, taking Mardana with him. As far as we know, these two were the first to combine evangelistic preaching with music. They were the original Moody and Sankey, and were an instant success. There is something in music which renders the soul of man susceptible to the message of an earnest evangelist.

The problem at the very first was to secure audiences. India was full of traveling ascetics and fakirs, but Nanak discovered, probably accidentally, a method of publicity which startled and attracted great crowds. It grew out of his central teaching. He was endeavoring to correlate the two powerful religions of his day. India had been invaded sometime before by Muhammadan missionaries who had met with considerable success, and in Nanak's day, Islam and Hinduism were great rivals.

13 Ibid., p. 37.

When Nanak announced that there was really no Hindu and no Muhammadan; when he, a Hindu, chose as his co-worker a Muhammadan, and especially, when he dressed himself in a startling costume combining, contrary to all precedent, the traditional garb of both religions, he attracted considerable attention wherever he went. His hat was Muhammadan, but just beneath it was the yellow mark on his brow which indicated that he was a Hindu. His necklace of bones confirmed that fact. A yellow jacket with a white sheet draped about it completed the confusion.[14] Whether those he met were Muhammadan or Hindu, all paused to see this strange garb, and while they were wondering whether he belonged to their religion or to that of their rivals, he had an opportunity to point out that there was an underlying religion which was greater than either. He said,[15]

I have appeared in this age to indicate the way unto men. I reject all sects, and only know one God, whom I recognize in the earth, the heavens, and in all directions.

Nanak's Missionary Journeys

Nanak resembled Jesus in that he preached a religion which underlay Moslemism and Hinduism, just as Jesus set forth a faith superior to that of either Sadducee or Pharisee. But he resembled Paul in the extent of his travels. We read of missionary journeys which took him for thousands of miles. The first of these occupied twelve years, and Nanak and Mardana covered, evidently on foot, practically the whole of northern India, wisely selecting for their preaching stations the places where religious people were accustomed to gather. By the end of the twelve years, his companion Mardana was more than ready to go home, for the adventures and dangers and sufferings also paralleled those of Paul.

Mardana was wondering whether his relatives were dead or alive. He remarked that Nanak might be able to get along without eating or drinking or entering a village, but that he himself could not stand it any longer. Nanak granted Mardana permission to go home and accompanied him until they were only a little way from the village. Then the great Guru stopped and refused to visit his own

14 Ibid., p. 58.
15 *World's Living Religions*, R. E. Hume, p. 88.

home. But he told Mardana to visit Kalu's house without mentioning Nanak's name.

There was a great home-coming reception for Mardana, but he soon got away from it and went to the home of Nanak, whose mother embraced him and, crying for joy, asked about Nanak's welfare. Mardana remained faithful to Nanak's command and would not even tell the old mother how her son was. But mother wit was clever enough to wait patiently and, when Mardana started off, to follow quietly until, as she had suspected, Mardana came to where Nanak was waiting.

The Guru saluted his mother, and she, stating that she adored the very ground he walked on, begged him to stop his journeyings and come back and live at home. In reply he sang a song to Mardana's accompaniment. In the song he indicated that he was satisfied with the work of the Lord. Pitifully the mother begged him to put on the new clothes and eat the choice food she had brought him. But he refused and sang two more hymns.

His father appeared with a horse and asked him to mount it and come back home. Another rhapsody on spiritual horses followed. The father refused to be quiet and said that he had built a new house which he wished his son to see, and suggested that he might at least come and visit his own wife. Nanak sang of the House of the Lord, and of the sin of marital happiness.

Kalu still refused to be silenced, and even offered to get his son another wife if he did not like the one he had. The conversation continued for some time, but without changing the determination of the Guru to continue his wandering. He said, "Father dear, mother dear, I have returned home. I have been until now a hermit. Obey God's order and let me again depart. . . . Mother, agree to what I say; consolation shall come to thee."[16] Then Nanak and his musician set off on the second missionary journey, which took them into comparatively distant lands.

We see Nanak preaching to the king and queen of Ceylon. Again we read of him visiting the Himalaya Mountains and localities far in the northwest. Even to Mecca, Bagdad and Medina the prophet of peace made pilgrimage. He produced a sensation by preaching a sermon on God's universality in front of the Kaaba, the sacred stone of the Moslems. He went disguised as a pilgrim,

16 MacAuliffe, *The Sikh Religion*, Vol. I, p. 101.

but his ignorance of prescribed etiquette in the sacred city nearly got him into trouble.

One night he slept with his feet toward the Kaaba. He was rudely awakened by an Arab priest, who said, "Who is this sleeping infidel? Why hast thou, O sinner, turned thy feet toward God?" Nanak replied, "Turn my feet in the direction in which God is not." At this point history ends, and legend begins. For the story continues that the priest took Nanak's feet and pulled them around to the proper Muhammadan position, whereupon the sacred Kaaba temple itself turned around, following Nanak's feet in their semicircular revolution.

Nanak's Message

The theology of the traveling missionary was very simple and yet rather advanced for his time. The teachings of Buddha and Mahavira in India, and of Muhammad in Arabia, had long since been overlaid with miracle and adulterated by relapses to primitive animism. A reform had again become necessary. Nanak was especially opposed to the animistic stone worship, a form of idolatry which he found not only among Moslems at Mecca but also among his own countrymen. He said,

The ignorant fools take stones and worship them. O Hindus, how shall the stone which itself sinketh carry you across?[17]

He even turned on his old friends, the ascetics and fakirs, and pointed out that they did not have the true religion. He announced,

He who worshippeth stones, visiteth places of pilgrimage, dwelleth in
    forests,
And renounceth the world, wandereth and wavereth.
How can his filthy mind become pure?[18]

He resembled Paul again in his ability to make even those who arrested him listen to his message. His preaching to a Muhammadan official who had imprisoned him, thereby securing his release, makes one think of Paul before Agrippa.

When he came in contact with criminals he was not so much concerned about his own safety as he was with trying to get them to

17 Ibid., Vol. I, p. 326.   18 Ibid., Vol. I, p. 339.

reform. One he advised to confess and make good the wrong he had done. To another group, who were robbers by trade, he preached with great effect, urging them to quit robbing and become farmers and to give to the poor the proceeds of their former thefts. The women of his day, as are many of the Indian women today, were almost slaves to superstition and magic. A large group of professional sorceresses, with their leader, Nurshah,[19] once tried to influence him with their magic.

The Guru was quite disgusted with these women and was really rude to them, suggesting rather sarcastically that those who used soap did not need musk. In the face of such frankness the usual charms did not seem to work. We learn that when Nurshah found her efforts unsuccessful she decided that it was due to her own sins. Probably Nanak's rather pointed remarks assisted her in reaching that conclusion. Nurshah thereupon tried him with the temptation of wealth, piling jewels, gold, silver, and coral at the feet of the Guru, which gave him the opportunity to preach another sermon to her. He discoursed with such earnestness that she and her women all became his followers.

Nanak was quite careless of the formal demands of Hinduism; indeed, he openly attacked certain of their practices. Once at a religious fair he felt the need of food, and cooked a portion of venison from a deer which had been given him. Of course, the Brahmans rebuked him for eating flesh. In a most caustic address he pointed out that it was foolish for man who was born of flesh and who lived continually in the flesh to object to eating flesh. He pointed out that those who were most meticulous about not devouring the flesh of beasts sometimes devoured men by oppression.

They who forswear flesh and hold their noses when near it, devour men at night.
They make pretences to the world, but they know not divine knowledge or meditation on God.[20]

At another time he attacked the Hindu practice of telling beads, which in his mind was associated with hypocrisy.

But when ye take rosaries in your hands, and sit down counting your

19 Ibid., Vol. I, pp. 73-78.   20 Ibid., Vol. I, p. 48.

beads, ye never think of God, but allow your minds to wander thinking of worldly objects. Your rosaries are therefore only for show, and your counting beads is only hypocrisy.[21]

Nevertheless, intelligent Hindus recognized that what Nanak was really accomplishing was the spiritual regeneration of Hinduism, just as the more intelligent Moslems likewise appreciated his efforts. Nanak had said,

He is a Musalman who clears away his own self, who is sincere, patient, of pure words . . .
That Musalman will go to Paradise . . .
Then the people, Hindus and Musalmans, began to say . . . that God was speaking in Nanak.[22]

He expressed very clearly the unsatisfactory character of the religions of his day and their sacred scriptures,

I have consulted the four Vedas, but these writings find not God's limits.
I have consulted the four books of the Muhammadans, but God's worth is not described in them.
I have consulted the nine regions of the earth; one improveth upon what the other saith.
Having turned my heart into a boat, I have searched in every sea;
I have dwelt by rivers and streams, and bathed at the sixty-eight places of pilgrimage;
I have lived among the forests and glades of the three worlds and eaten bitter and sweet;
I have seen the seven nether regions and heavens upon heavens.
And I, Nanak, say man shall be true to his faith if he fear God and do good works.[23]

The Temptation

A temptation in the wilderness is told as having been presented to Guru Nanak by the Indian Satan, Kaljug. This temptation by the devil was similar to those of Jesus and Buddha. Like Jesus,

---

[21] Ibid., Vol. I, p. 51.   [22] *Adi-Granth*, p. xiii.
[23] MacAuliffe, *The Sikh Religion*, Vol. I, p. 179.

Nanak was tempted by the offer of the wealth of the world, and we detect a similarity to Buddha's temptation in the offer of Kaljug to bring to him "very beautiful women." He also offered him the ability to work miracles, and the rulership of all the kingdoms of the world. Nanak informed Kaljug that he was not interested in ruling anywhere, as he had given up all that sort of ambition. The account[24] tells us that, finding Nanak unresponsive to his offers, the devil worshiped him and left him.

Confessions

The principal difference between Jesus and Nanak seems to have been the latter's frequent assertions of his own sinfulness. Jesus' admissions of guilt are very few. Some have found one in the fact that he accepted baptism at the hands of John. But that inference has been seriously contested. At one time Jesus said, "Why callest thou me good? There is none good but one, that is, God." But, in spite of that, Christian tradition has uniformly maintained that Jesus had no consciousness of guilt. Nanak, on the other hand, speaks of himself as a sinner. He said, "My sins are numerous as the waters of the seas and the ocean."[25] On another occasion he said, "I am not chaste, nor truthful, nor learned; foolish and ignorant am I."[26] Still again he confessed, "I am base and worthless. I covet my neighbor's house. Lust and anger, which are pariahs, dwell in my heart . . . I am a cheat in a country of cheats. . . . How can I, who am weak and dishonest, show my face! Humble Nanak expresseth his thoughts."[27]

The Death of the Guru

At length, Nanak's exertions and privations told upon his remarkable strength. When he knew that his end was near he returned to his childhood home and planned for someone to succeed him. His two sons had not been particularly impressed by their father's teachings, and he did not deem either of them fit to carry on the work. As his successor he selected one of his disciples named

24 Ibid., Vol. I, pp. 78–80.   25 MacAuliffe, Vol. I, p. 30.
26 Encyclopedia of Religion and Ethics, IX, p. 183–b.
27 MacAuliffe, Vol. I, p. 184.

Angad. When Nanak raised over Angad's head the umbrella which typified spiritual leadership, and when he bowed reverently before his designated successor, the people knew that the end was near.

Crowds came to bid him good-by. The old man announced that he forgave all his enemies. He sat down beneath a withered acacia tree to die. Legend says that it became green and produced leaves and blossoms. As the relatives, friends and disciples gathered about the dying man, he composed a beautiful ode to the Creator, and said, "We must assuredly proceed onwards like a guest . . . That which pleaseth the Omnipotent shall come to pass."[28]

Just before the Guru passed away an unseemly quarrel arose among his followers. Moslems and Hindus had joined in the religion which the Guru had preached, but they now reverted in part to their former beliefs. The Moslems announced that they would bury Nanak; but his Hindu disciples insisted upon cremation. They asked the dying man to decide this important detail. He said, "Let the Hindus place flowers on my right, and the Musalmans on my left. They whose flowers are found fresh in the morning may have the disposal of my body."[29] Then a hymn was sung and Nanak drew a sheet over his body and breathed his last. The legend goes that when the sheet was lifted the next morning, nothing was found underneath it, and both bunches of flowers were discovered to be in fresh bloom.

Nanak's followers have always appreciated beauty in nature and art. The fourth Guru established, as a holy place of the Sikh religion, a temple on an island in the lake near Lahore. He called this place "Amritsar," which means "immortality." There is only one temple in India, the Taj Mahal, which rivals in beauty the Golden Temple at Amritsar in its water-mirror setting.

The Sikhs

There were eight Gurus after Angad. And these ten holy men (including Nanak and Angad) have ever since been much reverenced by the followers of Nanak, who are called "Sikhs." They maintain that in each of the succeeding Gurus the spirit of Nanak was incarnated by a sort of progressive immortality. It is even asserted that there was but one Guru who appeared in ten bodies.

[28] Ibid., Vol. I, pp. 188, 189.   [29] Ibid., p. 190.

314] THE GREAT RELIGIOUS LEADERS

As in all religions, the original teachings of the founder have become obscured by later additions and changes. Nanak preached a gospel of peace, but the last Gurus were very warlike, for the tenth, Gobind Singh (1675–1708), trained the Sikhs to be warriors to defend their faith against the Moguls. But Gandhi's influence recently started a trend among the Sikhs to return to the pacifism of Baba Nanak. And it is reported (*The New York Times,* March 4, 1958) that some of the 3,000 Sikhs now in British Columbia, Canada, are even abandoning their traditional beards, long hair, and turbans for American hats and haircuts. Certainly both Indians and Americans are proud of Dalip Singh Saund, our Sikh congressman from California, who, as a member of our House Foreign Affairs Committee, recently received an ovation when he addressed a joint session of the Houses of Parliament in his native India.

In 1849 the last king of the Sikhs surrendered to the British and, as a token of his submission and his friendly feeling toward the conquerors, made a present to Queen Victoria of the enormous and beautiful Koh-i-nur diamond. But a century later the Sikhs again became independent. As a result of the recent division of India into the Hindu Republic and the Moslem State of Pakistan, many Sikhs moved into the East Punjab. Seven Punjab states then united (May 5, 1948) to form the new Sikh State. Probably it is too much to expect that the present British queen will return the "mountain of Light" as a token of friendly feeling. Will faith move that mountain again, or are diamonds a girl's best friend?

The Sikh Bible is the most difficult book in the world to read. It is called *The Granth,* The Book. The *Adi-Granth,* the original book, is a collection of the writings of Nanak and other teachers, gathered by the fifth Guru. There is another *Granth* compiled by the tenth Guru.

In no religion is such respect paid to the sacred scriptures as the absolute idolatry with which three million Sikhs regard the *Granth-Saheb,* the Lord Book. At Amritsar the volume is treated like a real deity. "Every morning it is dressed out in costly brocade and reverentially placed on a low throne under a jeweled canopy. Every evening it reposes for the night in a golden bed within a sacred chamber."[30]

---

[30] Monier-Williams, *Brahmanism and Hinduism,* p. 177, quoted in *World's Living Religions,* p. 95.

XV

❧

LUTHER

[A.D. 1483–1546]

WHO RESTORED LIBERTY TO RELIGION

M ORE BOOKS have been written about Martin Luther than about any other except Jesus Christ. He has been most extravagantly praised and most bitterly condemned. Whereby we know him to have been truly great.

For many years Catholics would hear nothing but evil of Luther, and Protestants nothing but good, but lately these two impossible views are receding and we have the former admitting his virtues and the latter his faults. Rome has not forgiven the great reformer but she has learned to respect him. The blind hero-worship of Luther by Protestants has changed to a saner appreciation of his historical significance. Because Luther was so much a child of his time and reflected so accurately the storms of sixteenth-century conflict in church, in state, and between church and state, some cannot see that he was also a mighty personal force in those conflicts, a powerful molder of public opinion, a defender of human liberties, a man not only of his times but of the ages.

The Inner Man

With a sublime disregard of criticism, Luther bared his soul to the world. His letters are among the most humanly interesting documents in existence. Even his mealtime and fireside conversations have been preserved, six volumes of them, taken down in shorthand by student boarders in his home. This "Tabletalk" of his, now brilliant and now tender, one moment sublime and the next obscene, is one of the most amazing character revelations in history. Augustine's *Confessions* seem sententious preachments beside it. Was Luther arrant egotist or the most nearly humble of all men?

All his blustering bravado and virulent verbal assaults on his enemies must have had a cause embedded deep in his personality. Nor was it all bluster. It took real courage to face his enemies, to challenge the great powers of his time. When the tests came, he met them boldly and always added a little impudence for good measure.

At the Diet of Worms, the supreme crisis of his life, when all Germany was wondering if he would recant, and when the stern examiner Eck bade him give a direct answer *"non cornutum"* (without horns, i.e., without sophistry), the embattled Luther replied, "I will give you one without horns or teeth." Many writers have wondered why Luther added the phrase "or teeth" and what he meant by it. It was an emotional rather than an intellectual response. The little incident revealed the man's tremendous fear complex. His flippant bravado on this and many other occasions indicated a defense mechanism built up in childhood and through years of intense mental suffering.

The Child Was Afraid

That childhood was darkened by frequent periods of terror. It is hard to say which the boy feared most, his father, God, or the devil. The father tried to break the boy's somewhat stubborn spirit by terrible beatings. Luther said in manhood, "My father once whipped me so severely that I fled from him and it was hard for him to win me back. . . . My mother once beat me until the blood flowed, having stolen a miserable nut." And again, "Where such fear enters a man in childhood, it can hardly be rooted out again as long as he lives. As he once trembled at every word of his father and mother, to the end of his life he is afraid of a falling leaf."

Little Martin literally feared the God of whom they told him, a cruel, wrathful Judge, a super-bogeyman of the skies, but most of all he was in mortal terror of the devil, witches, and malicious evil spirits. Even in his maturity when he had ceased to be afraid of God and thought of him as "a mighty fortress, a bulwark never failing," he yet feared the devil and added in the same stanza of his famous hymn,

> *For still our ancient foe*
> *Doth seek to work us woe;*
> *His craft and power are great,*
> *And armed with cruel hate,*
> *On earth is not his equal.*

At night as a child he crept to his attic straw trembling from cruel paternal blows, to tremble still more at the goblin-haunted dark. Picture the little Martin, shivering in cold perspiration, almost insane with stark fear; and contrast with that the man of thirty-seven defiantly burning the papal bull of excommunication. The Reformation was an outlet for the dammed-up antagonisms of a dynamic personality.

Schools

In the Mansfeld school the boy found no escape from fear, for the monitor, who visited dire punishment on any boy who lapsed from Latin into German, even in conversation, was called by the boys *Lupus,* the Wolf. The most important book in the school was the Latin grammar of Donatus, written nearly twelve centuries before, a tough morsel for young teeth. "What a time we had," said Luther, "with the *Lupus* and Donatus! My teachers made us parse everything, and made obscene jokes. The examination was like a trial for murder." It is no wonder that Luther looked back upon school as "hell and purgatory," for in a single forenoon he once received fifteen whippings!

In 1497, when the boy was thirteen, his parents sent him to a school in Magdeburg, where he had to beg his food on the streets.

He nearly died from starvation, so they transferred him to a school in Eisenach where the begging was better. The fourteen-year-old Martin was singing for his supper in the streets of Eisenach when his sweet voice attracted the attention of the motherly Frau Cotta, who soon took him into her home to live. The starved soul of the boy expanded in the genial environment, and his school work began to reveal his unusual mental ability.

Meanwhile his father's affairs improved so that in May 1501, at the age of seventeen, the boy matriculated at the University of Erfurt. We know little of his university days, but he must have made prodigious progress, for in 1502 he took his Bachelor of Arts degree and in the spring of 1505 his Master's degree, second in a class of seventeen. His father, who had planned to make his boy a lawyer, was delighted and bought him a costly set of law books, which Martin studied but two months. Suddenly, in July 1505, he left the university and entered the Augustinian monastery at Erfurt and a year later took the irrevocable vows of poverty, celibacy, and obedience.

Why should a young man of twenty-one with excellent worldly prospects so suddenly abandon them for the cloister? The immediate cause was fear, a return of the old terror of his childhood days which the happier associations of Eisenach and Erfurt had banished for a time. The plague came to Erfurt in the spring of 1505. Some of the students died and there was a general exodus from the town. Two of Luther's brothers died in the plague and he left for home toward the last of June but returned immediately.

The Storm

On July second, as the young law student neared Erfurt, something happened, the correct details of which we shall probably never know, as the terror-stricken youth could give no complete account afterward. We know that in the midst of a severe thunderstorm, Luther, who was always disturbed at such times, had some sort of emotional crisis. He says that he threw himself to the ground after a lightning flash and cried, "Help, dear Saint Anna! I will become a monk."

Another factor in the situation was the strange sudden death of a friend by Luther's side that fateful spring, whether from the plague, a murderer's hand, a lightning bolt in the storm, or some other accident, we do not surely know. But it immediately preceded Luther's sudden panicky decision to renounce the world and become a monk. His friends afterward compared that lightning flash on the road to Erfurt with the blinding light on the road to Damascus which led Paul of Tarsus to cry, "Lord, what wilt Thou have me to do?" Perhaps it was the fear of the devil rather than the call of God which sent Luther to the ground in prayer. Among the miners where he spent his boyhood, the devil rode abroad in thunderstorms. It is significant that it was upon Saint Anna, the patron saint of the miners, that he called in his trouble.

The Monk

But why the vow to be a monk? Because he had already an inclination that way. There were twenty cloisters in Erfurt, and the family of his beloved Frau Cotta had endowed a monastery, with whose gentle Franciscans the youth had been good friends. Two weeks after the thunderstorm Luther gave a merry party to his friends, men, maidens, and matrons, and the next day made good his vow by entering the monastery and beginning his year of probation. In the monastery he continued his studies so successfully that in the fall of 1508 he was assigned to the new University of Wittenberg to teach ethics and philosophy. He was not finding in the cloister the peace he had expected. In a perfect frenzy of devotion he went to excesses of ascetic privation which quickly won him a reputation for sanctity but brought no peace of mind. He not only prayed for hours at a time but so tormented his poor body by freezing, starving, and otherwise mistreating it that he never fully recovered from the effects.

"By Faith"

Sometime in 1508 or 1509 as he was sitting in his tower cell at Wittenberg reading the first chapter of Paul's Letter to the Romans, light and peace came to his soul when he read the seventeenth verse, "The just shall live by faith." He had been trying to find salvation by hard works of penance, self-mortification, and many prayers. But if justification were by *faith,* these works were utterly beside the point. Faith in Christ was the all-important thing, if Paul was right. A sense of freedom came to him and a great burden seemed lifted from his fear-tortured soul.

Martin Luther did not know it, but the Protestant Reformation had begun.

Rome

His work of teaching was interrupted in October 1511 by a five-month trip to Rome on foot with John von Mecheln on Augustinian business. When the two dusty pilgrims walking single file came in sight of Rome, Luther fell to his knees and said, "Hail. Holy Rome! Thrice holy thou in whom the blood of the martyrs has been poured out!" In a very few years, he did not talk so reverently about Rome, but in 1511 he was simply another credulous devout pilgrim. Still, he kept his eyes open, and at least once revolted against a custom of the pious, if we accept a story told by his son Paul many years later.

In Rome was a sacred staircase, supposedly from Pilate's judgment hall in Jerusalem The Pope had announced a nine-year indulgence for every step of the twenty-eight climbed by a pilgrim on his knees in prayer. Luther was part way up when he recalled his favorite verse in Romans, "The just shall live by faith." Immediately he stood up and walked back down the steps. The incident, if true, is indicatory of the conflict still waging in his mind between two mutually contradictory ideas of religion.

He brought back from Rome impressions of beauty, culture, and luxury, which made his home folk seem uncouth, but he returned sadly disappointed at the low moral tone and religious decadence of Rome. He said afterward, "I would not take a thousand gulden not to have seen it, for I never would have believed the true state of affairs from what other people told me, had I not seen it myself." On his way home another question presented itself to his inquiring mind. He returned through Milan and doubtless visited the spot where St. Ambrose baptized St. Augustine more than a thousand years before. In Milan he found priests who differed from any he had met. They denied allegiance to the Pope and followed St. Ambrose. It was a thoughtful journey home, plodding single file and silently.

Wittenberg

Luther reached Erfurt in February 1512 and was soon back in Wittenberg lecturing. He had already received his degree of *Baccalaureus ad Biblia* in 1509, which permitted him to lecture on the Bible, and in October 1512 he became a Doctor of Theology. The five years from 1512 to 1517 were busy years of hard work, studying, lecturing, and preaching, and his reputation grew rapidly. He lectured on the Psalms, Romans, Judges, and Galatians. The lectures were a treat for the students, who flocked to hear the popular new doctor. With keen wit and apt parable he illustrated his points, referring to current events and homely matters in a way hitherto unknown. He even used German phrases in his Latin lectures and made the Bible seem a living book. Other professors were glad to sit at his feet and hear his refreshing, original interpretations.

All through the lectures one can trace the growth of the doctrine of justification by faith. He found himself much in sympathy with the humanists, the advanced-thought group of the time. When Erasmus, the greatest of the humanists, published his Greek Testament in 1516, Luther immediately secured it and used it thereafter. The young professor followed Paul and Augustine and attacked the positions of Aristotle and Thomas Aquinas, the revered authorities of the day. Imagine the consternation in the theological world when it was noised abroad that the Wittenberg monk, Doctor Luther, had called Aristotle a "damned heathen"! In May 1517 he wrote an old friend, "Our theology and that of Saint Augustine, by the grace of God, are making excellent progress and gaining control in our university. Aristotle is gradually declining and his permanent extinction is not far off."

In his almost childlike glee Luther did not realize what a storm was gathering around his head. Pope Leo X needed money to complete St. Peter's church in Rome and was raising it by offering through his agents remission of sins to those who bought indulgences. A few miles from Wittenberg a monk named Tetzel was doing a thriving business selling indulgences to simple peasants whose native fears he stirred by his powerful preaching of hell and purgatory. Luther protested in several sermons, to no avail, and then boldly resolved on a master stroke. All Saints' Day always

drew crowds to Wittenberg to view the sacred relics of the saints
exhibited in the castle church.

The Halloween Theses

The night before, October 31, 1517, there was a vigorous tapping
on the door of that church, and the next day the people read a
placard there challenging to a debate those who would defend the
indulgences. Ninety-five propositions or theses were stated in force-
ful language. Debate challenges had appeared on that door before,
but none like this. There was instant recognition that a great event
had occurred. Eager students made copies, and in a short time
Nuremberg presses had printed them in Latin and German. Said
one man who read them,

"Ho, ho, he is come who will do what is needed."

In two weeks all Germany was discussing the theses. Doctor
Luther, to his astonishment, had suddenly become a national figure.
He had expected only discussions with theologians. He had not
realized the power of that new-fangled thing, the printing press,
nor the interest of the common people in theological matters. But
the clamor did not lead him to retreat from his stand. Dr. Jerome
Schurf called him to account, saying, "You would write against the
Pope? What do you hope to accomplish by it? They will not suffer
it." Luther said simply, "What if they must suffer it?" Among the
theses, several were especially challenging, for instance,

21. Those preachers of indulgences err who say that a papal pardon
frees a man from all penalty and assures his salvation.

31. They who believe themselves made sure of salvation by papal
letters will be eternally damned along with their teachers.

36. Every Christian truly repentant has full remission of guilt and
penalty even without letters of pardon.

82. Why does not the Pope empty purgatory from charity?

"Quiet That Man"

Such dangerous words soon reached Rome, and the Pope ordered
the head of the Augustinians to "quiet that man, for newly kindled
flames are easily quenched." Luther was called to Heidelberg the
next spring and ordered to recant. He refused, and defended his

theology so ably that he won converts. He was then charged with "suspicion of heresy" and ordered to appear at Rome in sixty days. The place was soon changed to Augsburg and the time to "at once." The Pope's representative in Germany, one Cajetan, was ordered to hear Luther and if he did not recant, to send him bound to Rome, or put him and his followers under the ban.

Cajetan's talks with Luther did not bring about a recantation, for the professor easily refuted all arguments. Every conflict only made Luther more confident. He wrote from Augsburg to a friend that Cajetan was "an obscure and ignorant theologian . . . as well fitted to manage this affair as an ass to play the harp." The monk's friends soon and wisely spirited him out of Augsburg and back to Wittenberg.

Events then developed rapidly. The Pope sent his chamberlain, Von Miltitz, to get Luther somehow and bring him to Rome, but the chamberlain found all Germany aroused. He reported that an army of 25,000 would be insufficient to get Luther out of the country. In July 1519 Luther debated in Augsburg with a cleverer opponent than any he had yet met, Dr. John Eck, who trapped him into defending some of the doctrines of John Huss, who had been burned for heresy a century before. Excommunication or worse was now confronting Luther. The Pope began to prepare his formal bull, or letter, of excommunication.

The Presses Hum

Meanwhile Luther was working feverishly. Besides all his regular work, he was keeping several printing presses busy. In 1519 he published nearly thirty treatises, including three large books. During the summer and autumn of 1520 he published three of his greatest treatises, "An Appeal to the Christian Nobility of the German Nation," "On the Babylonian Captivity of the Church," and "On the Freedom of a Christian Man."

The first of these called for extensive reforms in Germany, religious, social, and political. It had an immediate and enormous success and changed his fight with the Pope into a national affair. The second was such a bitter indictment of Rome that any reconciliation was seen to be impossible. The third was quite different, a charming constructive essay setting forth the new ideals of Christian conduct—namely, the godliness of simple service. In opposi-

tion to the monkish idea of otherworldliness, penance, and asceticism, Luther said simply, "What you do in your house is worth as
much as if you did it up in heaven for our Lord God. . . . That is
a right holy life, and cannot be made holier even if one fast oneself
to death."

Here was a new voice speaking, and the world sat up to listen,
shocked and thrilled. What would this amazing man say next! All
Christendom was looking at Luther. He knew it and staged a dramatic episode.

The Burning of the Bull

The papal bull, which reached Germany in the autumn of 1520,
condemned Luther's books and commanded Christians to burn
them. It expelled him from Christian pulpits and threatened to
ban anyone who supported or protected him. It cited in condemnation forty-one statements from his writings and finally pronounced
him excommunicated if he would not repent or recant in sixty days.
It was a formidable document.

On December 10 at Wittenberg before a large crowd Luther
deliberately burned the papal bull! The die was cast. On January 3,
1521, the Pope announced that Martin Luther was an excommunicated heretic. That meant death, ordinarily, but the Elector of
Saxony had been reading Luther's books and insisted that the professor be given a proper hearing before condemnation. The excommunication had been foreseen, and in November 1520 the
Emperor Charles V had asked the Elector Frederick to have Luther
appear and defend himself before a group of learned men at the
next Diet or Convocation of the empire, to be held at Worms in
1521.

The Diet at Worms

Accordingly in April 1521, Luther rode to Worms in a covered
wagon provided by the city of Wittenberg. It was a triumphal procession. As he rode into the city, people cried to him from the
windows not to recant. The great heretic entered the hall with a
smile on his face. On a table was a pile of twenty books. He was
asked if they were his and if he would retract in whole or in part.
He said they were his and that he had written many others. As to

whether he would retract or not, he asked for time to consider. He was given twenty-four hours and spent the entire night in consultation with his friends.

The next day he appeared before the diet again and made a long, carefully worded statement, the gist of which was that he would recant only if he were proved wrong by the Bible. When a direct yes or no answer was demanded, he said, "I cannot and will not recant anything, for it is neither right nor safe to act against conscience. God help me. Amen!"

A tumult arose as Luther uttered the fateful words. Spaniards hissed and Germans applauded. Western Christendom was splitting apart. The meeting was soon adjourned by the Emperor. Luther delightedly told his friends, "I am through! I am through!"

Private conferences were held with the monk to urge him even yet to recant, but his would-be persuaders found him, they said, like a rock. In a week he left Worms for home, but it was long before he reached Wittenberg. The Emperor Charles signed an edict May 26 branding Luther's doctrines as a cesspool of heresies, forbidding anyone to read his books or give him shelter, and ordering that he be surrendered to the authorities.

The Wartburg

Luther was safe, however. He had been arrested three weeks before on his way home by five armed men and secretly conducted to the Wartburg, a castle belonging to his good friend, the Elector Frederick. Here the warden treated him so royally that he soon suffered from too rich a diet. Ten days after arriving at this retreat he wrote to a friend, "I sit here lazy and drunken the whole day. I am reading the Greek and Hebrew Bible."

Melancholy grew upon him, partly due to ill health and partly because the lonely spot brought a return of his childhood fears. Some boys brought him some hazelnuts, and when a rodent rattled them in the night, he thought the devil was juggling the nuts. The story that in his little room in the Wartburg he once threw at the devil an inkstand, contents and all, is discredited by recent historians on the ground that he did not mention the occurrence in the many letters he wrote at the time, but the story is so typical of both his violence and his fear of the devil that it is quite credible without contemporary documentary evidence.

The story is certainly true symbolically, for many an evil spirit was laid low by the contents of Luther's inkstand. From May 1521 to March 1522, the period of the Wartburg exile, the inkstand in the lonely retreat must have been frequently refilled, for beside many lengthy letters, Luther wrote a large volume of sermons, a treatise "On Monastic Vows" dedicated to his father, and, in the last three months, a very carefully wrought but brilliantly original translation of the entire New Testament into German from Erasmus' Greek.

The Revolt Spreads

Meanwhile the religious revolt was spreading with incredible rapidity. Reformers sprang up overnight. In a few months Wittenberg instituted so many reforms that a condition bordering on anarchy resulted. Certain wild prophets from Zwickau proposed the immediate overthrow of religious and civil government. A strong hand was needed, and Luther prepared to return, ban or no ban. He felt called on to organize and establish on a firm foundation the reformation he had started.

His friend the Elector warned him that Duke George might take him and turn him over to the Pope. Luther said he didn't care if it rained Duke Georges for nine days running. He returned March 1, 1522, and with characteristic vigor preached eight sermons in eight days which almost magically cleared up the Wittenberg chaos. His first sermon was on the text, "All things are lawful for me but all things are not expedient." Then he proceeded to other towns, preaching and co-operating with the civil authorities, helping put down sedition and establishing the new order of religion.

The Protestants

He found himself already the acknowledged head of a vast movement spreading through all central and northern Europe, a movement having enormous political and social as well as religious significance. While he lay hid in the Wartburg, the seed he had sown in his books had brought forth a few weeds, it is true, but for the most part a bountiful harvest of new wheat.

When the Emperor Charles made his second visit to his German possessions to hold the great Diet of Augsburg in 1530, he found that conditions had changed greatly in the nine years since the Diet of Worms. He had been so busy in his French and Turkish wars that he had not had time to attend to the enforcing of the Edict of Worms against the heretic Luther. To enforce it now was a practical impossibility, for five powerful princes and the people of fourteen free cities had agreed to defend the new religion and to protest against the enforcement of the edict in their lands.

These protesters were therefore called Protestants.

Home Life

The Emperor found also that the lonely monk was no longer lonely nor a monk, but a happily married man with two children. Luther had been married just five years before to Catherine Von Bora, a former nun, who had escaped with eleven others from a Cistercian cloister in 1523, the year after Luther had left the Wartburg. There had been great excitement when the marriage was announced. Now that a renegade monk had married an escaped nun, the Catholics said, we may expect that they will have a child which will be Antichrist himself. Erasmus is said to have replied that in that case Antichrist must have come long since. Erasmus spoke bitterly, for he was himself the illegitimate son of a priest.

Luther confessed that he did not marry for love but "to please his father, vex the Pope, and spite the devil," a statement probably more clever than true, for the marriage was a happy one. "Katie" was an efficient housekeeper, rising so early that he called her "the morning star of Wittenberg." It must have been a pleasant change for him, for he tells us that for a year before his marriage his bed was never made up!

The "Table Talk" reveals the charming home life of the reformer in the old monastery, made over into a comfortable home by the capable Katie. They had six children of their own, practically adopted eleven others, and boarded many students besides. In this hospitable home, the after-supper conversations alternated with song fests, where Luther tried out his newly composed hymns before sending them out to help spread the Protestant Reformation. Attempts were made by the Emperor at the Diet of Augsburg and later to reconcile the two religious parties, but in vain. They were opposed on the fundamental question of the basis of authority in religion. The Catholics held to church and pope, the Protestants to the Bible and conscience. Conferences, diets, and councils only widened the breach, which for four centuries since has divided Western Christendom.

The Last Years

Luther's last years, until his death from heart disease in 1546, were occupied in writing, preaching, and conferring with other reformers. From the time of his return from the Wartburg he was inclined to be conservative, taking the stand that nothing should be altered in Catholicism save what was contrary to the Bible. He fought in pamphlets and letters against the more liberal Erasmus and Zwingli. The reformation movement rolled on and left him in an inlet. In many ways the religion of Luther's later days was nearly as conservative as Catholicism itself. It might be said that he merely exchanged one infallibility for another, an infallible church for an infallible book. He was even called the Protestant pope, but if anyone ever deserved that title, it was John Calvin.

We can hardly admire Luther's attitude at the time of the death of Zwingli, the man who carried the Reformation into Switzerland and with whom Luther quarreled over the meaning of the communion service. Luther said that Zwingli's death was a judgment of God for the Swiss reformer's "mad and furious blasphemies." A scientific age like ours must smile when it reads that Luther called reason "the Devil's harlot" and said that Copernicus was a "great big fool" for supposing that the earth went around the sun when "the Holy Scripture clearly shows us that Joshua commanded the sun, not the earth, to stand still."

Erasmus, the humanist scholar, whose studies made Luther's work possible, "who laid the egg that Luther hatched," was regarded with suspicion and even hatred at last by Luther, who considered him an atheist, and said, "Erasmus is bad through and through." Furthermore, Luther's reputation suffers severely for his attitude toward the Peasants' Revolt, an uprising of the poor which really grew out of Luther's own writings on Christian liberty, but which he feared would endanger his reforms. When the oppressed peasants rose in rebellion and demanded their rights, Luther advised the rulers to kill them as they would mad dogs, and wrote a strong pamphlet "Against the Thievish, Murderous Hordes of Peasants." Again, his advice to Henry the Eighth of England and

Philip of Hesse in their marital troubles was certainly most immoral.

   These undesirable elements in Luther's character were due to
his earnest desire to see the triumph of the Gospel, his version of it,
and to his consequent belief that anyone who threatened its success,
whether that one were pope, humanist, another reformer, or an
ignorant peasant, was inhabited by the devil himself. If Luther had
believed less in the devil and more in the God of love, not only
would his own reputation have been brighter but the Reformation
would have been more successful.

   Nevertheless the world owes him more than any other reformer,
for he changed the emphasis in Christianity from heaven to earth,
from asceticism to service, and laid the foundations of democracy
and civil government. Adolf Harnack put the matter succinctly
when he said, "Luther freed religion, and by that he freed all
things."

OTHER REFORMERS

Wycliffe (1320–1384) *Huss* (1373–1415) *Savonarola* (1452–1498)
Erasmus (1466–1536) *Zwingli* (1484–1531)
Melanchthon (1497–1560) *Calvin* (1509–1564)

   The Protestant Reformation is forever associated with the name
of Luther, but it began long before Luther, and his uncompleted
task was carried on by others after his death.

JOHN WYCLIFFE (1320–1384)

"The Morning Star of the Reformation"

   When Luther called himself a "Hussite" he was really acknowl-
edging himself a Wycliffe-ite, for Wycliffe of England was the
acknowledged teacher of Huss of Bohemia. And when he maintained that "St. Paul and Augustine were Hussites" he was giving
his spiritual genealogy, for Paul, Augustine, Wycliffe, Huss, and
Luther were brothers all in spirit, all insisting upon the freedom of
the individual Christian.

   In Yorkshire, England, about the year 1320, there was born to
the Wycliffes of Wycliffe (or Wiclif) a son named John. Of his
childhood nothing is known. He first appears as a scholar of con-

siderable prestige at Oxford University as Master of Balliol College about the year 1360. His whole career is closely connected with Oxford, and yet, for a scholarly person, he had a remarkable influence with the common people, whose hard lot he understood. He once said, "Poor men have naked sides, and dead walls have great plenty of waste gold."

It might almost be said that he lived three lives. He lived the cloistered life of a scholar at the university writing Latin theses which defended rather liberal views in theology. He had a notable public career. In 1366 he was given a seat in Parliament as an authority on ecclesiastical affairs, especially expert on the respective jurisdictions of the English Government and the Pope of Rome. In 1374 he was named a member of an important commission of Englishmen which met the representatives of Pope Gregory XI on the neutral ground of the Netherlands. His third career was that of an educator. His cardinal principle was the right of the individual Christian to decide religious matters by going directly to the scriptures and interpreting them in the light of his own reason.

But there was no Bible to which Englishmen of his day could go. Scholars could read the Latin Bible, but there was no English Bible. In fact, the English speech itself was then just taking shape. Consequently, he translated the Latin Bible into English, and as fast as he completed a section he would have it copied by students who went forth on foot throughout England, clad in a peculiar red robe, giving to the delighted peasantry the scriptures in their everyday speech. Thus he sowed the seeds which long years afterward bore fruit in the English Reformation.

This versatile man was in favor with the rulers of his day because of his ardent patriotism. He justified the acts of the government in refusing to accede to the rather domineering claims of the papacy. When, however, his theological views were seen to be radical he was summoned to appear at St. Paul's in London. As he walked down the aisle, Lord Percy and Duke John of Gaunt, two powerful nobles, walked beside him. The judge of the day was the Archbishop of Canterbury; the prosecutor, the Bishop of London. Lord Percy urged Wycliffe to be seated. The bishop said an accused man should not sit. The lord and the bishop quarreled loudly and soon the church was the scene of a disgraceful fight between their followers. Meanwhile, Wycliffe slipped quietly away.

The next year, 1378, he was again accused but was defended by the Queen Mother herself and given only a mild reproof. In 1381 he attacked the Catholic doctrine of transubstantiation—the belief that the wafer and wine become in the mass the literal body and blood of Christ. Wycliffe maintained that Christ was present only in a spiritual sense.

He was forbidden to publish these ideas but continued to do so quietly yet effectively. His views were condemned by the Archbishop of Canterbury at a great assembly in 1382. But Wycliffe's luck still held. An earthquake occurred while the assembly was in session and was deemed by Wycliffe and his followers to be a judgment of God against the assembly. He was that autumn called before a provisional synod in Oxford but nothing definite was done. By that time the common people of England had received Wycliffe's Bible and esteemed him so highly that the High Church authorities hesitated at any overt act. He died of a stroke of paralysis the last day of 1384.

But the Council of Constance, in May 1415, decided that Wycliffe was a heretic. His views were condemned, and it was ordered that his bones be dug up, burned, and the ashes scattered. The command was carried out twelve years afterward. The ashes were thrown into the little river Swift. His followers were fond of saying "as the Swift ran into the Severn, and the Severn into the sea, so did Wycliffe's views spread around the world."

JOHN HUSS (1373–1415)

The Heretic

The very council of Constance which proclaimed John Wycliffe to have been a heretic and ordered his bones to be dug up and burned also, a few days later (July 6, 1415), tried, condemned, and burned alive his Bohemian follower, John Huss, and scattered his ashes on the Rhine.

In the year of the earthquake which saved Wycliffe, 1382, Anna, the sister of Good King Wenceslas of Bohemia, married Richard the Second of England, and thereafter there was much going to and fro between the two countries. Oxford scholars traveled to the University of Prague and carried with them Wycliffe's heresies. In the year 1396 a peasant boy named John, from the village of Hussynecz, and therefore known as John Huss, received the Master of Arts degree at the University of Prague and became rector of the University in 1402.

He had read Wycliffe's writings with great interest and enthusiasm and made them the basis of his university lectures. He translated them into the Bohemian language and preached Wycliffe-ism from the pulpit. He was a good preacher, a well-known scholar, and was confessor to the Queen herself. Consequently, his advocacy of Wycliffe's heresies became widely known.

In 1403 the university authorities ordered him to cease proclaiming Wycliffe's doctrines. Pope Alexander V issued a bull against the heretic Wycliffe, and his writings were publicly burned in Prague. The warnings were clear and plain. But John Huss was made of stern stuff. Not only did he keep on preaching, even if he was excommunicated by the Pope. He even attacked the theory of indulgences. This so stirred the papal authorities that in spite of the friendship of powerful nobles his days were numbered. Huss was summoned to the great Council of Constance. A safe-conduct was given him by the Emperor himself.

Huss's progress from Prague to Constance was one of great triumph. Every town he went through greeted him as the needed reformer. But the dice were loaded against him. He was seized and thrown into a filthy prison cell, where he very nearly lost his life through sickness. He was kept there for months and removed only to be thrown into another prison, where he was chained day and night. In June the council which had condemned Wycliffe as a heretic only a few days before brought Huss before it for trial. Although not given a fair hearing, he boldly proclaimed his doctrines and refused to recant.

On the ninth day of July he appeared before the council for the last time. His priestly robes were stripped from him and he was asked again to recant. He replied, "How can I recant when I am innocent?" The bishops said, "We deliver thy soul unto Satan." He replied, "And I commit into Thy hands, Lord Jesus Christ, the soul Thou hast redeemed." They led him past a bonfire of his books to a stake surrounded by a pile of wood. He was given one more chance to deny his faith, but refused and sang a hymn as they lighted the fire, praying until the flames stopped his voice.

They burned his body and they burned his books. But upon his death there arose a mighty revolution of the Bohemian people, and his words were carried far and wide by faithful disciples. Today he is one of the most honored of the Christian martyrs and is recognized as one of the greatest of the reformers.

GIROLAMO SAVONAROLA (1452–1498)

The Martyr

Still another river was to bear a martyr's ashes to the sea: the Arno, this time, in Italy.

In 1490, in the monastery of San Marco in Florence, a Dominican monk of less than forty years of age began preaching sermons which were characterized more by fire and enthusiasm than by homiletic polish. He attacked the wickedness of his day, hurling his shafts right and left, without fear or favor. Church and state alike suffered his scathing comments, and delighted people flocked to hear him. The ruling Medici family, patrons of the revival of learning known as the Renaissance, tried to bribe the monk, Savonarola, by promises of patronage. But he resisted the temptation.

Florence had, not long before, been a democracy, so, basing his appeal on the democratic spirit of the people, Savonarola sought to create a great democratic Christian state. A party of his followers, called the Piagnoni, grew in power until Savonarola practically controlled the city. The people were aroused by the fiery preacher until they abolished the licentiousness and vices of the city.

But Savonarola had more enthusiasm than common sense. The fickle people soon found his idealistic standards beyond their reach. In the enthusiasm of the revival they had given up gambling and dancing, had burned their pornographic books and pictures, and had even given up singing secular songs. The natural reaction was taken advantage of by the Medici party, and when Pope Alexander VI, irritated by Savonarola's criticisms, became his enemy, the tide turned against the bold preacher.

He was denied his pulpit and was summoned to Rome. When he refused to go he was excommunicated. This was in 1497. But Savonarola still had friends, and it was agreed between the two parties that there should be a trial by fire. Two champions were to walk down a lane between two long fires. A Franciscan was to represent the Medici party, and one of Savonarola's Dominican brothers was to represent him. The preacher was not in favor of such an ordeal, but his followers agreed to the public test. A great crowd gathered, but the two parties debated for hours as to whether one of the monks should carry a cross or a sacred wafer. While they were disputing a rainstorm came up and the crowd went home disappointed, unjustly blaming Savonarola for the fiasco.

Now that the people were turned against him his enemies felt they could take steps to put him out of the way. He was arrested and tried for heresy. For a long week he was tortured on the rack every day. Under the terrible pain he confessed, but as soon as the torture ended he retracted his confessions.

On May 23, 1498, saying, "My Lord died for my sins; shall not I gladly give this poor life for him?" he walked to the gallows and was hanged. His body was burned and the ashes cast into the Arno. He left no organized movement, but his memory was an inspiration to other reformers. With prophetic vision he called himself "a forerunner and a sacrifice." For, when Martin Luther was journeying to the Diet of Worms, there to stand trial for his opinions, a priest who admired him brought from his study a picture of Savonarola. Holding it before Luther, the priest said, "Stand firm in the truth thou hast proclaimed and God will as firmly stand by thee." Luther was much impressed by the incident, and there is little doubt that when at the diet he refused to recant, he was mindful of the words of the priest and the example of Savonarola.

DESIDERIUS ERASMUS (1466–1536)

The Greatest Scholar of the Reformation

It was the custom of college students in those days to travel from one great European university to another with their beloved *Stammbücher* or *alba amicorum* (friendship albums, forerunners of present-day autograph albums) inscribed with original Latin verses by their professors. These albums served as communication channels between universities, as well as passports, introductions, and certificates of scholarship. This custom was somewhat responsible for the spread of the opinions which gradually led up to the Protestant Reformation. Oxford students carried Wycliffe's ideas to Prague, where they lived again in the intrepid John Huss, and the process of the dissemination of ideas continued throughout the next century.

When the Turks captured Constantinople in 1453 it became

necessary for Europeans to find new avenues of trade. The search for new trade routes opened commerce and exploration, resulting not only in the discovery of America and the circumnavigation of the globe but also in the broadening of men's minds. The breaking down of the barriers of the scholasticism and conservatism of the Middle Ages period first showed itself in the Renaissance at Florence, Italy, and as soon as news was received in university circles of what was happening, the more progressive students made long journeys to come in contact with the new culture.

Among those who went from Oxford to Florence was one John Colet. He was in Florence during the heyday of Savonarola's power and was much influenced by the fiery prophet. When Colet returned to England in 1496 and began lecturing at Oxford on Paul's Epistles he brought with him not only the seeds of the Renaissance of arts and letters but the yeast of a religious reformation as well.

Another student who desired to go to Italy in order to perfect his knowledge of Greek was a young Dutchman named Erasmus. He was the illegitimate son of a priest, had been well educated in early youth but had been robbed of his patrimony by the guardian appointed after his father's death. He was placed in a school of the monks and, later, in an Augustinian monastery. After ten years as a monk he left the monastery in the year Columbus discovered (1492) America, and after a period at Paris began a roving, knockabout career during which his income depended upon his literary compositions, as precarious a provision then as now.

That income was so meager that he was unable to go to Italy as he desired, and as the next best thing, he determined to get somehow to England, where, at Oxford, he could learn about the Italian Renaissance secondhand from John Colet. It was the fall of 1499 when he reached Oxford and he left there the next year. But during that brief period he made important English "contacts," such as with Thomas More, and caught enough of the spirit of the Renaissance to influence his life thereafter. For thirty-five years he wandered about western Europe seeking a patron who would guarantee him sufficient income to ensure him the freedom to write the books his fertile brain was continually planning.

Erasmus was a "character." He revealed his unique personality in the hundreds of letters he wrote to his many friends, and anyone who has read half a dozen of them would quickly recognize any of the rest even unsigned. He was neither saint nor hero but a very "human" person. His letters were filled with quaint complaints at the poor accommodations then afforded travelers. The roads and the inns and the beds and the wine were all wretched, it seemed. Everybody was mendacious but himself, but he certainly knew how to write artful, begging letters.

Authors at that time did not as a rule enjoy the benefits of a stated royalty on their books. The publisher gave the author a few copies, sold as many of the rest as he could, and kept the proceeds. The only recognized way by which an author could get money was by dedicating his book to some rich man, who promptly returned the compliment by sending a gift of a sum of money or some splendid present which might be sold. The resultant dedications were marvels of eulogy. If we are inclined to call Erasmus a fawning sycophant we must remember that it was a matter of bread and butter to him. In spite of the whining complaints with which his letters are filled one learns to admire the cleverness of the poverty-stricken scholar as he treads his difficult path through an unsympathetic world. On first acquaintance Erasmus rather repels the student of history, but after a while one learns to love him. He impressed his contemporaries in much the same way.

Without doubt, Erasmus was the greatest scholar of the Reformation period. He companied with the learned men of his time, and where he sat was always the head of the table. Nevertheless, his great contribution to the progress of religion is to be discovered in what he did for the common people. He was the father of all modern humanizers. The learning of the Renaissance and the doctrines of the Reformation he made available to the rank and file of the people. This he did in two ways: first, by publishing collections of classical sayings with pithy comments by himself, and, second, by his famous translation of the New Testament.

His first edited collection came about almost as an accident. When he left England in the year 1500 he had about twenty pounds with him which he had managed to get together. This he intended to use for the expenses of the journey to Italy, for his appetite had only been whetted by what he had learned at Oxford from John Colet. But the English customs officials at Dover stole the money from him and he found himself in France practically penniless. Always a sensitive soul, sometimes finding slights where none were intended, this real blow he took with considerable dignity. He said afterward, "Returning to Paris a poor man I understood that many would expect I would take my revenge for this mishap with my pen, after the fashion of men of letters, by writing something venomous against the king or against England."

What he did do, however, was throw together rather hastily a collection of quotations from classical writers which might serve as a model for those who wished to improve their Latin style. Appended to the collection was a poem in which Erasmus stated that he was not angry with either England or the king even though they had deprived him of his money. These *Adages* were immediately popular and went into many editions. Later, he published a collection of metaphors, allegories, and wise sayings which he called *Parabalae,* and near the end of his life, a collection of amusing anecdotes called *The Apophthegmata.* The parables and apothegms were as successful as the adages and carried Erasmus' fame far.

His greatest success, however, was his famous book, *The Praise of Folly,* a clever composition in which Folly praises herself. It afforded the author an excellent vehicle for pointing out the hypocrisies and excesses of the time. In a typical passage, Folly says, "Without me the world cannot exist for a moment. For is not all that is done at all among mortals full of folly? is it not performed by fools and for fools?" In the book Erasmus holds up to ridicule especially the superstitious worship of saints, the rivalries and immoralities of the monks, the popular craving for miracles in religion, and even the sale of indulgences, that corrupt practice which eight years later drove Luther to post his ninety-five theses and launch the Reformation.

One other of Erasmus' many writings deserves mention for its influence on the common people. He had, even before 1500, collected samples of colloquial conversations in Latin which he used as models for his pupils. An acquaintance named Caminade had pirated the collection, and a copy got into the hands of a publisher, who printed it without Erasmus' knowledge in 1518. Erasmus was so offended that he published an authorized version of the *Colloquia* in 1519. Inside of three years it had run into twenty-five editions, in ten cities from London to Vienna. Thereafter it gained even wider popularity and was a best seller for many years. One copy certainly reached Stratford-on-Avon.

It was really only a collection of dialogues or one-act plays, but every one was beautifully done from the point of view of dramatic unity and literary style. The subject matter, however, was what won the *Colloquies* their popularity. The people chuckled as they read the keen characterization of the absurd practices and foolish views of the priests and monks. The trade in relics, so wittily exposed by Erasmus, fell off as the *Colloquia* circulated. It will always be a debatable matter whether the Protestant Reformation was most aided by Luther's valiant defiance of the Pope or by Erasmus' trenchant pen portraits of the vices of the church.

When we realize that, besides these popular books, and an enormous correspondence (3,000 letters are known), Erasmus was constantly turning out editions of Aristotle, Demosthenes, Plutarch, Lucian, Terence, Cicero, Livy, and Euripides, to say nothing of editing the writings of many of the church fathers, we stand in wonder at the accomplishments of his prolific pen. He had in mind, however, a greater work than any of these: a translation of the New Testament. The Vulgate Version, based on Jerome's work, was the best available until Erasmus. What was needed was a careful and critical revision of the Greek manuscripts and an accurate translation into Latin—the *lingua franca* of the day.

It was a monumental task. We know from a letter he wrote to Colet in 1512 that he had at that time made considerable progress in the study of the old Greek manuscripts. In 1516 he published at Basle a parallel-column edition of the New Testament. In one column appeared the original Greek, carefully compiled from many manuscripts, and in the other, Erasmus' own translation of the Greek into Latin. In the preface to the book he said, "I wish that they [the gospels and epistles] were translated into all languages so that . . . the husbandman should sing portions of them to himself as he follows the plow, that the weaver should hum them to the tune of his shuttle, that the traveler should beguile with their stories the tedium of his journey."

The publication of the New Testament was one of the great events of the sixteenth century. It produced an immediate sensation. On the one hand the orthodox clergy protested vehemently because they considered the old Vulgate the very Word of God. The ignorant monks, never having been told that the Greek was the original, were shocked that the sacred scriptures should appear in such an heretical language as Greek. But, on the other hand, a great welcome awaited the book. Within three months Luther, in concealment at the Wartburg, translated Erasmus' Greek testament into the language of the common people of Germany, a version so vivid and idiomatic that it is still in use.

Erasmus' New Testament, his paraphrases of it, and its translations into other languages became the book of the Protestant Reformation. Heretofore the people had not known the Bible. When its democratic message reached them in their own tongue, autocratic religion lost its prestige and power. To Luther doubtless belongs great credit, but his work and that of the other reformers would have been almost impossible without Erasmus behind them.

The surprising thing about it all is that Erasmus remained a Roman Catholic. Luther and others sought to draw him into the active work of the Reformation, but he was always hopeful that the old Mother Church might itself be reformed without a schism. But at his death, Erasmus the Great Humanist refused confession and the last rites of the Catholic Church, and in his will left no money for masses for the repose of his soul, preferring to establish a trust fund for the education of poor but talented young men, for dowering poor girls, and for the support of infirm and aged folk.

He died July 12, 1536, suspected by both Catholics and Protestants because he refused in spite of pressure and bribes either to endorse or to condemn the Reformation. Yet he is today honored and respected by both.

ULRICH ZWINGLI (1484–1531)

The Reformer of Switzerland

It is quite possible that if Luther had not led the Protestant Reformation, a Swiss reformer, born just a year later, would have assumed that position. For he reached conclusions similar to those of Luther and independently of him. He first drew attention as a reformer when he preached against the indulgences with such good results that the sale was stopped in his vicinity. He was strongly inclined toward Erasmus' humanistic ideas and achieved great popularity in Zürich by preaching directly from the scriptures.

He was fortunate in having the support of his superiors and of the temporal authorities of Switzerland. An ardent patriot, he not only served as chaplain in the Swiss Army but met his death on the battlefield in 1531 fighting against the Forest Cantons in defense of the Swiss Confederation.

In 1520 he published a pamphlet declaring his sympathy with Luther's work and outlining a practical program of reform. The nation followed his leadership, and the Swiss Reformation was accomplished with less difficulty than the German one. He came into conflict with Luther on account of a different interpretation of the meaning of the Lord's Supper. A conference arranged at Marburg in 1529 to effect a reconciliation failed, and Luther was guilty of bitter words against his fellow reformer.

Zwingli was inclined to be more democratic than Luther, and the clash over the Lord's Supper was due to his willingness to allow a common-sense interpretation of the rite, while Luther always conservatively clung to the policy that nothing in the Roman Church should be changed unless it was absolutely necessary. When Luther turned against the common people in favor of the powerful princes, Zwingli chose the path of democracy. Here was the real difference between them. Zwingli was always cordial to Luther, even to the extent of allowing Luther's writings against himself to be sold in Switzerland, but when Zwingli held out his hand amicably to Luther, he refused it, saying, "No need of brothering and fellow-membering; you have not the right spirit."

When Zwingli was dying he remarked calmly, "They can slay only the body, not the soul."

PHILIP MELANCHTHON (1497–1560)

The Greatest Teacher of the Reformation

Another great scholar of the Reformation, second only to Erasmus, was the brilliant young Philip Melanchthon, whose learning and temperate spirit did so much to prevent Luther from making any more mistakes than he did.

Young Philip entered the University of Heidelberg at the age of twelve and got his Bachelor's degree two years later. At seventeen he was giving lectures on rhetoric and the classical authors. Before he was twenty he published his translation of Terence which ran into many editions. The year he reached his majority found him occupying the chair of Greek at Wittenberg. He stood by Luther through the whole Reformation period. He refused ordination and found his chief joy in his lectures to the students. The townsfolk and gentlefolk of Germany crowded by thousands to hear him.

Melanchthon acted as a sort of editor for some of Luther's work and was constantly seeking to reconcile opposing groups. To him is due the irenical tone of the famous Augsburg Confession of 1530. He differed somewhat from Luther in his interpretation of the Lord's Supper and irritated the great reformer by the compromise he was willing to make with Luther's opponents. His greatest work was as a teacher and he published many needed books, from text-books on Latin, Greek, and ethics to popular theological treatises.

JOHN CALVIN (1509–1564)

Who Systematized Protestant Theology

The Lutheran reform spread northwest into Norway, Sweden, and Denmark. But English-speaking Protestants derive from Calvin rather than from Luther.

John Calvin was a Frenchman, Jean Cauvin, who left his native country because of persecution and began his reforming work in Basle at the age of twenty-seven, in the year that Erasmus died, 1536. In that year Calvin first published his famous book known as *The Institutes of the Christian Religion.* Protestant theology had produced no document comparable with this work of a young man still in his twenties. He kept rewriting and revising it, however, all his life. It could be compared, for logical completeness and consistent argument, only with the work of Augustine, from whom, indeed, Calvin received his characteristic doctrines. He had been brought up in surroundings of wealth and culture and used Latin as if it were his native tongue.

Even in his youth he was severe and dignified, so much so that his fellow Latin students nicknamed him "the Accusative." He was by temperament a Puritan, and his vice of intolerance was only the exaggeration of his virtue of conscientiousness. There is no doubt that his excessive devotion to study undermined his constitution and that his consequent poor health is reflected in his gloomy theology. His law studies at the University of Orleans provided a strong foundation for his later work in systematizing theology, but he left Orleans to go to Bourges, where he became proficient in Greek. It was during this period at Bourges that he began preaching, and his early sermons there already showed his inclination toward Protestantism.

Soon he was in Paris, where his interest in the reform movement grew. On All Saints' Day, 1533, at the inauguration of a friend named Cop to the rectorship of the University of Paris, Calvin delivered an oration which really contained the essence of his later theology. He spoke strongly of the need of church reform and called for a new theology based on the New Testament. The oration by the twenty-four-year-old Calvin was a challenge to the old order very like the Wittenberg theses of the thirty-four-year-old Luther exactly sixteen years before. France was so strongly orthodox at that time that young Calvin and his friend were both obliged to leave Paris.

Calvin wandered about France for three years but found no welcome anywhere. Thereupon he sought refuge in Switzerland, and there, in Basle, managed to get his "Institutes" published. With great boldness he dedicated the preface of the book to King Francis I. From Basle he went to Italy, thence to his old home in Picardy, sold his property there, and started for Strasburg. He had to take a roundabout route through Switzerland. All these journeyings had been made rapidly, and it was only July 1536 when he arrived in Geneva on his way to Germany.

In the Swiss city a young man named Farel was endeavoring to establish the Protestant Reformation. He sought an interview with Calvin and boldly threatened the young Frenchman with the curse of God if he did not stay in Geneva and help in the work of reform. Calvin stayed. The time was ripe, and the whole city welcomed Calvin's program of reform, both religious and political. Even before Calvin arrived, the people of Geneva had declared their freedom from the authority of the Roman Catholic Church and from the temporal power of the Duke of Savoy.

It is doubtful that ever in history a community was so rapidly changed. Almost overnight the gay city of Geneva became a place of Puritanical piety. It was too much for human nature to stand, and in April 1538 Calvin found himself not only able to continue his journey to Strasburg but compelled to do so. The immediate occasion of Calvin's sudden exit was an Easter sermon which he preached from the pulpit of St. Peter's. The young-old man of twenty-eight had been aroused by the return of the people to frivolity and announced from the pulpit that he would not permit the people to partake of the Lord's Supper that day because, in their present condition, it would be a desecration of the sacred rite.

The next morning the indignant citizens banished him and Farel. Through a storm Calvin made his way to Strasburg. He utilized his unexpected leisure in two ways: he studied theology and he got married. After three years' absence, during which he began a beautiful friendship with Melanchthon, Calvin was recalled to Geneva by its repentant citizens, who implored him to become their pastor. He accepted the call.

Pastor, indeed, he was, and more. His position in the city was practically that of a Protestant pope with complete temporal power. Church and state were united, and Calvin dictated the constitution for both. For twenty-three years after his return to Geneva in 1541 to his death there in 1564, Calvin ruled the city with an iron hand. His earnestness and single-eyed devotion to his own interpretation of Christianity seemed to him sufficient excuse for the intolerance he showed toward those who differed from him even in minor matters.

Credit must be given him as a pioneer in both theological and social reform. He took up the Reformation where Luther left off. His early theology centered around the thought of the sovereignty of God. It was a magnificent structure, but his pursuance of its implications led him to extremes which modern Christian thought rejects, even in the Presbyterian, Baptist, and Congregational churches whose theology is founded upon his system.

Even Presbyterian candidates for the ministry are no longer required to affirm the famous Five Points of Calvinism in the sense in which their author intended. And the exponents of the present-day fad of "Neo-Calvinism" wisely say little about such incredible barbarities as Calvin's belief that "non-elect" infants are precondemned by God to eternal damnation in the perpetual fires of hell. Modified Calvinism, sometimes called "Mortified Calvinism" half a century ago and more (1903) amended the Westminster Confession of Faith to read, "We believe that all dying in infancy are included in the election of grace, and are regenerated and saved by Christ through the Spirit."

It was not without many bitter struggles that Calvin maintained his power in Geneva. The group which had driven him out and which had governed the city during his three-year absence opposed many of his extreme measures and still held enough power so that fifteen years elapsed before he succeeded in expelling these "libertines," as they were called, from Geneva.

Calvin had a caustic tongue and did not bridle it. He used it with much bitterness on his three personal enemies, Castellio, Bolsec, and Servetus. Castellio was a humanistic rationalist, and Bolsec opposed Calvin's favorite doctrine of predestination. They were both banished from the city. Servetus, the Unitarian, was bold enough to attack the Trinity itself. For such unspeakable heresy Calvin permitted the public burning of Servetus in 1553. It will ever remain a disgrace not only to Calvin's memory but to all Protestantism.

Calvin's great purpose was to meet the challenge of organized Roman Catholicism, based on an infallible church, with an equally well organized Protestantism, based on an infallible Bible. He very nearly succeeded, but the weakness of his system is inherent. The Bible is no more infallible than the church. Before he died, however, he saw his theology accepted by thousands of congregations in France, his native land, which had driven him out. The tragic but glorious history of the Huguenots perpetuates his faith.

He was reincarnated spiritually in John Knox (1513–1572), who introduced Calvinism into Scotland and founded the Presbyterian church there. In him, as in the man whose disciple he was, was combined both theological and political ability, and he maintained his views with fanatic enthusiasm. "He was lyke to ding the pulpit in blads and flie out of it." Knox contributed nothing original to theology but simply handed on what he had learned during two long visits in Geneva.

Not only were the Scotch Covenanters followers of Calvin, but also the English Puritans, by whose side they fought to overthrow English Episcopalianism. The Puritans and Separatists who left England and founded New England carried Calvinism with them and, it must be admitted, were as ready to persecute those who differed from them as was the man whose theology they had accepted. Let it be also said, however, that intolerant as Calvinism was in its founder and his leading disciples, there never was a religion which produced men of stronger character, willing to suffer everything for what they considered to be the Christian truth.

XVI

❦

NICON

[A.D. 1605–1681]

THE LUTHER OF RUSSIA

I F ONE WERE TO TAKE the reforming zeal of a Luther, the preaching power of a Chrysostom, the political ambition of a Wolsey
and the sensitive suffering spirit of a Jeremiah, and imagine all of
these qualities dwelling inharmoniously in the huge, seven-foot
frame of a burly peasant, the result would resemble the great Russian reformer, Nicon, who was in some ways the Rasputin of the
seventeenth century. Until recently almost nothing was known of
Nicon in the religious circles of English-speaking countries, save
that he was one of the most important of the group of patriarchs
who ruled Russian ecclesiastical affairs during the seventeenth century. But time is a great revealer of values. When the obscure and
almost inaccessible sources of information are made available,
Nicon will come into his own.

The Eastern Church

Roman Catholics and Protestants have been so occupied in their
quarrels with each other for the last several centuries that they have
almost forgotten the existence of the original Christian church

known as the Greek Catholic or Eastern Church. Its members call it the Orthodox Church (the "Holy Orthodox Catholic and Apostolic Church"), because they consider Roman Catholicism an heretical schism.

The great Eastern Church, the grandmother of Protestantism, was divided geographically into separate churches, such as the Coptic, Abyssinian, Syrian, Nestorian, Georgian, Armenian, Greek and Russian, each of them claiming to be orthodox although insisting upon certain peculiarities of dress and liturgy. Mar Athanasius Jesus Samuel, the Syrian Archbishop and head of the Jerusalem Monastery of St. Mark, who bought a few of the "Dead Sea Scrolls" for $140 and sold them in New York for $250,000, considers his church to be the original and oldest of all Christendom. For weren't the disciples first called Christians at Antioch in Syria?

In the seventeenth century, when the Russian branch was the strongest of all the divisions of the Greek Catholic Church, a great reformation arose comparable in some ways to that of Luther. This reformation was largely due to the efforts of Nicon, although Peter the Great got most of the credit for it.

The Child Nicon

Moscow was the political and ecclesiastical center of Russia when, two hundred and fifty miles away as the crow flies, in a suburb of the city of Nishni Novgorod, the child Nicon was born in a peasant home in the year 1605. Nothing is known of his parents, but from the single story we have of his childhood we infer that his mother died when he was still quite young, and that he was brought up by a stepmother. It is possible that some of the later eccentricities of Nicon were reflections or results of his hard experiences in childhood.

One cold winter day, the poorly clad boy, in search of warmth, crawled into the great Russian stove in which a certain measure of heat remained, although the coals had been raked out of it. His stepmother, peering into the stove, saw that the boy was sleeping. She was a most inhuman creature, and, probably inspired by jealousy of the boy's place in his father's affections, seized the opportunity to get rid of him. Pretending not to notice him, she crammed the stove with logs of wood in such a way as to prevent his escape and then, having lighted the fire, went out of the house and left the boy to his doom. The heat soon awakened him and, finding his escape blocked, he shouted so loudly that a neighbor woman, named Xenia, heard and rescued him.[1]

In some way the child came in contact with books. It is unlikely that they were in his father's home, but he may have made friends with some monk. At any rate, he learned to read, and loved the scriptures. They made a great impression upon his childish mind, and records of his later life say that his education was almost entirely based upon the Bible.

When he ran away from his uncomfortable home it was very natural that he should head for a monastery. Just as he was about to take the vows as monk in the monastery at Jeltovodsky, his father, who had missed and followed him, arrived. He either commanded or persuaded the boy to return to his home. There seems to have been a compromise arrangement. Probably what the young man objected to was the presence of the hateful stepmother. That difficulty was removed by an arrangement which the father made for the boy himself to marry. Nicon's desire to spend his life in the service of religion was satisfied, at least temporarily, by his father's permission for him to become a parish priest.

Nicon the Monk

Nicon was afterward convinced that he had made a great mistake when he yielded to his father and returned to Nishni Novgorod. When all his children died he took it as a sign from heaven that God disapproved of his having relinquished his plan to become a monk. Consequently, at the end of ten years of married life, he persuaded his wife to enter a convent, and himself went far to the north to the monastery of Solovetsky. His passion for self-immolation still not satisfied, he went still farther north after a while and lived with an old hermit named Eleazar, on the Isle of Anzer in the White Sea, on the edge of the Arctic Ocean.[2] How many years were spent in this almost inaccessible region, in conditions so difficult that it is hard to conceive how he managed to keep his body alive, we do not know. We do know, however, that he left this island several times.

[1] William Palmer, *The Patriarch and the Tsar*, Vol. I; *The Replies of Nicon*, Intro., p. xv.

[2] Mouravieff, *History of the Russian Church*, p. 194.

The first trip southward was made necessary by the fact that his wife refused to take the final step which would make her irrevocably a nun. After he had persuaded her to take that step he returned to Eleazar, with whom he left on a second expedition to go to Moscow in order to collect funds. After they had returned to their lonely station, the two hermits quarreled over the disposition of the money, and Nicon left the island for the last time. He came near losing his life, because the boat in which he left the island was in poor condition, and a storm arose. He managed to get to another island and finally made his way to the monastery of Kojeozersky.

Near that monastic retreat was an island on which Nicon built himself a rude shelter and proceeded to live such a life of asceticism and privation that even the monks were astonished. When the head of the monastery died, the entire body of monks urged Nicon to become their head. It took a great deal of persuasion, but finally he went to Novgorod and was ordained by the bishop of the province, the Metropolitan Aphthonius.

Moscow

After three years in the monastery it became necessary for him to visit Moscow on official business. From the moment of his arrival, the tall ascetic began to bulk large in the world of affairs. This visit was made probably in the year 1646 when Nicon was forty-one years old. He was in the prime of his powers and must have presented a most unusual appearance.[3]

The Czar of Russia at the time of Nicon's visit was Alexis, who had come to the throne four years before. He was not one of the strongest of the Russian Czars, but was progressive and had an open mind. He knew that the general moral condition of the nation was such that a reform was needed. He was also impressed by the backwardness of Russia compared with the civilization of the rest of the world.

If Alexis was not particularly strong himself he did realize the importance of securing the assistance of powerful men. When he first saw Nicon he was struck with his unusual personality. When he heard him speak he was even more impressed, for the monk of the north spoke with burning and eloquent words. Determined to know more about him, Alexis made inquiries and discovered that

3 Stanley, *History of the Eastern Church*, p. 457.

Nicon was considered by his fellow monks to be unsurpassed in his devotion to religion. Compared with his contemporaries he was a learned man. The Czar knew that such a combination of qualities was unusual, and acted quickly to attach this born leader of men to his entourage.

The Archimandrite

He began by making him archimandrite, or abbot, of the monastery in which the Czar's own ancestors, the Romanoffs, had been buried. The significance of this appointment in the life of Nicon and the history of Russia can hardly be overestimated. Intimate contact with Nicon confirmed and strengthened Alexis' first impressions, and the two were soon inseparable companions. Alexis not only listened eagerly to all the monk's public utterances but also sought every opportunity for private conversation.[4]

In the charms of his conversation Alexis Michaelovich found consolation to his soul, and from that time accustomed himself to be guided by his sage counsels; he found in him a zeal for the Church not inferior to his own, and the loftiest view not only of ecclesiastical but also of political matters, which in Nicon proceeded solely from the originality of his mind and from his bold openness of character.

Alexis found Nicon's advice in religious matters so wise that he consulted him on affairs of state as well. In short, Nicon had as great an influence over Alexis as Rasputin later did over Nicholas II, although both the monks were of lowly peasant origin. It did not take long for the observant courtiers to learn that the surest way to secure the accomplishment of any object was to get the favor of Nicon.

The Metropolitan

There was no surprise in Moscow when, only three years after his emergence from the northern wilderness, this singular monk was made Metropolitan of Novgorod, succeeding Aphthonius in 1649. When he was inducted into office he was consecrated by no less an authority than the Patriarch of Jerusalem. This new appointment increased Nicon's growing power. As Metropolitan he

4 Mouravieff, p. 195.

was next in authority to the Patriarch, and inasmuch as the patriarchate of Moscow was vacant, it took no great prophet to predict who the next Patriarch would be.

During Nicon's term as Metropolitan of Novgorod he achieved still greater distinction in several ways. Affairs in that city were in a turmoil, and Nicon endeavored to bring peace and order. In the streets of the city he went boldly into the heart of a riot and met a mob face to face. When they had finished with him he was left for dead in the city square. When his timorous friends arrived to take his body away for burial they found he was still breathing and was fully determined to face the mob again. As soon as they had raised him to his feet, he insisted upon going into the building where the malcontents had gathered. The very boldness of the stroke won the day for him and he was soon in control of the city.

In Novgorod and Moscow, religion was the main interest of the people, and they were at first startled and then delighted by an innovation which the new Metropolitan introduced. Men and women had been accustomed to stand for hours in the cold Russian churches listening to the long liturgical services, much of which they did not understand. Nicon began to preach. His sermons brightened the whole service. He knew the Bible and made it live again in the language of the people. It became necessary for them to arrive in the church early if they expected to get near enough to hear him. To his reputation for personal bravery was added a recognition of his talents as a preacher, and the popularity of Nicon grew proportionately.

A third occurrence in the eventful years of his service as Metropolitan of Novgorod still further increased his reputation. To a western Christian, that event seems to belong more to the realm of superstition than of religion. But in the seventeenth century in Russia it was hailed as a great religious achievement.

In one of their frequent conferences Nicon proposed to Alexis that the Czar call together a great public meeting to honor the memory of former leaders. Upon that occasion their bodies were to be brought to the Church of the Assumption. Nicon had found that the superstitious lower classes of Moscow firmly believed that the spirit of the former Czar, Ivan the Terrible, was still lingering in Moscow ready to work mischief.

Now Ivan the Terrible deserved his name. A single incident will suffice to show the character of the man. At one time he had condemned seven huge monks to be killed and eaten by wild boars. Ivan enjoyed the spectacle and made it more interesting by allow- ing the unwieldy monks to defend themselves each with a single spear, which only further infuriated the fierce animals, who soon made an end of them.[5] This and many other events were fresh in the minds of the people. There was only one way to "lay the ghost." One of Ivan's victims had been the hermit Philip, whose body had been laid at rest in the Solovetsky Monastery.

Nicon bore with him to that monastery a petition from the Czar addressed to the spirit of the saint, which was conceived of as still hovering over his body. When Nicon brought back the corpse and its attendant ghost to Moscow, where the body of Ivan was interred, the people were happy, not only because of the many miracles of healing which took place around the coffin but especially because they knew that the lost soul of the terrible Czar would now be quieted by the saintly spirit of the martyr.[6]

The Patriarch

After his successful three years as Metropolitan of Novgorod, Nicon was appointed Patriarch of Moscow by the Czar Alexis in the year 1652, but it was with great reluctance that Nicon assumed this high responsibility.

It is a tradition among the bishops of every branch of the Chris- tian religion that they should modestly protest their unfitness for such a high honor, but in Nicon's case there were real reasons for him to hesitate. He knew very well that for a monk who was un- known six years before to be elevated to the highest position in the Russian Church would be to incur the jealousy of other disap- pointed candidates.[7] Two groups were sure to oppose him. Among the clergy there were many who disliked the high-handed way in which he had upset their most cherished traditions, for he had not only introduced the extempore sermon, which seemed to them un- dignified, but he had also made other changes which appear insig- nificant to us but which were of great importance in so ritualistic a religion.

The other group of his opponents were the boyars of the Czar's

5 Stanley, *History of the Eastern Church*, p. 456.
6 Adeney, *The Greek and Eastern Churches*, p. 415.
7 Adeney, p. 415.

court. These nobles and princelings were very much disgruntled because of Nicon's sudden rise to power and were already plotting against him. His appointment as Patriarch would make him more vulnerable to their weapons of intrigue. Nevertheless, Nicon accepted the patriarchate and immediately commenced sweeping reforms, evidently with the hearty concurrence of the Czar. The only precautionary measure he took was to insist, as a condition of his accepting the patriarchate, that both the temporal and spiritual officials of the realm should swear a solemn and unbreakable oath of obedience to him. One can imagine the grace with which the boyars submitted to this decree.

Nicon's Ambition

With this rather precarious foundation beneath his feet, Nicon proceeded to erect a structure of ambitious proportions. He had more in mind than even the Czar suspected. In order to understand his later somewhat enigmatic conduct, it is necessary to glance at the organization of the Eastern Church. Christendom had been anciently divided into five great patriarchates: Jerusalem, Antioch, Alexandria, Constantinople, and Rome. But when Rome seceded from the rest of Christendom and set up the western branch, which was to be known as the Roman Catholic Church, it seemed necessary that another city should take Rome's place. Christianity had for several centuries been spreading northward into Russia, and in the year 1582 Moscow was chosen as the seat of the fifth patriarchate. And the patriarch Jeremiah of Constantinople solemnly inducted the Metropolitan Job as the first patriarch of Russia.

There were, unfortunately, other considerations which led to the establishing of this patriarchate. More than a century before, Constantinople had been captured by the Turks, and while the Ottoman ruler magnanimously allowed the Christians to maintain their form of worship in Constantinople, the income of the patriarchate there was gradually reduced until it was in dire straits. It seems to have been partly in consideration of substantial help for Constantinople that its patriarch instituted the patriarchate of Moscow.

Now, when Nicon was made Patriarch of Moscow in the year 1652, he conceived the ambitious project of making his city the third and greatest Rome. Constantinople had been spoken of as the second Rome after the city on the Tiber had seceded.

It will be seen that Nicon had two objects in mind: two tasks which must be accomplished simultaneously in the face of great opposition. The Czar of Russia must rule the world, and the Patriarch of Moscow must control the Czar. The fealty which Nicon compelled the boyars of the king to swear to himself as newly elected patriarch was an important link in the chain. Another link was his own intimate friendship with the Czar. He could not foresee that both these links would break when the boyars, out of jealousy, should prejudice the mind of the Czar against him.

The Reform of Ritual

With such a huge task before him Nicon proceeded with more vigor and energy than discretion. He seems to have had in mind as the basis of a world-wide Christian creed and ritual a return to the early Greek forms, as nearly as they could be discovered. As a beginning he proposed to change the Russian ritual to make it conform in certain details of worship with the original Greek customs.

Most of these changes seem to Protestants quite insignificant. That, however, is because in many Protestant churches today the worship, and even the recited creeds, are quite divorced from the actual belief of the people. For instance, it is customary, even among the clergy, for one to recite the Apostles' Creed in church while making mental reservations on more than one clause. In Russia, however, in the time of Nicon, every word or gesture was strictly expressive of the faith of the congregation. The slightest change of position or the omission of a single word was heresy.

Two Fingers or Three

When, therefore, Nicon attempted to change the making of the sign of the cross with two crossed fingers of the right hand to making it with three fingers, he raised a storm of protest. The use of two fingers signified that Christ had two natures, human and divine; the use of three fingers indicated belief in the Trinity—Father, Son, and Holy Ghost. Only a century before, a Russian Synod had decreed,[8] "If anyone does not bestow his blessing with two fingers, as Christ did [!], or does not make the sign of the Cross in the same way, let him be accursed."

[8] *Encyclopedia of Religion and Ethics*, Vol. XI, p. 335.

When Nicon commanded, then, that three fingers should be used, the perplexed people had the choice between incurring the displeasure of their Patriarch or the anathema of the whole church. Whether the blessing should be made with two fingers or three may appear unimportant, but when one realizes that the making of the sign of the cross was practically the only physical part which the people themselves took in the worship, and when we also realize that the people did not read, nor did they come into contact with religion in any other way than by the church service, it is easy to understand the consternation which greeted Nicon's decree. Yet, if the Greek practice was the true apostolic method, Nicon was right.

Restoring the Creed

Shortly after Nicon's induction into office, he found a vestment which had at one time been worn by a Metropolitan of Russia before the patriarchate was established, and which had been brought from Greece in the early fifteenth century. On this vestment, elaborately worked in pearls, was a copy of the Christian creed. When Nicon compared it with the creed which was used in the Russian Church in his day, he found differences. A council was called immediately by the Czar, and members of the council voted unanimously, with the concurrence of the Czar, that the liturgy and all books in Russian should be corrected to conform with the ancient Greek version.

This discovery started Nicon off on a frenzy of investigation and research. He persuaded the Czar to give orders that there should be brought to Moscow all the ancient manuscripts from the monasteries of the vicinity. Moreover, a messenger was sent to Constantinople to bring back an accurate copy of the Nicene Creed. With it he brought a letter from the Patriarch of Constantinople, who commended Nicon for his efforts to unify the practices of all five patriarchates but gently intimated that the zealous Russian leader should not be too precipitant in the making of changes within his own jurisdiction.

Another messenger was sent southward from Moscow bearing rich gifts and seeking ancient manuscripts. Five hundred Greek books were brought back from Mount Athos, including an ancient copy of the Gospels. The other patriarchs learned of Nicon's activity and donated so many valuable manuscripts that soon Moscow found itself in the unwonted role of a center of Biblical learning. A new service book was printed, followed by other books, based upon the old manuscripts. But when it was attempted to substitute these new books for the old ones, which the churches and monasteries had had for so long that they thought they were the very words of God, trouble began brewing.

Nicon's Iron Hand

Meanwhile, the foreign relations of Russia were becoming important. The Czar led an army off to the Polish War in 1654. The entire administration of civil as well as religious affairs was left in the hands of Nicon. The nobles had to bow to his will and he took care that they bowed low. Every morning a bell was rung, and the boyars were obliged to assemble in the palace immediately and listen to Nicon's decisions on matters of state business. If anyone was late he had to wait for several hours before he could see Nicon. Some of the nobles brought back with them from the Polish campaign certain religious pictures or icons painted after the Western manner. They also set up a new musical instrument, the organ, in their homes.

For these heresies Nicon punished them by confiscating the organs and ordering the eyes of the portraits cut out and the mutilated remainder carried in a jeering procession through the city. He even called the offending nobles by name in the public service of the cathedral.[9] But if he was hard on the secular boyars, he was even more severe with the ecclesiastical leaders. One of our main sources of information about Nicon's manners is a diary which was kept by a certain archdeacon named Paul, a traveling companion of the Patriarch Macarius of Antioch. Macarius had come to Moscow to solicit contributions for his work from the comparatively rich Russians. Archdeacon Paul says of Nicon's attitude toward his subordinates,

He is a very butcher among the clergy. His janissaries are perpetually going around the city, and when they find any priest or monk in a state of intoxication they carry him to prison, strip him, and scourge him.

[9] Mouravieff, p. 214.

His prisons are full of them, galled with heavy chains and logs of wood on their necks and legs, or they sift flour day and night in the bakehouse.[10]

The Punishment for Smoking

The Metropolitan of Mira came up to Moscow on a visit and was having a jolly time with some boon companions, indulging in the new hobby of smoking tobacco. They were discovered by the janissaries of Nicon, and all of them, except the Metropolitan, were sent into banishment. The Metropolitan was reserved for a worse fate.

Archdeacon Paul tells us how at one of the banquets given by Nicon in honor of Macarius, the host provided interesting entertainment of an unusual sort. There filed into the room, at Nicon's command, some thirty men of most repulsive aspect. They were chiefs of a Mongolian tribe from the far north, called the "dog-faced" men.

It was not their appearance so much as their habits that shocked the visitors from Antioch. Nicon said to these men, in the presence of his guests, "Is it true that you eat the flesh of men?" They laughed and answered, "We eat our dead; we eat our dogs; how then should we not eat men?" Nicon said, "How do you eat men?" They replied, "When we conquer a man we cut away his nose and carve him away and eat him." He said, "I have here a man who deserves death; I will send for him and present him to you that you may eat him." Hereupon they began earnestly to entreat him, "Dear Lord, whenever you have any men deserving death, do not trouble yourself about their guilt or their banishment; but give us them to eat; you will do us a great kindness."[11]

But when Nicon's servant went to bring the victim, the Metropolitan of Mira, they could not find him, for he had escaped. Whether Nicon actually intended to deliver the Metropolitan to such a horrible death, we do not know. Perhaps he only intended to frighten him. He certainly scared the archdeacon later when he pretended to deliver the fear-stricken visitor from Antioch into the hands of the savages. Archdeacon Paul relates also how Nicon banished three deacons who had ventured to marry again after their

---

10 Stanley, p. 463, *History of the Eastern Church*, quoting from Paul's Journal.
11 Stanley, p. 464, quoting Archdeacon Paul's Journal.

wives had died in the plague. They were bound and confined in a cell, condemned to die of starvation, but Macarius intervened and persuaded Nicon to set them free.[12]

The Plague

While the Czar was absent on the Polish campaign a terrible pestilence broke out in Moscow. There were so many corpses in the city that they could not all be buried. Nicon's ability showed itself in the way he handled the situation. He sent a pastoral letter to comfort the people and instructed them in preventive sanitation. With wisdom and energy he assumed charge of the royal family, in spite of the fact that the Czaritsa was opposed to him, and moved them about from place to place as the plague spread. When Alexis returned victorious from his Polish conquests and found his family safe, he was so grateful that he gave Nicon a new honor, the title of "Great Lord."

Affairs were then going very well for Russia. In the far east of Siberia another army was making conquests, and a group of ambassadors was negotiating in Pekin with the Emperor of China. Astrachan and Moldavia became part of Russia, and all the neighboring rulers were seeking alliances. Nicon's dreams of world empire seemed likely of fulfillment. But the tide turned.

Although Alexis was victorious in another campaign in Poland, all his hard-won victories there were set at naught by a clever Jesuit, the Austrian envoy, Allegretti, who succeeded in negotiating a peace advantageous to Poland, whereby the Czar was promised the crown of Poland if he would embark on a war against the Swedish people. When he did so he was sadly repulsed at Riga, and returned home to find that his family had been saved again by Nicon from the plague, which had broken out afresh.[13]

Nicon's Foes

Meanwhile trouble was brewing in Moscow for Nicon. The boyars had united and had secured the help of some of the princes of the realm. The Czaritsa, probably from jealousy of Nicon, was inclined to aid the plotters. At this time, in the year 1655, the follow-

12 Stanley, p. 465.   13 Mouravieff, pp. 212, 213.

ing groups were secretly arrayed against Nicon: the clergy whom he had oppressed and humiliated, the boyars and princes of the Czar's court, the Czaritsa, and most important of all, the great mass of the people, who were offended by the changes which Nicon had made in the services of worship. Nicon's only ally was the Czar himself.

But such was the power of the patriarch's personality that he actually succeeded in March 1655 in convening a synod and forcing the endorsement of three propositions, namely,

(1) That the creed was to be cleaned of Russian additions and that a return was to be made to the Greek form;

(2) That the sign of the cross must conform to Greek instead of Russian practice;

(3) That re-baptism was not necessary in admitting members of another branch of Christianity. Heretofore only triple immersion had been recognized as real baptism in Russia; hence the sprinkled members of the Western Church, for instance, could not commune in the Russian Church until they had been re-baptized.

Nicon was not satisfied with these victories and went even further. Before a large congregation in February 1656 he preached a sermon against the two-finger form of making the sign of the cross, which was customary in the Russian Church. His sermon was particularly offensive because he called the two-finger form the "Armenian" form and charged that those who used it were guilty of the Armenian heresy. Now at this time in Moscow the Russians had no dealings with the Armenians. If a Moscovite passed an Armenian church he stopped his ears lest he should hear the infidel music. And if an Armenian entered a Russian church during service, the service was stopped immediately. It is easy then to imagine the consternation aroused in Moscow by this sermon.[14]

Nicon succeeded in getting another synod, in the year 1656, to endorse all his changes in liturgy and even had Macarius apply his patriarchal curse upon those who ventured to continue the old customs. Whatever official sanction Nicon secured for the changes which he wished to make had little effect upon the opinion of the great mass of the people. Their suspicion of him was reflected in the council of the boyars. The latter soon saw that the only way to overthrow the powerful patriarch was to foment misunderstanding between him and the Czar, so they kept telling the Czar that Nicon

[14] *Encyclopedia of Religion and Ethics,* Vol. XI, p. 336.

was impudent, and they further magnified his defects. Soon there was a diminution in the number of conferences held between Nicon and Alexis. Probably the Czaritsa did her part. It became the fashion in the court to smile, simply smile, when the name of Nicon was mentioned. By such subtle ways the breach was widened.

Defeated by a Dog

The climax came when one of the nobles secretly trained a dog to sit up and bestow the patriarchal benediction with his paws crossed, imitating one of the innovations of Nicon. When the noble had the dog well trained he brought him into court and announced that the dog's name was Nicon. When the animal went through his performance the court was convulsed, and everyone knew that the fall of the patriarch would be only a matter of time.

A little later, in a procession, one of the courtiers openly insulted one of the followers of Nicon. When Nicon learned of it he insisted that an apology be made. When the boyars refused, Nicon notified the Czar that he would meet him at a certain time and place for an explanation. The nobles, eager to widen the breach, arranged matters so that the Czar was kept away from the appointment. Nicon, waiting at the appointed place, was openly insulted by the prince who came to tell him that the Czar would not be able to keep the appointment.

Nicon Resigns

This prince taunted Nicon with his pride in being called "Great Lord." Nicon was exceedingly angry. He managed to go through with the church service, but at the end shouted in his loud voice that he was resigning his patriarchate, "I leave my place conscious of my many sins before God which have brought this plague and woe upon Moscow."[15] His scepter of office was the staff of the first Metropolitan, Peter, who helped Ivan I in 1325 to establish Moscow as the religious and political capital of Russia. This staff Nicon laid on the most sacred picture in the cathedral; then he removed his robes of office, wrote a letter to the Czar and sat down in the cathedral to wait for the answer.

15 Stanley, p. 477.

The reason for this hasty action was probably deeper than most of his biographers have realized. It was no mere fit of temporary passion. His whole plan for himself and for Russia was being disrupted. The thing that was especially disturbing to him was the losing of the Czar's friendship, which was really the keystone of the ambitious structure which he was erecting. If the Czar became estranged, then the patriarchate would lose all its recently won power, and even if Russia did become the ruler of the world, the Russian Church and Nicon would not share in that glory. So as he waited in the cathedral for an answer from the Czar he knew that his own fate and that of the Russian Church hung in the balance. But no answer came. The nobles intercepted the message.

Exile

As the hours passed, the people became aware of the importance of Nicon's action. In spite of his austerity they loved and reverenced their patriarch. So they closed the doors of the cathedral to keep him from leaving. They even took the horses from his carriage so that he could not get away, but the broken Nicon crept out of the cathedral and went on foot to a nearby monastery, and from thence to one farther away, finally making his way to the Krestnoi Monastery near the White Sea of the north.

From the first moment of his resignation he had expected the Czar to send a message begging him to resume the patriarchate. He had not dreamed that the estrangement had gone so far. Meanwhile the weak Czar, who entertained no personal animosity toward Nicon, was prevailed upon by the boyars to allow the breach to remain. The patriarchate was declared vacant. One of Nicon's few friends in the city, however, sent a message to the northern monastery and urged the patriarch to return quietly and appear in the cathedral as if nothing had happened. Nicon overcame his pride and followed the suggestion, to the surprise of all Moscow.

But the bold stroke did not succeed. The Czar ordered Nicon to a monastery, there to wait until he should be tried by a great council. This message from the Czar finally convinced Nicon of his failure. Up to this time he had presumed that reconciliation was possible and that the Czar wished him to be patriarch but was hindered by the nobles.

The Trial

It was true that the Czar wished Nicon to be patriarch, but the boyars held the upper hand. The council was convened and thirty serious charges were made against Nicon, to all of which he made replies. The records of the proceedings are very lengthy. In Palmer's six-volume study, called *The Patriarch and the Tsar,* the entire first volume of nearly seven hundred pages is occupied with the "Replies of Nicon." Many of the points covered in these replies are far from interesting, but there are occasional flashes of the old Nicon. He exhibits a wealth of learning which is surprising, considering the lack of opportunity in his youth for becoming acquainted with the learning of the ancients.

He knew his Bible as few men have known the book and was very familiar with the writings of the early church founders. He shows also a keenness of wit and a certain dry humor. One of the charges against him was that he had used a comb and a looking glass "although bishops are forbidden to adorn themselves." In his reply Nicon pointed out that the priests of Moses' day were positively ordered to beautify themselves, both with beautiful garments and with unguents. He sets forth the duty of a priest to conceal the evidences of his suffering, and quoted Christ's words, "When thou fastest, anoint thine head, and wash thy face, that thou appear not unto men to fast."

Anyone who reads Nicon's replies to the charges against him in that great debate, which finally resulted in his condemnation on the twelfth of December 1666, will be surprised at the verdict, for the honors of the debate certainly went to Nicon. But like most church trials the result was a foregone conclusion. Nicon was doomed before he opened his mouth. All through the proceedings Alexis sought to save his former friend. The Czar even left his throne and came over and affectionately took the patriarch by the hand, saying,[16] "Oh! most Holy father! why hast thou put upon me such a reproach, preparing thyself for the council as if for death? Thinkest thou that I have forgotten all thy services to me and to my family during the plague, and our former friendship?"

But the hurt was too deep for Nicon to forgive. Looking around

[16] Stanley, p. 483.

upon the hostile nobles he said to Alexis,[17] "Why do you not bid them take up stones? So they would soon put an end to me; but not with words, though they should spend nine years more in collecting them." When the sentence was finally given, Alexis absented himself. Nicon was sentenced to spend the rest of his life in a distant monastery doing penance.

Unhatted

It was the Russian custom to unfrock deposed ecclesiastics by unhatting them. Nicon's khlobuk was a particularly valuable headdress, richly embroidered in pearls, and he refused to take it off. But they removed it by force from his head, and he went forth from the council disgraced. The next day the Czar sent a gift of money and rich furs to protect the exile on his long journey, but Nicon proudly refused to accept anything from his former friend. He would have perished from cold, but that a tenderhearted archimandrite threw a winter cloak over him as he set out. For nine years Nicon ate his heart out in the remote monastery near the Arctic Ocean. Then Alexis sent him gifts and begged his forgiveness.

Nicon was preparing to leave his retreat and return to Moscow to be buried in one of the monasteries he had built when he was at the height of his power. But his plans were changed by the death of Alexis, who sent from his deathbed a pitiful plea for forgiveness in which he called Nicon "Great Lord" and "Patriarch." The exile sent his forgiveness, but when the messenger reached the royal palace Alexis was dead. Nicon in his cell exclaimed,[18] "The will of God be done! What though he never saw me to make our farewell peace here, we shall meet and be judged together at the terrible coming of Christ." With his last protector gone, Nicon's lot became worse. His jailers were instructed to treat him more severely.

A Plot to Make Nicon Pope

The tutor of the young Czar Theodore was a strange monk possessed of a wild idea that there should be four patriarchs and over them a pope. Only one man would do for pope—the exile Nicon. He managed to convert the young Czar to his plan and found an

17 Ibid.   18 Ibid., p. 486.

ally in the Princess Tatiana, the sister of Alexis, who had never joined Nicon's enemies in their schemes. She worked with the monk and together they persuaded the Czar to urge the new Patriarch, Joachim, to agree to the return of Nicon. By some strange presentiment Nicon, now a broken old man of seventy-six, anticipated the coming of the messengers.

The Return

Early in the morning he prepared himself and persuaded his attendants to place him on a sledge as if for a long journey. Shortly after he started he met those who had been sent to bring him to Moscow. It was a long journey, and the frail body of the former patriarch weakened as the destination drew near. Yet it was a triumphal journey. Everywhere he stopped, the sick begged for his blessing. Religious officials along the route paid him honor. Just before he died he turned suddenly as if somebody had spoken to him, and then carefully arranged his hair, his beard, and his clothes and composed himself for death as those about him read the prayers for the dying.

Triumph at Last

Meanwhile Czar Theodore had sent the royal carriage to meet the returning Nicon. But before Nicon had reached Moscow he had breathed his last. Great honor was done him in his death. The Czar himself walked humbly in front of the enormous coffin in the funeral procession. In the place he had long before chosen he was buried, in the Monastery of the New Jerusalem.

Over his tomb they placed the great iron chains which he had long worn about his body as a penance for his sins, and for centuries that sepulcher was a place of devout meditation for Russian Christians.

The Importance of Nicon

To Western eyes the career of Nicon does not appear as important as it really was in Russian Church history. When we compare him with Luther we see that although he shared with the German

reformer a great talent for preaching, a love of the original languages of the scriptures, and a certain rough-and-ready energy in
getting needed reforms accomplished, nevertheless there was lacking in Nicon a grasp of the fundamental verities of religion. It is
hard for us to comprehend how there can be much importance in
the details of liturgy. But we must remember that in Russia liturgy
was practically the whole of religion. It is not that the people were
not devout. It is simply that the Russian temper was such that every
minute part of their religious forms was supercharged with tremendous meaning. If Nicon changed one jot or tittle of their creed
he was accomplishing a whole revolution in religion.

Orthodoxy anywhere, whether based on an infallible liturgy, as
in Russia in Nicon's day, or on an infallible church or pope, or on
an infallible Bible of the Fundamentalists, always insists that the
foundation is fixed, and not to be altered in any detail. The Bible
must be believed to be literally true "from kiver to kiver."

Yet all human institutions, whether claiming divine origin or
not, do change when thinkers arise within them, and there can be
no doubt that the tremendous disturbances in Russian religion
during Nicon's patriarchate were due to him and that the soil was
stirred for the planting of seeds of reform.

Peter the Great, who was a boy of nine when Nicon died in 1681,
was the one who carried out successfully the movement of reform
which Nicon initiated. It is significant that the very council which
condemned Nicon and sent him into exile approved his reforms
and condemned his opponents, especially Avvakum, the leader of
the party within the church which had consistently fought against
Nicon's ecclesiastical reforms. This was the old Catholic party
which stood for the retention of the familiar Russian version of the
liturgy and the Russian form of the making of the sign of the cross.
So, although Nicon did not live to see it, his reforms succeeded and
became the official Russian religion. The defenders of the ancient
Russian form seceded and were known later as the Raskolniks.

A student of history is struck at once by the fact that the difference between the Lutheran and Niconian reformations is this: that
in the Western countries the reformers seceded from the church,
while in Russia it was the orthodox who seceded. One would be
correct in saying that from an ecclesiastical point of view the Lutheran Reformation was a failure and the Niconian Reformation

a success. Luther did not reform the Roman Catholic Church. He simply formed another church. But Nicon's reforms obtained in the church itself, and his orthodox opponents were left outside the pale.

The Raskolniks

In their passion for insisting upon the maintenance of the liturgy of their fathers in its literal form, the Raskolniks ran true to orthodox form. As Nicon's reforms were urged upon them they shouted in dismay, "Why, they are taking away our Christ!"[19] The Russian fundamentalists were very faithful to their views, and three of their leaders, including Avvakum, were publicly burned in the year of Nicon's death.

Since the blood of the martyrs is the seed of the church, the Raskolniks thrived upon persecution. They became fanatical in their adherence to the Russian forms and refused to make the slightest concession in favor of the changes which were introduced through the influence of Nicon. "Hiding from persecution, the Old Believers filled all the forests of inner Russia with their secret cells. The spread of the sect was still further helped by the strict measures taken against it. Only in 1905 did the sectaries gain the right to religious freedom."[20]

These Raskolniks, or orthodox secessionists, divided in later years into many strange sects. One group, the Molokani, differed from the rest in insisting upon drinking milk through Lent. Several others fostered peculiar sexual practices which were made a religious requirement. Their indescribable customs, verging frequently upon insanity, afford a remarkable field for investigation by students of comparative religion. The best known of these sects is the Doukhobors, many of whom migrated to Canada where they are noted both for their industry and for their fanatic adherence to the peculiar forms of their religion, including periodic nudism.

When Communism, or State Socialism, came into power in Russia four decades ago, strenuous and continuous attempts were made to abolish religion as being the opiate of the people and a bourgeois delusion. But a very recent report by an eye and ear witness Quaker (*The Christian Century*, March 12, 1958) asserts that in spite of years of atheist propaganda and education, "religion is booming in

[19] *Encyclopedia of Religion and Ethics,* XI, p. 337a, note.
[20] Ibid., X, p. 871b.

Russia." Mr. Sidney Bailey reports over a half million Russian Baptists, each with "a miniature Billy Graham in his heart," 25,000 Seventh-Day Adventists, one Roman Catholic church in Moscow with a thousand regular attendants, but nearly two and a half million Roman Catholics in the Baltic regions, a Jewish synagogue and seminary in Moscow, a Moslem mosque crowded with worshipers, and 8,000 other mosques with fifteen million Moslems in the Soviet Union. Mr. Bailey visited the Russian Orthodox Metropolitan Nikolai and found that the church has "reached an accommodation with the state" and has thirty-three churches in Moscow and 25,000 outside, and printed half a million Bibles last year. Even the Raskolniks, Nicon's old opponents, now have 500 churches in the Soviet Union, with 1,500 worshipers in the Moscow church.

XVII

WESLEY

[A.D. 1703–1791]

WHO REVIVED RELIGION
IN ENGLAND

JOHN WESLEY revived religion by taking it out of sacred buildings into the open air, as Jesus had done before him. Incidentally the fresh air saved and prolonged his own life. The fifteenth of nineteen children of a mother who was herself the twenty-fifth child of her parents, he ought by all expectation to have died in infancy of low vitality, as nine of his brothers and sisters did.

An Astounding Life

As a matter of fact, Wesley lived to be eighty-eight, having traveled a quarter million miles, mostly on horseback, and having preached an average of fifteen sermons a week for fifty continuous years. Ministerial pension funds today expect a clergyman to retire at the age of sixty-five, but when Wesley was eighty-five, he delivered eighty sermons in eight weeks, with much hard travel between appointments.

Besides his preaching and traveling, he read more books and

wrote more books than seems credible, kept the most voluminous diary-journal ever known, wrote innumerable letters, founded schools, orphanages and churches, championed social reforms, and, above all, founded a religious fellowship which has survived nearly one hundred and seventy years since his death and now numbers considerably over thirty million adherents, the second largest branch of Protestant Christianity. (The Lutherans are the largest Protestant denomination in the world.)

The Secrets of His Power

What was the source of such power? For one thing, "I have no time to be in a hurry," said Wesley. For another, his flair for system led him to budget his time. He rose at four and preached at five. From then until nine or ten at night, every hour and half-hour had its planned task. No time was wasted. Even with the great folk of his time he would not tarry. Dr. Johnson complained, "I hate to meet John Wesley. The dog enchants you with his conversation, and then breaks away to go and visit some old woman. . . . He is always obliged to go at a certain hour. This is very disagreeable to a man who loves to fold his legs and have his talk out, as I do."

Such a careful budgeteer of precious time was an anomaly in the leisurely eighteenth century, so his contemporaries had a nickname for this efficiency expert born out of due time. They called him and his likewise methodical disciples "Methodists."

But the great source of John Wesley's power was prayer. Difficult as it is for this generation to give credence to the statement, Wesley deliberately planned and accomplished two hours' private prayer every day, an hour in the morning and another in the evening, for over fifty years. The emphasis he placed on these periods of devotion reveals their importance in his life. Upon the first page of every diary he wrote his resolution to keep these prayer trysts, "no pretense or excuse whatsoever."

The transforming power of an intimate personal experience with God was the basis of his whole theology. He lived it, preached it, and demanded it of his followers. He collected and recorded the "narratives" of the personal religious experiences of his disciples as if they were precious pearls. His Journal is a mine for modern students of the psychology of religious experience. The most interesting and valuable of all these narratives is the story of Wesley's own life, his long and painful search for reality in religion and his longer period of perfect repose of spirit after he had found God.

Susannah Wesley

Of the human influences in the life of John Wesley, there was one person who outweighed all others together, his most amazing mother. Susannah Annesley's nineteen sisters and five brothers, all older than she, might have spoiled her or might have extinguished her personality through sheer weight of numbers, but she towers above them all. Her father was a noted Dissenter, "the St. Paul of Nonconformity," but this chit of a girl, the baby of the parsonage, at the age of thirteen had examined the entire controversy between the Dissenters and the Established Church and had joined the latter!

The girl evidently had the freedom of her father's library, and in a day when the literary education of young women was discouraged, succeeded in learning Greek, Latin, French, and theology. At the age of nineteen she married Samuel Wesley and by the time she was forty had borne him nineteen children. John, her fifteenth, was her pet and pride, but she was fair and impartial to all her children. She conscientiously "conquered their wills" and taught them to "cry softly" when they were a year old. Six hours of each day she devoted to their education. The day a child was five years old, he or she was taught the entire alphabet in the six hours. The next morning he began reading the Old Testament. With such a start, progress was rapid. The youngest child, Keziah, could read the Greek New Testament at the age of eight.

The mother was not only an accomplished linguist but a well-read and thoroughly competent theologian. Her diary and letters reveal her as an abler theologian than her father, her husband, or even her famous sons. The entire management of the household fell on her and much of the parish work as well, for her husband, Samuel, spent his time either in writing reams of impossible verse in his study or in working in the garden, where his very impractical notions wasted much of the scanty yearly income of one hundred and fifty pounds. When he was attending ministers' convocations or was detained in prison for debt she conducted wonderfully in-

teresting and well-attended Sunday-evening meetings in the barn
and was severely rebuked by him for such unconventional proceedings.

The Fire

Epworth was in a marshy country and the people of the parish
were mostly ignorant fen-men. Samuel Wesley's obstinacy and lack
of tact infuriated and alienated his parishioners, who retaliated by
killing the family cow and by several attempts at arson. When they
finally succeeded in burning the house, they charged him with having set the fire. The family escaped with their lives, but stark naked
and practically destitute. In a few months they were back in the
partially rebuilt parsonage. Susanna Wesley's chief regret over the
fire was that her careful cultivation of systematic habits in the children had been interrupted and that they had learned slothfulness
and impudence during their stay in other homes. One most important result of the fire was the effect it had upon the six-year-old
John, both directly and through his mother's interpretation of its
significance.

In the confusion of the sudden exodus from the burning house,
little Jacky had been left behind and was not missed until heads
were counted. The father attempted to go back but was unable to
force his way up the blazing staircase. As he knelt in prayer to God
to receive the soul of the doomed child, some neighbors saw the
boy at a rear window. They made a human pyramid and rescued
him just as the roof caved in. His mother saw in this miraculous
escape a message from Providence. The child had been spared for a
special purpose, a "brand plucked from the burning."

The Charterhouse

The father accepted the rescue as a direct answer to his prayer
and he, too, seems to have considered the boy thenceforth as one
set apart, for he admitted him to communion at the very early age
of eight and sent him two years later to the Charterhouse school in
London to prepare for Oxford. At the famous Charterhouse young
Wesley did not particularly distinguish himself. It was here, however, that all unconsciously he was preparing physically for his
great mission.

It was the traditional privilege of the older boys to appropriate the daily ration of meat allowed to the younger ones. By virtue of this enforced vegetarianism the lad discovered that meat was not a necessity for him. In fact, he throve better without it. In later years when devoted female disciples, overanxious concerning his welfare, brought him a meat broth to strengthen him, they only made him ill. But bread and milk restored him to health. The only recreations he seems to have had at Charterhouse were studying Hebrew and running three times around the schoolhouse yard every morning before breakfast.

The Epworth Noises

The real thrill of his schooldays, however, came from the ghost stories in the letters from home. The "Epworth Noises" are notable in the annals of spiritualism and received considerable attention in their day and later. The daughters of the rectory first discovered the ghost and talked much about it. Probably they could have told more than they did. Life was very dull for lively girls in strict eighteenth-century parsonages. If the girls created the ghost, they did their work well. Old Jeffrey, as they named him, was disconcertingly versatile. He knocked, clashed, jingled, scared the family dog, and even pushed the parson about irreverently. Mrs. Wesley had to request him not to make noises during her hour of devotion from five to six. He obeyed so promptly as to arouse our modern suspicions. Poltergeists are not usually so obedient. We wonder how much Mother Wesley suspected. But John, away at school, was much impressed with the possibilities of the unseen world and ever afterward was rather gullible about ghosts.

Oxford

Wesley entered Oxford in 1720 on a forty-pound annual scholarship, which, with a few small sums hardly spared by his poor parents, barely enabled him to get through his five uneventful college years. Toward the end of his course he began to consider religion as a vocation. He was naturally serious and grew more so. He began to meditate and pray longer and read devotional books. He conducted a long correspondence with his mother on the doctrine of

THE GREAT RELIGIOUS LEADERS

predestination. She, ever mindful of him as the "brand plucked from the burning," advised him to seek ordination as a deacon and he became one in September 1725.

His election as a fellow of Lincoln College, Oxford, the next spring, however, seemed to impress him more than his ordination. The election carried a small salary and light duties as instructor. He interpreted the fellowship as an opportunity for study and mapped out a prodigious amount of work. He shut himself out from acquaintance with any persons, saving "such only as would help me on my way to heaven." For twelve years, from his election as fellow in 1726 until his conversion in 1738, there ensued a period in the life of the young man when his unconscious egotism and uncompromising ascetic piety made life a torment for him and for all those who had any dealings with him. Those who would have been friends with him at the college, he repelled. Any conversation not on religious or scholarly subjects he looked on as a sinful waste of precious time. He wrote to one of his pupils, "You, who have not the assurance of a day to live, are not wise if you waste a moment."

Wesley taught and studied at Oxford until 1735 except for two years, 1727–1729, when he served as curate to help his aging father and had charge of the little parish of Wroote, adjoining Epworth. It was a desolate hamlet of two hundred people as sodden as the bogs in which they lived. Wesley simply performed the duties of the office and probably never preached a sermon his hearers could understand. He was then more concerned about his own salvation than theirs.

The Holy Club

While John Wesley was acting as curate, his younger brother Charles at Oxford had formed a friendship with a young man, probably Robert Morgan, and had begun to practice with him a very strict and regular habit of life, with frequent devotions. When John returned to Oxford he and another young man joined in the practice and John was soon the acknowledged leader. The group grew in numbers and strictness and was dubbed the Holy Club. They met for serious discussion, were given to frequent celebration of communion, to self-examination, to hourly silent prayer, and soon began to practice poverty by giving away to the poor in the slums and prisons every shilling they could save. They were really young monks and friars without realizing it.

By 1734 John's austerities and fastings had so weakened his health that severe hemorrhages appeared. The next year his father died, disappointed that none of his sons had applied for the Epworth living until it was too late. John had refused because he could "be holier in Oxford than anywhere else," thoughtlessly disregarding all family obligations.

Georgia

His self-centered attitude was further demonstrated in the fall of 1735 when he and his brother Charles, with two others of the Holy Club, set sail for Georgia to convert the Indians, leaving his old mother and sisters to get along as best they might, with the sole help of the other son Samuel, whose income hardly sufficed for his own needs. To be sure, John asked his mother about his going before deciding. "If I had twenty sons," she said, "I should rejoice if they were all so employed, though I never saw them more." Just before sailing, John wrote, "My chief motive is the hope of saving my own soul . . . I cannot hope to attain the same degree of holiness here which I may there."

The picture of the Four Holy Young Men on pilgrimage to the New World would be ludicrous were it not pathetic. The glorious spiritual stature attained by the Wesley brothers later is a refreshing contrast to their quixotic, almost insane, pharisaic piety on the voyage and during the brief stay in Georgia. The daily program on shipboard John Wesley described in his Journal thus,

From four in the morning till five, each of us used private prayer. From five to seven we read the Bible together. . . . At seven we breakfasted. At eight were the public prayers. From nine to twelve I usually learned German, and Mr. Delamotte, Greek. My brother writ sermons, and Mr. Ingram instructed the children. At twelve we met to give an account to each other what we had done since our last meeting, and what we designed to do before our next. About one we dined. The time from dinner to four we spent in reading to those whom each of us had taken in charge, or in speaking to them severally, as need required. At four were the evening prayers. . . . From five to six we again used private prayer. From six to seven I read in our cabin to two or three of the passengers. . . . At seven I joined the Germans in their public service. . . . At eight we met again to exhort and instruct one another. Between nine and ten we went to bed. . . .

The Germans referred to were Moravian colonists whose general behavior and calm poise during the storms which terrified the other passengers, including Wesley, made a great impression on him. They seemed to have something which he was seeking but had not, and he learned German that he might talk with them.

Georgia in springlike February was an entrancing place to the voyage-worn travelers, but the Indians did not prove as charming and amenable to the gospel as Wesley had fondly expected. He found them "gluttons, thieves, dissemblers, liars, and murderers." General Oglethorpe, who was in command of the colony, desired Wesley to confine his ministrations to the English colonists, and Wesley began to set up a rigid discipline and program fitted for high church worship in England but utterly unsuited to the Georgia wilds. He was tactless and dictatorial and was in trouble all the time, largely because of his great capacity for minding other people's business.

One man told him frankly, before Wesley had been five months in Georgia, "They never heard of such a religion before. They do not know what to make of it. And then your private behavior: all the quarrels that have been here since you came have been 'long of you. Indeed, there is neither man nor woman in the town who minds a word you say. And so you may preach long enough; but nobody will come to hear you." Wesley thanked him for his "openness" and walked away. Such rude remarks were but a part of the hardships in which he gloried with the zeal of a martyr. Three times a week he fasted, and maintained his vegetable diet the rest of the time. His unfamiliarity with pioneer life increased his sufferings so that his Journal during his Georgia sojourn reads like the diary of a tenderfoot.

Sophy Hopkey

The cause of his greatest suffering and the reason for his leaving America was a love affair in which Wesley's part was not admirable, although one can only pity him. He was much in love with Miss Sophy Hopkey and she with him. They would probably have been a happy couple, for she adapted herself to his eccentricities and appreciated his good qualities. Wesley, however, was torn between his love and his profession. He was more than half convinced that celibacy was his duty. For months he suffered the tortures of indecision. His friends of the Holy Club intervened in the affair at last and persuaded him to resort to sortilege, the casting of lots to determine God's will in the matter. Several decisions were written on slips of paper and the one drawn was inscribed, "Think no more of it." Sadly he gave up the idea of marrying her. Four days later she married a Mr. Williamson, "a person," wrote Wesley in his Journal, "not remarkable for Handsomeness, neither for Genteelness, neither for Wit, or Knowledge or Sense, & least of all, for Religion."

The naïveté of John Wesley can be inferred from the fact that he expected the bride to continue to meet him for long sessions of spiritual advice and the reading together of pious books. Her husband very naturally objected, much to Wesley's surprise. When Sophy decided to obey her husband, Wesley considered her disobedient to her pastor and publicly excluded her from communion. When pressed for a reason, he said that she had not notified the curate on the day before of her intention to partake of communion. Strictly speaking, such notice was required, but others had partaken of communion without notice. Many in the church took sides with Sophy and her relatives, and a real church "row" developed. In the little colony some who had scant interest in religion sided against the rector because they considered him ungallant and a poor loser. Besides, they were weary of his punctiliousness.

The Voyage Home

Wesley stuck to his guns for a while, but his usefulness there was over. In December he sailed home, after two unhappy years in Georgia. Charles had also failed and had already left. The six-week voyage home was the hardest part of his life. In his diary he recorded as he neared England,

I went to America, to convert the Indians; but O! who shall convert me? . . . I think verily, if the Gospel be true, I am safe; for I not only have given and do give all my goods to feed the poor; I not only give my body to be burned, drowned, or whatever God shall appoint for me;

but I follow after charity, if haply I may attain it. . . . But in a storm I think, "What if the Gospel be not true?"

The reason the homeward trip was so hard for him was because he forced himself to the unpleasant task of self-analysis in a way he had never done before. It is customary for biographers to date the great change in his life some months later, as he himself did, but it is very evident from his Journal that the real struggle occurred during those winter days and nights when the storms through which the ship labored were matched by the tempests within him. It was his "dark night of the soul." Perhaps the bravest thing he ever did was to admit to himself his failure in America,

This, then, have I learned in the ends of the earth: That I am fallen short of the glory of God; . . . I want that faith which St. Paul recommends to all the world, . . . which enables everyone that hath it to cry out, "I live not; but Christ liveth in me."

The Awakening

In London on February seventh, four days after landing, he met a young Moravian missionary en route to the Carolinas. That Wesley was already undergoing a change is indicated by the fact that he sat humbly for several weeks under the personal instruction of Peter Böhler and learned how the confident assurance of faith comes through a vital religious experience of communion with God. Wesley had had no such experience, knew not how to get it, and hesitated to preach again until he had it. Wise young Peter Böhler cut the Gordian knot, saying, "Preach faith till you have it, and then because you have it, you will preach faith," which was poor logic but good psychology.

On the very next day, Monday, March 6, Wesley wrote, "I began preaching this new doctrine though my soul started back from the work. The first person to whom I offered salvation by faith alone was a prisoner under sentence of death." To Wesley's surprise, the prisoner accepted, and went to his death with "a serene peace." In that spring of 1738 a new Wesley went about England, preaching and teaching faith, preaching to crowds in churches, teaching individuals on the streets, in taverns, and anywhere a man would listen.

So Wesley preached faith, and faith came to him, gradually and then with heartwarming power. On the evening of May 24 in a little meeting of a society of pious folk on Aldersgate Street, London, after a day when the presence of God had seemed very near to him, the assurance of soul which he had so long desired came suddenly to him while "one was reading Luther's preface to the Epistle to the Romans." Paul, Augustine, Luther, and Wesley; Roman Jew, Carthaginian, German, and Englishman, how they clasp hands across the centuries!

Three weeks after, Wesley was on his way to Germany to learn more from the Moravians, leaving behind him a very puzzled group of friends. "What Jack means by not being a Christian till last month, I understand not," said his brother Samuel. In Germany Wesley found confirmation of his new faith, and, although he did not approve of all the ways of the Moravians, he came back aflame with an enthusiasm which electrified his hearers and an urge to preach which never left him. The day after his return he preached four times and thereafter as often as a pulpit was open. By the end of the year, however, he had been debarred from practically all London pulpits. His enthusiasm was in bad taste and very irregular, the clergy thought.

Whitefield

But the problem of a pulpit was already in process of being solved. Another member of the Holy Club of Oxford had previously caught fire with this strange new enthusiasm while Wesley was in Georgia. In 1737, George Whitefield, a brilliant young preacher of twenty-one, had addressed great crowds in the churches of Gloucester and Bristol. Wesley had invited him to Georgia. On his way, Whitefield stopped in London, and for three months was the sensation of the city, preaching to unheard-of crowds and collecting a thousand pounds for the missionary work in Georgia.

Whitefield sailed the day before Wesley's return, though neither knew it, and had as great success in Georgia as Wesley had had failure. In December 1738 he returned. He was welcomed by Wesley but not by the churches, because the clergy feared he was tainted with this same "enthusiasm" of Wesley's. Within a month, no rector in London would let Whitefield preach in his church. Bristol, too, barred him.

Open-Air Preaching

Here were two talented young preachers, bursting with a new message for the times, forbidden to preach in the churches. There was only one thing to do, and Whitefield did it first: he preached in the open air to the colliers of Kingswood, near Bristol. The first time he preached, his audience was a hundred; the fifth time, ten thousand. The common people heard him gladly. The great revival was on. At Bristol on a bowling green vast multitudes assembled and listened reverently.

Whitefield wanted to preach in London but dared not leave his new converts. He sent for John Wesley, but Wesley was still something of an aristocrat and a stickler for propriety. He had lived for fifteen years in the classic shades of Oxford University, a fact frequently overlooked by those who think of him merely as an evangelist of the "shouting Methodists." He came to hear Whitefield preach, however, and although he disliked the whole performance, he yielded to Whitefield's urging, and on the next day, April 1, 1739, preached his first outdoor sermon to three thousand people on the text "The spirit of the Lord is upon me, because he hath anointed me to preach the gospel to the poor." Within a month he had addressed forty thousand in all, and his doubts about outdoor preaching had disappeared. His other doubts faded away also. Moreover, his health grew steadily better. John Wesley had found himself because he had found his work. For over a half century henceforth, he passed up and down the highways and paths of England and Wales, Ireland and Scotland, preaching with apostolic fervor and astonishing power to a multitude no man could number.

Emotion

During the first summer of Wesley's preaching there were a number of emotional disturbances in his audiences, especially at Bristol. Men and women fell prostrate as if dead, or writhed in seeming agony. Naturally, these happenings brought censure upon the preacher. Even Whitefield protested to Wesley but found that the same demonstrations occurred under his own preaching when he came to Bristol. The disturbances ceased at the end of the summer and, since most were in crowded rooms, were probably due as much to fainting from bad ventilation as to overstimulated emotions.

In the early years of his long itinerancy there were other disturbances from ruffians and unfriendly authorities. Stories were spread that Wesley was a Papist and others that he was in the pay of foreign enemies of England. In the simple accounts in his Journal we read of his almost uncanny power in quelling rowdies and rioters.

He would sometimes pick out the leader of the mob, go directly to him, and, speaking quietly, fix the man with his piercing eye. Frequently the leader would not only be turned from his purpose but would even volunteer to protect Wesley from the rest of the mob. Hands raised to strike him would drop to stroke his hair; sticks would be strangely diverted in the moment of their descent. There was something in John Wesley's straight look which made men change their evil intentions. He passed through hostile crowds unharmed, as did his Master before him, and by the same power of personality.

Organization

Wesley's genius was shown as much in his organization of the new movement as in the wonderful preaching which initiated it. His new religion was primarily personal, but it was ethical and social also, and he demanded good citizenship as well as frequent prayers.

Whitefield was a great orator, hurrying from one audience to the next: Charles Wesley was the hymn-writer of Methodism, and his compositions were greatly instrumental in spreading the faith; but John Wesley organized permanent bands, classes, and societies with such carefulness and such understanding of human nature that the system still flourishes with only minor changes. He also established orphanages, schools, loan funds, prison visitation, and poor relief. It was noticed that smuggling and vote-buying ceased wherever Methodism gained a foothold. In short, Wesley's life was, after his conversion, spent entirely for others. He gave away all his income above his bare necessities. His home was the highway; his study, the saddle. He had no real home of his own, for the simple reason that he was not designed to be a husband.

Love and Marriage

Love came into his life again in 1748 when Grace Murray nursed him back to health. Again one of the Holy Club, ever jealous of the affections of its great leader, interfered. His own brother Charles practically forced the young widow to marry another, to whom indeed she had been engaged when she promised herself to John Wesley.

The third time, in 1751, he told no one until he had married another widow, Mrs. Vazeille. It should be said that it was too bad that the Holy Club was asleep this time. But it all happened very quickly. He slipped and hurt his ankle on London Bridge and was taken to Mrs. Vazeille's house. She nursed him while he worked on a Hebrew grammar and a lesson-book for children. On the eighth day after the accident he married her. She led him a terrible life because of her insane jealousy. Once a friend found her dragging him around the floor literally by the hair of his head.

But he had his beloved work and did not permit his marriage to interfere with it, insisting that he should not be expected to travel a mile the less. He simply kept on his way serenely, letting her rave and lecturing her occasionally.

Wesley had no children, "except," as someone has said, "the Methodist Church." He died, ten years after his wife, in 1791, with many friends around him, to whom he said at the last, "The best of all is, God is with us!"

Wesley's Place

The importance of John Wesley in the long history of religion is due to his patient search for the living essence of religion and to his careful observation of it in himself and others when he found it.

He was the first of all religious leaders to recognize, assemble, and preserve the data for a scientific study of religion. When violent emotional disturbances occurred among his hearers at Bristol in the summer of 1739, he entered an account of them in his Journal almost as terse and dispassionate as a clinical report. He warned his hearers that these faintings and writhings "might be from God and they might not." Again he said, "I relate just what I saw. Some of the circumstances seem to go beyond the ordinary course of nature. But I do not peremptorily determine whether they were supernatural or not." And he added, very significantly, "Much less do I rest upon them either the proof of other facts or of the doctrines which I preached."

He was much more interested in the human documents describing the exact feelings and thoughts of his converts. These careful and detailed "narratives," painstakingly preserved for posterity in his Journal, and in his *Arminian* magazine, are still fresh and warm with life, for they were written down and verified by witnesses shortly after the events occurred. Sometimes Wesley read them in the presence of the witnesses that they might be checked and corrected. These valuable narratives are irrefutable arguments for the reality of religious experience. They can be explained in psychological terms, but they cannot be explained away.

Wesley knew that religion made things happen in the lives of men, transforming real "sinners" into real "saints." With the patience and the inductive method of a true scientist, he labored to catch this elusive spiritual power and to pin it down in words. We may not agree with his deductions from his observations, but we are fools if we doubt or ignore his documented and attested facts.

The religion of the future may not be Methodism, but it will be vastly indebted to the founder of Methodism. Darwin's voyage in the *Beagle* and his careful observations of biological facts made possible the theory of evolution. Wesley's horseback journeys about England and his methodical and voluminous records of the religious experiences of himself and others may someday give us the key to this universal and infinitely precious but not yet understood phenomenon called religion.

OTHER ENGLISH LEADERS

BUNYAN (1628–1688)   FOX (1624–1691)   MURRAY (1741–1815)
BOOTH (1829–1912)

JOHN BUNYAN, THE BAPTIST PURITAN

The seventeenth century in England produced two notable religious leaders whose influence among the common folk doubtless prepared the way for Wesley's work in the eighteenth century. These two men were John Bunyan, the Baptist Puritan, and George

Fox, the Quaker. Their lives ran parallel: Bunyan's from 1628–1688; Fox's from 1624–1691.

Bunyan, in his late teens, was a soldier in the Parliamentary Army. After the war was over and he had attained his majority he married a woman as poor as he was, and that was "poor as poor might be, not having so much household stuff as a dish or spoon." But if his wife did not bring him worldly goods she brought him "godly books." This was not John Bunyan's first contact with religion, however. In his boyhood he had listened to the Calvinistic preachers telling of the torments of the flames of hell, and he had vivid dreams that the devil was carrying him off.

But his army experience had somewhat dimmed the terrors of his boyhood, and it was only when he began reading the books his wife brought him that his conscience began to trouble him again. He passed through a period of religious anxiety, gradually dropping comparatively innocent amusements because he thought they might cause him to lose his soul. In his later piety he looked back upon the sins of his youth as having consisted of bell-ringing, dancing on the green, and playing a simple little game known as tipcat! During this period of religious self-examination he became morbid almost to the point of insanity. It seemed to him that the devil kept whispering evil suggestions in his ear. He spent hours in prayer and feared that his soul was lost. He had read that faith as small as a mustard seed could move mountains, but his faith was not strong enough even to dry up the roadside puddles. Therefore, he argued with himself, he had no faith; therefore he was utterly lost.

He finally joined the Baptist Church in Bedford, but even as he partook of his first communion he had a wicked impulse to startle the little group of believers by cursing aloud. He began to preach but was much disturbed by ungovernable impulses to interlard his sermon points with shocking words of wickedness. Bunyan affords a perfect picture of a divided personality. Peace came to him in a strange way.

He had been a preacher for about five years when Charles II came to the throne of England and restored Episcopalianism. The Puritan preachers were obliged to conform or cease preaching. John Bunyan refused to conform and was clapped into jail for twelve years. He could have been released almost any time if he had promised not to preach, but he said boldly that if they let him out he would preach at the first opportunity. Even the hunger of his wife and children did not move his resolution. He managed to earn a little money in prison by making "long, tagged, thread laces." In prison he preached to his fellow prisoners. He had only two books with him: Fox's *Book of Martyrs* and the Bible. These he read and reread until they were part of his very life.

Then came his great inspiration. He would write a book telling of the difficulties of the journey of a Christian through the world. He was released from prison in 1672 because of the passage of the "Declaration of Indulgences" and was immediately elected pastor of his old church. But the "Declaration" was repealed three years later and again he was cast into prison as a nonconformist preacher. This second imprisonment, although it lasted only six months, enabled him to complete his book, which was published in 1678 under the title *Pilgrim's Progress.*

The book was first circulated in cheap, unattractive form among poor people, but its immediate popularity made necessary the issuance of one edition after another. Bunyan published a sequel in 1684 telling of the adventures of "Christian's" wife, and the combined book was second only to the Bible in popularity in England and America for many years. It was practically a manual of pious counsel for Protestant Christians. Part of its popularity was due to the fact that it was the only story which Puritans allowed their children to read. He wrote other books: *The Life and Death of Mr. Bad-Man,* a contrast to *Pilgrim's Progress; Grace Abounding,* a spiritual autobiography; and the *Holy War,* an allegory, and became so well known and loved in England that he was much in demand and traveled far and wide preaching in villages and even in London itself. He was called "the Bishop of the Baptists."

GEORGE FOX, THE QUAKER (1624–1691)

England produced no more striking personality in the seventeenth century than George Fox. His opinions were far in advance of his time, so much so that little attention would have been paid to them if it had not been for his striking and unusual habits of speech and dress. He had a religious reason for all his eccentricities, but that did not hinder him from taking advantage of the incidental publicity which those habits attracted. He wore his hat at all times as a protest against the exaggerated etiquette of the day.

In court or in church he refused to remove it, so he found himself the center of attention wherever he went. He would not wear buttons on his clothes and in other ways made himself conspicuous.

As a lad he had no schooling and was an apprentice shoemaker for some years. In his late teens he began to take long walks in quiet places meditating upon religion. He found no satisfaction in the sermons of Puritan preachers nor in the Episcopal services and was in much distress of soul. He consulted with one preacher after another but got little help. One of them made light of the young man's troubles and told him that what he needed was to use tobacco and sing psalms. He says, however, ". . . tobacco was a thing I did not love, and psalms I was not in a state to sing." Another preacher recommended "physic and bleeding."

He ceased attending church when he was twenty-two and decided that Christianity was a way of life rather than a collection of doctrines. He gathered about him a group of young men of similar opinions and trained them to spread the new gospel of the simple life. His "Valiant Sixty," as he called them, had before long persuaded fifty thousand people to follow Fox. He and his followers were persecuted, but it only seemed to increase their zeal and their numbers.

His first imprisonment was in 1649 when at the close of the sermon in a church in Nottingham he arose and contradicted the preacher, who had stated the Calvinistic doctrine that the source of religious authority is in the scriptures themselves. Fox shouted out boldly, "No, it is not the scriptures; it is the spirit of God." Upon his release he repeated his rather impudent proclamations in season and out of season.

About 1650 his followers were called "Quakers." Fox himself says in his journal that the name was given by a certain justice, Bennett, because Fox had told some magistrates that they should "tremble at the word of the Lord." It is possible, however, that the name "Quaker" had a similar origin to that of "Shaker." The Shakers received their appellation because in the emotional excitement of their religious exercises they trembled and vibrated from head to foot in a sort of fit until frequently they fell upon the floor. We know that the early Quakers were subject to similar physical tremors and contortions induced by religious emotion.[1] Fox was

[1] *Encyclopedia of Religion and Ethics,* Vol. VI, 142, and the New Murray Oxford English Dictionary, under "Quakers."

not averse to excitement, but he did exercise a wise supervision over the more violent of his followers, and the physical manifestations soon ceased. Not so the public excitement over his methods.

One sees in him an incarnation of the old Hebrew prophets, especially when he walked into Lichfield and strode up and down the streets shouting at the top of his voice, "Woe to the bloody city of Lichfield." One of his followers, named William Simpson, was even more startling in his appropriation of the methods of the prophet Isaiah, for he chose to walk naked for three years as a "sign" that God would strip Cromwell of his power. Just as Jeremiah broke the earthen bottle, so Fox's followers were fond of breaking bottles in churches and before Parliament.

Fox's central doctrine was the belief in "the inner light." He believed that God spoke directly to men in the seventeenth century as he had in Bible times. The authority of this inner voice, or spiritual force, was to be preferred to that of the Bible, or of the church. Whatever that voice told him, he did; whatever message it gave him, he spoke boldly. And unconventional as were his methods, there is no doubt that he preached great humanitarian principles.

He and his followers preached against slavery and against war at a time when both these institutions were taken for granted. The abolition of slavery in English-speaking countries and the gradual growth of the peace movement are due directly to the spread of the teachings of the Quakers. For their principles and their refusal to conform with established customs they suffered probably more than any other single group. Brave Quaker missionaries traveled to foreign countries and frequently underwent martyrdom. Four Quakers, one of them a woman, were hanged on Boston Common for their faith, between 1659 and 1661. Ten years later Fox visited America and strengthened the faith of his followers there. Pennsylvania, Rhode Island, Long Island, New Jersey, and Maryland had Quaker settlements of considerable importance.

The early eccentricities of the Quakers were gradually modified. They retained for some time, however, their very plain dress and their use of the primitive personal pronoun thee. Their simple meetings, with no preacher but with all waiting quietly for the spirit to move some one of the men or women to speak, were characterized by quiet spiritual fervor and were really early examples of what is now termed "group therapy."

It is in their influence upon other people rather than in the increase of the sect itself that Quakers have shown their power. Today they are among the most respected of Christians. Fox himself after a life of considerable hardship but of consistent adherence to his principles, much of it spent in prisons for disturbing the peace, died in London, January 1691, mourned even by his persecutors. One of his most eminent followers, William Penn, summed up George Fox's life in a sentence of eulogy, "In all things he acquitted himself like a man, yea, a strong man, a new and heavenly-minded man, and all of God Almighty's making."

JOHN MURRAY, THE UNIVERSALIST (1741–1815)

One of the direct results of Wesley's preaching was the conversion of John Murray. Murray had been born in England in 1741 but had lived for a time in Ireland during his boyhood. He rejoiced in the evangelistic speeches of Wesley and Whitefield but found a book by James Relly that interested him even more than the Arminianism of Wesley or the Calvinism of Whitefield. James Relly believed in the final universal salvation of men. Inasmuch as this was directly opposed to Calvinism, when Murray agitated Universalist views he was excommunicated from Whitefield's tabernacle. He fell upon hard times, lost his money and his wife, and was hounded because of his opinions. So he fled to America.

In a little church in New Jersey, in September 1770, he preached his first American sermon and thereafter visited the New England states, preaching, wherever opportunity offered, his doctrine of universal salvation.

He was much misunderstood and was even taken to be a Papist. He was suspected of being an English spy in 1774 while he was living in Gloucester. Although he was asked to leave the town, his friends intervened, and after a short period in the army he became pastor of a little Universalist church in Gloucester. In 1793 he went to Boston and preached until his death eighteen years later.

Universalism spread rather rapidly because the way had been somewhat prepared for it by the natural revolt against the preaching of Jonathan Edwards. Murray's belief in universal salvation did not prevent him from being orthodox in other respects. But his successor as leader of the Universalist belief, Hosea Ballou, was more liberal. Murray had taught that elect saints go immediately upon death to heaven, while the others are cleansed by fire until the day of judgment. Ballou abolished hell altogether and preached that all men at death are saved by the love of God.

Universalism has continued to become liberal and except for a dwindling orthodox wing is practically Unitarian in its theology. It is small in numbers but within a century has seen its cardinal tenet cause a complete change in the theology of other Christian denominations. Those who a century ago were calling Universalists derisively "No-Hellites" have now practically given up the preaching of hell and eternal punishment. Although it remains in the creed of many churches, the doctrine of hell is practically obsolete except in the more orthodox communions.

Now the progressive Universalists are giving their historic name a new but eminently fitting and timely interpretation by studying other ethnic faiths as well as Christianity and emphasizing the universal elements in all religions.

WILLIAM BOOTH (1829–1912) AND THE SALVATION ARMY

The evangelical enthusiasm released among the common people by Wesley's revival found expression in many ways outside the Methodist Church. One of the most striking and best-known of these is the movement known as the Salvation Army. A young Methodist minister named William Booth noticed in the 1860s that many of the poor people of England were not in any way connected with the churches. In July 1865 he began holding open-air meetings which met with almost immediate success and were transferred, first to a tent, then to an old warehouse in an unused Quaker graveyard. At first it was spoken of as the East End Mission and then as the Christian Mission. The ordinary evangelistic methods were used.

It started in a quiet way but soon took on the proportions of a real revival. Booth expanded the work by sending out evangelists to other cities. Although he was really working in the spirit and by the methods of Wesley, the New Connexion Methodist Church of which he had been a member considered his methods too radical, and he left their fellowship. It was a bold step because he was married and had three small children. His wife, however, encouraged him, and he went ahead with the work. The great success of his movement was due to a comparatively insignificant circumstance.

One of his mission workers in a seaport took the title of "Captain" that he might have more prestige among the sailors. William Booth went to visit this city and was billed as the "General." This gave him the idea of organizing his Christian work along military lines, and the "Salvation Army" was soon organized "to destroy the fortresses of sin in the various communities." To carry out the symbolism, Booth procured complete equipment for his workers. They appeared on the streets in uniforms and carried flags. They blew cornets and beat drums. At first they were greeted with hoots and cat-calls, and such crowds gathered that Booth's followers were arrested for making a disturbance. It was not long, however, before the new religious organization won its way into the hearts of the poor people of the slums of English cities.

Booth discovered, however, that although he might drum up a crowd and then preach salvation to them, the results were compara-tively meager because many in his audiences were literally starving. He made a quick decision, and from that moment the religious work of the Army was supplemented by social service of the simplest sort. The "Salvation Army" became the "Soap, Soup, and Salvation Army." The charities and reforms fostered by the organization have been almost numberless. The work done, especially among the lowest of the poor and for neglected children, has been most commendable.

By a wise combination of religion and social reform, permanent good has been accomplished. Down-and-outers have been brought back to lives of self-respect and usefulness. Drunken bums have, to their surprise, found themselves washed, clothed, fed, and in their right minds listening to the earnest message of some Salvation Army captain or lassie private, and have signed the pledge and resolved to lead clean lives. Some slip back into lives of sin, but thousands have been redeemed, many of whom have taken their place in the ranks of the Army.

The work done by Salvation Army workers in the World Wars increased the prestige of the organization, which is now practically world-wide in its service. Even those who do not agree with the evangelistic theology of Booth's Army nevertheless approve so highly of its social-welfare work that generous contributions have been made by the general public. Many hotels, homes, and nurser-

ies are owned by the Army, and special relief work is done during
the winter, largely provided for by small-change collections from
the public at Christmastime.

The efficiency of the Army is well known, and few relief organiza-
tions can make a dollar go as far. This is partly due to the fact that
the soldiers are unpaid volunteers who earn their living, and donate
their services after working hours. Each of the eleven thousand
corps is expected to raise money to cover its own expenses. Even the
officers are given nothing but food, clothing, and shelter, plus
modest transportation allowances.

As for doctrine, the Army creed is simple. Theological discussions are taboo. A simple evangelistic Christian faith is preached
of salvation from sin by the power of God through Jesus Christ.
There is rather more emphasis upon the blood of Christ than
modern Christian sentiment approves. But the "salvation" which
the Army soldier attributes to the blood of Jesus is due, at least in
part, to the kindly interest shown by the soldier himself. The sudden discovery by a "down-and-outer" that a person of fine character
cares enough for him to stay by him and help him through into a
better way of living is frequently sufficient in itself to bring about
"salvation." There is more psychology than theology involved.[2]

William Booth died in 1912 leaving behind him the well-organized Army, the famous magazine, *The War-Cry,* selling a million
copies a week, and many writings. His book, *In Darkest England
and the Way Out,* has had a wide circulation. He was succeeded by
his son, Bramwell Booth. Another son, Ballington Booth, in 1906,
after a quarrel with his father, founded with his wife, Maud Ballington Booth, a similar organization known as The Volunteers of
America, which has done excellent work in the prisons. The Booth
dynasty was deposed in 1929 in spite of the strong protests of the
aged General Bramwell Booth, and Edward J. Higgins was elected
to take his place. On assuming office General Higgins promised that
"the great purpose" of the Army to fight "against wrong and oppression, and want and sin" would remain the same but that "constitutional changes" would be made because "methods proper in
1878 were inadequate for conditions prevailing in 1929."

2 See James, *The Varieties of Religious Experience,* pp. 201–203.

XVIII

꧁꧂

AMERICAN APOSTLES

(Roger Williams, Jonathan Edwards, William Ellery Channing, Joseph Smith, William Miller, Robert Ingersoll, Phineas Quimby, and Mary Baker Eddy)

INTRODUCTION

IN THE THREE CENTURIES since the landing of the Pilgrims there have been no really new religions born in America. For that matter there have been no new ones born anywhere during that period, even in Asia, the birthplace of all great religions. But it might well have been expected that a new land, inhabited by an imaginative people, would prove fertile soil for new faiths.

What has actually happened has been that when the seeds of the old faiths were sown in the new land certain "sports," varieties, and abnormalities appeared. Some of these have been of great help to thousands of men. Others have been of doubtful benefit, and some have been positively detrimental. We are not here concerned with the merits of cults which have flared into temporary attention and died out without leaving more than a passing record; rather our task is to discover those leaders who have contributed something to American religious life. The Bible, either the Old Testament or the New, seems to have been the initial inspiration of most of the cult leaders of America, although their interpretations of its message have varied greatly.

When Christianity came over the ocean it appears to have suffered a sea change. Even the orthodox varieties of religious faith were unconsciously and inevitably liberalized to some extent by the necessity of adapting themselves to new conditions. When an Anglican came to this country and became an Episcopalian he followed the same forms of worship but felt a subtle influence which sometimes changed his point of view. Perhaps it was due to the attitude of mind with which the emigrant from the older countries approached the shore of the new. It was the "land of liberty" to which he was going, and the breeze of freedom blew away many a dusty theological dogma, and in a few years caused the newly made Americans to cut queer religious capers.

All the American apostles find their common denominator in the word *freedom*. The sects and cults which they established became, in some instances, quite orthodox and conservative in their later development. But when we study the lives of the great prophets themselves we find them all, in one way or another, asserting the right to liberty in religious development.

ROGER WILLIAMS

(1604–1684)

THE APOSTLE OF SOUL LIBERTY

Roger Williams is easily the leading figure in the first century of American religious life. There is a breadth of vision and a deep appreciation of human rights, an admirable conjunction of the qualities of the statesman and the prophet, which recalls at once the greatest prophets of Israel. His political ability is shown by the fact that through a half century of continuous unselfish public service he created the state of Rhode Island in spite of almost insurmountable difficulties. His religious genius is revealed in his announcing, defending, and establishing, practically singlehanded, the principle of freedom of conscience, with its corollary, separation of church and state. It is due to Roger Williams and such spiritual successors of his as Thomas Jefferson that the United States permits everyone to worship as he pleases.

We know very little of the period of Roger Williams' life before he landed in Boston in 1631, a young man nearly thirty. In his early teens he opened a door for himself by the aid of stenography. In the London courts and churches he took down speeches and sermons in shorthand, transcribed and presented them to Sir Edward Coke, who thereupon concerned himself to see that the enterprising boy got an education. He attended the Charterhouse School and Pembroke College and earned a degree. He tried and gave up the law and became chaplain to an English lord.

When he appears in New England he is already an ardent champion of very liberal theological opinions far in advance of his time. He evidently came to America expecting to find a more liberal atmosphere than in England, but he was immediately and constantly in trouble in the Massachusetts Bay Colony. For two brief periods he was assistant minister in Salem, and in the interim preached in the Plymouth colony. He achieved a rather unwelcome notoriety because of his opinions and for a considerable time was censured by every session of the Massachusetts General Court.

He was banished by this court in 1635, when he had been in the new world only four years. Because of his ill health the execution of the sentence was delayed, but his obstreperousness in persisting in preaching to groups in his own home led to an attempt to seize him and deport him to England early in the year 1636. He escaped before they could capture him, however, and fled south through the winter wilderness to the Blackstone River, then known as the Seekonk. He had been secretly advised by the Governor of Massachusetts to seek refuge among the Indians. The savages, whose acquaintance he had made during his Plymouth sojourn, extended him the hospitality which his fellow countrymen had denied, and he established in the fall of that year a new town, which he gratefully named Providence. To him fled the discontented and persecuted liberals from the other colonies, and although he had originally hoped to spend much of his time converting the Indians to Christianity he found himself almost constantly engaged with the pressing problems of administration.

Due to his great wisdom and broad humanity he was able to steer his little craft through the dangers which beset its early course. As with every prophet of liberty, his greatest difficulties came from those who overardently interpreted liberty as license. Providence and the other communities which were soon founded nearby were peopled largely with individualists, and it was exceedingly difficult to secure their co-operation in matters necessary for the common good.

His town was one of the outposts of the white settlements and would have been wiped out had it not been for his ability to win the esteem of the Indians. He not only saved his own colony but with great magnanimity exerted himself at considerable personal sacrifice on three occasions to prevent an Indian uprising against the other colonies. The first of these occasions was in the autumn of the year 1636, and it stands to his great credit that he thus saved the lives of the citizens of Massachusetts who had driven him from them within the twelvemonth.

Twice also, at the sacrifice of his own and his family's welfare, he made extended trips to England to secure and defend a charter for the state he had founded. He was never paid for these services, nor even fully reimbursed for his expenses. Throughout his long life he never was possessed of sufficient income to render comfortable his wife and six children, although he had wonderful opportunities for amassing wealth. He died in poverty and obscurity so unnoticed that not even the date of his death is surely known.

The appreciation which was denied him during his lifetime has been awarded him in increasing measure in more recent years. He stands out today as one of the major prophets of American religious history. To him more than to any other one man is due the fact that liberty of conscience and freedom of religious belief obtain in America today. We see now that what his contemporaries took for mere obstreperousness and obstinacy was really a conscientious and persistent effort to defend and establish these great principles in the little colonies of his day.

There is no doubt that his manner was belligerent and provocative upon occasion. When he first landed in Boston and was asked to preach he refused to do so for two reasons. The first of these was the fact that the Boston Puritans had not openly repented of their former association with the Church of England. Williams was distinctly and emphatically a "come-outer." He had separated himself from the Church of England and belonged to the group that were known as Separatists. The people of Plymouth were of that persuasion and that is why he was comparatively happy there, but the people of Boston had not gone so far: they were simply Puritans.

The second reason why he refused to accept the invitation to preach was because the civil magistrates in Boston were required to enforce the Ten Commandments. Williams had no objection to the enforcement of the last six commandments which were known as the second table of the law and which were concerned with man's duties to man but was strongly opposed to the enforcement of those commandments which had to do with man's relation to God. He not only believed that the Christian had a right to worship Jehovah as he pleased, but, with remarkable breadth of mind, also insisted that the Turk and the Moslem should not be molested in their forms of worship. It is sometimes asserted that freedom of worship in the United States was first established in the Catholic settlement of Lord Baltimore in Maryland in 1634. It is true that an act was passed there in 1649 which permitted freedom of worship to all followers of Jesus Christ, but Roger Williams did not confine his tolerance to any one religion. He stood for the absolute freedom of the human soul. He even maintained that atheists should be allowed to refrain from all worship, an opinion which was, at that time, the rankest of heresy.

On the statute books of the Massachusetts Bay Colony there were laws against blasphemy and heresy which were enforced by the whole machinery of the state. These laws, Williams maintained, were an infringement of the rights of the individual. What went on between man and man was the concern of the state, but the relation of the individual to his God was entirely that individual's concern. Williams' entire heresy centers in that point, and his insistent and consistent advocacy of its corollary, the separation of church and state, places him among the pioneers.

It is one thing for a clergyman to advocate freedom of worship, but a more difficult thing for him to establish and govern a state where utmost freedom of worship may be permitted. It was not mere bigotry which caused the Massachusetts officials to punish and expel those whom they called heretics. The problem was vitally connected with the peace of the community. Most of these heretics were very irritating and disturbing people. Their publicity methods were disruptive of civil harmony. The early Quakers advocated peace between nations, but their conduct was productive of anything but peace in the communities which they entered. They were as irritating in Boston as Jeremiah had been in Jerusalem. The severity which the authorities in Massachusetts used against them drove them to Rhode Island. Roger Williams welcomed these strange people, along with representatives of other advanced cults. Dealing wisely with them, he overlooked their peculiarities and built their worth-while qualities into the structure of his little colony.

One other group which entered Providence very early was not only welcomed by Williams, he even joined their company. These were the Anabaptists or, as they are better known, the Baptists. The prefix *ana* means again, and they were so named because they required their converts to be immersed even though they had been baptized in infancy by sprinkling. When a few of these Anabaptists straggled into Providence, Williams listened to their views and permitted one of their laymen, Ezekiel Holliman, to baptize him, thereupon becoming the first Baptist clergyman in the New World. He then baptized Holliman and a small group of other Anabaptists and was promptly excommunicated by the church he had served in Salem.

Although he separated from the Baptists in about four months he is regarded by their descendants as their outstanding American prophet. There is no doubt that the thing that attracted him to them was his discovery that they also advocated complete freedom of worship. Twelve years before, there had existed in England a dozen Baptist churches advocating complete soul liberty. It is quite possible that Williams may have had his first contact with them before he reached America. The reason he gave for severing his connection with the Providence Anabaptists, that "their baptism could not be right because it was not administered by an apostle,"[1] seems inconsistent with his other beliefs.

Thereafter he preferred to be called a "seeker." A "seeker" was an independent. The sensitive spirit of Williams rejected all sectarian yokes. It almost seemed as if his intensely felt spirit of hospitality to all faiths led him to the extreme point of refusing to be connected with any one of them, lest he give offense to the others. There was an element verging on agnosticism in Williams' belief from his late thirties until he died. His faith and his doubt seemed to counteract each other in a strange synthesis. The historian Edward Eggleston refers to Williams' later philosophy of life as "devout and contented uncertainty."

[1] Richman, *Rhode Island*, p. 110 note.

JONATHAN EDWARDS

(1703–1758)

AND

THE GREAT AWAKENING

Jonathan Edwards was one of the shortest-lived of all the great religious leaders. But although he died at the age of fifty-five, he accomplished much because he began very early, the child of a Connecticut parsonage in a period when that experience itself was a guarantee of a background of education. At the age of ten he wrote a pamphlet on the question of whether or not the soul of man is material. At twelve he composed a scientific treatise on American spiders. That same year he entered the Collegiate School at Saybrook, which later became Yale College. When he was thirteen he read Latin, Greek, and Hebrew with facility. At sixteen he was graduated from Yale. At twenty he was preaching in New York. At twenty-one he was a teacher in Yale. At twenty-four he was an assistant to his grandfather, Solomon Stoddard, in the Congregational church at Northampton, Massachusetts.

Nor was his early precocity belied by his later intellectual development. It is held by some that he had the greatest intellect of any American. Certainly in philosophy and theology he had no equal in his day. He preached in Northampton until he was expelled from the pulpit in 1750. The remaining eight years of his life were spent in writing theological treatises, in preaching to the Indians at Stockbridge, Massachusetts, and, for the last few weeks, in the duties of the President of Princeton College. The unique combination in Edwards of evangelistic fervor and clear-cut logic fitted him for the needed task of the time—namely, the formulation of a consistent system of evangelical theology.

Edwards' own religious experience and the careful records which he preserved of the experiences of his converts afford us material of the highest order for the study of the effect of religion in the lives of men. One is constantly reminded of Wesley, who was born the same year. The difference between the two men, however, lies in this, that Edwards' intellect was keener and found satisfaction in the logic of a Calvinistic interpretation, emphasizing God's sovereignty, while Wesley was Arminian in his theology, accepting God's love.

Throughout his boyhood Edwards enjoyed an increasing consciousness of the presence of God. He was fond of retiring to secret places in the woods where he meditated upon God. Consistent with his precocity was the fact that his great religious experience, his sort of theophany, came at the age of twenty, a decade earlier than that of most prophets. He tells us that on January 12, 1723, he gave himself to God: "I made this solemn dedication to God and wrote it down, giving up myself and all that I had to God, to be for the future in no respect my own."

This sense of God-consciousness, a certain mystic exaltation of spirit which reached crises at times when he felt actual union with God, dominated his entire subsequent life and colored his whole theology. God was omnipotent, supreme, and had entire freedom of will. Early in life Edwards made seventy resolutions for the guidance of his own conduct. Several of these seventy emphasize his consciousness of union with God, such as the fourth, "Resolved, never to Do, Be, or Suffer anything in soul or body, less or more, but what tends to the glory of God," and the forty-third, "Resolved, never to act as if I were in any way my own, but entirely and altogether God's."

There is a difference between Jonathan Edwards and most of the great religious leaders, which makes his experience invaluable for the student of religion, and that is Edwards' remarkably happy married life. Most religious leaders, especially those who have felt this God-consciousness keenly, perhaps because of that fact, have been very unhappy in their marital life. There seems to exist a conspicuous incompatibility between complete devotion to God and the experience of human love. But not only did Edwards' relation to his remarkable wife, Sarah, not interfere with his own religious experiences, it seemed, rather, to heighten and deepen it. Insufficient attention has as yet been paid to this aspect of Edwards' life.

These two souls were so devoted to each other, and yet so devoted to God, that their two personalities blended in a remarkable unity. Their separate religious experiences united to produce an unusually rich spiritual life. He describes her vivid, trancelike periods of God-contact so sympathetically that we feel he shared them deeply. In his narrative of the revival in New England he quotes her as saying,

"Last night was the sweetest night I ever had in my life. I never before, for so long a time together, enjoyed so much of the light and rest and sweetness of Heaven in my soul, but without the least agitation of body during the whole time. . . . All night I continued in a constant, clear, and lively sense of the heavenly sweetness of Christ's excellent love, of his nearness to me and of my dearness to him; with an inexpressibly sweet calmness of soul in an entire rest in him. I seemed to myself to perceive a glow of divine love come down from the heart of Christ in heaven into my heart in a constant stream, like a stream or pencil of sweet light. . . . There seemed to be constant flowing and re-flowing of heavenly love and I appeared to myself to float or swim in these bright, sweet beams like the motes swimming in the beams of the sun or the streams of his light which come in at the window.[2]

The student of the psychology of religion will recognize in this confession of Mrs. Edwards not only a valuable contribution to the study of photistic theophanies but also a realistic description of the phenomena of the borderland between two similar types of ecstasy.

It is significant that Jonathan Edwards' complete dedication of himself to God occurred at the time when he first became acquainted with Sarah Pierrepont, and that his description of the "rare and lustrous beauty of this thirteen-year-old girl" is as extravagantly enthusiastic as his eulogy of God himself. He married her when she was seventeen, and their union was productive of not only great happiness in their mutual spiritual life but also of a family of children of great ability. The children of Jonathan Edwards and their descendants are the most consistently brilliant and eminent family group known in the history of eugenics.

Edwards' keen appreciation of the power of God in his own soul was immediately reflected in his theology. When a man becomes impressed with the omnipotent majesty and matchless purity of God, and is able by his eloquence to convey that thought to other men, he is a great preacher indeed.

Edwards' ministry was pre-eminently a teaching ministry. When he was asked to take the presidency of Princeton College he demurred at first because he wanted to write a history of redemption.

2 Quoted, with comments, in William James' *The Varieties of Religious Experience,* p. 276.

But after he died Dr. John Erskine of Edinburgh was able to compile a history of redemption from the manuscripts of a series of sermons preached by Edwards at Northampton. His sermons were a course in theology. He viewed the whole Christian plan of salvation through the windows of his own experience and was therefore able to make that plan so very real and vivid to his hearers that before the young preacher knew it, a great revival had sprung up in his parish at Northampton. It is important to remember that the period of the "Great Awakening" in New England, consequent upon Edwards' preaching, coincided with the revival in England which resulted from the work of Whitefield and John Wesley.

One can get an idea of the impression Edwards made upon his audiences if one reads carefully his masterpiece: the treatise on *The Freedom of the Will,* the greatest theological work ever produced in America. This treatise is a devastating defense of determinism. With consummate skill and unanswerable logic he proceeds from premise to conclusion, and leaves his readers, as he left his hearers, with an appalling conviction of the inevitable consequences of sin.

A great mass of criticism has been hurled at Edwards because of the views of eternal damnation he expressed in such sermons as his famous one, "Sinners in the Hands of an Angry God." One is apt to picture Edwards as a monster who reveled in the thought of the eternal torture of the damned. It is true that he called children "little vipers." It is true that he told his hearers they were loathsome in the eyes of God and that the only thing between them and hell was the hand of God, who was holding them over the burning pit as one would hold a spider or loathsome insect over a flaming fire. It is true, although incredible to us today, that he maintained that the happiness of the saints in heaven would be increased when they looked from heaven into hell and saw their unsaved relatives writhing in torment.

Nevertheless, the bare recital of these apparently sadistic sentiments does not do Edwards justice. His reason for considering man vile was his overwhelming sense of the power and purity of God. There was in it also an element of righteous indignation. The times were bad. The people of old England and New England alike were indulging in sinful practices of indescribable immorality. What religion there was, was cold and formal and did not reach the life of the people. Dynamite was needed to blast through their indiffer-

400] THE GREAT RELIGIOUS LEADERS

ence, and dynamite it was that Edwards brought. We are told that so powerful was his preaching, especially about hell, that the auditors in the church actually grasped the pillars to hold themselves from slipping into the everlasting fire.

The effects were tremendous. First individuals, then families, and finally almost the entire community were converted after extraordinary scenes. It seems at first strange that a theology so intellectual should have produced a religion so emotional. But there was another factor—namely, the deep emotion of the preacher himself. Apart from his personality, his sermons might have convinced the intellect but would hardly have produced writhings, prostrations and foaming at the mouth such as characterized the revivals of the time.

A reaction was inevitable. The break came with his congregation when he refused to give communion in his church to the unconverted. Membership in the church in Massachusetts before his day was almost synonymous with citizenship in the community. When he demanded proof of Christian experience from all those who presented themselves at the communion table, he found a strong group in the church opposing him. While this controversy was going on, Edwards discovered that books he considered obscene were being freely passed about among the young people of the parish. A psychologist of today would recognize that there was a connection between the emotionalism of the revivals and the circulation of these books, for many of the revivals since the time of Edwards, especially at the camp meetings,[3] have been accompanied by waves of sexual immorality.

How widespread was the interest in these salacious books in Northampton is revealed by the fact that when the austere preacher announced in the pulpit the names of the guilty and the names of those whom he proposed to question in the matter, there was hardly a family in the church untouched by the scandal. Probably Edwards seemed to his parishioners fanatic, indiscreet, and tactless. At any rate, they took immediate measures to have him removed from their pulpit, which was done by a council in the year 1750.

But the wave of revivalism which Edwards started was not so easily stopped. It spread throughout the English world and has continued to this day in sporadic outbreaks. All the phenomena of spasmodic jerkings of the body and other similar manifestations

[3] Seldes, *The Stammering Century*, pp. 56, 66.

can be observed even to the present day. Revivals have long been considered evidences of the outpouring of the spirit of God, but of late years there has been growing in the Christian consciousness a conviction that such emotional outbreaks are not conducive to the best things in the Christian life. Consequently, Edwards is not as highly esteemed as once he was. It is well, however, to separate the Jonathan Edwards who was the father of revivals from Jonathan Edwards the great theologian. No man ever thought more deeply, or expressed himself more clearly on fundamental Christian doctrines.

The best results in American religion, however, from the work of Edwards have been of a negative sort. It was the reaction *against* the Edwardsian theology which produced the liberal wing of Protestantism. The common people of the late eighteenth and early nineteenth centuries repudiated the idea of hell and formed the Universalist denomination. The educated classes of Boston and vicinity revolted from the determinism of Edwards and formed the Unitarian wing of Congregationalism. Moreover, outside these two denominations, the same feeling of opposition to austere Calvinism spread both within and without the Christian church, so that, except in the most orthodox communions, the hell of Jonathan Edwards is a byword and a joke.

WILLIAM ELLERY CHANNING

(1780–1842)

AND

THE UNITARIANS

When the rigid Calvinism of Jonathan Edwards came into contact with the soul liberty of Roger Williams the result was the Unitarianism of William Ellery Channing. Channing was born in Newport, Rhode Island, in 1780, and although Roger Williams had been dead for almost a century his spirit still pervaded the very life of the state, and the principles of liberty and freedom were absorbed by young Channing from his very environment.

Channing came into contact with Jonathan Edwards indirectly. The Northampton Calvinist had for one of his pupils Samuel Hopkins, who not only continued the work of Edwards in Massachusetts but wrote his biography. Hopkins went to Newport in 1770 and preached there until 1803. He was not minister of the church which young Channing attended, but when the latter church was closed after the Revolutionary War, the Channings attended Hopkins' church for a period, and there the sensitive spirit of William Ellery Channing received the full impact of the hell horrors of the Edwardsian theology as expounded by Samuel Hopkins. Hopkins out-Edwards-ed Edwards and is most noted for his famous statement that one ought to be willing "to be damned for the glory of God." Channing himself, in describing Hopkins, later said,

He was distinguished for nothing more than for faithfulness to his principles. He carried them out to their full extent. Believing as he did in total depravity; believing that there was nothing good or generous in human nature to which he could make an appeal; believing that he could benefit men only by setting before them their lost and helpless condition, he came to the point without any circumlocution and dealt out terrors with a liberal hand.

When Channing was a small boy his father took him to hear one of the most famous hell-fire preachers of his day. The boy was very much impressed by the vivid picture of the punishments which the speaker had insisted were in store for the majority of mankind. As they were leaving the church he heard his father say to a friend, "Sound doctrine, sir." To the small boy this seemed the final note of authority. His father was confirming what the preacher had stated. Lost in gloom, the boy sat by his father's side on the ride home but was suddenly shocked by hearing his father whistle in a sort of happy unconcern.

When they reached home young Channing was astounded to see his father sit down in the easychair by the open fire, the very sight of which was terrifying to the young mind still under the spell of the preacher's words. Life went on as usual, and the boy decided that what the preacher had said could not possibly be true, for if it had been true people would not be so unconcerned about it. There is no doubt that this incident of his childhood had a powerfully determining effect upon Channing's theology. The boy's education confirmed the views which were rapidly developing in his keen mind. His father was a graduate of Princeton and had planned to have William Ellery follow in his footsteps. But before the boy started for college his father died, and his mother's family, the

Ellerys, who were great believers in Harvard, insisted that the boy be sent there.

Channing's biographers are fond of imagining what would have happened to him if he had gone to conservative Princeton instead of liberal Harvard. But inasmuch as the boy's mind was already in revolt against Calvinism, it is very doubtful that he would have become a rigid Presbyterian. He might have been driven into agnosticism as so many young men of the time were. Infidelity and atheism always grow rapidly in periods when the prevailing religion is extremely orthodox. Both Calvinism and Fundamentalism have in their days been directly responsible for the sudden flowering of atheist societies in the colleges.

At Harvard, strange as it may seem, Channing had his theophany. Under the willows of Cambridge he was reading Hutcheson one day when, as by a light from heaven, he had a vision of the beauty and worth of human nature. Hutcheson was the exponent of a theology which opposed that of Edwards and Hopkins. They emphasized the vileness of human nature and the impossibility of man's becoming good by his own efforts. Hutcheson, in his moral philosophy, taught that there is a certain native benevolence in man from which arises an impetus toward good conduct.

From that moment of inspiration we can trace in Channing's life and writings the rapid growth of his central contribution to religion—namely, that there is a seed of divinity in every human breast which, with proper cultivation, will flower into a noble Christian life. In other words, he opposed the current religious philosophy of his time with its insistence upon the natural *depravity* of man and emphasized, antithetically, the doctrine of the natural *divinity* of man.

Channing had entered Harvard at the age of fourteen, and in spite of his extreme youth easily led his classes, receiving the highest honor upon his graduation at the age of eighteen. Notwithstanding his interest in theology he had not at the time of his graduation selected his lifework. But in the fall of that year, October 1798, just as he was leaving Newport to go to Richmond, Virginia, as a tutor, he wrote to a friend that he had chosen the ministry as his profession. The purpose of his southern trip was to earn sufficient money for his support while pursuing his professional training for the ministry. A year from the following July he returned an invalid.

Inasmuch as he had been in good health when he went to Virginia something must have occurred during his southern sojourn which affected him very seriously. He afterward looked back upon those eighteen months as the most important period of his life. Over forty years later he wrote a friend,[4]

> I spent a year and a half there [Richmond], and perhaps the most eventful of my life. I lived alone, too poor to buy books, spending my days and nights in an outbuilding, with no one beneath my roof except during the hours of school-keeping. There I toiled as I have never done since, for gradually my constitution sank under the unremitting exertion. With not a human being with whom I could communicate my deepest thoughts and feelings, and shrinking from common society, I passed through intellectual and moral conflicts, through excitements of heart and mind, so absorbing as to banish sleep, and to destroy almost wholly the power of digestion. I was worn well-nigh to a skeleton. Yet I look back on those days and nights of loneliness and frequent gloom with thankfulness. If I ever struggled with my whole soul for purity, truth, and goodness, it was there. There, amidst sore trials, the great question, I trust, was settled within me, whether I would obey the higher or lower principles of my nature—whether I would be the victim of passion, the world, or the free child and servant of God.

It was a time of great searching of heart and great chastening of body. When we read of the asceticism which he practiced and the extremities of application to which his eager spirit goaded his body, we have a feeling of irritation that he should have been so devoid of the elements of common sense. But a more sympathetic appreciation finds in the Richmond period of Channing's life the struggle which every great prophet has had immediately following his self-dedication to God. The heavens may open and a man may feel himself called to God, but theophanies are usually followed by periods of temptation.

At Richmond he denied himself proper clothing, proper shelter, and even sufficient food. But what he missed most was understanding companionship. While there he wrote, "I cannot find a friend with whom I can even converse on religious subjects." His unhappy experiences in Virginia remind one of the sad period which Wesley had spent in Georgia just sixty years before. Both were extremely pious, given to asceticism, and self-tormented by morbid fancies.

4 Channing's *Life*, pp. 75, 76.

They took themselves altogether too seriously. Regular athletic exercise would have helped them both.

Channing's voyage home to Newport on a leaky coal ship did not improve his health any, and he was to suffer all the rest of his life from the privations of the Virginia experience. For a year and a half after his return he continued his theological studies at home, meanwhile tutoring two boys. Early in 1802 he was back at Harvard again acting as regent, a position which gave him a better opportunity to study and support himself while doing so. His college friends were surprised at the change which had come over the spirited young man. It was not merely that his physical condition was changed from health to debility but that his whole spirit seemed softened almost to effeminacy.

In the fall of 1802 he began to preach. His first sermon was on the text, "Silver and gold have I none, but such as I have, give I thee." The sermon attracted immediate attention throughout the Boston district and he was at once called by two important churches in that city. He chose to go to the Federal Street church and was ordained June 1, 1803.

His ministry there was distinguished by the preaching of what was then really a new theology. At first Channing could not have been conscious of that fact, but it gradually became apparent to him that he was the spokesman of a new movement in Protestant Christianity. More and more his sermons tended to a recognition of the great possibilities in human nature. He loathed controversy and was occasionally guilty of what his friends thought was compromise. He refused to have a sectarian name fastened to him and did not like the word *Unitarian*. But the growing Unitarian movement in the Congregational Church in New England found in him its great apostle. Despite his antipathy to controversy, his sermon preached in Baltimore at the ordination of Rev. Jared Sparks in the year 1819 was, in fact, a theological treatise as important in its way as the theses which Luther nailed on the church doors at Wittenberg.

In that sermon he set forth the weakness of Calvinism and lined up the arguments in favor of Unitarianism. Largely because of that sermon one hundred and twenty-five Congregational churches, most of them the leading churches of New England, came out openly for Unitarianism, and in the year 1825 a group of young men formed the American Unitarian Association.

Channing was not the first Unitarian. The movement had really begun several centuries before. The last heretic burned in England was Edward Whiteman, a Unitarian who suffered martyrdom for his opinions in 1612, as Servetus had in Geneva in 1553 with the approval of John Calvin. Lindsay and Priestley in England, about 1775, had led a Unitarian movement, and echoes of it had reached New England. In 1787 King's Chapel in Boston became Unitarian, and the movement had been growing ever since. What Channing did do was to bring the movement to a head and give it a consistent theology. Later on Theodore Parker and Ralph Waldo Emerson were to contribute to the development of Unitarianism.

The actual membership of Unitarian churches is small, but the influence of Channing was not confined to his own ecclesiastical group. It spread far and wide, and in many so-called orthodox churches in America today the theology preached from the pulpit is pure Channing Unitarianism. The churches of America have received from Channing not only the doctrine of the divinity of man but also a turn toward social Christianity. At the time that undergraduate Channing at Harvard was reading Hutcheson's works he was also eagerly devouring Adam Ferguson's essay on civil society. That book gave him his unusual appreciation of the importance of social progress and the relation of Christianity to it.

He had been amazed to find in Virginia, sponsored by Christianity, social conditions which seemed to him the very antithesis of the spirit of Jesus. Slavery, especially, appalled him. From the beginning of his ministry he began to strike the social note, and it increased as he grew older. He advocated woman's rights, the amelioration of the horrors of slavery, better systems of education, and the "elevation of the laboring portion of the community." He was one of the first to urge international peace. In a day when even the clergy were noted for their lack of sobriety he stood forth boldly for temperance. When charity was largely a matter of relieving one's own feelings of sympathy, he urged the organization of philanthropy on a practical basis. He was much concerned with the ethical duties of citizenship.

One is astounded today in reading his works to discover the number of reforms which he advocated and the very modern point of view which he took in all matters relating to social progress. His sociology grew directly out of his theology. If man were not a "worm of the dust" but, rather, a being of divine possibilities, then those possibilities ought to be wrought into actualities. Any injustice which prevented the growth of the human soul into beauty and goodness must, as a Christian duty, be removed.

On Sunday morning, October 2, 1842, as Channing lay dying, he heard the church bells ring, and told the friends gathered about his bedside that they should go to church. They reminded him that it was a part of true religion to nurse the sick. He replied, "True, you may stay." Then he asked them to read to him from the Sermon on the Mount, which he said was "full of the divinest spirit of religion." At sunset, when all the sky was aflame, they helped him to turn toward the window, and with the glory of the heavens upon his face, he passed away. His last words were "I have received many messages from the spirit."

JOSEPH SMITH
(1805–1844)
AND THE MORMONS

The incredible thing about Mormonism is that such a respectable religion could have derived from such a peculiar person.

Mormonism is little over a century old and yet it is one of the most successful religions on the American continent. Its more than a million membership is efficiently organized into ninety stakes or divisions which are subdivided into nine hundred and forty wards, each ward having a bishop and two counselors. All too little is known by non-Mormons, or "Gentiles," of the admirable civilization built up in Utah. By the use of a system of irrigation, the first in America, the Mormons made the desert an agricultural paradise. The town planning was intelligently done in a period when in the rest of the country communities merely straggled into existence. The fruits of the early system are now evident in the beauty and prosperity of the cities of Utah.

The first newspaper and the first university west of the Missouri were established by the Mormons. Their educational system, started early, embraces schools of a high order, literary societies, theaters and libraries.

The culture and prosperity levels of Utah are far above those of some other American states. Nor can the culture of Utah be separated from the religion of Mormonism, for that religion is inter-

woven with the fabric of the life of the state. If we are to accept the
dictum of Jesus, "By their fruits ye shall know them," we must rate
Mormons high.

There is reason for suspecting, however, that Joseph Smith, the
undoubted founder of Mormonism, was not only mentally disturbed at times, but also a shrewd schemer whose ethical sense was
poorly developed. In 1816, when young Smith was in his eleventh
year, the family moved from Sharon, Vermont, to the little town
of Palmyra in western New York, and thence, four years later, to
Manchester, six miles to the south. If one discounts the eulogistic
accounts of Mormons, and the equally prejudiced statements by
their adversaries, and seeks an unbiased history of Joseph Smith's
antecedents and early youth, he is forced to recognize the fact that
the boy was brought up in an environment of superstition and
credulity.

Lucy Smith, Joseph's mother, wrote a book called *Biographical
Sketches* in which she divulged family secrets. This book is repudiated by Mormons and they are said to have tried to suppress it, but
it bears the earmarks of veracity. According to this book, Joseph's
grandfather on his father's side, locally known as "crook-necked
Smith," was subject to fits, was reputed to have a weak mind, and
held peculiar religious views. This description was not due to
malice on the part of his daughter-in-law because she gives an
equally uncomplimentary picture of her own father, Solomon
Mack, who used a bodily infirmity as an excuse for begging and who
was an ardent follower of faith healers and dream mongers.

The boy's father, Joseph Smith, was a typical Vermont Yankee
jack-of-all-trades, who tried experiments and failed in several occupations. It is important to note that Joseph Smith senior anticipated his son in his firm belief in the Biblical doctrines of demon
possession and witchcraft. Young Smith admired his father and
naïvely defended him in his autobiography.

The boy was handicapped not only by his inheritance of the physical and mental peculiarities of his forebears but also by his environment. Western New York in the first half of the nineteenth century
was a hotbed of queer cults and offbeat beliefs. The mildest of
these were the Quakers, the Primitive Baptists, and an early variety
of Universalists known as Restorationists.

These were moderate, however, compared with the followers of
Jemimah Wilkinson. Miss Wilkinson had begun as a Quaker and

ended as a Shaker. After a critical illness during which she had fallen into a trance she claimed that she had literally been raised from the dead. She established a village which she called Jerusalem, where her followers were required to live a celibate life. The sect broke up three years after the Smith family arrived in that section. It was only ten miles from where the Smiths lived that the celebrated Fox sisters began their famous career and duped thousands with their mysterious rappings. They claimed that these sounds were due to spirit control, but in later life confessed that the celestial communications were due to manipulations of the great-toe joint. Western New York also saw the first success of William Miller with his doctrine of the imminent end of the world. Everybody was starting new religions, and it is no wonder that Joseph Smith founded another.

Smith had several theophanies. The first occurred when he was but a boy. He says, "When about fourteen years of age I began to reflect upon the importance of being prepared for a future state; and upon inquiring the place of salvation, I found that there was a great clash in religious sentiment."[5] It is no wonder the boy was confused amid the peculiar creeds of the time. He went "into a secret place in the grove" and began to pray. He describes his theophany as follows,[6]

While fervently engaged in supplication my mind was taken away from the objects with which I was surrounded, and I was enrapt in a heavenly vision, and saw two glorious personages who exactly resembled each other in features and likeness, surrounded with a brilliant light which eclipsed the sun at noon-day.

These heavenly messengers informed him that all religious denominations were wrong and that to him a revelation of the truth would later be made. About three years later he had another vision. The photism was more brilliant. It seemed to him "as though the house was filled with seeming fire." An angel of God told him that the time was now at hand for great things. He was further informed that he was the chosen instrument and that a sacred book would be revealed to him.

[5] Joseph Smith's own account of the "Latter Day Saints" written for Rupp's *Religious Denominations*, pub. in 1844, p. 404.

[6] Ibid., p. 405.

From this time on he had seven visions within seven years, in one of which, he claimed, an angel revealed to him the hiding place of the promised book, which was delivered into his hands "on the morning of the twenty-second of September A.D. 1827." He describes it as follows,

These records were engraven on plates which had the appearance of gold; each plate was six inches wide and eight inches long, and not quite so thick as common tin. They were filled with engravings in Egyptian characters and bound together in a volume as the leaves of a book with three rings running through the whole. The volume was something near six inches in thickness, a part of which was sealed. The characters on the unsealed part were small and beautifully engraved. The whole book exhibited many marks of antiquity in its construction and much skill in the art of engraving. With the records was found a curious instrument which the ancients called "Urim and Thumim" which consisted of two transparent stones set in a rim on a bow fastened to a breastplate. Through the medium of the Urim and Thumim I translated the record by the gift and power of God.[7]

The method of translation was interesting. From behind a blanket Smith dictated to copyists the translation which he saw by gazing through the "peepstone," or Urim and Thumim, at the golden plates. Mormons believe today that the translation of the sacred words appeared a sentence at a time and that each sentence refused to move on and give place to the next if the scribes had made an error. Only when the correct transcription had been made did the next sacred sentence appear. Fortunately there has been preserved the original transcription, and an expert alleges that "a recent inspection of it, with its crude superscription 'Caractors' and its partial back-handed autographs, shows it to be nothing but the automatic scrawl of the self-hypnotized crystal gazer."[8]

A "higher-critical" appraisal of the Book of Mormon, which was the result of this creative effort of Joseph Smith, would be extremely interesting. The book purports to be a history of two races which anciently inhabited America. "The first were called Jaredites and came directly from the Tower of Babel; the second race came directly from the city of Jerusalem about six hundred years before Christ. They were principally Israelites, of the descendants of Joseph. The Jaredites were destroyed about the time that the Israelites came from Jerusalem, who succeeded them in the inheritance of the country. The principal nation of the second race fell in battle toward the close of the fourth century. The remnant are the Indians who now inhabit this country."[9]

The book goes on to tell of the appearance of Jesus in America after his resurrection, and how the gospel was established. The people became wicked and were all exterminated, but one prophet who wrote their history and hid it in the earth, where it remained until it was discovered by Joseph Smith. He thus apparently capitalized the old legend of the lost ten tribes of Israel.

When we examine the book carefully we find evidence that the aboriginal personages in the Book of Mormon bear strange resemblance to some of the people whom Smith knew in western New York, and that the speeches quote parts of accessible books. "Thus the speech of Nephi contains quotations from the Westminster Confession of Faith, and the speech of Lehi, the heretical tenets charged against the Presbytery of Geneva, New York, in whose bounds Joseph himself lived. The book is also interspersed with the catch-words of the Methodist camp meeting exhorter; its last section in fact being a palpable imitation of the Methodist Book of Discipline."[10]

In 1827, the year which witnessed the great revelation of the golden plates, Joseph Smith went down into Pennsylvania and brought back a wife with him. Apparently she was not greatly impressed by his claims of supernatural communications but believed that her husband was not right in his mind.[11] For two years Smith kept at his work of translation assisted by several scribes, one of whom was his wife. For a while it looked as if the book would never be published because the wife of one of the scribes, irritated at her husband's interest in what she was sure was a fake, stole part of the translation and destroyed it.

But in 1830 the book was published at $1.25 per copy and peddled through the countryside by the prophet's father. That same year there was organized at Fayette, New York, a church which was later called "The Church of Jesus Christ of Latter Day Saints,"

9 Smith's account in Rupp, p. 406.
10 *Encyclopedia of Religion and Ethics,* Vol. XI, p. 86a.
11 Ibid., p. 85a.

more popularly known as the Mormon Church.[12] There were so many freak cults in western New York at that time, however, that Joseph Smith's new religion attracted very little attention locally. The next year a revelation was received that the church should move west.

At Kirtland, Ohio, an ex-Baptist preacher named Sidney Rigdon, of considerable education, had established a sort of communistic religion. When Smith and his followers arrived at Kirtland there was an immediate amalgamation of the two groups, and converts from all sides swelled the membership of the new church to two thousand. Success turned the heads of both Smith and Rigdon and they embarked upon business ventures which were unsuccessful. They formed the Kirtland Safety Society Anti-Banking Company, which was not as safe as the name implied. For practices of doubtful honesty the organizers were forced to depart suddenly for Missouri.[13] Smith's saints followed their leader and soon there were many Mormons in Missouri. But the native Missourians objected to the newcomers who were pouring into Independence, the new city of Zion. The Mormons were warned they must leave and were driven out in 1838.

But persecution did not seem to dampen the ardor of the new religionists. They simply moved on to Illinois and created in an incredibly short time the town of Nauvoo. By clever manipulation of one political party against another the Mormons secured a charter for Nauvoo which gave them great power. Late in 1843 or early in 1844 Joseph Smith, in an article on "Latter Day Saints" which he contributed to a history of the religious denominations of the United States, set forth in thirteen articles the Mormon Statement of Faith.[14] It is in the main a summary of the tenets of orthodox evangelical Protestantism. It differs, however, in several particulars. Article two reads, "We believe that men will be punished for their own sins and not for Adam's transgression." Article eight reads, "We believe the Bible to be the Word of God as far as it is translated correctly; we also believe the Book of Mormon to be the

12 The followers of Joseph Smith are called Mormons because their Book of Mormon was supposed to have been originally composed by the last leader of the Nephites, whose name was Mormon. It was Mormon's son, Moroni, who is believed to have appeared as an angel to Joseph Smith.

13 Ibid., p. 87b.

14 Rupp, p. 410.

Word of God." Other articles affirm belief in future revelation from God and the restoration of Zion upon the American continent.

A remarkable note of tolerance is struck in the eleventh article, "We claim the privilege of worshipping Almighty God according to the dictates of our conscience, and allow all men the same privilege, let them worship how, where or what they may."

The best-known feature of Mormonism is not named in this Statement of Faith although it took its rise at this very time. In 1843 Joseph Smith received another divine communication, permitting the practice of polygamy. Smith and the other leaders took to themselves many wives, but "celestial marriage," as it was called, was kept from the public for nine years and was not officially announced until 1852. Very cleverly it was proclaimed that no woman could enter heaven unless "sealed" to a good male Mormon. The Nauvoo period was also characterized by great missionary activity. In 1842 it took eight ships to carry to America the converts made in England. Thousands were flocking to the new faith.

But the polygamy idea was not altogether popular among the Mormons and some of them established a newspaper for the purpose of combating the doctrine. Only one issue of the paper appeared, for Smith and his satellites not only suppressed the paper but smashed the press, pied the type, and burned the building. This act cost Smith his life, for the newspaper owners had him arrested on a charge of riot. Smith was discharged by one of his own officials, but public opinion among the non-Mormons in Illinois reached such a pitch that it was decided to drive out the Mormons. Smith and his brother Hyrum were arrested on the charge of treason and placed in jail at Carthage, Illinois. A mob overpowered the prison guard and killed both the Smith brothers, on June 27, 1844.

A dispute arose as to Smith's successor. There were three candidates, but Brigham Young won. He, like Rigdon and Joseph Smith, was a former Vermonter. He had joined the Mormons twelve years previously and had been active in missionary and organization work. The year after Smith's death the Gentiles repealed the Mormon Charter, and Young realized that it was time for the saints to move again. The history of religion has witnessed only one other migration, the exodus of the children of Israel, to compare with the move of the Mormons to Utah.

The move was decided upon in 1847 and was completely carried out by the next year. One caravan of over fifteen hundred people

traveled in five hundred and sixty-six wagons. A complete new
state was established, the state of Deseret, in what was then New
Mexico but is now Utah. It is doubtful that the experiment would
have succeeded if it had not been for the fact that the Mormon
settlement became a way station for the gold-seeking Forty-Niners
on their way to California.

There was rebellion within the colony in 1856 which was put
down with a high hand. Those who attempted to escape were prevented by a specially trained band of "Wolf-Hunters." Gentiles
were informed that they were not wanted, and when they persisted
in attempting entrance severe measures were taken, such as the
Mountain Meadows Massacre, for which a Mormon bishop was
twenty years later put to death by the United States Government.
Meanwhile, in the rest of the country a second protest against polygamy was made, and in 1862 the Federal Morrill Act against the
practice was passed. It was ineffective, however. Another bill in
1869 was opposed by a Mormon delegate on the constitutional
ground that the Mormon marriage was a part of their religion and
therefore could not be legislated against. Matters came to a climax
when Brigham Young's private secretary was convicted of bigamy.
He appealed, but the Supreme Court ruled that religion could not
excuse a criminal act.

Several other acts were passed, and in 1887 the corporation of
"The Church of Jesus Christ and Latter Day Saints" was dissolved
by act of Congress. Four hundred and sixty-eight Mormons were
convicted of bigamy and other sexual irregularities. The Mormons
opposed this law but soon saw the error of their ways and their
president, Wilford Woodruff, in 1890, ordered Mormons "to refrain from contracting any marriage forbidden by the law of the
land." In 1896 Utah was admitted into the Union as a state, with
the proviso that bigamies, or plural marriages, are forever prohibited.

Mormons are now found not only in Utah but also in several
other states, especially in Idaho, Arizona, Wyoming, and Colorado.
They have colonies in Mexico and Canada and there are members
of the Mormon Church in every part of the world. Recruits to
Mormonism have for nearly a century been gathered from distant
lands. Many of these have been of good stock, and the resultant race
blend has produced a fine type of Mormon. For instance, a young
lady from Norway named Anna Kerstina Morrison and a young

man from Kentucky named Abraham Owen Smoot became the parents in Salt Lake City of Reed Smoot, the United States Senator from Utah. America has no better citizens than the Mormons. At first sight it is difficult to account for the evolution of present-day Mormonism from the teachings of such an erratic person as Joseph Smith.

There are several factors of importance, however, in the situation. In the first place, in spite of his visions and vagaries, Smith was undoubtedly a commanding and attracting personality. That fact has been testified to by both friend and enemy. In the second place, there were elements of power and worth in Smith's message. In the third place, the absurdities and abnormalities in early Mormonism were gradually sloughed off when they were found to be contrary to enlightened public opinion. Mormonism has been changed for the better by the common sense of its later leaders.

WILLIAM MILLER

(1782–1849)

AND THE END OF THE WORLD

In the second quarter of the nineteenth century western New York experienced a wave of Second Adventism. It was a direct result of careful Bible reading by the pious farmer. Whether he read the words of John the Baptist or Jesus, or Paul's Epistles to the Thessalonians and Corinthians, or pored over the strange prophecies of Daniel and Revelation, everywhere he found warnings of the approaching end of the world and the second advent of Christ to set up his kingdom. Earnest but ignorant folk sought by combining various apocalyptic prophecies to deduce the actual date when the dreadful day would come.

It mattered little to them that the date had been set time and again in the history of Christianity only to have the world roll on just the same. Jesus had expected the end of the world before his generation passed away. The author of Revelation who probably wrote during the persecution by Domitian expected the end of all things before A.D. 120. Ignatius and Polycarp were firmly convinced that they were living in the "latter days." Hippolytus expected it A.D. 500. All Christendom looked for it in the year 1000. It was expected again in 1260, in 1367, in 1660, in 1700, in 1715, and in 1734.

Early in the nineteenth century a wave of millennialism swept Great Britain. The American movement was an echo of the English excitement and had its rise in some of the English literature. Mormonism had its genesis in the millennial craze. Smith's great desire was to set up a new city of Zion ready for Christ's return. The several moves of the Mormons ever westward were due to difficulties encountered in each locality which prevented the setting up of the city of Zion, and it was finally established at the Salt Lake. The millennial character of Mormonism faded somewhat but is still to be detected in its theology and in its name, *"Latter Day Saints."*

It was in the year 1830 that Joseph Smith founded his church in Fayette, New York, and it was in 1831 that William Miller of Low Hampton, not far away, began his public preaching, actually announcing that Christ would soon appear in bodily form. Mormonism and Millerism, or Second Adventism, are sister religions in origin.

William Miller was the eldest of sixteen children and was not distinguished in boyhood save for the fact that he was the only one of the sixteen who loved books and that he did the letter-writing for the community.

The citizens of Low Hampton recognized his love of books and loaned him some which he otherwise could not have had an opportunity to read. His parents discouraged his bookish proclivities, but he disregarded their advice and looked forward to college education. That, however, was denied him and he was doomed to farm work. But his determination led him to continue his reading evenings and he soon became one of that group known as "self-educated men" who have done so much good in the world—and so much mischief. When his parents found that their son was looked up to by the neighbors because of his "book-larnin" they repented so far as to permit the young man to have a whole room to himself in the house. There he simply devoured books of all sorts, and his mind was soon crammed with a hodgepodge of miscellaneous information.

In June 1803, when Miller was twenty-one, he married a Miss Smith of Poultney, Vermont, and set up housekeeping there on a farm. He attracted attention by composing a patriotic hymn which was sung by the villagers on the Fourth of July. The young man began to prosper and joined the Masons, advancing rapidly to the highest degree. After serving a term as constable he was made sheriff in 1809.

Suddenly he took a strange notion to join the army. The motive which he confesses to was unusual. His historical studies had convinced him that men were naturally wicked. He said,[15] "I began to feel very distrustful of all men. In this state of mind I entered the service of my country. I fondly cherished the idea that I should find one bright spot at least in the human character as a star of hope; a love of country—Patriotism." Probably Miller was experiencing a spiritual conflict at this time. We know that he had been reading the works of Paine, Voltaire, and Hume and that the experience was rather upsetting to his Baptist faith. He went over to a sort of deism, referred to his former religion as superstition, and began to make fun of his pious relatives, several of whom were Baptist preachers. There was much consternation in the family over this change in William Miller's character. His mother's heart was nearly broken, his sisters reduced to tears, and his wife was much disturbed.

His entering the army in 1810 was therefore a sort of desperate gesture. He was seeking escape from the religious dilemma which he felt within himself. When war broke out between the United States and England in 1812, Miller was raised in rank from lieutenant to captain and found himself soon on the march to Burlington, Vermont. On the way an accident happened to him which nearly finished his career and may have had much to do with shaping it. While he was seated on the back of a wagon the horses started and he was thrown out. He landed on his head and lay for fifteen minutes as if dead. Still unconscious, he was put into the wagon and did not regain his senses until he had proceeded five or six miles.

At Burlington, army fever became epidemic, and Miller suffered from it all summer. The next year he took part in the battle of Plattsburg and wrote exultantly to his wife, "Yesterday was a day of great joy. We have conquered! We have drove them. . . . My God! What a slaughter on all sides!—out of three hundred on board of one ship, twenty-four alone remained unhurt. I cannot describe to you the general joy."[16]

The next year William Miller retired from the army and returned to the farm at Poultney. While he had been away at war his

---

[15] Sears, *Days of Delusion*, p. 8.   [16] Sears, pp. 17, 18.

father had died in Low Hampton and his mother was lonely; consequently William took his wife and son to New York State and built
himself a house on a farm near his mother's home. There he devoted himself to agriculture, endeavoring, in the hard work of
managing a two-hundred-acre farm, to drive away the thoughts
which were troubling him.

He had returned from the war an agnostic but a troubled one.
The death of a friend from fever made a great impression upon
him. He began to wonder what did actually happen after death.
Miller was not really an agnostic but a Deist. He believed in God
but did not believe in Christianity. He asked a Deist friend what
his idea was of the future life, and the reply was that human beings,
like trees, grew for a time and then decayed. "I was then satisfied
that Deism was inseparably connected with and did tend to the
denial of a future existence. And I thought to myself that rather
than embrace such a view, I should prefer the heaven and hell of
the Scriptures, and take my chances respecting them."[17]

Miller's return to Christianity occurred in a Baptist church in
Low Hampton, and immediately he plunged into Bible study with
the assiduity which had characterized his boyhood studies. The
obscurities of Daniel and Revelation particularly attracted him
and he was soon working out a scheme for determining just when
the end of the world would come. As early as 1818 he set upon the
date 1843, and for fourteen years spent his spare time working out
additional proofs of the correctness of the date. Toward the end of
the fourteen-year period of study he became increasingly convinced
that he should make a public proclamation of his discovery. He
tried out his arguments tentatively in conversation but found
people were not much impressed. He was disinclined to assume the
role of a public speaker, the more so because he was fifty years old
and felt older.

His theophany came one Saturday morning as he was about to
continue his fascinating Bible study. He does not tell us of any
light, but a loud voice said to him, "Go tell it to the world." At
first he refused, but the voice was insistent and he finally agreed to
go out if God would open the way for him. Again the question
came, "What do you mean by opening the way?" and he answered,
"Why, if I should have an invitation to speak publicly in any place
I will go and tell them what I find in the Bible about the Lord's

[17] Sears, p. 27.

coming." He felt an immediate relief because he did not expect that he ever would be called upon, as he never had had such an invitation. But half an hour later there was a knock at the door and a messenger from Dresden invited him to speak there the following Sunday.

From that date on, the amazed William Miller was the center of attention. The work for which he had been unconsciously preparing himself through many years of patient study began when the startled congregation in Dresden listened to the flaming prophet of the Lord who proclaimed that the end of the world was coming in twelve years, and proved it over and over from Scripture. A great revival began, and whole families were converted. Congregational, Baptist, and Methodist churches were thrown open to him, and opposing sects united to call William Miller to lecture in their town. Through New York and New England, and even eastern Canada, he journeyed. At first it was the eloquence and conviction of the man which captivated his audiences. Much to his own surprise, he discovered that he had preaching ability.

Very likely little further would have happened, and the Millerites would have died out, or, like the Mormons, they would have changed the emphasis of their religion. But Miller soon received startling approbation from heaven itself. In the fall of 1833, just before dawn on November 13, there occurred the famous meteor shower, concerning which the newspapers of the time were full. There is no doubt that the spectacle was unusually brilliant. A Yale professor called it the "greatest display of celestial fireworks that has ever been seen since the creation of the world."

One can imagine the effect of this "shower of stars" upon the already excited Millerites. It was immediately seen as the first sign of the approaching catastrophe. Bible students turned at once to the sixth chapter of Revelation and read the thirteenth verse, "And the stars of heaven fell unto the earth, even as the fig tree casteth her untimely figs when she is shaken of a mighty wind." According to that sixth chapter the rest of the program would include the rolling up of the heavens as a scroll. Rich men would hide themselves in tents and beg mountains and rocks to fall upon them. The prophets of doom were justified in saying, "The great day of his wrath has come and who shall be able to stand?"

Miller himself was ecstatic at the confirmation of his preaching. Thousands flocked to hear him, and hundreds were converted to his cause. With renewed diligence he returned to his chronological charts. His lectures were illustrated by strange numerical diagrams and pictures of the beasts of the Apocalypse. Millerism became a fad very similar to the later vogue of numerology, but with a deadly seriousness underlying it all. For ten years Miller traveled almost constantly, lecturing in the eastern states. In 1840 the Rev. Joshua V. Himes became his publicity agent and general manager. With good strategy Himes immediately took Miller off the rural circuit and started him in the great cities. He began in Boston and lectured to crowded houses, with many turned away. Himes had been a Unitarian and was a Baptist when he met Miller, but he soon became a Millerite and accompanied the prophet of doom on his travels.

As the date approached which Miller had set for the end of the world, the excitement grew intense. Many who had heard him preaching, themselves went forth to preach, and Millerism spread like a strange fever. Himes reproduced Miller's charts and trained preachers in their use. He printed thousands of pamphlets and sent them broadcast. There were many scoffers and egg-throwers, but the work went on. Miller's strength gave out and he suffered from abscesses on his legs. But the approach of the day of doom seemed to give him new strength. The New York *Herald* announced that the Millerites had set April third as the date. The irreverent said it should have been made April first. Miller himself had been careful not to set a definite date.

Then, to cap the climax, came the great comet of 1843. The scenes which followed would have been amusing had they not been pitiful. During the summer of 1843, camp meetings were held throughout the east. Unstable personalities were driven to insanity. One little girl said, "Mother, I want to die this summer; I do not want to live until next year and be burned up." People began to prepare their ascension robes. When 1843 came without the end of the world, prophet Miller set the date for the twenty-first of March 1844. He had previously suggested, occasionally, that it might be 1844 instead of 1843.

On March twenty-first thousands of people, clad in white robes, spent the night on hilltops and housetops. But when dawn came they made their way to their neglected homes. Many had given away all their property and all had neglected their proper business. The poor sick prophet Miller lay at his home in Low Hampton for four days as in a trance, but wrote to his manager, Joshua Himes, on March 25, "I am still looking for our dear Saviour, the Son of God from heaven. . . . I still believe the time is not far off." But the general public, having been fooled twice by Miller, left him, and his followers dwindled.

Several sects of Second Adventists, however, arose from his preaching, and a millennial flavor was imparted to other denominations. Those who today are inclined to scoff at the deluded Miller and his followers should remind themselves that there are even now many thousands who believe that "millions now living shall never die." The imminent second coming of Jesus is one of the cardinal tenets of Fundamentalism and will always claim the allegiance of those who believe in the literal interpretation of the Bible. The new menace of the atom bomb, H-bomb, and nuclear fission and fusion has revived Adventism, and the doom sects are harvesting many converts again.

ROBERT INGERSOLL

(1833–1899)

AND THE AGNOSTICS

Robert Ingersoll was the apostle of the religion of the unchurched. The common people of his day, vaguely resentful at the inhumanities of the religion proclaimed in the churches, turned with relief to the speeches and writings of their advocate.

If anyone is inclined to doubt the propriety of including Ingersoll's name among America's religious leaders, let such a one take notice of the fact that religion is not confined to those claiming monopoly of it. As this century grows older, much that seemed heresy in the nineteenth is regarded as commonplace, even in the churches from whose pulpits were thundered denunciations of the infidel Ingersoll. The "mistakes of Moses" are recognized now even in the Sunday schools. Clergymen often express opinions more radical than those of Ingersoll and still retain their pulpits.

In other words, agnosticism is becoming respectable. It is no longer a crime, except in rural communities, to admit that one does not know all about God and the hereafter. The more enlightened of mankind no longer confuse agnosticism with atheism, or either with immorality. An agnostic is a person honest enough to admit that he does not know, although he is looked down upon by many who do not dare to admit their doubt. But the present toleration of agnosticism was not evident in the days when Robert Ingersoll spoke. It took a brave man then to say, "The clergy know that I know that they know that they do not know," and it took a broad-minded sympathetic leader of men to announce,[18]

I have made up my mind to say my say. I shall do it kindly, distinctly; but I am going to do it. I know there are thousands of men who sub-stantially agree with me, but who are not in a condition to express their thoughts. They are poor; they are in business; and they know that should they tell their honest thought, persons will refuse to patronize them—to trade with them; they wish to get bread for their little chil-dren; they wish to take care of their wives; they wish to have homes and the comforts of life. Every such person is a certificate of the meanness of the community in which he resides. And yet I do not blame these people for not expressing their thought. I say to them: "Keep your ideas to yourself; feed and clothe the ones you love; I will do your talking for you. The Church cannot touch, cannot crush, cannot starve, cannot stop or stay me; I will express your thoughts."

Ingersoll's views were a direct reaction from his father's theology. John Ingersoll was a Congregational preacher of the old school—a typical hell-roarer of the early nineteenth century. When Robert was four years old his father subscribed to the Auburn Declaration and became a Presbyterian. The boy's mother had died when he was two years old, and Robert spent most of his time in company with his brother Eben, as his father devoted his entire time to the duties of the procession of parishes which he served in New York, Ohio, and Illinois. On the trip west through Buffalo the boys were delighted to see their father manhandle a Millerite preacher who insisted upon preparing the travelers for the end of the world which was coming in three years and who offered to show them the ascen-sion robes which he had in his traveling bags.

John Ingersoll's orthodoxy did not prevent him from becoming a champion of the anti-slavery movement, and Robert later re-flected his father's views about slavery. In Illinois Robert grew to young manhood and developed a liking for the law. He read widely, however, in general literature and early showed a greater fondness for Shakespeare than for the Bible.

An antagonism toward Christianity, born of his dreary childhood

18 Rogers, *Colonel Robert Ingersoll*, p. 214.

Sundays, began to assert itself. A group of Baptist revivalists who invaded his boarding house tried to induce him to discuss religion, because from his attitude they inferred that he was not a Christian. He refused to enter into discussion with them until they insisted that he give them his opinion of baptism. His answer was brief but to the point, "Well, I'll tell you, with soap baptism is a good thing." The next day the school board waited on him at the little school house, where he had been teaching to earn money for his education, and insisted upon his immediate departure, refusing to pay him even the back salary then due him.

Robert Ingersoll's early success in pleading before the bar established a local reputation for eloquence, and when he began to travel to neighboring towns and give lectures on religion he was always sure of an audience. In spite of the opposition of clergymen of all denominations, the people crowded to hear him. As his fame increased he traveled more widely and was greeted by ever larger throngs until those who had heard him really were members of a great unorganized group of Ingersollians.

When we examine the speeches of Robert Ingersoll we discover that the popular impression still obtaining in many circles is incorrect. Ingersoll was not an atheist. Nowhere in his writings can there be found a denial of God's existence. But he did assert his disbelief in the existence of such a God as the Jewish Jehovah of the Bible, against whom he launched most brilliant and scathing denunciations. He said, "Let me say once and for all, that when I speak of God I mean the being described by Moses: Jehovah of the Jews. There may be for aught I know, somewhere in the unknown shoreless vast, some being whose dreams are constellations and within whose thought the infinite exists. About this being, if such an one exists, I have nothing to say."

Ingersoll's first public appearance as a defender of heresy occurred at a Baptist picnic when he was but twenty-three years of age. The preacher who was expected to deliver the speech of the afternoon had been taken with sudden illness, and young Bob Ingersoll was asked to take his place. For two weeks he had been reading carefully the works of Thomas Paine and took the opportunity to defend his new-found hero. The young orator had a few minutes of mild stage-fright until he suddenly felt a desire to refute the aspersions cast upon Paine. Warming to his subject, he discovered in himself a strange power of influencing his audience. The speech was a success and young Bob's reputation as a heretic was established.

Alternating political speeches with ones of a religious nature, Ingersoll soon found there were more demands upon him than he could fill. No doubt his personal appearance helped a great deal. He was large, but well proportioned, and had a noble bearing. He won instant attention when he stepped upon a platform and held that attention by the charm of his speech and the purity of his diction.

Ingersoll's political career is well known. Many considered his speech nominating James G. Blaine in June 1876 as the greatest of his career. There is no doubt that it gave him the reputation of being America's greatest orator. Had it not been for Ingersoll's anti-Christian views, openly expressed, he could have been President of the United States. But he found greater delight in discussing religion than politics. To him the common religion of the day seemed largely superstition, and against superstition he fought his whole life long. It irritated him to see how the priest, taking advantage of the awe inspired by his supposed influence with the gods, made his fellow man a cringing hypocrite and slave. His own mind was so free that he regretted the slavery of his credulous fellow men, and he summed up his philosophy when he said, "There is no slavery but ignorance."

But Ingersoll's teaching was not all negative. It is true that his strength lay in attack, but he did have a real faith of his own: a sort of humanism, which attracted thousands who were disgusted with the absurdities of current Christianity. For him worship was not a matter of incense and intonations; rather, "To do justice; to defend the right, to be strength for the weak—a shield for the defenseless; to raise the fallen; to keep the peace between neighbors and nations: this is worship. Work is worship. Labor is the best prayer. To fell the forest, to subdue the earth; to develop in mind for the love of man: this is worship. To build a home; to keep a fire on the hearth; to fill with joy the heart of her who rocks the cradle of your child: this is worship. . . . He who loves, worships."

If he hated Jehovah, Ingersoll admired Jesus. The theological Christ he held to be "the impossible union of the human and divine," but, regarding the human Jesus he said, "For the reformer who loved his fellow men, for the man who believed in an infinite father, who would shield the innocent and protect the just, for the martyr who expected to be rescued from the cruel cross . . . for that great and suffering man, mistaken though he was, I have the highest admiration and respect."

For the Bible, too, he had a deep appreciation, although he refused to worship it as most Christians of his day did. With an anticipation of the modern approach to the Bible he said, "Is it not infinitely more reasonable to say that this book is the work of man, that it is full of mingled truth and error, with mistakes and facts, and reflects, faithfully perhaps, the very form and pressure of its time? If there are mistakes in the Bible certainly they were made by men."

Ingersoll's speeches against orthodox religion were very widely circulated, especially in paper covers among the laboring classes. They contributed greatly to the exodus from the Christian churches which took place after the Civil War. The fact that half the population of the United States at the present time is not affiliated, even nominally, with any religious denomination is partly due to Ingersoll's lectures and the speeches of his soap-box successors. His influence on religion was therefore mainly negative, but he deserves recognition because of two things. He prepared the minds of many people for the reception of the seeds of liberal religion, and by pointing out the absurdities of orthodox churches, he enabled them to clean house by discarding certain outworn dogmas and by revising many other tenets.

He had no great ability as a theologian and his arguments were occasionally faulty in their logic. But eloquence attracts the people whom theology drives away. What Unitarianism did for the educated classes was accomplished by Ingersoll for the masses of folk who would never have entered a Unitarian church. When Humanism writes its history, it should acknowledge Ingersoll as one of its John the Baptists who laid the ax to the roots of many a dead tree and cleared a way for the coming of a better religion.

PHINEAS QUIMBY

(1802–1866)

AND NEW THOUGHT

The year after Channing died, the year before Joseph Smith was martyred, the year when the Millerites were expecting the end of the world, the year when ten-year-old Robert Ingersoll was moving west with his father—in short, in the year 1843—Phineas Quimby, down in Maine, was neglecting his trade of watch- and clock-making to experiment with mesmerism as an aid in drugless doctoring. Curing without drugs or medicines has always possessed a fascination for mankind. The early medicine men and shamans, the witch doctors and the voodoo quacks, have ever been able to dupe the credulous with their incantations, charms, and absent-treatments. In the early nineteenth century hardly a New England village but had its "healer," "bone-setter," or "doctor" without a medical degree. One did not need a medical education to be a doctor; all he needed was a theory. Patients there were a-plenty.

Quimby continued his experiments in mesmerism for some time. The name was applied to the practice which is now recognized scientifically and called hypnotism. Quimby sometimes called it animal magnetism. A sort of trance or sleep may be induced in impressionable people by the monotonous repetition of sounds, continuous strokings, or by the focusing of the hypnotist's eye upon that of the patient. When the nerves of hearing, touch, or sight are thus subjected to continued stimulus, the trance state is produced and then the patient is responsive to suggestion.

Discovering one young man, Lucius Burkmar, who was particularly susceptible to hypnosis, and who in the trance state became clairvoyant, Quimby traveled around in Maine with his subject and gave exhibitions, not primarily for financial reward but because he was essentially an experimenter in the delicate mechanisms of the human mind. Early in his experiments he believed that Burkmar, under hypnosis, could see inside the bodies of sick people and report their diseases. But a little later Quimby noticed that Burkmar's diagnosis of the case always corresponded with what someone present at the trance considered to be the matter. Sometimes it was the patient's ideas which Burkmar reflected, sometimes those of another.

Quimby had found what he wanted. Right then and there the modern history of mental science began. For when he had established to his own satisfaction that the symptoms existed primarily in the mind of the patient, Quimby resolved to cure people by treating their minds instead of their bodies.[19] Thereupon he dismissed Lucius Burkmar and began to work out a system for curing

19 Dresser, *The Quimby Manuscripts*, p. 32.

disease through the mind. For a while he retained mesmerism as part of his process. A little later he discarded the mesmeric trance and simply sat by the patient, placed his left hand upon the patient's abdomen, and with his right hand rubbed the supposed seat of the disease.

His early theory was that a sort of electric connection was thus established, and that the disease passed out of the patient through the body of the doctor. But before long he gave up any physical contact with his patients and concentrated upon convincing them that mental healing could cure their disease. In other words, he attempted to relieve the deranged state of their minds and to remove the wrong beliefs which they had. He began to talk about the "science of health."[20] His patients rapidly increased because, in certain types of disease at least, he was having great success. In 1851 he was treating three hundred patients a year, and five years later five hundred.

He definitely considered his cures to be connected with religious faith. There was nothing miraculous about them, though; it was all purely scientific. "In proportion as we understand Science we understand God."[21] He linked his cures with both science and religion by stating, "The Science of True Religion is Health, Happiness and Deliverance."[22]

In 1859 Quimby began practicing in Portland, and the files of the newspapers of that city a century ago contain many reports of Dr. Quimby's cures, some of them written by the patients themselves. One of the most remarkable cases was that of Captain John W. Deering of Saco, Maine, who was suffering from a contraction of the muscles of the right side so that his leg was drawn up into a most unnatural position. Over his signature, Deering made the statement,[23] "Without calling on the spirits of the departed for aid, without mesmerism and without the use of medicines of any kind, he succeeded in completely restoring the muscles of my side and leg to their proper functions, and I am now as well as ever."

This cure inspired one of Quimby's other patients to write a sonnet lauding the power of the new healer. That sonnet was composed and signed by a "Mary M. Patterson," of whom we shall hear later. Quimby's practice at Portland, 1859–1865, was a great success,

20 Ibid., p. 67.
21 Ibid., p. 209.
22 Ibid., p. 196.
23 Ibid., p. 104.

and when he retired, one of the newspapers had the following announcement,[24]

The doctor has been in this city for nearly seven years and by his unobtrusive manners and sincerity of practice has won the respect of all who know him. To those especially who have been fortunate enough to receive benefit at his hands—and there are many—his departure will be viewed as a public loss. That he has manifested wonderful power in healing the sick among us, no well-informed and unprejudiced person can deny. . . . By a method entirely novel, and at first sight quite unintelligible, he has been slowly developing what he calls the "Science of Health."

Evidently Quimby had felt the approach of his own death in some form which even the science of health could not control, for he passed away in Belfast, Maine, in January 1866, only a few weeks after he had retired from his Portland practice. The work of Phineas Quimby was that of a pioneer, and his voluminous writings contain suggestions which may bear fruit in years to come. He must be recognized as in a general way the "Father of New Thought" in all its branches, including Christian Science. But only in a general way, for New Thought owes as much to Ralph Waldo Emerson, and Christian Science owes infinitely more to Mary Baker Eddy.

MARY BAKER EDDY

(1821–1910)

AND CHRISTIAN SCIENCE

There are two things which immediately impress the student of the life of Mary Baker Eddy. The first is that she is the most compelling figure in American religious history. The second is that there is no sign whatsoever of that greatness in the first half of her long life, although her admirers, including herself, have tried rather pathetically to find such signs.

Between the saccharine eulogies of her followers and the caustic criticisms of her foes, the unprejudiced observer is hard put to it to discover the real truth about Mary Baker Eddy. Still, if one bases his adverse criticism on the unconscious revelations in Mrs. Eddy's

own writings and gathers his bouquet of praise from the admissions
of her enemies, he avoids extravagance in either direction.

Mary Baker was born in 1821 on a farm in Bow, New Hampshire,
the youngest of six children. The child was named Mary for and by
her grandmother, who took much interest in her, and therefore
naturally made a great impression on her. Little Mary was the pet
of the family and stood in danger of being spoiled by her doting
brothers and sisters, and especially by the grandmother. The child
was "delicate in health from her birth."[25]

In Mrs. Eddy's autobiographic reminiscences[26] she says, "In the
Baker homestead at Bow I was born, the youngest of my parents'
six children and the object of their tender solicitude." We are left
a little in doubt as to whether it was the parents, or the children,
or both, that were solicitous, but we get a good idea of the atmosphere in which the child grew up. Educators recognize such an
environment as likely to create an exaggerated sense of self-impor-
tance. She was early interested in books and was much impressed
by the fact that her great-grandmother, who was also named Mary,
had written poems. Her grandmother permitted her to see the
actual manuscripts. The child became obsessed with the idea of
writing poetry herself and, perhaps, someday, a book.

In her autobiography she further relates that when she was eight
years old she kept hearing a voice calling her by name. When she
went to her mother and asked her what she wanted, the mother
replied that she had not called. The voice continued, at intervals,
for a year, and caused considerable consternation in the family.
Thereupon, Mrs. Eddy tells us, her mother read to her the Bible
story of little Samuel and told her when the voice came again to
say, as Samuel had, "Speak, Lord, for thy servant heareth." When
she did so answer, the voice ceased ever after. It should be noted
that Mrs. Eddy's account of the voice was written over sixty years
later. Possibly, little Mary had read or heard the Samuel story
before she heard the voice. Alarmed by the voice incident, the
father gave orders that books should be taken away from the child
because "her brain" was "too big for her body."

A little later she went to school but "could not endure the severe
routine of the district schoolroom where restless farmers' children,
with noisily shuffling feet, droned through their lessons and in-

25 Sybil Wilbur, *Life of Mary Baker Eddy*, p. 17.
26 *Retrospection and Introspection*, p. 5.

dulged in occasional rude pranks that ended in birchings. . . . Mary, who could not endure to hear the calves bawl or the pigs squeal in their own farmyard without an effort to comfort them, was depressed or excited by the turbulence of school life." She picked up some education at home by studying with an elder brother during his vacation from college, "I gained book knowledge with far less labor than is usually requisite. At ten years of age I was as familiar with Lindley Murray's grammar as with the Westminster Catechism; and the latter I had to repeat every Sunday. My favorite studies were natural philosophy, logic, and moral science. From my brother Albert I received lessons in the ancient tongues, Hebrew, Greek, and Latin. . . . After my discovery of Christian Science most of the knowledge I had gleaned from school books vanished like a dream. Learning was so illumined that grammar was eclipsed."[27]

The education she received from her brother was supplemented by attendance at Professor Sanborn's private school, where, we are told, she specialized in rhetoric.

Mary's religious life developed normally. She rebelled at the doctrines of predestination, hell, and election, which her father and her preacher maintained, and she found in the idea of God's love all the theology she wanted. She liked to argue theology with her father and could hold her own with him. He is reported to have said, somewhat ambiguously, "If Mary Magdalene had seven devils our Mary has ten." She "professed religion" at the age of twelve. When she was fifteen the family moved from Bow to a farm near Tilton. In the Tilton Congregational Church which she joined two years later she learned much from the educated minister, Rev. Enoch Corser. She admired his learning and he recognized her intellectual ability, and gave her a class of children to teach in the Sunday school.

In 1843, after a brief courtship, George Washington Glover and Mary Baker were married by Dr. Corser. Mr. Glover was a contractor and builder from Charleston, S.C., whither he took his bride. She begged her husband to free the slaves he owned, but he refused. It was the young woman's first contact with slavery and she was much disturbed by it. The next June, while on a visit to Wilmington, N.C., Mr. Glover died of yellow fever, after a sickness of only nine days. It was a terrible blow to his young wife, but she received loving care in her New Hampshire home. In September

[27] *Retrospection and Introspection,* p. 10.

a boy was born to her, but the state of her health prevented her from taking care of her child. George Glover, Jr., was too much for his mother to handle; she could not bear even to have him in the house. When the nurse who took care of little George moved some forty miles away, the child was taken along.

Mrs. Glover turned to literary pursuits—that is, she continued her poem writing and contributed political articles to a Concord newspaper. For a while she was substitute teacher in an academy and then opened a kindergarten for children. But she was not capable of sustained effort. Her naturally weak constitution which caused "tender solicitude" on the part of the family from her earliest childhood still hindered her from carrying out the schemes which her active brain devised. She kept her bed for months at a time. For three years she made her home with her married sister, Abigail, who, although ill herself, lavished much affection upon her. Her sickness was "a spinal weakness which caused spasmodic seizures, followed by prostration which amounted to a complete nervous collapse."[28]

Much of the time she had to be carried from place to place. In 1853, when she was thirty-two, another man entered her life; this time a dentist. "Dr. Patterson . . . a fluent-speaking, full-bearded, broad-shouldered optimist in broadcloth . . . was always something of a dandy, and even in the mountains wore broadcloth and often linen, kid gloves, topping all off with a silk hat."[29] She wrote many years later, "My dominant thought in marrying again was to get back my child, but after our marriage his stepfather was not willing he should have a home with me. A plot was consummated for keeping us apart. The family to whose care he was committed removed to what was then regarded as the Far West."[30]

For the first three years of their married life Dr. and Mrs. Patterson lived in Franklin, N.H., a factory town, and then moved to Groton, a remote village in the foothills of the White Mountains. It appears that the reason Mrs. Patterson urged her husband to move to Groton was because her son was living there. She rejoiced for a time in seeing her boy again, but Dr. Patterson claimed that his visits excited her. Immediately sister Abigail became jealous of her Mary's health, and evidently concocted a scheme with Dr. Pat-

28 Wilbur, p. 54.
29 Ibid., 56.
30 *Retrospection and Introspection*, p. 20.

terson to have the Cheneys, with whom the boy was staying, move west. This is the plot to which Mrs. Patterson refers in the passage quoted.

The boy later ran away from the Cheneys and enlisted in the northern army during the Civil War. Whether it was due to the visits of the boy or to his removal from her, or to something else, Mrs. Patterson was certainly not well during the Groton period. A woman who visited her then said, "She was all alone in her home, and I heard her bell ringing. I went in and found her lying rigid with foam on her lips. I brought her around with cold water. She motioned to her medicine chest and I gave her what she wanted. Then I sat with her until she got better."[31]

The Groton experience was, altogether, very trying, not only on account of Mrs. Patterson's illness but because her husband was more successful with the ladies than with his dentistry. From Groton the Pattersons moved to Rumney Station, where Mrs. Patterson made desperate efforts to regain her health through careful attention to diet and with homeopathic medicines. "The nervous seizures continued to occur with increasing violence."[32] Dr. Patterson went to Washington to get an appointment as a physician in the army, but while he was viewing the Battle of Bull Run he was captured and put in Libby Prison. Just at this time Mrs. Patterson heard that her boy had enlisted. Her cup of sorrow was full. But in New England they say it's always darkest just before dawn.

Shortly before leaving for Washington Dr. Patterson had come into possession of a handbill[33] which told of the remarkable cures by Dr. Phineas P. Quimby of Portland, Maine. The fact was emphasized that he gave no medicines and made no outward applications. The handbill spoke of the cure of patients being by "correcting their error." In italics was printed, "The truth is the cure."[34] Dr. Patterson himself had a very open mind toward new methods of cure, which he called "high medical attenuations."[35] Ever optimistic, he had written immediately to Dr. Quimby and asked him to come to Concord if possible; if not, he would take his wife to Portland. Quimby replied that he was too busy but felt confident that he could cure Mrs. Patterson if she were brought to Portland.

While Dr. Patterson was in Washington Mrs. Patterson reread

31 Wilbur, p. 59, 60.　　34 Dresser, *The Quimby Manuscripts,* pp. 150, 151.
32 Ibid., p. 67.　　35 Wilbur, p. 55.
33 Ibid., p. 71.

the handbill and the letter. In May 1862 she wrote Dr. Quimby herself. She had detected in the phrases of the handbill a hint of a new
philosophy of health and she told him that she wanted to come and
study his method and be healed. With the energy which always
characterized her when her mind was made up, she made plans to
go as soon as possible to Portland. She wrote asking her sister Abigail to help her get ready. Abigail protested against Mary's going,
told her that Quimby was a quack, and insisted that Mary go to a
"water cure" at Hill, New Hampshire. Mary assented, but when
the water cure failed, determined to go to Portland by herself. In
October 1862 she managed to reach that city but had to be assisted
into the doctor's office.

Mary Baker was at that time a frail shadow of a woman, an abstracted
student, given to much thinking and prayer. With great blue eyes, deep
sunk, yet arched above with beautiful brows, she looked into the friendly
face bent above her and she looked with the deep intense gaze of the
seer.[36]

It is important to note that Mrs. Patterson came to Dr. Quimby
in an attitude of great expectation, and it must be remembered that
there was a religious element in her faith. She had been devout
since childhood and believed in the power of faith and prayer.
There is something tremendously appealing in the simple, almost
childlike, faith with which she forced her weak body to make the
journey to Portland and in the eagerness with which she contemplated the new physician.

When Mary Baker entered Mr. Quimby's office he sat down beside
her, as was his custom with his patients, to get into the sympathetic and
clairvoyant relation with her nature which he called rapport. Gazing
fixedly into her eyes, he told her, as he had told others, that she was held
in bondage by the opinions of her family and physicians, that her animal spirit was reflecting its grief upon her body and calling it spinal
disease. He then wet his hands in a basin of water and violently rubbed
her head, declaring that in this manner he imparted healthy electricity.
Gradually he wrought the spell of hypnotism, and under that suggestion
she let go the burden of pain just as she would have done had morphine
been administered. The relief was no doubt tremendous. Her gratitude
certainly was unbounded. She was set free from the excruciating pain

36 Ibid., p. 78.

of years. Quimby himself was amazed at her sudden healing; no less was he amazed at the interpretation she immediately placed upon it, that it had been accomplished by Quimby's mediatorship between herself and God.[37]

Mrs. Eddy's official biographer, Sybil Wilbur, suggests in this quotation, and elaborates the idea in following paragraphs, that Quimby was an unreligious, materialistic mesmerist who was surprised at his first meeting with Mrs. Patterson to have her interpret his healing as accomplished by the power of God and Christ. Quimbyites, however, point to a manuscript written by Dr. Quimby in February 1862—months before he met Mrs. Patterson. This manuscript was written to answer fifteen questions raised by one of his patients. In it he distinctly interpreted his healing as being by the power of God: "God is truth, and there is no other truth, and if we know God, the same is known to us."[38] He also had much to say about science, matter, and error, and ascribed his healing to the removal of wrong ideas in the minds of his patients.

Mrs. Patterson required several treatments and spent some time in Portland. The records of that period are interpreted in exactly opposite ways by the Christian Scientists and the followers of Phineas Quimby. The latter are inclined to believe that Mrs. Patterson, recognizing the value of this new method of treatment, secured from Dr. Quimby or one of his assistants the "Questions and Answers" manuscript stating the philosophical basis of his cures. It is supposed that this manuscript and the other things she learned from Dr. Quimby became the nucleus of her later book, *Science and Health*. The Quimbyites consequently believe that Mrs. Patterson should have given Dr. Quimby due credit for the discovery and should not have claimed the entire glory for herself.

On the other hand, the Christian Scientists maintain that Mrs. Eddy had the germ of her idea before she ever saw Quimby; that the help which she derived from him was largely due to her own faith; that his method was purely hypnotism or animal magnetism; and that whatever manuscripts Dr. Quimby's heirs may possess which resemble Christian Science teachings were written by Mrs. Patterson herself and signed by her with Quimby's name.[39]

The opposing views are set forth at considerable length—the one

37 Ibid., 86, 87.   39 Wilbur, p. 97.
38 Dresser, p. 167.

in Horatio Dresser's *The Quimby Manuscripts,* especially chapter twelve, and the other, in Sybil Wilbur's *The Life of Mary Baker Eddy,* chapters six, seven, eight, and nine. The controversy later got into the courts. A former student of hers, named Arens, had published a pamphlet entitled, "Theology or the Understanding of God as Applied to Healing the Sick," and containing unacknowledged quotations from Mrs. Eddy's book. He contended that Mrs. Eddy's book was not original but was copied from Quimby's manuscripts. Mrs. Eddy's claims were upheld by the Massachusetts court, but an element of doubt remained because Mr. Quimby's son, George Quimby, refused to permit his father's manuscripts to be used as evidence. The son seemed to have a great fear of Mrs. Eddy and refused to allow his father's manuscripts to go out of his possession, even temporarily, as long as "that woman" was alive, even though the papers were desired in order to confute Mrs. Eddy.

It is not necessary to presume duplicity on the part of either Dr. Quimby or Mrs. Patterson. Christian Science probably grew out of her contact with him. Just what proportion of the credit should go to either it is impossible now to determine. She put some of her ideas into his mind and absorbed some of his. Her original appreciation of his wisdom, as shown in two rhapsodical poems[40] which she composed in extravagant praise of her teacher and healer, dwindled with the years, until finally she asserted that he "was in no wise connected with" her discovery of Christian Science.[41]

Dr. Patterson was finally released from prison through the intercession of his wife, who carried letters from the Governor of New Hampshire to President Lincoln. In 1864 he set up a dentist's office in Lynn, and Mrs. Patterson joined him there. They lived in the suburb of Lynn called Swampscott, and Mrs. Patterson contributed articles of local interest to the Lynn newspapers.

On the evening of February 1, 1866, Mrs. Patterson was injured by a fall on the ice on a Lynn street. She remained unconscious for some hours and thereafter suffered considerable pain. The physician thought that she had sustained a concussion and perhaps a dislocation in the spine. The following Sunday morning, February 4, having refused to take the medicine which the doctor had left her, she dismissed all who were in the room and, taking her Bible, read the story of Jesus' healing of the palsied man. Immediately she

[40] Dresser, pp. 156, 160.   [41] *Retrospection and Introspection,* p. 24.

underwent a strange spiritual experience. She believed that God spoke to her and said, "Daughter, arise!" All her pain disappeared. She arose, dressed herself, and walked into the parlor, to the utter astonishment of the group of friends there who had thought her dying. This was the experience from which she later dated the beginning of Christian Science, and is now referred to by her followers as the "Great Revelation."

The fact that after this, in the latter part of February 1866, she ardently praised the recently deceased Quimby is explained by Christian Scientists as being due to her domination by the "power of error called mesmerism or magnetism."[42] Nearly ten years elapsed after the "discovery" of February 1866 before the first edition of *Science and Health* was published, so it is quite evident that Mrs. Patterson's discovery was not a complete one. Versions of the episode vary.

It was not long after his wife's accident in 1866 that the philandering Dr. Patterson eloped from Lynn with the wife of one of his wealthy patients. Upon the return of the lovers Mrs. Patterson refused to take back her repentant husband, but interceded with the husband of the woman and persuaded him to take her back. Mrs. Patterson never again lived with her husband and secured a divorce from him in 1873. A small alimony was agreed upon which was paid for several years.

The chronicle of the decade from 1866 to 1875 records a period of suffering and hard work, the perusal of which excites deepest sympathy for the lonely woman struggling toward her great work. It was a period of wandering in the wilderness for Mrs. Patterson. The wandering was both geographical and theological. A chart of her peregrinations from boarding house to private home and back again would show a zigzag network over eastern Massachusetts. She lived in Lynn, Swampscott, Stoughton or Avon, Taunton, and Amesbury, and by the middle of the decade was back in Lynn again.

Much of the time she lived with spiritualists, who now assert that she herself was a spiritualist, which Christian Scientists vehemently deny. The truth appears to be that she made experimental investigations of spiritistic phenomena. She also associated with Universalists and Unitarians. In 1870 she took a pew in a Unitarian church in Lynn. Those who are inclined to date the beginning of Christian Science from 1866, when Mrs. Eddy says she discovered it, have to

42 Wilbur, p. 122.

account for the fact that as late as 1872 she was still praising Dr. Quimby and his work and was allowing the pupils she had by that time assembled to practice a form of mesmerism in their cures.

Her first pupil was a Mr. Crafts, a spiritualist, whom she taught as early as the year 1866, but whose instruction she had to abandon because of the jealousy of Mrs. Crafts. She had been successful enough with him, however, to enable him to earn his living for a while performing mental cures. Wherever she traveled during the decade she was constantly seeking to discover likely pupils to whom she could impart the principle which she was then evolving. She was also quietly testing her system of mental cures upon the sick with whom she came in contact. She was satisfied herself that she had cured several, but the patients were inclined to be doubtful about it.

In 1870 Mrs. Patterson, who now was calling herself Mrs. Glover, and a young man named Richard Kennedy rented the second floor of a house in Lynn, the first floor of which was used for a girl's school. There Mrs. Glover conducted classes in mental science, and Mr. Kennedy had an office as practitioner. Most of her students during this period were shoe-factory operatives and they were constantly coming and going. She lost a number, including Kennedy, when in 1872, as the result of a "vision," she announced that mesmeric practices, such as head-stroking, must cease to be a part of the mental science practice. She had considerable trouble with several of her students, who set up in the healing business for themselves and practiced methods not approved by Mrs. Glover.

From 1872 to 1875 she lived in a number of homes and boarding houses, but in the spring of 1875 purchased a two-and-a-half-story house at 8 Broad Street, Lynn, part of which she sublet, but where she was able to have a ground-floor classroom and an attic study. The accommodations were of a primitive sort but afforded her a better opportunity for work than she had had for some time. Her classes increased, and the book she had long been working on was at last completed.

This was the first edition of *Science and Health*. To trace the evolution of that manuscript and its journeyings from Portland, Maine, to Broad Street, Lynn, would require a book by itself, if one included the controversies which have raged concerning its origin. Mrs. Eddy wrote in her "Message for 1902," "Its title, *Science and Health,* came to me in the silence of night, when the steadfast stars watched over the world—when slumber had fled." But Dr. Quimby's frequent references to his method of healing as "The Science of Health" may have given her a suggestion years before which cropped up from her subconscious mind "in the silence of the night."

The acquisition of the house on Broad Street was a good move. In spite of the work involved in completing and publishing her book, Mrs. Glover was able to build up a large class of pupils although the tuition had been increased from one hundred to three hundred dollars. Among her new pupils was an East Boston bachelor, a quiet man of sterling character, whose success as a sewing-machine agent had been hindered by ill health. Mrs. Glover healed him and persuaded him to become a pupil. There had been difficulties in the disposal of the first edition of *Science and Health*. Students who had peddled it from door to door had not met with much success, and Mrs. Glover decided to make different arrangements for the disposal of the second edition. She took the agency from the hands of one Barry and gave it to one Spofford. Spofford had been graduated from her class and had built up a successful healing practice in Lynn. She persuaded him to give his full time to the selling of *Science and Health,* and to hand over his practice to the sewing-machine agent. This caused a mixup all around. Everybody was dissatisfied, and a real quarrel broke out in the "Christian Science Home" at 8 Broad Street.

Mrs. Glover solved the problem in a rather unusual way. She married the sewing-machine agent, whose name was Asa Gilbert Eddy. The ceremony was performed January 1, 1877, by Rev. S. B. Stewart, minister of the Unitarian Church of Lynn. For a brief time the quarrels ceased, but they soon broke out again, and Messrs. Barry and Spofford caused considerable trouble. There were several lawsuits. Mr. Eddy and Mr. Arens were actually arrested in October 1878 for murdering Daniel Spofford. An indictment was found by the superior court in December, but the case was dismissed without trial. The whole thing was very absurd. There seems to have been no evidence against the prisoners.

Meanwhile, Mrs. Eddy had begun Sunday-afternoon lectures in Boston, and from this time on her career was one success after another. Boston took to Christian Science with amazing enthusiasm. Influential citizens allied themselves with the work. A church society was incorporated in 1879, known as The Church of Christ Scientist, with Mrs. Eddy as president. She was also elected pastor in 1881. Mrs. Eddy was very insistent that things should be done in her way. Eight members withdrew from the society and charged her with "frequent ebullitions of temper, love of money, and the appearance of hypocrisy."[43] But Mrs. Eddy was equal to the emergency. "She took from them the right to resign by expelling them from the ranks of her church, thereby preserving the rights of the charter.[44]

This year, 1881, was a time of great activity on the part of the sixty-year-old woman. In January she had organized the Massachusetts Metaphysical College with chairs of Pathology, Ontology, Therapeutics, Moral Science, Metaphysics, and their application to the treatment of diseases. She reserved the presidency for herself and made the six teachers directors. In that same year she issued the third edition of *Science and Health,* a much improved piece of work. She also made her plans to leave Lynn and establish herself in Boston. Early in 1882 she leased a house on Columbus Avenue, Boston, and there in June Mr. Eddy died. Mrs. Eddy has been criticized because she called a regular physician to attend her husband. Dr. Noyes prescribed digitalis and strychnia because he had diagnosed the illness as heart disease. The official biography by Miss Wilbur plainly implies that some enemy was exercising occult powers.[45] Whether Dr. Noyes' medicine was used or not, neither his visit nor the treatment of Mrs. Eddy prevented the death. Just before he died Mr. Eddy said, "Only rid me of this suggestion of poison and I will recover."[46] An autopsy was performed, and Dr. Noyes pointed out to Mrs. Eddy that his diagnosis had been correct because the valvular trouble was very evident, but Mrs. Eddy refused to believe the evidence and stated that "mesmeric poison killed her husband."[47]

Until late in life,[48] and probably to her death, Mrs. Eddy retained a fear of what she called "mental malpractice" or "malicious animal magnetism." She thought her enemies could, from a distance, exert a baleful influence upon her and her friends. Students of comparative religion will recognize in this fear an example of "the almost

43 Wilbur, p. 259.
44 Ibid., p. 261.
45 Ibid., p. 268.
46 Ibid., p. 269.
47 Ibid., p. 270.
48 See *Message for 1901,* pp. 19, 20.

universal dread of witchcraft."[49] Ignorant folk believe that by a sort
of absent treatment a voodoo doctor or a witch can work a spell!
upon a victim miles away. In southern Pennsylvania it is called
"hexing."

The widow, so soon called to lose the companionship of one who
was very dear to her, carried on admirably, however. After a summer in northern Vermont she returned to Boston and with incredible energy began laying even broader foundations for her work.
Calvin Frye was chosen as steward of her household, which released
her for larger duties. The college was reopened, the curriculum enlarged, and plans laid for the magazine which later became *The
Christian Science Journal.*

Mrs. Eddy was soon so popular in Boston that it was difficult for
her to accomplish her work because of the adulation and flattery of
her followers. There were stormy days before the journal was really
successful, and soon the extension of Christian Science beyond the
confines of Boston brought other problems. She still kept up her
classes, wrote numerous letters, and was lecturing Thursday evenings and Sunday mornings. In 1884 she spent a successful month
in Chicago. The graduates of the metaphysical college spread far
and wide, and as early as 1888 there were thirty academies in various parts of the United States.

Another revision of *Science and Health* was made, and Mrs. Eddy
was wise enough to employ a retired Unitarian clergyman, named
Rev. J. H. Wiggin, to edit it. Mr. Wiggin's work included not only
the indexing of the volume and the correction of minor mistakes
in phraseology but also the rearrangement of the chapters. The
most significant change in the edition, however, was the addition
by Mrs. Eddy of a chapter which was really a Christian Science
commentary on the Bible Book of Revelation. Mrs. Eddy's young
womanhood had coincided with the period of American religious
life when the favorite occupation of religiously inclined folk had
been the interpreting of the so-called prophecies of the last book
of the Bible.

Her first marriage occurred in the year which William Miller had
set for the coming of the end of the world. It may have been a long
latent desire to give her own interpretation to the Book of Revelation which led her to add this chapter to the new edition. It may

[49] Frazer, *The Golden Bough,* Vol. III, p. 281, and index in Vol. XII.

have been something even deeper, and may mark the public announcement of the final accomplishment of her girlhood ambition to write a book. For in this new section Mrs. Eddy definitely identifies the "little book," mentioned in the tenth chapter of Revelation, as *Science and Health,* and the "woman clothed with the sun," of the twelfth chapter, as herself. She felt that she had earned the right to so identify herself. This was the first indication of a peculiar attitude toward herself and her work which at times verged on self-glorification.

Every great prophet develops a certain defiant ruthlessness and rides roughshod over accepted methods. The truth they have to present is so precious that they feel justified in doing anything to pave the way for it. Much of the egotism of Mrs. Eddy (and certainly to a Gentile her writings seem full of self-satisfaction and the complacent acceptance of praise) was due to her consciousness that the glorious message she brought reflected its radiance upon its apostle. The adulation and reverence she demanded was simply a part of the respect she coveted for her religion.

One detects also a feeling on her part that the arduous years of preparation which she spent before she could triumphantly announce herself as the "Discoverer and Founder of Christian Science" entitled her to a place among the world's prophets. But it may well be that the real cause of her noticeable self-appreciation lay deeper. She was coddled by her parents, her sister Abigail, and her husbands. This intensified her native sense of her own importance. On the other hand, we must not overlook the probability that it was to that very attitude of hers that much of her success was due. If she had not taken herself so seriously, her pretensions would have been laughed to scorn. When one speaks with sufficient authority, there are bound to be listeners.

Did Mary Baker Eddy think she was on a spiritual level with Jesus Christ? She denied that she was the "second Christ"[50] but in the same letter implied that she had, more than others, the "Mind which was in Christ Jesus." She insisted that in the services of worship in her church her book should be given equal position with the Bible. She spoke of herself as "Mother Mary," and always reserved for herself supreme control of every activity of Christian Science.

[50] *Pulpit and Press,* pp. 74, 75.

But the surprising thing is not that she should make these claims. It is, rather, that her followers accepted them and were always eager to give her greater honors than she was willing to receive. Again, it is not at all astonishing that the tremendous success which her religion achieved during her own lifetime led her to class herself as second only to, if not on a par with, Jesus Christ. When he died, all his disciples forsook him and fled; he did not see with satisfaction what the travail of his soul had accomplished. Before Mrs. Eddy died she was able to receive in person the homage of tens of thousands of devoted followers. He did not live to see a single copy of his biography; her works went into many editions long before she died.

Did she hypnotize her disciples with a mesmerism learned from Quimby? Most certainly not. The adulation given Mrs. Eddy was earned. No one but a prejudiced bigot can deny her credit for having made available to hundreds of thousands of sufferers a method of healing which literally gave them new life. The reason she spoke with authority and not as the scribes was because she was sublimely conscious of the fact that she had a message of great worth for mankind.

The methods of Christian Science may be open to criticism. It may have deluded many people and has doubtless been given credit for many cures which it did not make. Nevertheless, and there is evidence abundant enough to convince the most skeptical, it does cure disease with even more success than the bones and relics of saints at Roman Catholic shrines. And if attendance at church and testimony meetings and a general air of joy and happiness are true indexes, then Christian Science is vastly more successful than the average Protestant church.

During the remainder of her long life Mrs. Eddy kept her hand on the helm and steered her ship through many dangerous waters. Her administrative ability was remarkable and her sense of publicity value unusual in a religious leader. The "demonstration" of a church building adequate to house the new movement was accomplished in a very short time and a beautiful structure was dedicated in Boston January 6, 1895, free of debt. The movement continued to grow, and in June 1906 an enormous new church building was dedicated, so vast that the ten-year-old one by its side was dwarfed. At the dedication of the new building thirty thousand Christian Scientists from all over the world crowded the building in relays and testified enthusiastically to what Christian Science had done for them.

Much has been said against this religion, but even its foes must admit that it is widespread and firmly established. Its growth is in startling contrast to the decay of those Protestant denominations from which its recruits have largely come.

Mary Baker Eddy was a very astute woman. She was the best sales person religion ever had. Hers is the first Bible that included testimonials from converts as an appendix. Her business ability was further shown by the fact that she was the first to charge high prices for her religion. What people pay for they respect. You can get the Christian Bible for a few cents, or even for nothing; but you have to pay real money for *Science and Health*. Christian theological seminaries offer substantial scholarships and give so much aid that a young man can enter one penniless and come out with money in his pocket. But Mary Baker Eddy taught four thousand in her metaphysical college and charged them $300 for seven lessons.

Christian Scientists give generously to their churches. They contribute not only what the ordinary church member gives but also what he would allow for physicians and medicines in the family budget. Consequently Christian Science churches are dedicated free of debt, and the congregations avoid the disruptive effect of continual financial "appeals." Businessmen chuckle at such financial acumen; then they join the church, now that it has become rich and respectable, because they admire such methods.

Still another evidence of Mrs. Eddy's knowledge of the psychology of salesmanship is the fact that she was clever enough to permit Christians to retain Jehovah, Jesus, and the Bible. She made Jehovah and Jesus seemingly sponsor Christian Science. She interpreted the Scriptures in such a way as to suggest that every Bible verse fore-indicates Christian Science, but she was careful to omit mention of the verses that positively oppose it. She took a leaf from Moses, who told the children of Israel that Yahweh was really the God whom they had been worshiping as El Elyon and El Shaddai. She presented Christian Science, not as a new religion, but as a new interpretation of an accepted religion.

When a Christian picks up *Science and Health* and looks at the symbol on the cover, he feels at home at once. The Christian Science seal is a cross thrust through a crown, both in a circle bearing the motto "Heal the sick, raise the dead, cleanse the lepers, cast out demons." She must have known the meaning of the symbol in Christian history, where it always signifies that the crown of immortality is attained only by bearing the cross of suffering. The Christian martyrs welcomed suffering, believing it would bring them the crown of life. But Mrs. Eddy considered suffering "an error of sinful sense."[51] So she had to reinterpret the cross, "Your good will be evil spoken of. This is the cross."[52] There is some incongruity, also, in having the words "raise the dead," "cast out demons," on the cover of a book which claims to be an exposition of science.

But Mrs. Eddy knew that people are not reasonable: they are emotional. What better design for the cover of *Science and Health* than the old beloved cross and crown, wreathed round with familiar Bible words? Suspicion of the new cult would be disarmed immediately in the hesitant prospect. The symbol cannot be justified logically or theologically, but psychologically it is perfect.

When she realized that the end of her long life was approaching, Mrs. Eddy carefully planned for the continuation of the work by organizing for the future all Christian Science activities. One of her latter duties was the proper disposition of a personal fortune of at least two million dollars. She maintained her activity until the last. The day before she died she was up and dressed and about her usual work. Her passing was peaceful. The medical examiner said, "What struck me most as I looked into the dead face was its extraordinary beauty . . . I do not recall ever seeing in death before a face which bore such a beautiful, tranquil expression."[53]

Her mission was complete. She had even solved the problem which troubles most religious leaders and frequently divides their disciples into quarreling sects—the problem of the successor upon whom the mantle of leadership shall fall. She became her own successor! There were ambitious and able women who desired to succeed her, and they made trouble for a long while. But even though dead, she still spoke with authority.

She had written in a letter to her "Beloved Students" after her retirement, "You can well afford to give me up, since you have in my last revised edition of *Science and Health* your teacher and

51 *Science and Health*, 23:9.   53 Wilbur, p. 385.
52 Ibid., 254:29.

guide."[54] Her wishes have been respected. Through her master-piece, reflecting and perpetuating her personality in every line, read every Sunday in all Christian Science churches, she still leads her followers. The book dreamed of in her girlhood and brought forth with much travail in her womanhood has taken its place among the bibles of the world.

[54] *Miscellaneous Writings,* p. 135, quoted by Wilbur, p. 387.

CONCLUSION

THE FUTURE OF RELIGION

THE STORY of religion has not yet been told. When we chronicle all the evidence in the history of religion, even to the present hour, we have not told the story of religion, for that story is still in the making. Only the first chapter has been written. Centuries hence men will look back to our day and will place all that has hitherto happened in the first chapter of *their* history of religion and will entitle that first chapter, "Primitive Superstitions."

Religion today is still in the stage in which chemistry was in the days of the alchemist, and astronomy in the days of the astrologer. Until magic was eliminated from the minds of those who studied the elements and the stars, no real progress was possible, and until the supernatural is eliminated from the minds of men we shall not be able even to comprehend the nature of religion.

Strange as it may seem, science is to blame for the lack of progress in religion. No scientist can afford to laugh at the backwardness of religion: that religion is still so primitive is an equal shame to both religion and science. Hitherto, the scientist has turned his instruments upon comparatively easy subjects. Stones and stars, trees and birds, living animals and extinct varieties, flowers and geological strata are all comparatively easy things to study. It was when the scientist began, a few years ago, to turn his instruments upon himself that he realized he faced a real challenging task.

We have been hearing about sociology and psychology for the last few decades, it is true, and some inexact persons have referred to them as sciences, but they can hardly be dignified by that name as yet. Science has, until lately, neglected the psychic phenomena, so plainly evident in the lives of most founders of religions. The scientific study of religion, although it has attracted a few pioneer workers, is even less developed than sociology and psychology.

Theology used to be a metaphysical study. It concerned itself with imaginary beings and imaginary relations between those beings. The science of religion, however, which is just coming into existence, deals with religion, not as up in the sky but as in the lives of men. It is, after all, the study of the religious experience of human beings, and the reason religion is still so backward is because, as Wieman reminds us, "the datum of religious experience is so exceedingly complex that no method has yet been devised which is fit to treat it scientifically."[1]

There is an immense amount of material already available for the scientist who chooses religion as his field. We have attempted to show in the pages of this book that the religions of the world have been developed from the religious experience of typical individuals of unusual susceptibilities. The accounts which they have left of their conflicts and struggles afford ample data for the scientist. Take such a person as Wesley, for example, who not only left us the record of his own long battle to find peace, but also preserved detailed accounts of the religious experiences of hundreds of his converts. The material left by Wesley alone should be sufficient to enable a patient and original scientist to ascertain what this thing called religion really is; nay, more, what it may be when it is understood and its laws followed. Not only are the religious libraries of the world overflowing with material for the scientist of the future, but all around us are developing types of religious experience in most fascinating variety and profusion.

Some spiritual or psychic power has been sensed and somewhat comprehended by the millions of followers of various New Thought cults. They do not understand this power, and are only occasionally able to get direct results, but they are groping toward it, however blindly, and joyously use what of it they can find. We need an Edison or an Einstein of the spirit to discover that great force, formulate its laws, and make it available for the sons of men.

There is one striking affirmation made by some of the followers of New Thought and that is that this power, they are sure, is

1 H. N. Wieman, *Religious Experience and Scientific Method,* p. 23.

within themselves, now, whatever its ultimate origin may have been. In other words, there are untapped resources within the human personality waiting for release. Great souls in times past have plumbed the depths of their own consciousness and brought forth vast treasures for the enrichment of the world. But these were only surface scratchings compared with what shall be revealed when men shall courageously explore the unknown continent of the human spirit.

There are those today who claim that religion has no future, that it is outgrown, that it is synonymous with superstition and has long since survived its usefulness. Such assertions are based upon a very superficial view of life and religion. To put it in a very crude and somewhat shocking form, religion has a future co-terminous with the future of mankind because religion is a magnification of the first law of nature—self-preservation.

In a German book by Bender on the science of religion, entitled *Wesen der Religion* (p. 38), the significant sentence occurs, "Religion is that activity of the human impulse toward self-preservation by means of which man seeks to carry his essential vital purpose through, against the adverse pressure of the world, by raising himself freely toward the world's ordering and governing powers when the limits of his own strength are reached." Self-preservation's primal powers, however, are within as well as without.

Way back in the dawn of sentient life lie the roots of this primal impulse toward self-preservation. It is really part of the life urge itself. Religion is unseparated from life and life from religion. When man finds his desire to live, and to live richly and abundantly, thwarted and hindered by what seem to him blind forces and material needs, he looks about for allies and reserves. In earlier ages he sought to find these allies outside himself. At first he thought he had discovered them in natural objects, and that stage of religion was called Animism. To stocks and stones, to the rolling thunder in the mountains, to the majestic mountains themselves, to the all-powerful sun and the silent stars of night he called for help, and sometimes he thought help came.

This nature-worship period was followed by what has been called Polytheism, which is simply an extension of Animism by the attribution of personality to the spirits of the natural objects. If the great stone of the hilltop in Palestine, or the black meteorite at Mecca gave him help, then it must be due to the spirit resident in that place—the guardian angel of the stone; so he named the spirit and endowed it with godhood.

Then arose a war in the minds of men between various gods and goddesses. There was conflict on Olympus. Finally, one great god gained the ascendancy over the other gods and ruled the Pantheon. Jupiter became supreme. In another country Yahweh triumphed over Baal, Chemosh and Ashtoreth. To the greater gods men cried in times of trial. To them they brought thank-offerings in times of victory. From them they thought were derived the reserves, the extra ounce of strength, the magical access of power, which enabled men to overcome their enemies.

Still later the minor gods were eliminated from the Pantheon, and Monotheism arrived. Moses heard Yahweh say, "Thou shalt have no other gods." The next step in the progress of man's thought was the gradual improvement of the morals of the one god. The jealous Yahweh, Lord of Hosts, who commanded the slaughtering of innocent children and the murder of captive men, and the rape of captive women, who condoned trickery if by trickery greater sacrifices and spoils were dedicated to him, became transformed through the teaching of earnest prophets into a god of justice, of truth, and finally, of love and beauty. Man's god had grown with man himself.

Despite atavic survivals, retrograde movements and aversions to change, there had been a steady growth in religion. Man's cravings for God had become less erratic.

The race has been like the individual in the dark. At first the child is afraid of the dark but, with age, becomes less fearful—not so much that the dark is less abhorrent, but that he bravely takes a light and peers into the shadowy corners. The race is taking the light of science and is looking into the dark areas and is coming to recognize that a blind faith is not so high a religion as a seeing faith. In the dark places where blind faith had tried to assure the race that God existed, there the race, in the light of science, has discovered mighty laws. "Some call it evolution and others call it God."

We have not explored all the corners, nor even many of them, but we have gradually enlarged the lighted area. Magic, mysticism, and ritualism still survive, and long will, but religion is approaching a period of self-recognition which is analogous to the emancipation from infantile and handicapping fears. Of late man is beginning to suspect that these reserves of power upon which he may call in times of need may be within himself. The transcendent God of Heaven has become the immanent God in man. The Kingdom of God, Jesus discovered, is within us rather than outside. Socrates advised men to know themselves. But in the two thousand years or more since, comparatively little progress has been made in that direction.

Deep within us still is this instinct of self-preservation, sublimated now into various psychic trends toward self-recognition, self-development, and self-expression. It has been softened, too, by a recognition of social responsibility, into self-giving. The self-sacrifice which once was considered the highest form of religious conduct is now changing in the minds of leaders of men into intelligent self-giving of a creative sort socially. Even the superficial observer, the traditional "man of the street," has noticed the far-reaching change which religion is now undergoing. In such a period of transition it is difficult to chart the course and plot the curve of the progress of religion so as to predict future developments.

Certain trends, however, can be discerned, and give us some intimations of the possibilities of the religion of our distant descendants. In America, denominational lines have for some time been blurred and are, in some sections, disappearing. Throughout the world racial religions are exhibiting phenomena remarkably similar to each other. Buddhism and Islam have in the last few years undergone changes parallel to those previously experienced by Christianity.

Besides these more evident signs of the changes in denominational and racial religions there are other indications in religion itself which give hints as to what may be before us.

Christian Sunday-school classes are now studying the festivals of other faiths, such as the Jewish Purim and Hanukkah and the Buddhist Wesak. It is too early for the effects of that study to be fully apparent, but without a doubt great developments are now budding. It is impossible for a youngster of average intelligence to study sympathetically the other religions of the world without perceiving at once the great common area shared by all religions. We are entering an era of the exchange of ideas between representatives of various religions, a quiet by-product of the United Nations. For several years groups of young people in America have been holding symposia at which Buddhists, Moslems, Jews, and Christians have amicably discussed the varying emphases of their respective religions. What will happen when this interchange of ideas becomes common?

Professor Whitehead said[2] a generation ago, "The decay of Christianity and Buddhism as determinative influences in modern thought is partly due to the fact that each religion has unduly sheltered itself from the other. The self-sufficient pedantry of learning and the confidence of ignorant zealots have combined to show up each religion in its own forms of thought. Instead of looking to each other for deeper meanings they have remained self-satisfied and unfertilized." One thing that is surely occurring today is the interpermeation of Christianity and Buddhism to their mutual enrichment. Oriental and Occidental ideas are now mixing. West met East when Emerson and Mary Eddy began preaching slightly disguised Vedantic philosophy, and East met West when Gandhi included Thoreau with Rama and Jesus to make his trinity.

The cross-fertilization of religions, desirable as it is, is bound to produce strange hybrids, and some of these have already made their appearance. Anyone reading the religious announcement columns of Saturday newspapers in either New York or Los Angeles can see that process going on at the present time. Most of these hybrids are unfertile and die out in a short period, but from the "sports" and variants new species will arise. The interchange of ideas will, in the long run, however, increase the common stock of knowledge and decrease that suspicion which is the sister of ignorance. Whether the religion of the future will be an amalgamation of existing religions on the basis of their common human experiences or whether it will be a new variety of religion altogether we cannot at present foresee.

Another sign of the emerging religion of the future is the fact that religion is becoming self-conscious. It is attempting to define itself. Anyone who tried to make a collection of the definitions of religion would find that new ones are born every day, and the ones which have been written in the last few years differ very greatly from those current only a generation ago. The common characteristic of recent definitions of religion is their almost uniform insistence on a much wider outlook. Whereas not long ago men always defined religion in terms of man's relation to the supernatural, the definitions now place their chief emphasis upon the religious experiences of men. It is not that men are becoming morbidly intro-

2 *Religion in the Making*, p. 146.

spective, but that they are realizing that any scientific approach to the subject of religion must be concerned with those phenomena which are available in the feelings and reactions of men.

A third sign of the emerging of the religion of the future is the great dissatisfaction with existing religious institutions. The churches founded on the old conception of religion were empty, or nearly so, for a long while. Then, in mid-twentieth century, they began to fill up, much to the surprise of the preachers and the old faithful few in the pews.

The cry has recently been, "Back to God, back to Christ, back to the Church!" But when they get there, the cupboard is bare, for them. The new churchgoers simply do not know what the preacher is talking about (even if he does), because he is using religious terms and theological concepts meaningless to them today.

They and their parents left the church, perhaps, for various reasons, but largely because it did not fit into their busy lives. They had probably other more attractive interests. But they found they needed religion and came back to the church. Yet the old orthodoxy, even when rewrapped in the plastic package called Neo-orthodoxy, is a disappointment, because the modern mind finds no inspiration or spiritual sustenance in superstitious supernaturalism, however artfully and casuistically camouflaged. But these modern seekers *are* nevertheless interested in *religion*. This fact is shown in the new market for books on religion. Dealers used to sell religious books to religious people and would not stock a book that spoke disparagingly of religion unless it was the religion of the "heathen," which everyone knew was not real religion but idolatry and paganism. Now, however, dealers also sell, and in increasing volume, books about religion to non-churchgoing people who wonder how conventionally religious people "get that way," and wonder, too, if they themselves would be happier if they got that way also.

It is possible that a larger, greater religion will develop in America if the fundamental American principle of religious liberty obtains for a long enough period. Here all the religions of the world have met, and in due time out of their meeting and blending may arise a new one, just as in Rome, from the synthesis of many religions, Christianity arose.

It may be that this new American religion will be a revamped, enriched Christianity. There are evidences already that certain native elements are in process of incorporation into Christianity. For example, Emersonian transcendentalism is being inserted into Christianity by way of the religion of New Thought. Many members of Christian churches are also members of New Thought groups and are a leavening influence in their churches. Another movement, which might be called Walt Whitmanism, and which is essentially an American version of the ancient worship of Pan, is mitigating the severities of that imported English variety of Christianity sometimes called Puritanism.

Still another and more powerful trend is the infiltration of psychological explanations of problems of conduct which for centuries have been explained theologically. What once was termed the "Old Adam" in us is now often explained by amateur clerical Jungians as the "racial unconscious." And sexual immorality is by young Freudian neophytes apt to be interpreted as mere aberrations to be "understood" rather than sins to be repented of, or atoned for by penance.

Clumsily, perhaps, but powerfully, psychology is pushing in and usurping theology's throne in the world of religion. The most crowded churches and halls are those where the preachers translate Christianity in psychological terms.

One thing which still somewhat hinders the more rapid development of the religion of the future is the fact that despite the studies of the small group of forward-looking folk, religion is not yet commonly recognized for what it is and is not yet differentiated from its primitive beginnings. For the common run of folk, religion is yet closely allied to superstition and magic.

If religion is due to the urge for self-preservation and the desire for a more abundant life, religion will be concerned more and more with the attempt to make proper adjustment between man and his environment and will thereby supply the initiative for social experiments. No more significant indication of the trend of the times can be found than the fact that Sunday schools are becoming "Schools of Human Relations." It is being recognized that it is not so important for a child to be able to recite the books of the Bible in order or to name the kings of Israel and Judah as it is for him to learn how to live amicably and helpfully with his fellow men.

It is evident then that if religion is to be conceived as man's making the proper adjustment with his environment we shall derive considerable assistance in our task by studying those who, in times past, did make satisfactory adjustments. Progress will come by a careful analysis of the great spiritual leaders. Help has been derived in the past by such studies. Jesus "saves" men not because of any magical potency inherent in him, not through any miraculous quality of his "saving blood," but because when we study and contemplate a great personality who succeeded in making a conspicuously successful adjustment, we ourselves are instructed and inspired for the tasks before us.

Maladjustment is conspicuous today. We are not as successful in our world as our fathers were in theirs. There seems to be a lack of unity in our lives. Formerly all men's activities were synthesized by or in religion. Now, science, education, politics, philosophy, and morals are separate departments of life. We need a new synthesis. It is inevitable that the mind of man should seek to unify his experiences. Therefore there is a great future before religion. The tremendous advance in various human activities will make the new religion of the future vastly superior to the religion of the past.

There are many students of religion—an increasing number— who hope that the study of parapsychology, or extra-sensory perception, may afford a scientific basis for a new philosophy of religion. Surely, if man is even partially freed from the sense world, the existence of an X quantity or psi factor in his mind may indicate man's possession of something like what religion calls a "soul." If mind can function in a realm where time and space do not limit it, we may yet find a respectable foundation for belief in "immortality," but of a different sort from the old idea.

We should keep our minds open to this possibility and not be such scientific snobs as some who try to ridicule Dr. Rhine and the thousands of researchers in the field. But as even they admit, the present situation is well illustrated in the old priest's sermon on miracles: "Of course they's miracles, for Holy Writ says so. But nowadays they's scarce, and irregular, and you can't depend on them."

The Gospel "good news" of Christianity was that man could lay hold on a power which illumines and transforms his life. That power has hitherto been interpreted as outside man, but we are suspecting that it is within him. Lives which have been transformed by this power will be studied scientifically. It is suspected that the so-called supernatural is really natural and therefore susceptible to investigation. When science has developed instruments keen enough to dissect, and minds great enough to comprehend, the elements of personality, then, perhaps, theology will be again the queen of the sciences. But it may not be called theology. The "science of religion" is already being adopted as a better term. When we actually know what religion does for and to the individual, and how a person's powers are increased by an intelligent understanding and appropriation of religion, life ought to be infinitely more worth living.

By laying hold on that power in an intelligent way man will find himself better able to initiate great ethical projects, will find that in crises his religion is the weight in the balance which tips it to the right side and determines his conduct for good, and that this power enables him to sustain and maintain a certain course of right action which he has decided to pursue. But the greatest ability which the scientific study of religion will develop will be the creative power of man. Man has long said that God was the Creator. That belief has had curious abnormal developments, such as attributing to an anthropomorphic God the making of a physical earth and the creating of man out of the dust of the earth. These ideas were naïve and primitive, but they embody a central truth. The creative ability of this power, which men have called God, is available for man. The world is yet to be made.

APPENDIX

LEADERLESS RELIGIONS

(Including Egyptian, Babylonian and Assyrian, Hindu, Greek, Roman, Teutonic-Scandinavian, Shinto, and Mexican)

THE STATEMENT that every great religion is the religious experience of some great soul written large would appear to be contradicted by the fact that there have been a number of religions which have had no outstanding personality connected with their history: at least none of enough importance to have sufficient impress upon their times so that their names and activities were recorded by their fellow countrymen. The ancient religions of the Assyrians and Aztecs, of the Greeks and Romans, and existing religions such as Shinto and Hinduism cannot be studied through the biographical approach.

Nevertheless, this fact is not a contradiction of the thesis that all great religions develop under the guidance of great souls. The leaderless religions were *not* great, simply *because* they did lack great leaders. They all remained at an arrested stage of development. Most of them never evolved further than the primitive sort of religion known as animism or nature worship. A few reached the next stage, polytheism. These leaderless religions remained behind in the path of progress. Those which did not die long ago are today the least ethical and most immoral religions, because the least developed. Those which are no longer in existence succumbed before the vigor of some religion founded on and inspired by the experiences of a personal leader.

It is not necessary to go into detail regarding these leaderless religions because they exhibit the same phenomena which are found in the early stages of those religions which were led forth from animism or polytheism by some great prophet. They include, arranged chronologically, the Egyptian religion, the Babylonian and Assyrian religion, Hinduism, the Greek religion, the Roman religion, the Teutonic-Scandinavian religion, Shinto, and the ancient Mexican religion. In this group also belong the primitive religions of Africa, the Indian tribes of America, and the islands of the sea, which afford the student so many parallels to the early stages of what may be called the historical religions, but which do not call for treatment in this book, as they contain no features not already discussed.

The Egyptian Religion

The Egyptian religion belongs among the leaderless ones because, although Akhenaten was a religious genius and might have led his people out into monotheism, he was so far ahead of his time that his strenuous endeavors to establish belief in Aten left scarcely a ripple on the religious life of the Egyptians themselves. The records of their religion show almost no progress from the dawn of history to the conquest of Egypt by the Romans. It is astounding to find this race so highly developed in architecture, in art, in literature, and in mechanics, while remaining so very primitive in religion.

The very earliest Egyptian religion of which we have record, reaching back four or five thousand years before Christ, is animism, with a tendency toward polytheism. From that state there was practically no change made through millenniums. Gradually animism yielded somewhat to polytheism, but even in the later periods of Egyptian religion we find nature-worship and elements of fetishism and magic. The well-known animal gods of Egypt represented the highest native development of religion in the land of the Nile. Conservatism was so strong a characteristic in both priests and people that any tendency toward new forms of religion received scant support. As W. Max Müller says,[1] "It cannot be repeated too strongly that all deviations from conservatism were isolated and timid steps of a few most advanced scholars."

The fact that most of the surviving relics of early Egyptian life are tombs and their contents has produced a general popular impression that Egyptians were much interested in the future life. From that fact people have inferred that the Egyptians were deeply learned in religious mysteries, but that view is not correct. The religion of the masses of the Egyptian people, through long periods of time which make modern civilization seem very evanescent, was a simple nature-worship of a most primitive sort. Even the priests accumulated no fund of religious wisdom to which we may go for help. The very gods to whom they turned were recognized as fallible, subject to suffering, and frequently impotent to grant the prayers of their worshipers. They were believed to have "scarcely greater powers than one might hope to gain by magic and witchcraft of his own."[2]

When the Jewish diaspora brought Judaism and Gnosticism to Alexandria and when Christianity was established there later, it was long before they made much impression on the resident Egyptians. It took a militant faith like Islam to capture all North Africa by force and impose a somewhat higher type of religion.

Babylonian and Assyrian Religion

At first glance one might think that the Babylonian-Assyrian religion is an exception to the rule that leaderless religions remain essentially primitive. In very early times they had a pantheon, and before long there were tendencies toward monotheism. There is an evolution of the gods with a shifting of their attributes and the growth in permanence of the more powerful gods. As early as the seventeenth century B.C., in the time of Hammurabi, who developed a legal code which probably influenced the thought of Moses four centuries later, the sun god Marduk was the chief of the gods. It would be a mistake, however, to regard the religion of Babylonia in the days of Hammurabi as pure monotheism. The ascendancy of

1 *Religions of the Past and Present*, Edit. by James A. Montgomery, p. 48.
2 W. M. Flinders Petrie, Article "Egyptian Religion," *Encyclopedia of Religion and Ethics*, see Index.

Marduk was largely political. He was the guardian deity of the city of Babylon and increased in importance as Babylon became the leading Babylonian city.

Practically, the religion of Babylon, both then and later, was a polytheism characterized by the worship of demons and animal gods. Animistic polytheism is certainly to be recognized in the popular worship of the three great gods of the golden age of Babylon. The lives of the people were greatly influenced by their worship of the moon-god Sin, the sun-god Shamash and the planet-goddess Ishtar; the planet referred to being the one we call Venus. Of these, Ishtar was perhaps the most important. She was the great fertility goddess worshiped by rites which would now be considered very immoral. Ishtar was recognized as the consort of Marduk and was his rival for popular favor.

Although there were tendencies toward monotheism, the transition was never really accomplished. "Steps in this direction were made, but, after all, the force of the old animistic conceptions of the gods was too strong to lead to a definite change in the religion."[3] Great prayers have always been the mark of great religions, but in Babylon and Assyria prayer remained, for the most part, mere incantation and divination. When things were wrong, incantations were used to set them right. When it was feared that evil was approaching, divination was used to keep it away. No religion ever exhibited such a developed system of divination. They believed that almost anything could be predicted from the size, shape, markings, and peculiarities of the liver of a slaughtered animal, because the liver was believed to be the location of the intellect and the emotions: a belief which had its effect upon Hebrew theology.

Divination also found a field in unusual events of all sorts. The dreams of men, the motions of the stars, and the movements of animals, especially the flights of birds, were all significant. Astrology was developed to such an extent that it is popularly looked upon as the principal feature of Babylonian and Assyrian religion. The priests who did the interpreting and gave advice to those who sought the meaning of the stars and who desired to learn the will of the gods from the sacrificial liver were very wise men. Although they had remarkable opportunities for trickery and for personal enrichment it appears that on the whole they generally advised ethical conduct. The records which have come down to us show a strong

[3] Morris Jastrow, Jr., in *Religions of the Past and Present*, p. 62.

emphasis upon the value of honesty and fair play in business and personal relations. The code of Hammurabi reveals an appreciation of the value of justice. But Babylon and Assyria fell before any great religious leader arose.

Hinduism

Hinduism is reckoned the oldest religion now in existence and yet it may be seriously questioned whether it can properly be called a religion at all. "As a matter of fact, orthodox Hindus have believed in every kind of theism, polytheism, and pantheism. They have worshiped any object which they prefer, or virtually none. They have followed any standard of morality, or almost none. Yet they have been recognized as Hindus in good and regular standing, so long as they have not flagrantly violated the rules of caste and for that offense been outcasted."[4]

Hinduism presents the only example of a religion with a history reaching from 1500 B.C. to the present time in which one still finds the most primitive animistic practices. In other religions, when a great reformer has come, the entire religion has usually been raised to a higher level. But in India the followers of the reformer have always formed a separate sect and the old Hinduism has gone on parallel with its offshoots. There have been many reform movements in Hinduism, the best known of which were Jainism and Buddhism in the sixth century B.C., and Sikhism in the early sixteenth century A.D.

The vast mass of Hinduism, however, is still animistic. One of the most popular manifestations is the tendency of devout Hindus to go on pilgrimages to sacred mountains and rivers. Idolatry prevails and includes a widespread phallicism. The objects of veneration and worship in Hindu temples are very startling to travelers not familiar with the history of primitive religion. Of course, educated Hindus have rejected the primitive features and have developed a purer religion than that of the masses. The recent reform movements such as the formation of the Brahma Samaj, the Prarthana Samaj, and the Arya Samaj have been protests against certain religious practices, but their membership is very small.

Although Gandhi (1869–1948) was a character of great spiritual

[4] *World's Living Religions*, R. E. Hume, p. 19.

appeal, his followers can hardly be called a religious sect, as they are more concerned with political and economic matters than with religion.

The Greek Religion

It is easier to tell what Greek religion was not than to tell what it was. The student is baffled when he attempts to classify it, for it differs widely from most known faiths.

At the very beginning one is startled to discover that the Greeks had no sacred writings. One hunts in vain for dogmas, doctrines, and creeds. Religion is mentioned in ancient writings. Every page of Homer has references to the gods, but Homer cannot be regarded as the Greek Bible. Not only were there no sacred scriptures but there were no great revelations to men of the will of the gods. Furthermore, the gods themselves were conceived of as only a little better than men and were lacking in power, in holiness, and even in moral character.

The outstanding characteristic of Greek religion was the close relationship between the gods and men. There was a startling familiarity. Conversations between divinities and earth folk were frequent, and it was not uncommon for the mortal to reproach the deity for failure to keep promises or even to act decently. Greek literature is full of tales of loves between mortal men and goddesses, and between the gods and the women of the earth.

While Greek religion was polytheistic, emphasis should be laid upon the fact that it was an anthropomorphic polytheism. Intermingled with this polytheism were survivals of more primitive religion. Fetishism, animism, and even traces of totemism are found. Too, even in and alongside beautiful temples whose artistic lines reveal high culture, there were rude images, scarcely more than blocks of wood, which were devoutly worshiped. A very old statue of a goddess in the Parthenon itself was comparable to the rudest idols of African tribes. The statues of the gods developed from primitive stones and blocks of wood through a period characterized by blocklike human figures to the later developments when the image of God was simply that of a very beautiful man.

Mystery religions developed rather early in Greek religion. They were mostly importations from surrounding countries but were brought to a higher degree of development by the Greeks. The

Dionysian, Mithraic, Eleusinian, and Orphic mysteries were celebrated in rites which contained the germs of later Christian ceremonials, although the average Christian layman has not the slightest
suspicion of that fact. The religion of the Greeks was closely connected with their literary and artistic life. The phallic choruses of
the cult of Dionysus, so Aristotle tells us, were the source of the
great Greek comedies.

A popular development of Greek religion was the oracular form
of divination. By such signs as the rustling of the leaves of sacred
trees, by the murmurings of priestesses in a trance, or by dreams of
men sleeping in sacred places, the will of the gods was supposed to
be made known. The most famous oracles were those at the sacred
oak of Dodona, where Zeus was said to speak, and that at Delphi,
sacred to Apollo. Here the priestess, known as the Pythia, went
through an elaborate ceremonial which consisted of bathing, drinking sacred water, chewing sacred laurel leaves, and then sitting on
a tripod over a fissure, whence came vapor fumes. In the trance thus
induced she uttered almost unintelligible words which the priests
shaped into poetry and gave to the person desiring to know the will
of Apollo.

Greek religion was later supplanted by philosophy, which was
developed in a practical way to such an extent that Stoicism, for
instance, became even a religion; at least a guide to right living.
In all Greek history, however, we find no great prophet. The religion remained, until late times, a strange mixture of animism and
polytheism. When we read in Plato of the last hours of Socrates we
are startled to find in the midst of his philosophic utterances his
request to a friend that he sacrifice a cock to Aesculapius.

The Roman Religion

The adoption by the Romans of practically the entire Greek
Pantheon occurred so early in their history that it is difficult to
ascertain very much about the character of the early Roman religion. Tradition assigns to the legendary king, Numa Pompilius,
the founding of an international religion with the assistance of the
sacred nymph, Egeria, but the alleged career of Numa is so thoroughly obscured by myth that his very existence is doubted by
many scholars.

We know, however, that in early times the Romans who migrated from the Danube region were great believers in magic and spirits. These spirits developed into gods connected not so much with particular places as with certain daily and seasonal occupations of the people. Janus protected the door and Vesta, the hearth. Saturn was the god of the time of sowing. Ceres guarded the growth of the grain. Ops was the patron of the harvest, and Pomona was the goddess of fruit. These were all worshiped out of doors save Vesta, and the religion of the period might be termed agricultural animism.

Under the Etruscan Tarquins, father and son, real gods with temples appeared. Jupiter, Juno, and Minerva became the great Roman trinity. The temple to Jupiter on the Capitoline Hill, said to have been begun by the elder Tarquin and completed by his son, was regarded with great veneration by the Romans. It is likely that a strong monotheism would have developed, with Jupiter as the great god, but in the three centuries from 500–200 B.C. came the invasion of the foreign gods, particularly from Greece. Jupiter's growing ascendancy was checked. As neighboring cities were conquered by the Romans, the gods of the conquered were incorporated into the Roman Pantheon. Besides, the prosperity of Rome was due to her many immigrants, who brought with them their own gods and were allowed to worship them as they pleased. Whenever any great calamity seemed to threaten the Roman state the fickle Romans sought another god's help. For instance, in 293 B.C., when Rome was suffering from a great plague, the Greek god of healing, Aesculapius, was imported to check the pestilence.

One goddess who was welcomed with great acclaim nearly brought disaster to the whole Roman state. This was Cybele, the great mother. Connected with her worship was a sacred meteoric stone which probably resembled the Kaaba of the Mohammedans. But the worship of Cybele introduced a religious sanction for sexual excess. Combined with the rites of Bacchus, which has given us the adjective "Bacchanalian," the worship of Cybele became so popular that the Roman Senate, in spite of its fixed policy of religious toleration, had to check the degrading observance of the rituals of the mother goddess for the protection of the state itself.

In the century before the birth of Christ and in the century or two after, so many Eastern religions and mysteries entered Rome that very little was left of the original Roman religion. The great city was simply a hotbed of cults of all possible sorts which vied with one another for supremacy. From Egypt came the worship of Isis and Osiris, from Phrygia the cult of Attis, and from Persia via Asia Minor the powerful soldier religion of Mithra, dominant in the second century A.D.

Finally, a new religion from Palestine, little noticed at first but gradually gaining in strength because of the purity of its teachings and the faithfulness of its followers even unto death, grew, gradually ousting even its greatest rival, Mithraism, and appropriating Mithra's birthday, December 25, for the birthday of Christ. Then, early in the fourth century A.D., Constantine established Christianity as the official religion of the Roman Empire. Again a leaderless religion succumbed before the triumphant advance of a religion inspired by a great personality.

Teutonic-Scandinavian Religion

The singular lack of religious leaders which characterized Greece and Rome is noticeable in northern Europe among their Aryan cousins, the Teutonic and Scandinavian peoples.

The Aryan stock as it spread westward seemed to be sterile when it came to producing prophets, for the folk who were later known in various countries as Germans, Norwegians, Scandinavians, Danes, Icelanders, and Anglo-Saxons never had any religious geniuses to lead them out of animism and polytheism into a high ethical monotheism. The people of all those countries today are ethical monotheists but that is due to their conversion by Christian missionaries of long ago. Survivals there are, so that even Christian English-speaking countries call Tuesday, Wednesday, Thursday, and Friday after the old Scandinavian gods *Tiw, Woden, Thor,* and *Frigg.* Another survival is the name of the Christian springtime feast, from *Austro* or *Eostre,* the Teutonic goddess of spring, with her Easter bunnies and colored eggs, those non-Christian symbols of the old fertility faith.

When we study the Scandinavian gods we find them singularly like those of the Greeks and Romans. They are exceedingly human. Some of them have bad tempers; most of them are gluttonous; some are shrewd, and some are easily tricked. Along with the great gods were many demi-gods, spirits, and demons. The old Teutons lived in a world of dwarfs and elves, giants and trolls. Even Christianity has not driven from northern Europe a belief in various spirits, and religious folk customs still survive among the common people. Grimm's fairy tales perpetuate loved legends of old.

The religion was exceedingly simple. Thunder was believed to be caused by the blows of Thor's mighty hammer upon the pates of the giants. There were great trees, the most noted being "Yggdrasill," the "world tree," one root of which reached to hell and the other to heaven. In the place of the angels of Zoroastrianism, Essenic Judaism, and Christianity were the fierce valkyries who protected the warriors and guided them to Valhalla, the Teutonic heaven. The joys of heaven were those beloved by a race of fierce hunters and fighters, and consisted of fighting, feasting, and drinking every day. Frigg, the wife of Woden, resembled Astarte and Venus. An early Christian abbot, named Elfrich, about 1000 A.D. preached sermons in which he compared Thor to Jupiter, Mercury to Odin, and mentioned "the foul goddess Venus whom men call Frigg."

It is possible that the popularity of Thor would have given him the supreme place and prepared the way for monotheism, but the energetic, persistent, and ingenious missionaries of Christianity gradually persuaded the Norsemen to adopt the gentler religion. Interesting stories are told of the conflicts of the period of conversion. Very reluctantly the Teutons permitted their sacred stones, groves and hills, graven mounds and sacred enclosures, to be condemned, renamed, and their places taken by Christian churches. Eventually the hammer of Thor became the cross of Christ.

Shinto

Shinto, the national religion of Japan, is properly called *Kami-no Michi* in Japanese, which means "the way of the gods." When one translates that phrase into Chinese it becomes Shin-tao, shortened to Shinto, which is its popular name even in Japan. The Japanese claim that Shinto dates from the seventh century B.C. Scholars, however, date its origin much later and very much doubt the statement of the Japanese scriptures that the first land created was Japan and that the sun goddess herself gave birth to the first mikado, Jimmu Tenno.

The Japanese scriptures have two sections: the Kojiki, or "Records of Ancient Matters," and the Nihon-gi, the "Chronicles of Japan," which were composed in the eighth century A.D. The Kojiki is the most obscene of all holy books, and in the English translation many sections appear in Latin. There are other sacred books describing the ceremonial of Shinto and containing religious poems. Shinto is animistic polytheism. The Kojiki states that there are eight hundred thousand gods and goddesses, all of whom were descended from the two original deities, Izanagi and Izanagai. The anthropomorphism of Greek and Teutonic deities is almost divine compared with the filthiness of the Shinto gods. Advancing civilization has made it absolutely necessary for the Japanese people to revise their religion. In the last half century the phallicism which characterized Shinto for so long has been greatly suppressed.

The most important of all the deities of Japan is the sun-goddess, the heaven-shining one, Amaterasu. Popular religion venerates the sacred mountain, Fuji-yama. Religion and patriotism have been so closely intertwined in Japan that the various rulers have been considered practically as gods. It is only of very late years that the Japanese people have been permitted even to look at their rulers.

In the sixth century A.D. Buddhism made its way into Japan and mixed with Shinto. Confucianism and Taoism also came from China, and for many centuries the Japanese had a very much confused religion. In the eighteenth century there was a great revival of Shinto led by a group of scholars who restored primitive Shinto to a considerable extent. The tendency of Shintoists to be hospitable to other religions led to a movement to make Shinto an all-embracing world religion to include not only Buddhism, Confucianism, and Taoism, but Islam and Christianity as well.[5]

It is doubtful, though, that a religion so essentially national as Shinto could be made the basis of an international religion. An even greater hindrance to its spread is the character of its sacred scriptures and its well-known phallicism, considered by Westerners to be immoral. Because of its political nature, with strong nationalistic emphasis, it was officially banned as the state religion at the end of World War II, but it survives. No temples were closed. It is no longer tax-supported but is free to compete with Buddhism, Confucianism, Christianity, and the two hundred or more new religious health and faith-healing cults.

[5] *World's Living Religions*, p. 168.

The Mexican Religion

When one refers to the ancient Mexican religion, that of the civilization which flourished in the period roughly comprised between A.D. 1000–1500 is meant. Of the early part of that period little is known regarding the Mexicans. Traditionally, the Toltecs in the eleventh century are credited with having built up a civilization which disappeared when tribes from the north, the Nahuarians, invaded and conquered the country. Of these Nahuarians one tribe gradually gained supremacy—the Aztecs, and the civilization of Mexico from about 1300 to 1519, when Cortez conquered the country for Spain, is commonly known as the Aztec period.

A study of the Aztec religion reveals surprising similarities to those of the Egyptian. The *Teocalli,* or houses, of the gods were large pyramids not as well constructed as those of Egypt but resembling them in size and shape. The one at Mexico City measured 375 feet by 300 feet and was over 80 feet high. The *Teocalli* were really huge mounds of earth with carved masonry facing. They were dedicated to the worship of various gods. The rites included practices more horrible and revolting than those of any other religion. Countless thousands of men were thrown alive on the sacrificial block. Their arms and legs were held by four men while their living heart was torn out of the body and offered to the sun. Victims were uniformly prisoners captured in war raids. After the heart had been torn out, the body was given to the particular warrior who had captured that prisoner. This warrior, after cooking the corpse, partook of it in a great feast with his relatives, while the thigh bone was fastened to a pole near the warrior's house as a luck fetish. The skull was added to the pile of such trophies on the top platform of the *Teocalli.* The Spanish conquerors reported that in one pile they counted one hundred and thirty-six thousand skulls.

The favorite gods of the Mexicans were Tezcatlipoca and Huitzilopochtli. Tezcatlipoca was originally the god of the waxing moon but was sometimes spoken of as the god of the wind. Each year the most beautiful of the male captives was selected to represent the god for a year. He was supplied with all possible luxuries and was revered as if he were a god. A month before the time selected for his death he was given four beautiful maidens as wives. Then as the day of his death approached, his wives were taken from him, and as he mounted the *Teocalli* his beautiful garments were stripped away and he was sacrificed in the usual way on the top of the pyramid.

Huitzilopochtli was the popular god of Mexico City. His origin is not clearly known and he has been identified as the god of the morning star or the rising sun; but later he was well known as the war god. He was, according to tradition, miraculously conceived by his mother from a feather ball which fell from the sky. The Aztecs claim that he was born fully armed and immediately killed his sister, the moon goddess, and drove away his mother's four hundred other children. It is easily seen that this is a dramatization of the appearance of the morning sun before whose brightness the moon and stars disappear. There were other gods: of the earth, of the rain, and of the maize, besides many spirits who lived in springs, mountains, and caves. The female deities included goddesses of earth, fire, filth, flowers, and love.

No name is mentioned of any great religious leader among the Mexicans. Their civilization fell before a handful of Spanish conquerors. The Christian priests who accompanied Cortez were astounded to find that the religious customs among the Mexicans resembled those of pious Catholics: confession, penance, absolution, baptism, and communion existed. These were, however, in rather more primitive forms. One form of preparing communion bread, for instance, consisted of making an image of Huitzilopochtli out of dough into which was kneaded the blood of infants. The most surprising discovery by the priests was the widespread use of the cross by the Mexicans. They called it the "tree of our life." But instead of referring to sacrifice, it was a symbol of the four winds of heaven.

The militant conquest of the Aztec religion by Christianity is typified by the fact that in 1593 the foundation stones were laid for a great cathedral in Mexico City costing two and a half million dollars which was erected on the very spot where there had been a temple to one of the gods of Mexico.

The religion of Peru resembled in many ways that of Mexico but was of somewhat higher sort. Human sacrifice did not exist. Fire was sacred and the whole religion centered around the worship of the sun. The temple of the sun was attended by vestal virgins. The state and religion were practically identical. The ruling monarch was believed to be divine and his huge harem consisted of the virgin attendants in the sun temple. It was believed that the first Peruvian ruler, or inca, named Manco Capac, was virgin-born to redeem mankind.

INDEX

(Erasmus), 340 (Zwingli), 362 ff.
(Nicon), 444 (Mrs. Eddy)

Dead Sea Scrolls (Qumran MSS), 14,
27, 162 ff., 214–15, 346

Debates, 74, 75, 176, 202, 213, 295,
302, 322 ff., 361

Decalogue, 55 ff.; *see also* Commandments, Ten.

Deer's Cry, 262–63

Deism, 417–18

Deity, Deification, 27 (Moses?), 134
(Buddha), 151 (Buddha, Confucius, Lao-tse), 186–191 and
240 ff. (Jesus)

Delphi, 462

Demeter, 94

Democracy, 1, 21, 133, 160, 173, 198,
329, 333, 339–40

Demons, 43, 48, 68, 69, 72, 78, 160,
185, 191, 266, 408, 444, (Mrs.
Eddy's belief in) 464; *see also*
Devils

Depravity of man, 236, 402–03

Deserts, 38, 51, 62, 66, 164, 172, 183,
244–45, 270, 273, 281, 407

Desire, 131 ff.

Determinism, 399

Deutero-Isaiah, 120, 182

Deuteronomy, 89 ff., 104, 117, 180

Devadatta, 135

Devils, 42 ff., 62 ff., 67 ff., 72, 76, 78,
130, 183, 243, 266, 277, 306, 311–
12, 317, 319, 325, 329, 382; *see
also* Adversary, Ahriman, Angra
Mainyu, Asmodeus, Demons,
Evil, Exorcism, Gods, Hexing,
Kaljug, Mara, Satan, Shaddai-
Shedim

Dharma, 135

Diaspora, 197, 458

Diet of Augsburg, 327; *Augsburg
Confession,* 341

Diet of Worms, 316, 324 ff.

Dillmann, C. F. A., 55

Diodorus Siculus, 51, 98 n., 270

Dionysian Mysteries, 462

Dionysius Exiguus, 182

Disciples, 130, 180, 313

Dives, 208

Divine Comedy, 269

Divination, 459, 462; *see also* Necromancy

Divinity of Man, 403, 406, 407

Dodona, 39, 462

Dogs, 66, 74, 253, 283, 359

Dominicans, 291 ff., 333

Doukhobors, 365

Dragon, 141, 152

Drama, xvi, 227

Dreams, 122, 208, 245, 254–55, 260,
269, 408, 459; *see also* Visions

Dresser, Horatio, 435

Driver, S. R., 90

Druidism, 259 ff., 262, 269

Dualism, 63, 228

Dughdhova (Zoroaster's mother), 65

Easter, 52, 262, 266, 342, 464; *see also*
Resurrection

Eastern Church, 345; *see also* Greek
Catholic Church, Russian
Church

Ebed-melech, 112 ff.

Eck, John, 316, 323

Edbald, 9

Eddy, Asa G., 438–39

Eddy, Mary Baker (Glover, Patterson), 427, 428 ff., 451

Edison, Thomas, 79

Edom, 110

Edwards, Jonathan, 84, 386, 396 ff.,
401 ff.

Eena, mena, mona, my, 259, 260 n.

Egeria, 462

Egypt, Egyptians, 1 ff., 25–30, 33 ff.,
36 ff., 88, 92, 107, 116, 176, 239,
284, 457 ff., 464

Eight-fold Path, 131

El, Eloha, Elohim (Hebrew gods), 36,
43, 44, 92; *see also* El Elyon, El
Sabaoth, El Shaddai, Allah,
Baal, Helios

Elan vital (vital impulse, life thrust),
12; *see also* Powers

Eleazar, 61

Electrons, 209

El Elyon (God Most High), 43, 443

Elephants, 122–23, 126, 272–73

Eleusinian Mysteries, 598

Eliakim, 92

Elias (Greek form of Elijah), 254

Eliezer, 36

Elijah, 84, 85, 87, 187